About The Author

Photo taken August '96

When John Thomas began his pursuit of agelessness, his *calendar age* was only 27 while his *real* age, that is, his **bio-electric age** was 39. Today (1997) John is 53 years by the calendar, YET his bio-electric age has declined to just 19 years "young!" Thomas is living proof that aging reversal can be a reality for anyone who wishes to experience it.

John was heavily influenced by the exemplary lives of Paul C. Bragg and Jack LaLanne.

Thomas spent 26 years researching every aspect of aging, challenging accepted dogmas, and daring to "rock" the boat of both conventional and alternative medicine.

John discovered that "medical science" asks the *wrong* questions and generates useless answers—while "alternative" medicine labors under gross misconceptions and half truths that fail to produce long term results.

Thomas was encouraged to write *Young Again!* because he does **NOT** age! Time stands still for John because he uncovered the **mystery** behind the aging process, applied it, and thereby reversed his **bio-electric** age to only 19.

For a book like *Young Again!* to be *meaningful,* the author would need to have "personally lived" the subject matter AND be *living* proof that aging reversal and body rejuvenation are within every person's reach. The author would need a broad background in the sciences, philosophy, politics, history, and nutrition. He would also need to think "low tech" and incorporate a style of writing that would educate and ensure *communication* with the reader.

John wrote *Young Again!* as a practical, useful, guide book of information spelling out **exactly** what must be done to **recapture** lost youth, **reverse** disease, and extend one's life into the hundreds of years while "looking" and "feeling" young!

This book was NOT written for "experts" who claim to have answers, but whom cannot demonstrate evidence of it in their lives or in that of their patients.

Young Again! is a living *testimony*—a mosaic of nature's secrets pieced together for the very first time. It encourages everyone to talk the talk AND walk the walk! Enjoy!

Thoughts From Patricia Bragg

What a masterpiece! *Young Again!* is the best of the best! It will help millions of people.

We are a nation of half dead people! Cancer, heart trouble, high blood pressure, osteoporosis, etc. The health of our people is slipping fast. The question is why?

Good health is something that cannot be purchased from a doctor or in a bottle of pills. Good health is the product of a healthy lifestyle. America needs to know more about how to achieve health and vitality. Staying youthful, no matter what your age, is central to the health message and to the message of this book.

My father, Dr. Paul C. Bragg N.D., Ph.D. was a teenager dying of tuberculosis when he *chose* a life of health. Dad was ninety-seven years "young" when he died of a surfboard accident. During his life, he helped thousands of people find the path to agelessness. One of those people was Jack LaLanne.

Jack was a sickly boy. His health was so poor he was forced to drop out of school. Dad's message changed his life. Today, Jack LaLanne is a legend. He is living proof that the health message really works.

Dad said the world was lacking strong, courageous men and women who were not afraid to buck the trend of commercialism in the food industry and in the healing arts—people who could stand tall.

Here we have a strong crusader who *believes* in the health message and who *lives* what he preaches. John Thomas' wonderful book is his gift of love to the world.

Now, dear reader, it is your turn to experience a life of boundless energy and health. The keys are in your hand. Read and follow this book and it will change your life. *Young Again!* is the most thorough and concise message ever written on the subject of healthy living.

No excuses. You know right from wrong. Remember, what you eat and drink you become. It's either sickness or it's health. It's time to choose. Now! Today!

Young Again! is truly a personal guide to ageless living. I am honored to be a part of it.

Authored and published under the jurisdiction of
Title 4 U.S.C. 1 Flag of Peace of the united States of America
(see front cover)

Printed in the united States of America

young AGAIN!

How To REVERSE *The Aging Process*

John Thomas

Promotion Publishing
San Diego, California, united States of America

Authored and published under the jurisdiction of the
Title 4 U.S.C. 1 Flag of Peace of the united States of America
(see front cover)
Printed in the united States of America

young AGAIN!
How To Reverse The Aging Process
By John Thomas

Promotion Publishing
3368 F Governor Dr. Ste 144 San Diego, California 92121
Phone (619) 490-1400   Fax: (619) 490-1455
(800) 231-1776

Cataloging-In-Publication Data
Thomas, John
Young Again! How to Reverse The Aging Process / by John Thomas
p. cm. • References: p. • Includes index and glossary.
ISBN 1-884757-78-2 (4th edition)
1. Aging. 2. Rejuvenation. 3. Longevity. 4. Health. I. Title
RA776.75.T56   1997
613.04—dc20   94-65131

Printings: 20 19 18 17 16 15 14 13 12 11 10 9 8 7 6

LEGAL NOTICE

Aging reversal requires the investment of time, energy, and money by the reader/Citizen desiring the experience knowing that aging reversal is "personal and unique" to the indivdual. The **"intent of mind"** of the author and publisher in making *Young Again!* available in the public domain is limited to the dissemination of health related information for causing THINKING among Citizens and QUESTIONING of medical modalities/advice. Neither the publisher or author offer "medical" advice and the book *Young Again!* is not to be used for medical diagnosis. The author and publisher believe the information provided is complete and accurate, but mistakes both typographical and in content may be dicovered after printing, and therefore, the reader should use *Young Again!* as a general guide only and not as the ultimate source of information. Neither author nor publisher have liability or responsibility for any reader/Citizen respecting loss or damage caused or alleged for reliance on information in *Young Again!* **THE READER IS RESPONSIBLE FOR SEEKING "PROFESSIONAL" MEDICAL CARE BY THE READER'S OWN CHOICE.**

DEDICATED TO...

Robert McLeod—You will meet Bob in Chapter one. He became my mentor, a living example, and a good friend.

Dr. Paul C. Bragg N.D., Ph.D.—Paul Bragg was the point man of the health movement in the United States. Millions of people owe their lives to him. He served his fellow man well, and his Creator to the fullest. Paul Bragg saved my life!

Charles Walters—Charlie is the editor of Acres USA. He taught me to winnow the wheat from the chaff. He helped me establish the link between "live" food and "live soil." His editorial pen is the harbinger of TRUTH in matters of agriculture and national economics. He is another Thomas Paine!

Diane DeFelice M.S., R.D.—Diane was my upper level college nutrition instructor. She is unselfish in her effort to help students make the connection between diet, lifestyle and good health. She helped me realize that *Young Again!* simply had to be written.

Patricia Bragg N.D., Ph.D.—Patricia *challenged* me to write this book. She also challenged me to pick up the baton her father handed to her and to Jack LaLanne. Patricia is the daughter of the great Wizard—"Paul Bragg." Patricia is a mighty force in the health movement worldwide. She is a voice crying in the wilderness!

Jack LaLanne—Beginning in the 1950's, Jack LaLanne became "Mr. Fitness." He is a living example of the benefits that accrue from a healthy lifestyle and regular exercise. Jack has been the point man in the fitness industry for over forty years! He deserves our applause and thanks. Many people have been blessed by his work.

Leonard Ridzon—Of all the people I've known in 52 years, this farmer makes me think more than any other. Leonard is a simple man, but he isn't simple. He sees the Creator's handiwork and asks questions to whoever will listen. His questions can hold a pack of doctors at bay; they seldom risk an answer. And when Leonard talks, you had best be listening. He says as much *between* the lines as he does in words. Thank you, Leonard, for teaching me to observe, think and challenge!

TABLE OF CONTENTS

Acknowledgements

The author would like to take this opportunity to acknowledge and thank the following people who were involved, directly and indirectly, in bringing this book to fruition and/or to the attention of the public.

Robert Stephan D.D.S., Dr. John Briggs D.C., Dennis Higgins M.D., Linus Pauling M.D., Edward Arana D.D.S., Hal Huggins D.D.S., Dr. Helen A. Guthrie, Dr. Roger Lent, Joseph Kramer M.D., Ignaz Semmelweis M.D., Thomas Gerber M.D., Arnold Lorand M.D., Max Gerson M.D., Dr. Carey Reams, Drs. Paul C. and Patricia Bragg, Dr. Bernard Jensen, Guenther Enderlein M.D, Robert F. Hofman M.D.

Bob Mcleod, Jack LaLanne, Charles Walters, Mitchell May, Christopher Bird, Burt Stoker, Kyle McLain, Bob Greenebaum, Walter Grotz, Dean Stonier, Merlyn Anderberg, Diane DeFelice, J. Carmen Robinson, Leann Springer, Ray and Carolyn Teagarden, Carol Arana, Dan Poynter, Nancy Poehlann, Frank and Kay Morrow, Hanna Campbell, Linda Berthof, Linda Torretta, Ellen Rosbach, John Murphy, Werner and Janice Gerhardt, Tom Mahoney, Rita Ryan, Cathy Cameron, Keith Ries, and my immediate family as well as the family into which I was blessed to have been born.

Special thanks to Elizabeth Beryl, Marguerite Willner and Amy Alter for their assistance in editing and clarification and to Terri Lonier for her help and kindness.

Cover design by: Michael Anthony Lynch
4901 Morena Blvd., ste. 123
San Diego, CA 92117
(619) 490-9223

Introduction by Robert B. Stephan D.D.S.

Man's ways are the antithesis of Nature's ways. They have little resemblance to the natural healing process. Nature provides the basis of life and the potential to help man correct his tendency towards disease, but drug based medicine has chosen to increase health care productivity rather than identify the constraints which inhibit good health.

Allopathic medicine seems to be infatuated with technology, powerful drugs, and the suppression of symptoms. It prefers to *cut, poison,* and *burn,* when less would do. Medicine's world is physical and chemical.

We are moving away from this physical and chemical based system of disease care and into the realm of energy and spirit. This is not a new movement, but a rediscovery of ancient wisdom. It is a mix of "proven" wisdom combined with technology.

As we move away from a *disease* care system and into a *health* care system, we will need a compass and a road map to navigate by if we hope to find our way through the maze of exploding knowledge and rediscovered tradition that is fast approaching us.

Young Again! serves the dual purpose of a navigation tool and a survival manual. It is easy to read and it is a very complete gathering of information. It will guide you to a healthy, vibrant life *and* it will take you where Western Allopathic doctors fear to tread.

It is a divine privilege to be involved in the march to a preferred future, and it is a great pleasure to have John Thomas' wonderful book to use as a fount of information in my position as a Holistic Biological Dentist. Discover in this book the joy and path of good health!

Dr. Robert B. Stephan, D.D.S., B.S., F.A.P.D.
Spokane, Washington
Holistic Dental Association, Board of Directors
International Academy of Oral Medicine and Toxicology
American Academy of Biological Dentistry
Occidental Institute, Research Faculty
Environmental Dental Association

Introduction by Dr. John A. Briggs

Our body is an incredible work of art. Unfortunately, it does not come with an owner's manual—as does a car—that tells us *how* to care for our body.

Consider the master mechanic. He has knowledge of the workings of his car. He knows how to protect his investment. His world is a world of regular maintenance and mechanical details. He avoids the pitfalls of ownership through individual responsibility. He knows *how* to maintain his car's youthfulness and vigor.

The medical world is not like the world of the master mechanic. In my practice, I have seen people with the full range of health related problems—problems directly related to modern living—problems that could be avoided if people only had an owner's manual.

These people come to me willing to spend their fortunes. They have tasted the bitterness of disease and old age—they cry out for good health. They also DREAM of regaining the health of their youth.

I help them as best I can. I point the way, but my time is limited as is their money. What these people really need is an owners manual for the care and maintenance of their body. I have wished for such a manual.

My wish was fulfilled when John Thomas wrote *Young Again!* It contains all the information my patients need to maintain their youth and vigor.

Young Again! arms the reader with practical, valuable information. This book is correctly aligned with the concepts of Naturopathic medicine. It will help the reader to stay young no matter what their age.

Thomas' research is exhaustive. He has a thorough working knowledge of the healing arts. Most importantly, he drives home his points with simple examples designed to help the reader understand.

Read this book and follow the information it contains. If you do, you too can achieve the radiant health I observed when John Thomas first introduced himself.

Dr. John A. Briggs
Naturopathic Physician
Clatskanie, Oregon

Foreword by Charles Walters

"People can be fed to live peacefully or fight, to think or dream, to work or sleep, to be virile or pathologic, physically, mentally, and spiritually developed or retarded, and for any possible degree of advance or variation within the mechanical limits of the organism."

This was the late Albert Carter Savage speaking during the early years of WW II, and Winston Churchill took him seriously. After all, the health of England's fighting men was all that stood between the freedom of Englishmen and Hitler's thirst for world domination.

It was realized that food had to carry a fair complement of minerals in order to confer health, and the idea that vitamins could function without minerals was at least as strange as the concept that coal-tar drugs—capable of making a healthy person ill—could make a sick person well.

These few thoughts came to mind when John Thomas' manual *Young Again!* arrived on my editorial desk.

Individual health is too important to be left in the hands of physicians, but how can a person make informed decisions to not only preserve health, but to conquer sickness as well? Most books deal with individual problems—single factor analysis, we call it—but leave unanswered the silent killer in our lives, namely *shelf life.* For it is shelf life in the grocery store that annihilates the quality of life for the consumer.

When most of today's senior citizens were still youngsters, strange words in type too small to read became an indispensable part of almost every label. First came the emulsifiers and stabilizers—carrageenan in cheese spreads, chocolate products, evaporated milk, ice cream and dairy products. All evidence of mutagenicity, carcinogenicity, and teratogenicity remained neatly tucked away in the scientific literature.

Dioctyl sodium sulfosuccinate became the wetting agent of choice, even though infants suffered gastrointestinal irritation and reduced growth rates as a consequence of its use. There were also dozens of flavorings and colors other than Red Nos. 2 & 4, all inimical to sustained human health. Aspartame (Nutrasweet) is a sweetener with approximately one hundred sixty times the sweetness of sugar. The problem is that people with phenylketonuria can't handle it. It accumulates in the system and causes mental retardation and even death. Cereals, chewing gum, and gelatins are loaded with it.

As shelf life for foods improved, strange anomalies in the population multiplied. The public prints became filled with reports of bizarre crimes (youths dumping gasoline on old ladies and setting them on fire, for instance) and asylums for the insane became a growth industry, finally to emerge with credentialed practitioners and a new nomenclature—mental health!

Did shellac—a food grade version of furniture finish—used as a confectioner's glaze have anything to do with this? Or xylitol, a sugar substitute that is a diuretic and causes tumors and organ damage in test animals? Or propylene glycol alginate, or oxystearin (a modified glyceride), or glycerol ester of wood resin, or guar gum? All annihilate lesser life and whittle away at human health a bit at a time!

John Thomas' message in his manual on health is clear and to the point. Witless science has worked its mischief, but we are not helpless. We have only to take command of our own health and make sensible judgements without reference to higher approved authority.

Young Again! has little to do with mirror image vanity and everything to do with the "mechanical limits of the organism," as Albert Carter Savage put it, meaning the human body.

Young Again! has to be read with a box of marker pens handy. It is a matchless narrative and an encyclopedia of health. It covers the secrets of the ancients and projects forward to encompass the range of the electromagnetic spectrum. The advice—page by page, chapter by chapter—may not entirely reverse aging, but it is certain to put the process on hold.

Charles Walters
Editor, Acres USA
Kansas City, Missouri

Aim High!

This "object" of this book is to provide the reader with ANSWERS to health concerns and improve the quality of the reader's life. Hopefully, these are the reasons you are reading this book.

Your author's approach to health and longevity is total and BASIC! He does NOT believe in band aids or magic bullets. He wants readers to understand how loss of control of the body's terrain occurs and exactly what must be done to experience aging reversal.

It is not the author's *intent* to be absolute or over-zealous. Few people will be able to comply 100% with all of the suggestions contained in these pages. The reader is encouraged to advance in personal knowledge at his/her own pace. Do not feel doomed because you are unable to follow all suggestions at once. Please realize, the material presented represents the BEST you can shoot for—the goal—the ideal!

The ideal world of health is a lifestyle that includes wholesome food, pure water, moderate exercise, adequate rest, low stress, a clean body and a strong mind. These things are worth striving for even though the *perfect* lifestyle is very difficult to "live" in a world where disease and human suffering are the norm.

Hopefully, this book will help the reader find a middle ground where enjoyment of the best health life has to offer consistent with their own circumstances can be realized. We live in an imperfect world, and we fall short of the ideal. Sometimes we are subject to events and circumstances beyond our control. Yet, each day, we DO have the opportunity to make "choices" that affect our lives and health—and the lives of those around us—for good and bad. We must strive to make the BEST choices we can each and every day of our lives.

The reader is reminded that health and disease are **cumulative** states of being, and the *alternative* to good health is a sorry existence indeed. Poor health cheats us of happiness—and "life."

Aim high and do the very best you can. Good health is worth **whatever it takes** to get it and keep it!

Think About It!

"In the health arena, there are only two classes of people. Those who are young and healthy and those who are old or sick. The former want to hold onto their youth and the latter desperately want to reclaim what they have lost."
John Thomas

1

Something Of Value

*"If you want to look and feel as I do when
you are my age, you must begin!"*
Robert McLeod

It was a strange place for me to meet the person who would become my mentor. Stranger still were the circumstances—a restaurant meeting room in San Bernardino, California in 1971. The event: A district sales meeting for ARCO (Atlantic Richfield Company), formerly Richfield Oil Company.

Having graduated from college the previous September, I stood in awe of the grandeur of it all. The Company, the oil industry, and all that.

We had instinctively corralled ourselves into groups based on our position on the corporate ladder. Barnyard pecking order they call it.

And as a few of us were talking, I overheard my immediate superior and his cronies laughing and poking fun in a rather contemptuous way at one of their peers—a man named, Bob McLeod.

McLeod was not socializing with people of his own level ("status inconsistent" the sociologists call it). Instead, his peers had shunned him. As I listened to their gossip, something caught my attention.

"You know," one of them said, "McLeod is a vegetarian. He doesn't eat meat. He's...real strange!" "Yah! He's into health, whatever that is," said another.

It was difficult to compare McLeod to this arrogant, egocentric bunch of executives. I could NOT account for the differences between the *group* and the stranger, McLeod.

McLeod looked young. His smile, his eyes, his laugh—nothing squared with someone of forty-nine years. His hair was vibrant! His stomach trim and slim. I liked what I beheld!

The "other" executives, well, they all looked twenty years older than McLeod. Paunchy stomachs, grayed hair, bald heads, fat, cigarettes blazing—and booze. Many were ready for their gold watches. But by this time in history, gold watches had been replaced by the old glass hand, a slap on the back and the epitaph on the grave stone, *"He was a good old boy!"*

McLeod Knew

McLeod knew something they did not, for he was forty-nine years "young" and the others, who were in their late thirties and early forties, were, well,...older!

I took my first step into the world of ageless living as I navigated in McLeod's direction. Life would never again be the same for me. I was destined to be there on that day, at that moment, and Bob McLeod was destined to become my mentor. God works in strange ways!

I introduced myself to this forty-nine years *young* enigma and as we talked it became crystal clear that he was a very special human being.

Immediately, my mind was made up! "When I reach forty-nine, I am going to *LOOK* and *FEEL* like Bob McLeod!"

"It's a long story and you are going to have to search it out for yourself, but I would consider it a privilege if I can assist you," he said.

Instant friends we were! Fellow travelers for sure! Our paths only crossed a few times in the months that followed. When they did, he would take me under his wing and point the way.

"If you want to understand how I have managed to look and feel twenty years younger than I am, you will have to study. I recommend you begin by reading a book by Dr. Paul C. Bragg, entitled, *The Miracle of Fasting.*

"You will not find all the answers there, but this book is a good place to start," he said.

Six months after meeting Bob, I left the company and lost ALL contact with him until August of 1993. He still looks *young and vibrant!* If you saw him on the street today you would guess him to be in his late forties. Not too bad for someone age 69 years YOUNG!

Twenty-six years have passed and now it is my turn. As I approach fifty-three (53) years *young*, I am here to tell you that you **CAN** stop the clock and reverse the aging process—if you will follow my lead and stay on course.

Fear

People are reluctant to venture out, to break new ground, to sail uncharted waters—particularly when it involves being *different*. Perhaps it is social pressure. Perhaps they think they are giving up *something of value*. Regardless, fear and ignorance are the primary stumbling blocks that keep people from following the path of good health. Instead, they hang onto old bad habits that become the glue with which they seal their grave(s).

Most of my peers at that fortuitous meeting are well on their way into old age. All of them were past their anabolic PEAK at that time. Today, most of them suffer from degenerative conditions and some of them are dead. All of them are old beyond their years—each product of their "choices." There is no room for blame here. We are responsible for our CHOICES!

People do not think "they" are going to get old. They know they have to die, but it is the other guy who gets old, never them. One day they wake up and look in the mirror, and their mind says, "Heh! Better enjoy it while you can! Time is short!" As friends grow old and die, the image in the mirror is confirmed—disease and old age have arrived.

It's important to understand the difference between a disease and a condition. A disease is a condition that has "officially" been given a name. Diseases and conditions BOTH alter our lifestyle and prevent us from enjoying life as we normally would if we were in a healthy state of being.

We do not CATCH diseases. We DEVELOP conditions. Disease should be hyphenated. It should be spelled "dis-ease," and we will do so for the remainder of this book to drive home the point. We die of conditions, not dis-eases!

How we define our health problems greatly influences our **attitude** about aging and our ability or inability to take control of our lives and redirect those forces that cause the bio-electric body to grow OLD.

It's Your Decision

Would YOU like to become *Young Again*? All that is required is that you complete this book and apply its lessons in your life. If you want to experience the **miracle** of reversing the aging process, you MUST *visualize* the end result in your mind's eye. The miracle is available to *anyone* who wants it, but it is NOT free. You will become acquainted with the price as each chapter unfolds.

Once you understand HOW you become old, you will understand HOW to become *Young Again!*

PREVIEW: *In the next chapter, you will discover that you have four different ages. You will also determine your anabolic PEAK and learn about its significance in your life.*

GLOOM

SUNSHINE

YOUR CHOICE

UNHEALTHY LIFESTYLE   ← **?** →   **HEALTHY LIFESTYLE**

The choice of which road to take is up to the individual. He alone can decide whether he wants to reach a dead end or live a healthy lifestyle for a long, happy, active life.   – Paul C. Bragg

---

REALITY SELF CHECK

"When you look down the street, do you see a STOP sign instead of the horizon? Young people see only the horizon because their entire life is in FRONT of them.

"Don't lose sleep over the doctor's diagnosis—for it is nothing but a confirmation of yesterday's poor choices. Instead, focus on today and tomorrow will be yours.

"When you look in the mirror and the image looking back at you isn't the one you remember when you were young, you better believe the image looking at you!"

"In this book, the author goes a long way to provide hope that, in a world beset by health threatening pollution of all kinds, we are afforded some tools with which to build healthier, longer, and perhaps happier lives."

Christopher Bird, *The Scret Life of Plants*

2

young Again!

*"Youth is a wonderful thing. What
a crime to waste it on children."*
George Bernard Shaw

**Old age follows days filled with new hopes and new
dreams of good times to come.** Good times that go unfulfilled
because our body fails to keep up with our mind.

An old body with a young mind is a phenomenon where
conflict and misunderstanding abound. It is a condition where
the body we once knew becomes *lost* in Time and unable to
communicate with the mind. Flip sides of the same coin: a
young mind, an old body. Each expresses itself in a different
language with no interpreter to translate.

Aging occurs through ignorance—and by **CHOICE!**
People grow old because they do not know HOW to stay young.
They are becoming old much faster than they once did. This is
particularly true among the young—especially women between
ages 25-45. The young now experience the ONSET of old age by
year 24. Dis-eases that were once the domain of the old are now
the domain of the young. The problem can be reversed!

Despite the statistical claims of the *experts*, life expectancy is *not* greater today than it was yesterday. The statistics
used to support this claim of greater life expectancy have been
skewed by the number of children reaching adulthood. At one
time, half the population of the United States died prior to
reaching age twenty. Those deaths held life expectancy down.
The *statistical* rise in life expectancy over the last fifty years has

caused a gullible public to accept medicine's false claim of greater life expectancy. This is a serious mistake.

We are NOT better off today than we were yesterday. Degenerative conditions have replaced infectious conditions. Moreover, contagious conditions are on the rise and are returning with a vengeance. They are MORE than an old enemy returned. Their return spells ill for those who are unprepared and unwilling to conform to nature's plan.

A long, HEALTHY life is what we were meant to experience during our sojourn on Mother Earth. That is what this book is all about.

Dividing Line

At my initiation into the study of aging in 1971, it was considered difficult to turn the body's biological clock backward if someone had *survived* thirty-five years of NORMAL living. If we made the same statement today, we would have to reduce age thirty-five down to age twenty-four. The dividing line between youth and the ONSET of old age is falling—fast!

When we are young, our health is at its peak and the body is able to repair itself quickly and easily. The word *anabolism* best describes this state. Anabolism means the absence of breakdown in body tissues. It also implies normal body repair of muscle, skin and bones. It is a *building up* process.

As we age, body functions slow and we become fragile. Injuries do not heal as quickly. *Catabolism* best describes this state. It means the breaking-down of body tissue. It is the opposite of anabolism.

Catabolism releases energy. It is a kind of *self-digestion* where the body lives off the energy released from the digestion of its own tissues. This is bare-bones energy used to meet the body's *minimum* energy needs. Energy produced through catabolic activity is starvation energy. Catabolic activity can keep us alive, but it should NOT be equated with health and longevity. Catabolism has its roots in death.

When we are young we are anabolic. When we are old, we are catabolic. Of course, there are degrees within these two categories. In this book, when we use the words *anabolism* and *catabolism* we are referring to the OVERALL condition or direction of the bio-electric body and its implications to the aging process.

The age twenty-four dividing line we spoke of earlier is our **anabolic PEAK.** It is that point in Time when the young begin their slide into old age. Some people experience their anabolic peak earlier than age twenty-four. For others it comes a little later. The *point* is that its onset is arriving much too soon.

Once Upon A Time

There was a time when it was uncommon to see the first signs of old age until the fortieth or forty-fifth year—unless one was subject to hardships beyond the norm. Obesity, gray hair, balding, loss of sexual drive, wrinkled skin, and diminished vitality are all classic *SIGNS* of old age.

Before we can erase these signs of old age, we need to understand *why* they occur. We also need to understand *how* they express themselves. When we become AWARE of the passing of *TIME*, we also become aware of the invisible forces of aging—forces that cause the young to wake up old.

When we reach our **anabolic peak,** we are at the crossroads of Time. We are caught between the wonder of youth and the approach of old age.

Aging initiates quietly and without notice. It is a self-ordained process that speeds the passing of Time and hastens our date with death.

Change The Script

Life does NOT have to be this way! We can change the script if we *choose*—no matter what our age! We can *reverse* our course if we are willing to learn and then act upon our new-found knowledge.

It is not the idea of growing old that people fear. Rather, it is the idea that old age will *cheat* them of the enjoyment of the things they once took for granted. For most, the thought of old age gives rise to visions of a dead-end street, loneliness, pain, suffering, and finally death.

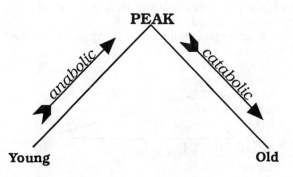

Anabolic Peak—That point in time when our youth is spent and the onset of old age has begun.

When I chose the title for this book, I wrestled between *Forever Young* and the present title, *Young Again!* The former title did not fit those people who are on the *anabolic* side of the pyramid. They will not read this book because they cannot grasp the meaning of the word *old*. Their world is *young*. They are never going to get old—or so they think.

Only those who realize that they have *passed* their anabolic peak understand the implications of the word *OLD*. To them, the idea of becoming *Young Again!* is only a dream.

Hosea proclaims, "My people are destroyed for lack of knowledge." However, it is not knowledge that mankind lacks, but the wisdom to discern the difference between false knowledge and truth. *Old age* and *old* are not necessarily synonymous. They do not have to mean the same thing.

The Doctor

When we are dying, we hear the pronouncements of medicine "Nothing can be done!" "Accept that which cannot be changed!" and other expressions designed to worm their way into our consciousness. These expressions numb our wits and excise our will to live.

Oral pacifiers, these pronouncements! Empty words designed to help us accept and rationalize the phenomena we call life and death.

In the beginning—when poor health manifests itself— the medical folks talk of recovery. In time, recovery gives way to high-tech jargon and HOPE.

For the terminal patient who has cast himself or herself before the altar of science, medicine quickly exhausts its mumbo-jumbo turning instead to steely words that chisel our name on the tombstone.

The doctor announces death's call. The patient answers that call with forced preparation and/or frustration and the questions "Why?" "How?"

The *mystery* of health and happiness, life and death goes unanswered.

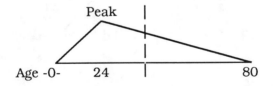

Aging Pyramid—note how far left of center the anabolic peak is located. In this case, it is shown at age 24.

The Clergy

Religious training convinces us that we have an "appointed time" and to "accept what God has foreordained"—soothing words that placate our emotions and numb the reality of the moment. Few people dare to question religion's pronouncements. There is little quarter for rationality here.

Instead, we elevate to dogma that which we do not understand. We blindly follow our beliefs, never pausing to question "Why?" and "How?" as life slips away.

We give up. We grow old. We accept what we have been taught, and we die decades ahead of TIME because medicine said, "Sorry!" and our religious leaders offered us little consolation—except a "hereafter."

The balance of society attempts to buffer the "Why?" and "How?" with cynicism set to music in songs like Peggy Lee's, *Is That All There Is!* Because we do NOT know where to find the answers, we keep dancing, pausing only to break out the booze.

Our inability to winnow truth from lies is *not* totally our fault. We have been schooled to accept the flood of distortions that emanate from our societal organs—government, newspapers and universities. They are bullhorns—all of them—wired to the halls of Science, the present god of our civilization. Science has become a cult, a national religion, but science fails to answer "*Why?*" *and* "*How?*"

Pilgrimage

Daily, we *voluntarily* make the pilgrimage to Science's cultic altar, paying homage to the idea that cause and effect can be explained using single factor analysis. We accept the *theory* that there is a bug responsible for every dis-ease, a pill to cure every ailment.

We are told we have a built-in alarm clock that signals our time to die, when longer days—good days—filled with health and happiness are within our reach if we will only act and accept our greatest gift of all—good health!

Science and medicine blame the bacteria and viruses for our health problems and Christianity blames Eve for bringing the curse of sickness and death upon Adam and his progeny.

Instead of taking responsibility for ourselves, we place blame as we prostrate ourselves before the *Altar of Science* and pay homage with the fruits of our labor. We buy medicines and pills that treat our symptoms but leave the causes untouched and more importantly, *unidentified!*

Palliation is a term that comes to mind. It says much about medical science in a few syllables. It means relief of SIGNS and SYMPTOMS without relief of underlying cause(s).

Drugs produce change in body function. They are prescribed to prevent, diagnose, or cure dis-ease. *Palliation* is the fourth reason pharmacology texts use to justify drug administration. Palliation *tricks* the patient and leads the physician astray.

How different life would be if people had a correct knowledge about dis-ease and the aging process, and then acted upon that knowledge. Sadly, mankind lives in a medically induced stupor, where the "Why?" and "How?" of life and death, health and disease goes unanswered.

Make no mistake, 99% of the aging process is under our direct, personal control. We can possess and maintain a young body AND a young mind—if we wish. This book was written to answer the "Why?" and "How?" and to point the way to the path of ageless living.

What Is Your Age?

How we define age can make a big difference in our *attitude* toward life. Our attitude dictates our daily actions. Our actions in turn draft our physiological future and our *bio-electric age*.

Age can be defined on the basis of chronological age, mental age, functional age, and most importantly, *bio-electric* age. *Carefully* review each.

Calendar age is how old we are in years upon this earth. We celebrate our calendar age each year with a birthday party. Unfortunately, we celebrate in *past tense* and in the *negative* by defining age in years *old*, instead of years *young!*

Mental age is defined by the way we think. Mental age is our perspective on life. It is a kind of mental cohort effect. A mental cohort is a "mental" time capsule where the person's mind is *stuck* in a past time period—like in the the Great Depression when the person grew up. Many older people are living proof of a *mental* cohort effect. These are people who are mentally young, but *physically* old.

Most of us know someone like this. Perhaps a loved one. Regardless of how young this person thinks, it is obvious that their body long ago passed its anabolic peak—losing cadence with their mind. *Old* body, *young* mind. Not a very exciting prospect is it?

Functional age is based on our ability to function. *Nursing* and bogus *holistic* medicine define functional health as our ability to experience normal, everyday desired activities.

These bogus medical definitions allow for one or more degenerative conditions, while *wellness* is based on the way we perceive ourselves, without respect to mental or physical limitations that deprive us of younger, healthier lifestyles.

The above plastic definitions bother me because they lead us astray! They *dodge* the issues and causes of aging and dis-ease! They are dead end statements.

We can only experience *peak* health in the ABSENCE of dis-ease. This book teaches you HOW to achieve that goal every day of your life for as long as you desire to live.

Reversing your **bio-electric age**, which is your body's *actual age*, is what this book is about. Your bio-electric age can be measured and manipulated downward. You will learn HOW in a future chapter. Hopefully, this prospect will motivate you to finish reading this book. When you learn how to manipulate and control the forces that influence your bio-electric age, TIME'S effect on your life ceases to be a concern. When you *LOOK*, *THINK* and *FEEL* young—you are *Young Again!*

PREVIEW: *In the next chapter, you are going to determine your REAL age and identify those things that are causing you to become old before your time. The information you provide will become YOUR foundation for the balance of this book. Are you ready?*

Brown Eyes Green

We are taught that eye color, balding, diabetes, obesity, and female problems are "genetic" in origin. But it's not so. Children are **born** with blueish eyes **before** they change to brown or black. Men **with** hair become bald after they **lose** it. People **become** diabetics! Women **develop** female problems. People **grow** fat.

I once had dark brown eyes. **Now,** the're half green. Men can **grow** hair again. Diabetics can **become** normal. Women can **recapture** feminine health. Fat people can **become** thin. "Genetic" problems are solved by purging the body of metabolic waste, by restoring hormonal balance and by consuming SUPER foods. "Genetic" problems are symtomatic **never** causitive. I "regrew" my hair and saw my life blossom AFTER 50 years of age—and so can you!

Who's In Control?

Question medical authority. Get up off your knees. It's YOUR body and YOUR life. Take control of your future.

NORMAL COLON AND SICK COLONS

A. The Normal Colon
The normal colon in the proper position in relation to other structures: 1) stomach 2) appendix 3) cecum 4) ascending colon 5) transverse colon 6) descending colon 7) sigmoid flexure 8) rectum

B. The Spastic Colon
The colon in spastic constipation.

C. The Engorged Colon
The colon in engorged constipation.

D. The Sagging Colon
Ptosis, or sagging, of the transverse colon, accompanied by displacement of the stomach.

Programmed To Die
We *program* ourselves to die by our actions, words, and thoughts. And as we prepare, the *reaper* takes our friends and siblings—a signal that "our" time is approaching. We do our best to make sure we are not left behind.

3

Any Old Road

*"If you don't know where you're going,
how will you know when you get there?
If you don't know how you got there,
any old road will NOT take you back."*
John Thomas

Aging is considered to be part of the normal life process. In actuality, it is the *abnormal* part of the process. Normal growth takes us from infancy to our anabolic peak. Abnormal aging takes us from our PEAK to our grave.

Aging follows a procession of TIME-related **events** we identify with symptomatic descriptions like: gray hair, menopause, balding, diabetes, wrinkles, loss of strength, low sex drive and obesity. These events document the passing of TIME. They are symptomatic, but they are also SIGNS of aging!

The aging process can be slowed, stopped and reversed. But these things are ONLY possible when we have correct knowledge supported with action. Informed action is *the* controlling factor.

People speed the aging process and the passing of TIME when they IGNORE the SIGNS along the way. 'Tuning-out' shortens their days on the Earth and they age by default. Instead, let us choose to *re-experience* TIME, **not** by reliving our experiences, but by *reliving* TIME itself—TIME that we have already spent.

Aging and Time are related, but they are not the same. Aging is the result of Time poorly lived, whereas Time is the *vehicle* of aging. For example, dis-eases like cancer are the product of Time *poorly* lived. Cancer causes the passing of Time to accelerate. When this occurs, our body experiences a slump in its *bio-electric* balance and we become OLD! Think of dis-ease as Time in motion. Dis-ease *warps* our concept of TIME! Aging is Time's trail—a confirmation of biological deterioration.

Rate Yourself

In a few lines you will be asked to *personalize* each of the types of aging we discussed in Chapter Two. This simple project will give the concepts of *aging* and *Time* more tangible meaning.

Use an erasable pen or pencil. *Estimate* and place *your* age on each line. Leave the last line blank until *after* you have scored your *bio-electric* age at the END of this chapter.

Mental Age	0_____	80 yrs
Calendar Age	0_____	80 yrs
Functional Age	0_____	80 yrs
Age You Feel	0_____	80 yrs
Bio-electric Age	0_____	**80 yrs ++**

Signs & Symptoms

Time poorly lived produces SIGNS and SYMPTOMS of *bio-electric* aging and dis-ease. Signs and symptoms represent *change* and diminished function in the vital organs and glands.

Symptoms of dis-ease are *subjective* changes in body function that are NOT apparent to an outside observer—like nausea, anxiety, pain, dryness of mouth, anorexia and low sex drive. Symptoms usually go unnoticed by the host. Symptoms, however, do indicate *subtle* alterations in body tissues, hormones, and fluids. Aging is a "NICE" word for slow-down. Slow-down eventually leads to shut-down.

Aging initially occurs in the "*invisible*" realm where the "electric" body resides. Eventually, aging is seen in the mirror and/or confirmed by the doctor's diagnosis.

Time Made Visible

Signs are different than symptoms. They are *external* events and are observable. SIGNS of—aging and/or dis-ease— can be observed and measured. Signs support a doctor's diagnosis of a morbid condition. Signs cause the host to become acutely aware of alteration of normal body function— like fever or inflammation. Hence, SIGNS are a *confirmation* of aging and the passing of Time. *Signs are Time made visible!*

Signs are *bio-electric* Time capsules.

Signs are *abnormal* events in the life process. They represent dis-ease and pathology. When we think of them as *normal*, we diminish their impact on our consciousness and we compound their effect. Aging and dis-ease are one in the same.

Dis-ease is like the unwelcome guest who drops in. Its *appearance* causes temporary upset. Yet, when it departs, dis-ease leaves its *shadow* upon us. Sometimes the shadow is self evident—as when we can no longer do the things we once did. More often than not the full manifestation of the aging shadow is delayed until we are in serious trouble. Only then does dis-ease remove its cloak and the passing of Time accelerates.

Damage to the vital organs is dis-ease's shadow. Slow down and loss of vital function should be our cue to change our lifestyle before it is too late.

Charting Your Bio-electric Age

The following list is your key to *your* bio-electric age. Additionally, it is the brush and canvas you will use to determine *how* and *why* your *bio-electric* age is what it is. This list is **your** *personal* road map to ageless living. It also points the way back in *bio-electric Time* —that is, if you absorb the simple lessons contained in the balance of this book. Each item on this list will be fleshed out as we proceed.

Each item reflects an assigned point value that is based on its long term **cumulative effect**. Most items are unisex and apply to both sexes while the male/female list applies to the respective sex only. *Contributing factors* that accelerate the aging process are also listed.

NOTE: This list is not a diagnosis of a particular dis-ease condition. Rather it is a list of markers. It gives you a close approximation of your *"bio-electric age"* providing you are honest with yourself.

Check the boxes that apply. Serious *past* health conditions should be counted if they have left their mark or are of recent vintage. If you are under care, or take medications for a condition, it should be counted. Complete this exercise NOW and again after you have completed the book when you better understand the significance of each item on this list. Each item will add direction and meaning to your quest for agelessness.

Please **do not** diminish or pass judgement on the items listed. The list is comprised of signs, symptoms, effects and contributing factors.

Let me assure you that every item deserves your *attention*. Their **cumulative** effect can easily BLOCK your path and prevent you from becoming *Young Again!*

Signs, Symptoms & Contributing Factors
Of Bio-electric Aging

Unisex

Height: Loss of physical height	
•1/4" shorter	50 ❏
•1/2" or more	200 ❏
Gout:	40 ❏
Eyes: •Crow's feet around eyes (mild)	8 ❏
•Crow's feet (heavy)	15 ❏
Skeletal Muscles: Deterioration of, loss of	20 ❏
•Soft or flabby	50 ❏
•Cramps/charleyhorse	18 ❏
Stomach (gut): Paunchy	8 ❏
•Pot/beer belly	40 ❏
Eyebrows: thick, bushy	15 ❏
Nose & Ear hair (external)	18 ❏
Clothes: Trousers/pants & Shirts/blouses	
•Progressively larger after age 24	20 ❏
Energy: Erratic, not level	25 ❏
Body Odor: Requires deodorant	20 ❏
•Overpowers deodorant	40 ❏
Bad Breath: Chronic	30 ❏
Teeth: •Decayed	40 ❏
•Cleaning required once a year	25 ❏
•Cleaning every 6 months	40 ❏
•Mercury amalgam fillings	150 ❏
•Root canal(s) present in mouth	40 ❏
•Gingivitis (inflamed gums)	30 ❏
Nails: finger/toe	
•Weak; break easily; spots; heavy ridges	20 ❏
•Slow growth	30 ❏
•Thickening of toe nails	40 ❏
Hearing: Poor; early onset; progressively worse	30 ❏
Skin:	
•Dry, scaly (includes dandruff)	10 ❏
•Psoriasis/seborrhea (scalp or body)	50 ❏
•Wrinkled (hands, face)	10 ❏
•Fat bumps on back of upper arms	10 ❏
•Pimples/acne/skin blemishes	30 ❏
•Do not sweat easily or much	20 ❏
•Brown *liver* spots on hands/body	40 ❏
•Bruise easily; painful to touch	60 ❏
•Heavy oil secretion	15 ❏
Hair, Mustache, & Beard:	
•Predominantly gray/white	30 ❏
•Bald head	30 ❏

•Loss of body (leg) hair   60 ☐
•Slow hair growth   30 ☐
•Head hair (once wavy, now straight)   40 ☐
•Gray or white pubic, axillary, or leg hair   40 ☐

Physical Activity:
•Inability to perform hard physical work   20 ☐
•Pain/inflammation during/after work   20 ☐
•Abnormal sleep/rest required to recover   30 ☐

Weight:
•Gain w/o increase in clothes size   30 ☐
•Gain w/o increase in food   20 ☐
•Unexplained large weight loss   40 ☐

Mental:
•Short or long term memory loss   20 ☐
•Fatigued; can't face day   30 ☐
•Foggy, can't gather thoughts   30 ☐
•Need coffee to get/keep going   20 ☐

Stools:
•Lack of medium dark brown color   30 ☐
•Hard, dry   20 ☐
•Defecation requires strain/effort   20 ☐
•Food transit time between mouth and
    toilet over 24 hours   40 ☐
•Overly foul gas/odor   40 ☐
•Bright red blood   15 ☐
•Less than a "complete" stool   20 ☐

Sickness/dis-ease:
•Often feel sick, but no fever   20 ☐
•Colds more than once a year   25 ☐
•Succumb to flu most years   20 ☐
•Diagnosed degenerative dis-ease   80 ☐

Eyes:
•Require reading glasses   8 ☐
•Sensitive to sunlight   40 ☐
•Inability to adjust to dark   20 ☐
•Brown spots in iris (colored portion)   30 ☐
•Shadows under eyes   30 ☐
•Drooping eye lids   8 ☐
•Eye lids don't open/close evenly   20 ☐
•Macular degeneration   50 ☐
•Retinitis/tunnel vision/galucoma   50 ☐

Cheeks:
•Sunken, hollow   8 ☐
•Jowls distended/sagging/inflated   25 ☐
•Flushed with spider capillaries   40 ☐

Joints:
- Joint pain (general) — 40 ❏
- Diagnosed arthritis, bursitis,
  rheumatism, or variations thereof — 60 ❏

Stature:
- Hunched-back (mild) — 80 ❏
- Hunched-back (severe) — 120 ❏

Minor Wounds:
- Scab drop-time for minor wounds
  requires over 1 week — 20 ❏
- Subject to secondary infections — 30 ❏
- Scars form easily — 40 ❏

Capillary Blood:
- Fails to form a "pearl" when
  finger is pricked (i.e. blood flows
  instead of forming a crown or pearl — 30 ❏
- Color is dark red; not bright red — 30 ❏
- *Less* than instantaneous color return
  to finger/toe nails when squeezed and
  released—both sides — 40 ❏
- Dizziness due to poor blood flow — 30 ❏
- Suffer w/sticky blood (Rouleau effect) — 50 ❏
- Use of blood thinners/aspirin — 50 ❏

Respiratory (lungs):
- Heavy breather/can't catch breath — 70 ❏
- Lungs fill with fluid — 80 ❏
- Angina-tightness — 40 ❏
- Asthma — 80 ❏

Colon/Bowels:
- Constipation (chronic) — 50 ❏
- On/off-irregular habits — 30 ❏
- Alternating diarrhea/constipation — 30 ❏
- Ongoing appendix problems — 50 ❏
- Appendix removed — 20 ❏
- Colitis — 75 ❏
- Diverticulitis — 75 ❏
- Removal of any portion of small intestine — 90 ❏
- Colostomy — 60 ❏
- Parasite activity or untreated for parasites — 90 ❏

Blood Circulatory System:
- Heart Attack — 80 ❏
- Low red blood cell count (chronic) — 40 ❏
- Low hemoglobin level — 30 ❏
- Diagnosed arterio/atherosclerosis — 100 ❏
- Poor circulation — 30 ❏

Lymphatic System:
- •Nodes chronically swollen/painful in groin/armpits/throat — 50 ❑
- •Lymph nodes surgically removed — 50 ❑
- •Cancer of lymph system (lymphoma) — 90 ❑
- •Spleen surgically removed — 60 ❑

Body Fat:
- •30-50 lbs overweight — 90 ❑
- •Body weight at top of "normal" scale — 30 ❑
- •Fatty tumors beneith skin over body — 50 ❑
- •Total fat intake over 20% of diet — 10 ❑
- •Use of ANY type margarine — 30 ❑
- •Use of soy/canola oils or products — 60 ❑
- •Severely restricted intake of dietary fat — 30 ❑

Urinary:
- •Chronic albumin in urine — 50 ❑
- •High urea level in urine — 40 ❑
- •Low specific gravity urine — 30 ❑
- •Prone to kidney stones — 40 ❑
- •Generally dark urine color — 25 ❑
- •Foul urine odor — 30 ❑
- •Sweet urine odor — 50 ❑
- •Bladder infections (female) — 75 ❑
- •Volume usually small (less than 4 oz) — 35 ❑

General Metabolic:
- •Drink less than 1/2 gal water/day — 40 ❑
- •Drink with your meals — 20 ❑
- •Drink chlorinated/fluoridated H_2O — 60 ❑
- •Substitute soft drinks for water — 60 ❑
- •Failure to drink at least 8 oz of H_2O every two hours — 30 ❑
- •Failure to drink at least 12 oz of H_2O every 15/30 minutes during hard physical activity — 20 ❑
- •Use fluoridated toothpaste — 30 ❑
- •Use common deodorants — 30 ❑
- •Drinking water comes from tap — 50 ❑
- •Drinking water source is bottled, distilled or common filtered — 30 ❑
- •Over counter medications for headaches — 40 ❑
- •Regularly take Rx drugs — 40 ❑

Liver/Gallbladder/Indigestion:
- •Diagnosed/prone to gall baldder problems — 60 ❑
- •Surgical removal of gall bladder — 60 ❑
- •Diagnosed for, or prone to hepatitis, mononucleosis, Epstein-Barr, malaria, or Chronic Fatigue Syndrome — 60 ❑

Saliva:
- Dry mouth — 20 ❑
- Must drink liquids to swallow — 30 ❑

Body Temperature:
- Chronic low grade fever &/or below normal temperature — 35 ❑
- Cold hands and feet — 60 ❑
- Sensitive to frigid temperatures — 30 ❑
- Inability to handle hot weather — 30 ❑

Connective Tissue/Energy
- Diagnosed w/systemic lupus/MS/myasthenia gravis/or degenerative nerve conditions — 200 ❑
- Have a diagnosed disorder — 20 ❑
- Stiff joints/loss of flexibility — 20 ❑
- Lack of energy — 40 ❑
- Must eat often to have energy — 30 ❑
- Subject to mood swings/energy drops — 30 ❑
- Meals slow energy & brain function — 20 ❑
- Sleepy/listless after lunch meal — 20 ❑

Stress and Headaches:
- Inability to function under stress — 30 ❑
- Regularly stressed-out — 40 ❑
- Chronic headaches — 40 ❑

Gastrointestinal Tract:
- Cramping after meals — 30 ❑
- Chronic gas — 50 ❑
- *Foul* gas — 40 ❑
- Bloated abdomen after meals — 50 ❑
- Diagnosed for colitis, diverticulitis Crohn's dis-ease — 60 ❑

Cancer:
- Diagnosis of any type of cancer — 200 ❑
- Received chemo/radiation therapy — 200 ❑
- Cysts or tumors of any kind — 50 ❑

Tobacco:
- Smoke or chew — 95 ❑

Tongue:
- Coated, pasty white-daytime — 40 ❑
- Coated upon rising in morning — 20 ❑
- Heavily grooved — 40 ❑

Sleep:
- Sleep less than 7 hours per night — 7 ❑
- Sleep less than 6 hours per night — 30 ❑
- Sleep broken; usually interrupted — 20 ❑
- Sleep with windows closed — 30 ❑
- Sleep under electric blanket — 50 ❑
- Walking Legs syndrome — 60 ❑

- •Insomnia (can't sleep) — 20 ❑
- •Hypersomnia (sleep all time) — 40 ❑
- •Narcolepsy (involuntary daytime sleep lasting about 15 minutes) — 40 ❑

Dietary:
- •Don't use multi-vitamins/minerals — 20 ❑
- •Use "non food based" vitamins/minerals — 20 ❑
- •Take calcium supplements — 20 ❑
- •Lump in throat (difficulty swallowing) — 50 ❑
- •Pulse picks up after meal — 10 ❑
- •Vomit often — 40 ❑
- •Eat when nervous — 30 ❑
- •Excessive appetite — 30 ❑
- •Increased appetite w/o weight gain — 30 ❑
- •Acid foods upset stomach — 30 ❑
- •Nervous stomach — 20 ❑
- •Always hungry — 60 ❑
- •Poor appetite — 25 ❑
- •Milk causes indigestion/bloating — 20 ❑
- •Spicy foods a problem — 20 ❑
- •Greasy foods cause indigestion — 50 ❑
- •Snack often — 30 ❑
- •Eat or snack more often than every 4 hrs — 25 ❑
- •Devour food...fast eater — 30 ❑
- •Salt food — 30 ❑
- •Eat lots of alfalfa sprouts — 20 ❑
- •Food not home grown — 40 ❑
- •Eat restaurant food regularly — 50 ❑
- •Eat lots of junk/packaged foods — 40 ❑
- •Own/use a microwave oven — 50 ❑

Computer:
- •In front of more than 1 hour daily — 8 ❑
- •Closer than 30 inches from face to monitor — 30 ❑

Florescent-Mercury—Sodium vapor Light:
- •Use for work light — 20 ❑

Electric price scanner: — 20 ❑

Cellular Telephone (use regularly) — 30 ❑

Radar:
- •Work with radar (police/military) — 40 ❑

Electronic Equipment: Exposed to daily — 30 ❑

Smoke Detector: Sleep/work under — 20 ❑

Exercise: Lack of aerobic activity 3x week — 30 ❑

Basal Metabolic Rate: Low — 50 ❑

Wake-up: Slow; requires several hours — 40 ❑

Resting Pulse Rate: above 75 — 20 ❑

Blood Pressure:
- Resting pressure above 90/130 — 50 ☐
- Resting pressure above 80/120 — 20 ☐

Emotions:
- Keyed-up, can't relax — 30 ☐
- Moods of depression/melancholy — 40 ☐
- Highly emotional — 30 ☐

Females Only

Menstruation & Menopause:
- Easily fatigued — 20 ☐
- Premenstrual tension (PMS) — 50 ☐
- Painful/difficult menses — 50 ☐
- Depression before menstruation — 20 ☐
- Ovaries/uterus removed — 80 ☐
- Frigid/loss of sexual desire — 40 ☐
- Menses irregular/skip often — 40 ☐
- Acne worse during menses — 30 ☐
- Painful breasts — 60 ☐
- Body painful to touch — 60 ☐
- Ovarian cysts/uterine fibroid tumors — 95 ☐
- Hot flashes — 95 ☐
- Can detect active ovary each month — 60 ☐
- Used birth control pills (ever) — 150 ☐
- Used any form of estrogen replacement — 150 ☐
- Thyroid condition/thyroid medication — 90 ☐
- Thinning vaginal walls/painful sex — 90 ☐
- Yeast/bladder infections; vaginal itching — 80 ☐
- Endometriosis — 200 ☐
- Food binges/cravings before menses — 80 ☐
- Foggy mindedness, confusion — 90 ☐
- Lack of sexual interest — 90 ☐

Male Only

- Impotentence — 90 ☐
- Prostate: (inflammation of, BHP) — 90 ☐
- Prostate removed — 80 ☐
- PSA count over 5 — 60 ☐
- Painful ejaculation — 60 ☐
- Urination dribble, can't release — 90 ☐
- Frequent night urination — 80 ☐
- Pain inside leg or heels — 30 ☐
- Leg spasms, cramps at night — 20 ☐
- Lack of sexual interest — 100 ☐

Total Score.. _____

Divide (men divide by 232; women by 244) |‾‾‾‾‾‾‾‾‾‾‾

Your *bio-electric* "reference score" is........... _____

   Add your points together and divide your score by 232 for men or 244 for women to obtain your *bio-electric* reference score. Example: If you are man and your score is 1838, divide by 232 to obtain a **reference score** of 7.92, and so on.
   Next, use the conversion scale to convert your reference score to your *bio-electric* age of 70 years. This is your **"real"** age!

Bio-electric Score Conversion Scale

   The number on the left is your reference score. The number on the right is your *bio-electric age.*

.18 = 18	.22 = 20	.30 = 22	.33 = 24
.66 = 28	1.1 0= 30	2.42 = 35	2.86 = 40
3.30 = 45	3.96 = 50	4.40 = 55	5.28 = 60
6.60 = 65	7.92 = 70	8.81 = 75	11.0 = 80+ etc.

   Your bio-electric age *should* motivate you to evaluate your lifestyle and the peculiarities of your particular body. **DO NOT panic or feel hopeless if your bio-electric age is older than you think it should be. It is only a reference age.**
   Remember, it took your entire life to reach your present *bio-electric* age. Allow yourself a little time to undo the damage. **Circle** your age and **transfer** your score to the chart earlier in this chapter. You should re-calculate your *bio-electric age* every year to determine if you are aging or growing younger. Your *bio-electric age* is a VERY important **reference** number.

Think About It!

   If your *calendar age* is twenty-seven years and your bio-electric age is thirty-nine years—as mine was when I began the reversal process—you are losing the battle. Consider the impact each additional *bio-electric* year exerts upon you. The younger you are, the less effect a few extra years will have. BUT, if you are already thirty-five, forty, fifty, sixty or MORE *bio-electric* years OLD, a few extra years can mean a lot and they must not be ignored or written off.
   The older you are, the faster Time flies and the faster you become old! You "know" you are in trouble when the SIGNS appear. Most signs appear between *bio-electric* age thirty and

fifty five. Female/male problems, fat/obesity, thyroid problems, low energy, arthritis, gray hair, cancer, stroke, multiple sclerosis, lupis, fibromyalgia, yeast bladder infections, etc.

Time is NOT on your side if your bio-electric age is equal to or greater than your calendar age.

There is NO time to waste! Don't look back! Make yourself finish this book and apply what you learn! The answers you SEEK are contained in these pages.

My calendar age is 53, but my bio-electric age is holding at 19 years YOUNG! Time is standing still for me—and it can stand still for you too—if you will do what needs to be done!

No one's situation is hopeless! The *bio-electric* body has AMAZING resiliency! Follow the steps outlined in this book and your body will heal itself. Let your body prove to you that you can become *Young Again!*

ACTION STEPS TO AGELESS LIVING

1. Evaluate your score & review items checked.
3. Complete your study of this book.
4. ACT upon your new knowledge.
5. Recalculate your score once a year.
6. Learn to GUARD your words and thoughts.
(Read *Your Body Believes Every Word You Say*)

Each thing you do to improve your health—no matter how small—will produce big benefits. Several small steps are more effective than one big step. The combined effect of many steps is *synergistic*.

PREVIEW: *In our next chapter, you will meet a few great people of science; get a glimpse of the behind the scenes maneuvering within medicine; be offered an explanation of mankind's present environmental dilemma.*

Female Problems

The LAST thing women need is calcium and magnesium. Contrary to popular belief, mineral intake is NOT the issue. Female problems have "one" common denominator—and you will discover what it is in future pages of this book.

All Played Out

Life is like a record player that plays in three speeds: 33, 45 and 78. At 33 life is great. At 45 you're not so sure. At 78, you're all played out. To avoid being a 78 at **45,** all you have to do is "reduce" your bio-electric age to decimal .33!

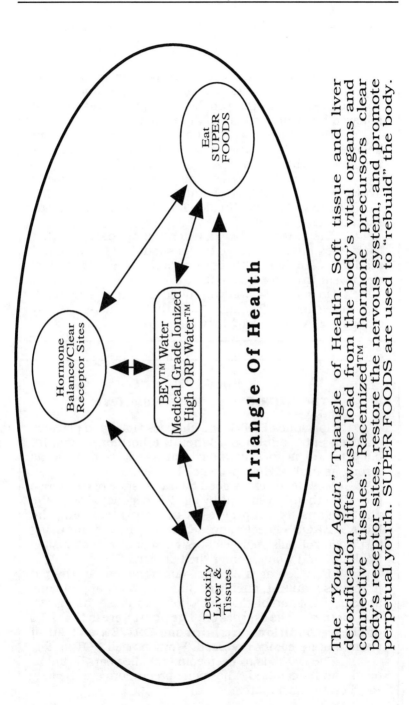

The *"Young Again"* Triangle of Health. Soft tissue and liver detoxification lifts waste load from the body's vital organs and connective tissues. Racemized™ hormone precursors clear body's receptor sites, restore the nervous system, and promote perpetual youth. SUPER FOODS are used to "rebuild" the body.

"The Experts"

When a system becomes overly *complex*, a cadre of *experts* soon appear with their agenda, codes, and private vocabulary. And in the people, this spawns resentment followed by skepticism as to the system's fairness.

Most of what we're taught and much of what we believe either isn't true or doesn't work. The experts understand this fact and so should you.

To learn the rules of the game and learn how to avoid "experts," read *If You Want To be Rich & Happy, Don't Go To School, Winning Through Intimidation,* and *Looking Out For Number One.*

The latter two books teach the **opposite** of what their titles imply. All three books should be "mandatory" reading—complete with book reports—every month of every year from grades K-12.

Do yourself—and your children a favor—by reading these classics. The only thing that counts is the way things are, NOT the way they ought to be.

PUBERTY
The "WINDOW" To The Middle Years

Hormones DRIVE the changes that take place as children enter adulthood. When the hormones kick in, baby fat turns to lean muscle mass. Boys become as strong as mules. Girls become shapely.

Most teens enjoy good health in spite of the abuse they deal themselves. But by age 25, degeneration of the vital organs is in progress. In young women, the **DISASTEROUS** effects imposed on the body from using birth control pills manifests as hormonal receptor sites "lock up" and women enter "hell on earth!"

Between ages 28-35, women pile on fat, thyroid problems manifest, energy declines, menstrual problems appear, yeast and bladder infections manifest , hair grays and/or thins—the list goes on. **The point here is that ALL of these conditions are hormone DRIVEN and all of them can be easily reversed.** Women need NOT suffer.

The GOAL is to keep your "middle years" window open—and racemized™ hormone precursors are the key. Read on to learn more.

4

See What You Look At

Said Dorothy to the Wizard:

"You're a very bad man!"
"Oh no!" responded the Wizard.
"I'm just a very bad Wizard!"

It's difficult to comprehend the human dilemma without some understanding of the forces within science and medicine that blur our vision and confuse our thought processes. Once understood, however, the reader will more fully grasp why he or she is discovering the path of agelessness in the pages of this book versus the media or medical system literature.

The truly Great Wizards of science and medicine are a breed of their own. They are often light years ahead of their time. They are also a problem for those who want to control and manipulate society. There have been many of these great people in science and medicine. Many of them lived out their lives on the fringe—away from mainstream medicine and science. We hear little about them, but the impact of their vision is all around us—often with another's name on their discoveries. A few hardy souls chose to function *within* the system. Their insight usually created craters that could neither be denied nor erased by the powers that be.

I refer to these people as WIZARDS. Wizards understand medical science's loss of direction and the dilemma of TRUTH vs. theory.

Medical science's tragic loss of direction did NOT occur by accident, rather, it was foreordained. It is a tale of manipulation and *behind the scene* control.

Let us paint the historical landscape of a few great men and women of REAL medical science so we will better understand the politics of medicine and why each of us must accept responsibility for our own lives and 'UNPLUG' from the medical system. Here's a brief history of a few medical Wizards.

The Great Wizards

Dr. Carey Reams was a Wizard. Reams had a sixth sense about nature and the energy forces of life at the subatomic level. He exhibited the instincts necessary for genius to express itself.

Like others before him, Reams knew that science and medicine had lost their way. They *refused* to see the obvious, choosing instead to face down TRUTH with calls for endless studies, procedure, and rubber stamped proof!

Reams *dared* to expose the connection between diet, lifestyle and dis-ease. He used simple, inexpensive testing procedures that only called for the pH of the urine and saliva plus the mapping of the blood capillaries in whites of the eyes. Reams chose NOT to follow allopathic medicine's path. He knew that health and vitality are *gifts* from God. He tried to give these gifts to the world and suffered professional ridicule and legal abuse for his efforts.

Dr. Linus Pauling was a Wizard! He gave us his monumental discoveries about vitamin C. He also suffered professional ridicule for the TRUTH he heralded. Dr. Pauling was the harbinger of the fantastic DNA molecule discovery in 1954. He was cheated of the credit, but was gentlemanly enough to congratulate Watson and Crick's presence at the finish line. Pauling died at age 94. He still taught at Stanford.

Millions of people are indebted to Dr. Pauling. He was a wonderful scientist and a monument to TRUTH. Truth separates a good scientist from a poor one. Truth comes before personal fame and fortune. Dr. Pauling was a servant to mankind. Medicine and science would do well to emulate him.

Dr. Guenther Enderlein was a Wizard. He proved that the blood is NOT a sterile medium. He heralded the pleomorphic nature of microbial life forms that are always present in the blood of healthy people. He further elucidated exactly why and how various life forms from viruses and bacteria to yeast and fungi predictably appear in the blood as people lose control of their body terrain. Also, Enderlein was the first person to use body fluid pH to detect the presence of cancer. Dr. Wilhelm Pfeffer of the University of Leipzig tested Enderlein's understanding of life with the question, *"What is the difference between plant and animal?"* Enderlein responded, *"There is NO difference!"* He was correct and his discoveries proved it.

Rene M. Caisse, R.N. was a Wizard. Rene was Canada's "cancer nurse." She reconstructed and resurrected an old North American Indian herbal recipe that "cured" thousands of people of all types of cancer and diabetes.

Rene was a good student and a keen observer of nature's ways. She understood life at the subtle energy level and she tempered her understanding with compassion for others. Rene was hounded by health officials, but her TRUTH lives on. We not only have her prized recipe, but we also have the EXACT source of her high resonance racemic herbs

Rene's tea is the ONLY *vibrational* product to ever be imported into mainland China specifically for the treatment of diabetes, cancer, and other degenerative conditions.

Dr. Max Gerson was a Wizard. His discoveries are of tremendous importance to the aging process. He immigrated to the United States from Germany in the 1920's. He was an excellent example of "low-tech" medical brilliance. Gerson leveled cancer's playing field by using uncommon good sense, instinct, and inexpensive therapies.

What made Gerson unique was that his therapies worked. He cared about people. He was an astute observer. He *cured* cancer with simple, inexpensive modalities and therein was the *rub*. Gerson was hounded mercilessly by the American Medical Association and various state medical boards because his work threatened medicine's dogmatic position on the nature of cancer. He died in 1959 tired and overworked.

Rachel Carson was a Wizard. She was the lady scientist who took on the military industrial complex by herself. In 1959, she wrote the book, *Silent Spring*. Rachel was the beginning of the *legitimate* environmental movement. Her findings shattered Science's litany of lies and brought the evils of pesticides into focus. She was proclaimed a witch and was verbally burned at the stake before and after she died in 1964. Her epitaph reads: TRUTH!

Dr. Ignaz Semmelweis was a Wizard. He has particular significance to medical science and our story. He was a physician in Budapest during the middle 1800's.

Semmelweis made the mistake of confronting a thoroughly entrenched male dominated profession that had only recently wrestled away control of the healing arts from female healers—midwifery in this case. His contribution to medical science was a simple one, but it involved the use of uncommon good sense—a dangerous commodity in the face of arrogance.

Semmelweis said, **"Doctors, wash your hands between patients!"**

There had been unrelenting outbreaks of childbirth fever (Puerperal Fever) among women and hundreds of deaths in area hospitals. The year was 1840. His detractors laughed good Dr. Semmelweis from the scene. They destroyed his reputation by character assassination—a ploy that leaves neither trail nor record of those in bloody robes. They also used professional ostracism—a time-tested tool of the trade. Today, they resort to revocation of a physician's license to practice— putting a doctor out of business. Ostracism, licenses, and belittling are *common* maneuvers used to this day to CONTROL physicians who dare to step out of line.

This codicil is offered to stimulate the reader's perspective. A doctor's status derives from the State. When the State grants its permission, the professional is created by way of a license. The doctor is a political being that exists at the whim of the State.

Licenses are supposed to protect the public. More often than not, they are a mockery that does little more than soothe. Behind the scenes, the professional boards and medical organizations badger and control the doctor who "sees truth" and dares to challenge scientific and medical dogma.

History provides us with a long list of good Wizards— Galileo and Copernicus for example—who were driven out and destroyed. Control is the name of the game. Control is ALWAYS carefully maintained despite brush-fire political events that are provided for their theatrical effect. Keep these thoughts in mind as future chapters unfold. In history, nothing happens by accident!

The history books tell us Dr. Semmelweis *suggested* that doctors should wash their hands between patients. They tell us *nothing* of the political maneuvering by his peers, nor of the women who died, nor of the money that was siphoned away from people who prostrated themselves at medicine's altar.

How It Happened

To understand how science and medicine lost their way and why mankind is at war with Mother Earth let us go to the roots of Christianity, for it is there that we will find our clue.

And God said to Adam, *"Take dominion over the Earth and every living thing thereon."*

This one command, credited to Deity, has done more to

pillage the Earth and its inhabitants—plant, animal and man—than any words ever put to task. The problem isn't the command, but its *interpretation* and *implementation*.

Misunderstood and certainly *misapplied*, the biblical edict to *"take control of Nature and hold dominion over Her"* set the course and destiny of history from the time of Christ to Isaac Newton and the present day order.

By *blaming* the sin and fall in the garden on Eve—instead of acknowledging that BOTH male and female made their own choice—*man* dogmatized jurisdiction over woman and proclaimed WAR against Nature and the Earth. It was done in the *name* of GOD. Mankind's present dilemma is the result of blame instead of mutual respect for life.

Adam & Eve

"Power and dominion OVER nature," shaped science and its tributary, medicine, into the cult it is today. Man over God. Man over the Earth. Man over Woman—for it says, "Eve caused Adam to sin."

Interwoven in this tragic story was the shift from mankind's original primeval state as a *matriarchal* society to that of a *patriarchal* one. No longer would the blood line flow through the woman. Instead it would flow through the man. No more would Woman be exalted and recognized as the *giver* of life. Instead, she would be looked upon as the *ONE* who caused *man* to sin in the garden.

"And from this day forward, you will experience pain in childbirth as a REMINDER of your transgression." And so, Woman became the villain. A commodity to be controlled, bought, sold, and most importantly, *"blamed"* for Adam's transgression—which was Adam's own choice.

It was into this arena that Dr. Semmelweis wandered. Little did he realize that the powers behind the scene did not care about Puerperal Fever. It was profitable business. *"So what if some women die as long as WE control access to choice in medical care, access to God, and, of course, control over the creation of a nations money supply."*

Control is the name of the game. If we want control over our lives and destinies, we must recognize that in matters of health and finance, things are NOT what they seem (please read *Winning Through Intimidation*, and *Looking Out For #1*).

TRUTH in medicine causes problems and the greater medicine's *backlash* to a Wizard's message, the greater the probability that TRUTH is on the loose.

In the business of medicine and science, TRUTH prospers OUTSIDE the mainstream—out on the fringe. The fringe is where we will be taking our lessons in reversing the aging process. On the fringe you can become *Young Again!*

PREVIEW: *In our next chapter, you will become acquainted with the "energy forces" that CONTROL the aging process and you will learn HOW to identify them.*

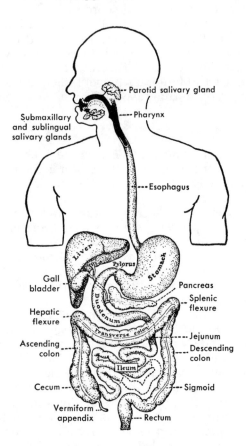

Visceral Organs Of The Abdominal Cavity

Dark Circles Under The Eyes

Circles under the eyes are a SIGN of liver overload, kidney malfunction, under-hydration, lymphatic congestion, and systemic toxicity. A change in lifestyle and diet can eliminate this SIGN of premature aging.

5

Energy And Matter

*"Reason, of course, is weak when measured
against its never-ending task. Weak, indeed, compared with the follies and passions of mankind,
which, we must admit, almost entirely control our
human destinies, in great things and small."*

Albert Einstein

Little in life is seen in concrete terms of black and white.
This is particularly true in the healing arts. For example,
consider the differences in the following modalities (therapies)
of healing presently in use.

Allopathic medicine (allopathy) attempts to heal using chemotherapy, which is *"chemically induced"* restoration of
health. It also includes surgical intervention, emergency medicine, and *palliation.* This is the predominant medical modality
practiced in the West today. It uses chemical drugs to force
'submission' and overpower body mechanisms to induce change.
Allopathy believes that "opposite cures opposite."

Homeopathic medicine (homeopathy) is the exact
opposite of allopathic medicine. It is called the medicine of
"similars." Homeopathy focuses on *unfriendly energy fields* in
the body that vibrate at anti-life frequencies—frequencies that

create stress in the vital organs and imbalances within the system. Homeopathy uses 'vibrational' *remedies* instead of chemical drugs. They are potent substances *tuned* to cancel renegade energy frequencies in the body—as represented by drugs, vaccines, etc. Remedies **erase the signature** of the offending energy field and return the patient to health or homeostasis (*homo*-the same. *stasis*-cause to stand; fix).

Chiropractic considers dis-ease to be the result of the incorrect alignment of the spinal column and the nerve plexus issuing therefrom. Poor alignment negatively influences the vital organs served by the central and peripheral nervous systems. Chiropractic has much in common with other vibrational modalities. This is the reason we often find chiropractors wearing several hats at once. Chiropractors are held in contempt by medicine. The reason: a good chiropractor is trained to be results and patient oriented, AND they are very open to alternative healing modalities.

Network Spinal Analysis (NSA) is a new form of chiropractic that integrates various "levels" of care in such a way as to *unfold* and *awaken* spinal energy flow. Healing occurs as a by-product of the freedom of the *body-mind* to utilize its natural, self-regulatory and self-expressive capabilities. In other words, healing is not the direct product of chiropractic, but of the "forces" of life itself *at the subtle energy level.*

The purpose of NSA is to determine the appropriate *timing* and *application* of mechanical forces to the tissues *before* chiropractic adjustment. NSA enables patients to release *non*-productive neurological patterns that block healing. NSA allows the *whole* person to express and experience their body's own self-intelligence and vital energy force.

[Insert] It is the author's belief that NSA brings about healing by helping the patient to become *aware* of negative energy *memory* patterns *at* and *below* the cellular level, and to "erase" them from the tissues.

Network Spinal Analysis produces significant improvement in patient self-awareness and ability to make life changes. This promising new healing modality was developed by Donald Epstein D.C. and is offered to the public by highly trained healers under the trade name *Network Chiropractic.*

Psych-K is wonderful new vibrational therapy. It helps people to deal with subconscious "beliefs" that direct their behavior. It is based on the idea that beliefs are the basis of our attitudes, and from these attitudes we develop behavior patterns—good and bad—that dictate our actions.

Psych-K helps people "reprogram" their subconscious mind similar to erasing a cassette tape and recording a new message. It increases self-confidence, releases old doubts and fears, and rids people of unwanted stress—and it works!

Psych-K is helping thousands of people who have heretofore been beyond the reach of traditional therapy. It is effective because it works at the *subtle energy* level of our existence. It was developed by Robert Williams, M.A. and is taught in business and public workshops nationwide.

Acupuncture promotes healing and numbs pain by manipulating energy meridians (pathways). Acupuncture uses tiny needles. It is a modality from the Far East.

Gua Sha s a 3000 year old "in home" modality that is easy to learn, very effective and can be used to relieve pain, promote healing and free bound 'chi' energy. John Thomas teaching video, special Gua Sha water buffalo tool, hyssopus balm are available. (See Source Page).

Bio-Magnetics heals through the use of magnetic energy flowing from *therapeutic* medical magnets. This promising modality has broad application for people who desire *personal* control over their health. It is an inexpensive, in home modality that is very effective.

Therapeutic magnets vary in size and shape and are used in seat and back cushions, shoe inserts and mattress pads. They are particularly useful against stress and they nullify the damaging effects of 110v electrical current. They protect the immune system and stimulate immune response. *Therapeutic* magnets are DC (direct current) energy fields. Their vibratory energy 'awakens' energy meridians and manipulates pain. Healing follows *repolarization* of cellular organelles and stimulates the production of ATP. These special magnets stimulate blood and lymphatic fluid movement.

Therapeutic magnets balance energy fields in and around injured or inflamed tissue. Millions of people get drug free relief and improved health through magnetic therapy. It is widely used in Japan. In the USA, the medical establishment says magnetic therapy is quackery. The fly in the ointment is the patient who experiences relief (see Source Page).

Vibrational medicine is a composite description that includes dozens of healing modalities that rely on the manipulation of the body's *energy* fields to induce healing. Vibrational medicine recognizes that health and sickness are manifestations of abnormal energy patterns at the subtle energy level of our existence and that healing requires that balance be established before a person becomes 'whole.'

Vibrational medicine is a *blend* of Western and Eastern thought and it is rendering wonderful results. Its roots antedate allopathic medicine by many thousands of years. There is no question that this form of medicine IS replacing the Frankenstein we call "allopathy."

A few examples of vibrational medicine are cold laser, photo-luminescence, aroma therapy, flower essences, Network Chiropractic, therapeutic magnets, qi gong, tai chi, DEEP breathing, essential oils, chiropractic, homeopathy, and the use of BEV™ and medical grade ionized waters. These heal naturally by avoiding the trauma of surgical intervention and by promoting energy flow within the *bio-electric* body.

Compare The Difference

Allopathic medicine is based on the *Newtonian* view of reality. Sir Isaac Newton saw the world as an elaborate mechanism. Newton so influenced allopathic medicine that for the past three hundred years, the body has been viewed as a grand machine that takes its orders from the brain, central, and peripheral nervous systems. This view has been replaced by a new model that sees the body as a flesh and blood biological computer. Nuts and bolts have given way to circuit boards and switches. These approaches fall short of the reality of life at the **subtle energy level** of our existence and lead us astray.

The Newtonian approach fails to account for energy forces like spirit, intuition, conscious and subconscious mental thought, biofeedback—all energy manifestations that form and compose our *sixth* sense. They belong to the Fourth Dimension because they are NOT physical. They CANNOT be measured by length, width, and height—the First, Second and Third Dimensions—a world of metaphysics (*meta*-beyond the physical). Strangely, Physical is but "frozen light" energy .

Paradigm Shift

Vibrational medicine (VM) sees the physical body as the *signature* or *footprint* of the invisible "electric" body. VM is based on Einstein's view of matter, which says, "matter will release energy when taken apart." For example, the splitting of an atom in an atom bomb. This is a MAJOR *paradigm shift* from Western medicine's approach to healing. The word *paradigm* means *para*-beside, *digm*-an example that serves as a model.

The Einstein model sees the human being as a network of energy fields that co-exist and commingle together, that is, condensed energy resonating at a healthy or sick frequency. (Mother Earth frequency is between 7.8-8.1 Hertz.)

Vibrational healing involves the *manipulation* of opposing energy fields, where allopathic medicine relies on negative energy drugs—to over power and **force** the body into submission—thereby bypassing the body's innate intelligence.

Vibrational medicine does not endorse the Germ Theory

of Disease. Instead, it recognizes that the TERRAIN of the bio-electric body controls the bacteria and viruses, and not the other way around.

Secondly, present day drug therapy is a mixture of *hoped for* therapeutic effects and KNOWN adverse effects—the good *hopefully* outweighing the bad! Vibrational medicine avoids the use of drugs, opting instead for a more therapeutic and less traumatic approach to the *bio-electric* body.

Drugs are drugs! They alter body function in negative ways. For example, arthritis medications are extremely potent negative, chemical energy. They do violence to the body and to the liver in particular. They ease the patient's suffering through *palliation* (the relief of signs and symptoms without cure of the underlying causes)—while ultimately killing the patient.

Health Through Manipulation

An example of energy manipulation could involve running a magnet over a computer disc or cassette tape. The magnet would neutralize the *energy* stored on the disc by cancelling the other frequency and *erasing* its signature.

If the energy message on the disc were a dis-ease condition in the body, a positive change in one's health would occur when the offending energy field is *neutralized*. Whenever positive energy forces gain the upper hand, the body returns to a state of health. Since life is energy and energy is matter, we must conclude that life and energy are manifestations of the same phenomenon. Vibrational medicine's focus is "energy."

Magneto Hydro Dynamics (MHD) is a relatively new field of vibrational medicine. Its focus is in the field of dentistry at the "consumer" level through prevention of dental problems.

Plaque formation on the teeth produces cavities. Prevent the formation of plaque and you prevent the formation of cavities, which a poor diet makes even worse. MHD is effective at preventing cavities and treating periodontal gum problems.

MHD utilizes a small counter appliance that pumps water through an **electromagnetic** field where hydrogen ions are freed from respective H_2O molecules. These 'free' ions carry a positive (+) charge. When this specially treated water is flushed against the plaque on the teeth—or under the gum lines—the negatively (-) charged plaque is dissolved and washed away. MHD is an inexpensive 'in home' dental modality for your family's teeth—and your dog's teeth, too! Add saliva pH management to MHD, improved diet, liver purges and racemized™ hormone therapy and dental problems ease or disappear.

Radionics is used by some alternative farmers. It involves broadcasting *energy* frequencies into the surrounding area where it will be picked up by soil, plants, animals and microbes. Compare this practice to a radio station that transmits a melody that is picked up by our radio so we can hear and enjoy it. Properly used, radionics can enhance the production of highly nutritious food while controlling weeds and insects.

Biodynamics is *homeopathic* agriculture. It is the *medicine of "similars"* applied to the soil. It involves the use of minute amounts of biodynamic *horn* manure (one pinch to 20 gallons of pure *energized* BEV ™ type water in such a way that an *energy fusion* takes place. This solution dramatically affects soil, microbes, crops, and weeds. The process involves packing fresh cow manure into a cow's horn and leaving it buried between the Equinoxes (Sept.—March) so it will absorb cosmic *energy* and undergo an ENERGY transmutation. The product is no longer manure, but a totally new, different, and potent energy force field (see Source Page for Biodynamics l, ll & lll).

Medicine & Science Conflict

Medicine and science are threatened by these paradigm shifts because they conflict with textbook mentality. They challenge theory that has been elevated to the status of *LAW* by way of the mumbo-jumbo called the *scientific method*. Misuse of the scientific method has gotten us into a lot of trouble. It should be abandoned because it shackles individual creativity. Vision MUST precede inquiry rather than the other way around.

Because vibrational medicine is replacing old dead theories with models that are bringing RESULTS, it behooves each of us to learn as much as possible about these new fields of thought and *apply* them in our daily lives wherever possible. Reversing the aging process relies heavily on the manipulation of *energy* fields within the bio-electric body.

Becoming *Young Again!* involves the application of vibrational medicine at the layman's level. Given the TOOLS and knowledge, we can produce amazing results in our lives and in the lives of our loved ones at minimal expense—and minimal risk!

This book provides a basic overview of the knowledge needed to bring about vibrational healing. Application of the techniques discussed and the response each person experiences will be *unique* to that individual.

New View

The universe is composed of but two things: *ENERGY* and *MATTER.* Our body is but matter in the form of frozen light. If this is true, then medicines and drugs, which are matter, must also be energy—and they are! However, they are NEGA-TIVE energy—energy that manipulates illness in the short term at the expense of health and longevity in the long term. No one can deny the advances allopathic medicine has made—especially in the replacement of body parts and in emergency medicine. But there is a negative side also. We must realize that medications and surgical intervention carry *substantial* risk and tradeoffs.

Aging is a cumulative process. The *combined* effect of personal neglect, dis-ease and drugs accelerates aging in the youngest of people.

Energy Shift

When we choose to ignore a healthy lifestyle, an energy *shift* occurs. This results in dis-ease and illness. Reversing the aging process involves learning how to manipulate these forces so these shifts either do not occur or are quickly returned to normal. When we talk about having an ageless body, we are talking about a body where the positive energy forces are in control—a body that does NOT require perpetual jump-starts with drugs and surgery—to keep it going.

Everything we do, eat, drink involves "energy" that influences the *bio-electric* body. We must learn HOW to decipher what is good for us and what is not. By learning HOW to identify these forces, we can also learn HOW to manipulate them *without* the use of drugs or invasive surgery.

Dis-ease is a manifestation of negative energy forces in the body. Vibrational medicine halts and reverses aging and dis-ease and offers the ordinary person CONTROL over their health and life.

We *must* recognize that we are more than hunks of flesh and blood, more than biological machines, and more than spiritual beings *trapped* in our bodies during our time on Earth. We are *energy*, and as such, we are part of the cosmos, and yes, we are created in the likeness of God who is also *ENERGY*—positive, beautiful energy!

Anions & Cations

Anions and **cat**ions are usable forms of **'electron'** energy that are released when a chemical reaction takes place—as in our gut and liver when we eat and digest food. The release of energy opposites—one (+) the other (-) produces the electrical activity that grants permission for life.

All matter is a combination of (+) and (-) energy forms. For example, it is the energy *pattern* of anions and cations that gives us steel. When steel is fashioned into a spoon, we identify it as a *steel* spoon. When the energy pattern of matter is altered through fusion, we may get lead or alchemist gold instead of steel. Break the bonds that hold a substance together and energy is released. That energy may be positive or negative.

Good & Bad Energy

The terms *positive* and *negative* energy mean the same as *good* and *bad* energy. *Good* energy is "right-spin" energy and *bad* energy is "left-spin" energy. We know good energy from bad energy by its EFFECT on our health and the bio-electric body.

Positive energy has a particular *spin* of its own—it *spins to the right*, meaning clockwise. NEGATIVE energy *spins to the left*, meaning counter clockwise.

Solar energy is **an**ionic energy. It is life-giving energy. The Earth's spin is the product of **an**ionic, clockwise, right-spin energy entering the Van Allen Belt (ozone layer). As these energy particles penetrate the ozone layer they are deflected and bombard the Earth causing it to spin. When Van Allen theorized this belt in 1948, he was laughed down by the *experts.* Later he was vindicated when NASA lost contact with astronaut John Glenn as he passed through this belt (ozone layer) on his return to Mother Earth.

Anionic energy can *pass through* matter. It is also very comforting and soothing. Have you noticed the difference in the heat produced by a wood fire compared to the heat produced by gas or electricity? If you have lived in a cold climate, you know that wood heat is wonderful heat and warms you clear to your bones.

Wood heat is **an**ionic energy; it comes from the Sun. Its effect is *right-spin* and it warms us because the **an**ions released by oxidation (burning) of the wood pass through our body and warms the cells. This is similar to how a microwave oven works—with one very important exception. Microwave energy is left-spin energy and VERY destructive to life forms.

Right-spin positive energy keeps you young. Left-spin negative energy causes you to become old. The former keeps you on the *anabolic* side of the pyramid as illustrated in Chapter One. The latter puts you on the *catabolic* side. One spins RIGHT, the other spins LEFT. We are interested in the way these energy forces affect living things and HOW they influence the aging process. Please check your understanding by reviewing the following drawings.

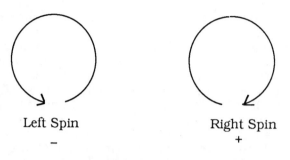

Left Spin   Right Spin
     –   +

How To Determine The Spin

There are several ways to determine the spin and/or predict the effect a substance will have on the bio-electric body.

For instance, look at a bottle of vitamin E and you will see that the word tocopherol is preceded by the letter(s) d or dl. "d" indicates that when infra red light is beamed through the tocopherol, the light is bent to the *right* or clockwise indicating that the vitamin E has life giving energy. The "dl" tocopherol is the opposite and steals life force.

Please note, when "d" vitamin E is carried in SOY or CANOLA oil, its positive energy is neutralized and converted into a negative substance. (Use only wheat germ oil capsules or dry forms of vitamin E. Avoid soy and canola like the plague.)

Those things that exert a negative influence on the body must be *neutralized*, disposed of quickly, or isolated. This applies to BOTH food and non-food substances like drugs, food additives, colorings, salts, and other noxious substances which we will discuss in more depth later.

Neutralize

The word **neutral** doesn't mean much to most people. It's kind of a *neutral* word. We must be more specific in its use. When we say that the body must *neutralize* toxic or left-spinning substances we mean that those substances which exert a negative influence on our body must be **de-energized** by the body. To de-energize something requires energy. Please recall our magnet and cassette tape example. Both are *stored* forms of energy. The magnet's energy neutralized the cassette tape's energy because it had an opposite spin.

The body handles negative energy in similar fashion. Consider a potato—which is a natural form of stored energy. It is stored carbohydrate energy put there by the plant for future needs. Depending on how the potato was grown, it may produce positive or negative effects in the body. All potatoes or carrots or peaches or apples, etc., are NOT equal!

A negative energy potato causes the body to forfeit some of its reserve energy in order to process and *de-energize* that negative energy field. If the body is unable to accomplish the task, the toxic energies in the potato circulate in our system doing violence to the vital organs and *bio-electric* body.

A left-spin substance turned loose in the body has **momentum.** It is like a boulder rolling down a hill. Stopping it requires the body to waste *vital* force and creates an energy deficit with a loss in health and vitality. In addition, the body is FORCED to remove the toxic energy from circulation or suffer further damage to the system. When the body is force fed left-spinning energy, vital force is squandered. The effect is *catabolic* and we grow OLD!

Back to the *spin*. When we say *right-spin*, I want you to think "good for my body." When we say *left-spin*, I want you to think "bad for my body." It might seem like oversimplification, but that's the way it is.

Kinesiology

Kinesiology is the study of fluid dynamics (the movements of fluids). In vibrational medicine, Kinesiology is concerned with the energy dynamics a substances imposes on the tissues and fluids of the bio-electric body.

Kinesthetics refers to muscle sense and is also known as **Dynamic Reflex Analysis** or muscle testing. Many health practitioners use it to diagnose and guide the healing process.

Kinesthetics is a useful diagnostic technique. It can be used to determine the 'immediate' effect that a substance will have on the body. Other dowsing techniques can provide further information, such as the 'long term' effect a substance will have on the body. Kinesthetics involves the gain or loss of strength in the fingers or limbs. It's a good testing procedure, but it requires training and skill. It should "NEVER" be relied upon by itself. For example, biologically active substances—like racemized™ products—produce healing crises and FALSE negative responses that "warp" test results. Racemization™ of energy fields seriously alters the rules which we'll discuss later.

Muscle testing is GROSSLY influenced by heavy metals in the tissues from mercury amalgam dental fillings. This procedure accesses body intelligence through the *autonomic nervous system* which is short circuited in the presence of heavy metals and will be explained in more detail shortly.

To summarize, substances exert one of two subtle energy EFFECTS on the bio-electric body and health. They are: Good • Positive • Right-Spin, or Bad • Negative • Left-Spin.

How To Test

All that is required is another person and the food, drug or supplement that is being tested. First, form a ring with the thumb and middle finger of your dominant hand. Next, have your friend attempt to gently, but firmly, pull your fingers apart. It is important that he or she note the amount of effort required to *separate* the fingers. In general, if it is good for the body, the fingers will become STRONGER. If it is bad, they will become WEAKER. You can place the item in question in the mouth to test by yourself. Do remember that racemized™ substances can and do produce negative readings due to their very high biological activity.

Sometimes, the body gives false results because it *instinctively* KNOWS that the substance will produce a healing crisis and force the bio-electric body to cope, cleanse, and heal. Rejuvenation—like growth—is stressful and the body seeks to minimize stress—especially when it **knows** that its owner doesn't really desire healing or is unwilling to cope. I see a lot of this phenomenon. Sadly, these people cannot heal.

The above procedure can also be done by extending the dominant arm so that it is level with the shoulder and having another person gently pull down while the person being tested holds the substance. Do a before and after to measure strength and arm resistance to movement.

Other Examples

People who drink too much alcohol have a cirrhotic liver (cirrhosis of). So will those suffering from hepatitis or mononucleosis. You can test them easily. Have them extend their arm. Next, pull down on the arm to get a feel of their strength. Then, pull down with one of your hands while at the same time you touch their liver area (just below rib cage on right front). If they have a weak liver, they will LOSE all of their strength.

My friend recently bought some tomatoes at the super market—the kind that grow mold before you get them home. I tested them using the above procedures. The results: *Total loss of strength!* They were returned to the store. If he had eaten them, he would have put a negative substance into his body and weakened his bio-electric status—and his aura—which is a reflection of the vitality of the body's vital organs and glands.

Foucault's Pendulum

A pendulum is one of my favorite ways to measure right and left spin energy. A pendulum is an antenna. It works just like the antenna of a radio station or the one on the roof of your house, except that it is a moving antenna. Antennas can send OR receive energy signals.

All substances emit energy signals! The body issues energy signals with a "spin." A body with HIGH vitality issues "right spin" signals. The opposite is also true. Body energy is sometimes referred to as the body's "aura." Rocks, drugs, food, and bodies all have auras. Kirlian photography can capture a picture of the body's energy aura.

When a pendulum is suspended by a string, horse hair, or chain, the pendulum will "spin" left or right when held over a substance like food, drugs, water, etc. Some pendulums are more sensitive than others, as are individual dowsers.

The pendulum's spin reflects the "status" of the energy field of whatever is being checked. For example, white sugar, soy, canola all emit left-spin signals and the pendulum picks them up and spins accordingly. Here, the substances are the transmiters, the pendulum is the receiving antenna, and the body is the interpreter. That is all there is to it! No hocus pocus or spiritual voodoo is involved.

Learning to use a pendulum **and** vibration chain requires practice. *The Pendulum Kit* and *Vibrations* are very good instructional works on the subject.

Other Vibrational Therapies

Therapeutic Touch involves the transfer of positive energy transfer. It is used in the fields of nursing and massage therapy. Here, energy from a healthy person is used to transform the sick person's energy fields.

Laying on of hands, a religious practice, and **Qi Gong**, an ancient Chinese modality are similar to therapeutic touch. We will develop these subjects in a future chapter.

Scars

While having my mercury amalgam fillings removed, my dentist noticed a one inch scar under my chin and asked when and how it got there. After I told him, he asked me to do the finger exercise we just described, only instead of placing a substance into my left hand, he had me touch the scar with my left hand. BINGO! No strength!

The EFFECT the scar was exerting was strong because it was directly in the path of a major *energy* meridian that flowed from my abdominal chakra (energy center) to the top of my head. It was *blocking* the flow of that energy.

Scar tissue are negative energy fields. Scars are recorded in the skin's holographic memory. (*holo*-light reflected around a central object; *graph*-a record; *ic*-pertaining to.) Scars are negative memory—a magnetic *energy* message like the information on a cassette tape or computer disc—no difference! (Read *The Holographic Universe*.)

To "temporarily" *erase* the scar memory, the dentist injected a homeopathic *remedy* along its length and instantly *full strength* returned to my joined fingers.

Trauma produces scars—be they internal or on the skin. Scars occur when the system is stressed. My scar resulted from a fall while in poor health at age ten. Had I used SOC™ capsules and lotion I would not have scarred (more later).

The tissues are composed of *functional* cells called parenchyma cells. Scar tissue is *non* functional tissue. Scar tissue in the vital organs alters function and accelerates aging. Altered body function is like a car driving on a flat tire. The further you go, the more damage you do.

Aging is the CUMULATIVE effect of negative energy forces on the bio-electric body.

Energy fields are *real!* They underwrite all of our life processes. They are the key to life's mysteries. They control aging. We must come to understand them and learn how to interpret and deal with them in our daily life.

It is important that the reader understand that we live in a world full of energy phenomena. Frankly, everyone should learn to dowse (locate, read, measure) and manipulate energy.

We dowse when we use our intuition to guide us in dealing with people, things, and events—so why not in medicine, healing, and dietary choices? You will learn more about dowsing as we progress.

PREVIEW: *Our next chapter is an overview of "high-tech" modern medicine and its "magic bullet" promises. It will help you to see the futility of relying on medicine's quick-fix techniques and to appreciate the value of good health.*

Scar Tissue & Stiff Joints

SOC™ erases scars, clears acne blemishes, softens wrinkles, dissolves internal scar tissue, restores burned skin, clears arterial plaque, grows hair, stops joint pain, renews joint cartilage and opens energy meridians.

SOC™ causes the body to become limber. Nerve and connective tissue disorders respond well, also. SOC™ softens cell membranes for increased bilateral movement of nutrients and wastes and it carries heavy metals OUT of the brain and OUT of the body (see Source Page).

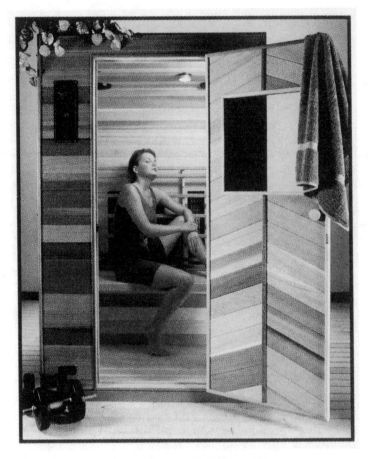

Far InfraRed Sauna™

A FIR™ Sauna does **NOT** rely on lights, steam or heat to do its job. FIR technology leaves you <u>refreshed</u>, never tired.

- No Water Or Plumbing Required
- Dissolves Acne & Acid Wastes In Skin
- Improves Blood & Lymph Circulation
- Burns Calories & Reduces Weight
- Eases Aches & Pains Associated With Disease
- Very Inexpensive To Operate (15¢/day)
- Portable • No Tools Needed • Beautiful

See Page 365 & Source Page For More Information

6

Magic Bullets

"We know life only by its symptoms"
Albert Szent-Gyürgyi
Discoverer of vitamin C

Allopathic medicine is no closer to understanding the *essence* of life today than it was a hundred years ago.

It understands little about basic functions like sleep, growth, pain, aging, and healing. Medicine attempts to manipulate these functions, but it does NOT understand them.

At the same time, we labor under an endless procession of new drugs and high-tech equipment concocted for the treatment of degenerative conditions like cardiovascular disease, cancer and arthritis—just to name a few. These conditions are *technology* driven. They require ever more expensive diagnostic equipment and a long line of *experts* to operate it.

We have substituted 'high-tech' medicine for the "take the pill, solve the problem" approach of yesterday. We have substituted the dis-eases of *civilization* for the contagious maladies of the past. The problems of dis-ease and aging are still with us despite our drive for technology.

High-tech medicine has become an extension of our national consciousness. It is the same 'magic bullet' approach used in the movies. We incorrectly equate medicine's heroic efforts with true healing. Magic bullet technology masks our health problems and allows them to grow worse. Magic bullets blur our vision and numb our reason. They cause us to accept life on *marginal* terms instead of enjoying PEAK health.

Yesterday & Today

Yesterday, medicine knew us as people. Today, we are numbers in a cattle line—stripped of our human dignity. The difference is the *system.* The system has quashed the human being on both ends of the continuum. The doctor is denied training in nutrition and vibrational medicine. The patient gets neither. Modern medicine has substituted technology for dignity. It believes in "magic bullets" and so do the people!

Medicine does NOT understand dis-ease at the subtle energy level. Medicine attempts to diagnose it with tests, X-rays, CAT scans, and Magnetic Resonance Imaging. It has "trained" people to take refuge in *magic bullets* and *hope* instead of dealing with the root causes of degenerative dis-ease.

Daily, newspapers gush with glowing reports of a promising new Flash Gordon therapy. Just as fast, people fill the stalls—like cattle in the slaughter yards—waiting for the *magic bullet* that will cure their misery. Desperate people doing desperate things, ignorant as to the cause of their agony.

Poor Health • Life Of Simplicity

Poor health isn't a sin, but it's awfully inconvenient and terribly expensive. There's a better way.

A life of simplicity allows you to take control of your life and health. It's the drive for money and things that stands between us and a life of simplicity. We must evaluate what is *really* important and learn to *walk away* from the rest.

If we lose our health chasing a dollar, we lose. Even if we catch lots of dollars, we still lose. When we fail to take care of our greatest treasure—our health—we give our dollars to the doctors and hospitals. When we become desperately ill, money and things mean little. They are a poor trade for good health.

We partake of *magic bullet mentality* because it offers us a quick, efffortless fix to our problems. People like smoke and mirror technology, but it's a **past tense** approach —a fancy bandaid at best.

We are confounded by *high-tech wizards* in white coats. We seem unable to see that there is NO difference between empty promises and a bucket full of "empty" hope. *Magic bullets* have become an excuse—a salve for an old body.

Just because you enjoy good health today, it does NOT mean you will enjoy it tomorrow. This is the assumption that people in every generation make over and over again. It is an erroneous assumption. I prefer to regain and KEEP my health.

It is foolish to squander your good health. Tomorrow is but a few days away. Just ask someone who is old.

Why experience the hell of old age when you can enjoy **perpetual** good health? Time stands still when you are truly healthy. So do whatever you need to do to get your *bio-electric* reference score under '.33.' When you are *Young Again! YOU* are in control and you don't need any of medicine's "magic bullets!"

PREVIEW: *In our next chapter you will learn WHY food fails to supply the ENERGY you need to stay young and WHAT you can do about it.*

The 65% Watery Human Being

BRAIN 74.5%

BONE 22%

KIDNEY 82.7%

MUSCLE 75.6%

BLOOD 83%

THE 65% WATERY HUMAN
The amount of water in the human body, averaging 65 per cent, varies considerably from person to person and even from one part of the body to another (right). A lean man may have as much as 70 per cent of his weight in the form of body water, while a woman, because of her larger proportion of water-poor fatty tissues, may be only 52 per cent water. The lowering of the water content in the blood is what triggers the hypothalamus, the brain's thirst center to send out its familiar demand for a drink.

"Pure Water Is The Best Drink For A Wise Man" – Henry Thoreau

---

The Hormone Connection
Hormones DRIVE the syndrome of HEALTH issues plaguing women of all ages. Learn how to deal with your body and you will experience "life" on a whole new level.

Spider Bites

Spider bites involve "energy." Some people experience severe reactions to them, while others suffer loss of body parts. We must come to understand the "nature" of the energy forces that produce these reactions.

In front of me is a story about a lady in Southern California who was bitten by a Brown Recluse spider, went into a coma, and awoke six months later missing her arms, legs, nose, and ear. I discovered that medicine has no *magic bullets* with which to treat most spider bites.

Here is "my" story. I awoke at 2 a.m. with my hand throbbing and swollen. I was in *severe* pain. My hand looked like a balloon! Quickly, I shredded an organic potato, combined it with some Epsom salts and made a poultice with plastic sandwich wrap. The poultice "drew" the poison into two boils. My physician could not help me!

I visited my "holistic" dentist. He duplicated the energy frequency and "footprint" of a *homeopathic* remedy in his MORA frequency generator and applied the "invisible" energy to my hand and body—cancelling the spider's venom at the *subtle energy level* of my being. Instantly, the pain was gone. No limbs were lost. I regained full use of my hand.

Had I depended on allopathic medicine, I could have lost the use of my hand or worse. Fortunately, I was in good enough health that the spider's venom did not cause permanent damage to my hand.

This story is proof of the effectiveness of vibrational medicine and authentication of the "energy" focus of this book. In future chapters, we will develop the "energy" thesis upon which peak health depends.

• Health disarms dis-ease •

Toxicity & Wavy Hair

What do chemotherapy, wavy hair, water on the lung, and appendicitis have in common? Toxicity!

Chemotherapy causes hair loss because it overloads the skin's waste processing capability. When hair regrows, it usually comes back wavy—even where the person previously had straight hair.

Systemic toxicity is behind wavy hair. It disguises blue and green eyes as brown and black. It dulls the hair and dims the brilliance of beautiful eyes.

7

Death By Chocolate Pie

*"Chew your liquids and chew your
solids until they are liquid."*
Dr. Paul C. Bragg N.D., Ph.D.

"Death by Chocolate Pie" read the sign. It reminded me that all food is NOT equal.

Some food is *alive* and promotes health, while other food is *dead* and promotes death. We are concerned with the differences in food and their influence on the aging process. We are specifically concerned with food's *energy footprint.*

Water has a similar story to tell, but there is a fundamental difference between food and water. Foods are listed in tables and are rated, one against another based on their nutrients, caloric content, etc. But water is NOT classified as a food because it contains NO nutrients—that is, it contains no proteins, fats or carbohydrates.

We are told that water is water, but there is MUCH more to the story. Water is more than just "wet." Water's *signature* powerfully influences life and health. Its *signature* is reflected in its spin and measured by its ORP potential.

Water is considered a *necessity* of life because we cannot live without it. Oddly, the *experts* tell us to limit *food* intake. Then, in the same breath, they tell us to drink as much water as we desire without regard to the type of water or its *vibrational* MEMORY, or its oxidation/reduction potential (ORP). Water is food and like food, all water is not equal!

We pick and choose our food on the basis of personal

taste, appearance, color, and aroma. Yet, we aren't concerned about the water we drink. We don't see water as food.

Water IS food. Water is THE most important food we put into our body. Water is not important for the nutrients it contains—it contains none. Water is important for the *ENERGY* that it *should* contain. Extremely pure water with a zero contaminant load, clean vibrational memory, therapeutic bond structure and high ORP can heal a sick body.

BEV™ water is pure FOOD and more. It has right-spin characteristics that people can feel and taste. It is **body friendly** because it energizes, hydrates, and detoxifies the system. People who drink it will tell you that it is "different!"

Live Food

Traditional food that is *biologically active* has a right-spin *signature* and it produces right spin effects in the body. It contains enzymes, charged ionic minerals, vitamins, and positive energy that are absolutely necessary for good health. These components of "live" food are the foundation of life itself. Let's discuss enzymes.

Enzymes are biochemical proteins. Enzymes are also *catalysts*. A catalyst accelerates a reaction or causes a reaction to take place that either would not occur or would occur at a much slower rate if it were not present.

Enzymes can be compared to oxygen's effect on a fire. No oxygen, no fire. Without oxygen, fire can neither start nor continue. "True" catalysts are used over and over. They are neither altered or destroyed in the reaction. An example is the platinum and rhodium used in catalytic converters on cars. These *noble* metals convert toxic gases like carbon monoxide to carbon dioxide and water. They do it through a series of oxidation and reduction (redox) reactions. *(In future chapters, you will learn how to use redox reactions to your benefit.)*

In the body, most biochemical catalysts are consumed, altered or destroyed in the reactions they fuel and must be continually *manufactured* by the body. The liver is our PRIMARY enzyme and catalyst manufacturing organ and therefore will always be a player in any health disorder.

The constant formation of new enzymes requires tremendous amounts of *right-spin* energy that must come from substances that are "live" and friendly to the bio-electric body. Dead food and dead water are negative energies. They are left-spin energy forces that not only fail to contribute to health, but actually BLOCK the benefits of substances with a right-spin energy *footprint* and *signature*.

Biocatalysts

Biological catalysts cause reactions to occur millions of times faster than what would occur if they were not present. Without biocatalysts, life as we know it could not exist.

Vitamins do not work unless all of the needed major *and* minor (trace) minerals are present in the body in balanced form. In biochemistry, vitamins are called *cofactors* because they work WITH minerals and enzymes. Because most vitamin supplements are synthesized (man-made) despite claims to the contrary on the label, they are useless at best and damaging to the vital organs at worst. Moreover, most mineral supplements are **useless** because they are in 'elemental' form—a form which we should avoid (more later).

Your BEST source of biologically active vitamins and minerals is garden fresh food. Almost "all" vitamin/mineral supplements are synthesized substances and negative energy fields that stress the vital organs creating secondary problems.

When we have **EXCESS** toxins and wastes in the system, biochemical reactions slow and blood and lymph circulation becomes difficult. **Excess** wastes and toxins interfere with vital organ function and hormonal balance, and their accumulation leads to "systemic" (whole body) degeneration and rapid aging. The use of Yucca herbal, the juice of one fresh lemon morning and night, PAC's, colon therapy, BEV™ and medical grade ionized water helps flush the system. Lymphatic "self" massage with a lymph roller is VERY helpful also.

Cooked Food

Cooking denatures enzymes. Denatured enzymes can't do their job because they have LOST the characteristics that caused them to work. Cooking food seldom improves quality. Improper cooking totally destroys food value and enzymes.

I am not suggesting you to stop cooking your food, but I am suggesting that you eat plenty of fresh, raw—and preferably—home grown green leafy vegetables and fruit. *(My favorite source of easy to grow, no work fresh greens is comfrey. It grows on its own from March to November every year and is available by mail or can often be found in your local area.)*

Avoid high heat and cook no longer than necessary. Steam instead of boiling. Use stir fry methods. Avoid microwave ovens and table salt, flavor enhancers, and dyes. These substances **zap** the body's energy fields and block crucial biochemical reactions. When you eat them you **cheat** yourself of good health and you lose vital energy.

Metabolism

Metabolism is a term that comes to mind. It means *biotransformation* and refers to the way food molecules are transformed into energy molecules in the body's energy pathways. Metabolism involves *fusion* reactions that join individual atoms into right spin *energy* molecules. This is the opposite of the kind of energy produced by nuclear fission (atom bombs/ nuclear power plant wastes, microwave ovens). Fusion reactions are right-spin and anabolic—they build up! Fission reactions are left-spin and catabolic—they tear down!

Metabolites are the waste products of biochemical reactions. Dissected the word looks like this: *meta-*beyond. *bol-*tranformation. *ite-*product of. Hence, a product that is **beyond** transformation. Metabolites are waste. When we speak of metabolic wastes, we are talking about toxins and/or metabolites. Included in this definition are chemicals of organic synthesis (poisons like pesticides and herbicides) all of which carry estrogen "analogs" that lock up hormonal receptors.

Animal Protein

Industrialized man eats high on the hog. He eats too much animal protein and not enough fruits and vegetables. Animal proteins come from the top of the food chain. If animals are healthy, their proteins will reflect a right-spin *signature* and their proteins will sustain us. But if they are not healthy, their proteins will have a left-spin signature and they will cause us to become sick and age prematurely.

Most animal proteins now represent *left-spin* energy in the form of concentrated metabolic and environmental wastes. Sick animals concentrate negative energy. Animals suffering from environmental stresses and excesses (bad food, air, water, and excess metabolites) become sickly just like humans.

Food energy derived from sick animals brings on dis-ease in man a thousand times faster than does food energy from sick fruits or vegetables.

Animal proteins can be an excellent source of *energy* and *nutrients*. but they can be a two-edged sword and must be used wisely. The "issue" with animal protein is: the *quantity* eaten, how we metabolize it, the levels of "analogous" estrogen like hormones, how the liver and kidneys process it and dispose of wastes, and transit time from the mouth to the toilet. (We will develop these points as the book unfolds.)

In his wonderful book, *Fatu Hiva*, Thor Heyerdahl tells how in 1937 he and his wife lived with the last surviving cannibal of the Marquesas, an island chain twelve-hundred miles northwest of Tahiti. The cannibal told them *"Human flesh is different than other animal flesh. It is sweet!"* And I would add, so is the flesh from a toxic cow that was in a *catabolic* state and sick when it was slaughtered. Toxic meat and fish have more flavor. Toxins are more concentrated in the animal's fats than in the lean tissues for reasons we will discuss in great detail later.

The Food Chain

Here is an example of what is meant by the statement, "animals are at the top of the food chain."

A rabbit eats food that is contaminated with pesticides. The poisonous residues are stored and concentrated in its flesh and fatty tissues. One day the farmer decides the rabbits are out of control and uses a toxic chemical to poison them. Next, an eagle comes along and eats from the carcass of the dead rabbit. Thus the poisons in the rabbit are now in the eagle's body—hence the poisons moved UP the food chain.

When we eat sick meat, fish, and fowl, we become the eagle and the poisons and metabolites concentrate in us. If you are going to eat animal proteins, derive them from healthy animals and in limited amounts.

Negative energy food from any source—animal or plant—is sick food. Sick food must be dismantled and *neutralized* by the liver. Left-spin food causes the body to squander vital energy that is needed to keep us healthy and young. When we eat sick food, we lose more than we gain!

Animal Proteins & The Bowel

Animal proteins MUST be eliminated from the intestines within 18 hours, maximum. If they remain in the gut longer than this, they putrefy and release extremely toxic, organic poisons. Substances like indoles, skatoles, and phenols. These set the stage for dis-ease, premature aging, and cancer.

Indoles, skatoles, and phenols are WHOLE molecules that are absorbed directly through the intestinal wall. Most molecules are broken down into pieces before they are absorbed, thus offering us some protection. Not so with many waste byproducts. Poor digestion is at the root of it!

Potatoes absorb toxic compounds from raw, non composted manure. These toxic molecules pass **directly** into the potatoe's tissues—**whole and intact.** When the potatoes are boiled, a sharp nose can identify the kind of manure that was used to grow them—pig, cow, or chicken.

Toxic molecules that are absorbed in this fashion

bypass our safety net and are a threat to good health. Undigested food rots in the gut, feeds the parasites, brings on obesity, produces foul gas and leads to colon related problems like colitis, diverticulitis, irritable bowel syndrome, appendicitis, and eventually cancer, arthritis, diabetes, and cardiovascular problems.

Mastication

Thorough chewing of food is critical to good health. In addition, I strongly advise the use of Disorb Aid™ and R/Hcl to insure 100% digestion and absorption of food nutrients. These things will help you to become *Young Again!*

PREVIEW: *Our next chapter deals with digestion, junk food, and WHY it causes us to become old.*

Collard Greens

Collard greens are easy to grow and thrive anywhere in the USA. You can grow them in pots, in a flower bed, or in the garden. They are a "non" hybrid vegatable.

Eaten raw in a salad or served in plain leaf fashion, they are sweet and crunchy. They promote a healthy colon and will stretch your food budget.

Collards winter over if planted in the summer and mulched with straw during the winter. In the spring, they come to life and produce fresh salad greens long before other vegetables can even be planted.

Insects don't attack collards. Pick the lower leaves and the plants will keep producing for you. Enjoy!

Comfrey Greens

Comfrey greens are heavenly! Comfrey roots produce copious amounts of leaves that make fantastic spinach when lightly steamed or stir fried and drenched with olive oil and apple cider vinegar.

Each March, comfrey grows freely. It is rich in nutrients. The pulverized roots heal ulcers. The FDA does not like comfrey, but people and animals do!

Chickens and milk goats relish comfrey. Comfrey is good for the colon. Everyone should grow comfrey. Plant comfrey once, and you'll have comfrey forever!

Water! The *Essence* Of Life!

Water has memory! It "absorbs" the *frequencies* of the contaminants it carries and it **continues** to *vibrate* at those frequencies long after the contaminants have been removed.

Contaminants are *energy* fields that leave their *footprint* on water by causing the molecules to **vibrate** at frequencies *unfriendly* to the body.

Conventional approaches to water purification are *incomplete.* Methods like distillation, reverse osmosis, carbon block and ceramic cartridges work at the mechanical level only. They are good as far as they go, they just don't go far enough.

The BEV™ process, on the other hand, is a Fourth Dimension approach that delivers water that tastes good and *feels different* in the body. People like it because it *awakens* natural harmonic frequencies *at* the cellular level and below.

BEV™ water **reprograms** the electrical *rhythm* of the body. It causes body cells to *dance.* Its energy *frequency* is body friendly. Its electromagnetic *signature* is complete. **BEV water is liquid *music!***

The BEV™ process "voids" waste energy fields in the water and alters hydrogen and molecular bond angles so molecules can **"dance"** and become **liquid music** and **electronic food** to the body and spirit.

BEV™ theory and application *transcends* traditional water testing and comparison techniques. It defies Newtonian physics. BEV™ water must be experienced to appreciate its profound significance to human health and longevity. **BEV™ has captured the essence of life on planet Earth in liquid form.**

The BEV™ process is a **proprietary** process. A full discussion of the theory and application of BEV™, and its relationship to aging and dis-ease is available in manuscript form (see Source Page).

BEV water is made from tap water with BEV™ equipment and tap water. The process we call BEV™ focuses on biologically *friendly* DRINKING water. Next to the air we breathe, we consume more water than any other commodity. *Make sure the water you put into your body is spelled BEV™.*

"Water Is MORE Than Wet. Water Is FOOD!"

Female Estrogen & Hormone Cycle

0 . . . . 4 : . . . . . . days . . . . 12 . . . . days 28

Estrogen production escalates day 4 of menstrual cycle and peaks at day 12. Estrogen causes the endometrium in the uterus to "proliferate" in preparation for fertilization. Ovulation occurs days 14-16 when a ovarian follicle forms the corpus luteum producing an egg, hence "ovulation." If ovulation fails to occur or the corpus luteum does not maintain itself through day 26, estrogens produced earlier "remain" causing PMS and fueling the growth of fibroid tumors in the breasts/uterus. Women using birth control pills or estrogen replacements, experience receptor site "lock up" and lose of control over their body and life—a condition that is "epidemic" among females and if ignored paves the way for female cancers and osteoporosis. Racemized™ hormone precursors "open" receptor sites and "remove" dangerous analogous hormones from the body. "ALL" menopausal women are unopposed estrogen dominant and suffer from EXCESS estrogens that weaken bones, cause hair loss, wrinkled skin, mental fog/memory loss, and eventually osteoporosis and formation of the "dowager's hump" pictured on page#100. Racemized™ hormone precursors prevent and reverse estrogen dominance in young and older women with noticable changes occurring in as little as 30 days, with long term improvement confirmable by bone density tests, normalization of monthly period, elimination of the SIGNS and symptoms of hormonal imbalance listed on page #212, and restoration of cartilage. Read *Our Stolen Future*.

8

Junk Diets & Stress

"There is no such thing as 'junk food', only 'junk diets'!"
Dr. Helen A. Guthrie

All food contains energy. It is the nature of energy and its electrical *footprint* that determines what effect—good or bad—food will have on the *bio-electric* body. To understand the aging process, we must concern ourselves with the "spin" of food energy. The direction of spin as well as the intensity of the spin determines foods ability to satisfy hunger and build and maintain healthy tissues and bones.

Nutritive tables measure nutrients. It is assumed that if we eat food listed on the nutrient tables that we will be nourished. It is also assumed that ALL nutritive food energy produces positive results in the body. These assumptions are INCORRECT.

We hear a lot about junk food because we are inundated with it. People identify junk food with quick snacks and fast food. Their association is correct. But instead of calling it junk food, let's call it bio-junk (food) because it better describes it.

Bio-junk food is composed of left-spin energy, and it greatly accelerates the aging process. If the body cannot break down or eliminate bio-junk energy from the body, it isolates it from the rest of the system. The body does this by entombing the toxic energy in body FAT that it makes specifically for this purpose. (We will develop this point in the obesity chapter.)

Dead Is Not Dead

Bio-junk food alters biochemical reactions because it has an anti life energy **signature.** It also destroys or blocks critical body pathways and cripples cellular activity. Bio-junk food has the ability to multiply its original sphere of influence by transferring its vibratory **footprint** to all of the body's tissues. Transference takes place at the subtle energy level of our being. Bio-junk food is the equivalent of "poison." It contains *radiomimetic* qualities—qualities that *mimic* the effect of nuclear *radiation* on the tissues. People who eat artificial foods eventually see the effects in the mirror.

Bio-junk food has the ability to CHANGE its *footprint* after it enters the body. Its presence in the GI tract triggers *bastard* reactions that form **free radicals** in the system. Free radicals do damage to the vital organs and especially to the liver and kidneys. The energy *footprint* of these substances is so volatile that they clash with the body's energy fields the moment of contact. They continue to interfere with normal metabolism UNTIL their presence is eliminated. In other words, they have a life of their own while in the system. It is impossible to keep all toxic substances out of the system because they are ubiquitous. We can, however, neutralize their effects with enhanced PAC's, Yucca blend and racemized™ hormone precursors to unlock your receptor sites.

A "bio-junk food" diet insures the accumulation of toxic energy fields in the tissues, lymph, and blood.

The Kidneys

The kidneys are crucial to good health and it behooves us to pay attention to anything that negatively affects them. Bio-junk food causes tremendous long-term damage to the kidney's nephrons (blood filters). The kidneys are second only to the liver in their ability to rid the body of waste, and a decline in function is a prerequisite of cancer and dis-ease.

Taoism teaches that the urinary system (kidneys and bladder) is related to the Water Element. Taoists believe that *Jing*—the very **essence** of life—is contained within water. They believe that careful management of the Water Element is the key to youthfulness. BEV™ and high ORP water keep the kidneys young and speed waste flow without overworking the kidneys. which were NEVER meant to do the liver's job!

Digestion & Liquids

If Pavlov's dog is any indication, digestion initiates

through visual/mental stimulation BEFORE food enters our mouth. In other words, the flow of digestive juices in the mouth, stomach, and intestines are linked to vision and thought.

Digestion begins in the mouth when we chew and mix food with saliva. The flow of saliva and digestive juices are dependent on fluid hydration levels in the body. When we drink our share of water, we secrete enough saliva to begin the breakdown process we call *digestion*. Saliva also lubricates food so it can be comfortably swallowed.

It is important to TRAIN ourselves to drink a cup of water every hour of our waking day. This habit maintains perfect fluid volume levels and moves waste out of the system. Lots of water is key to *avoiding* the need to drink liquids with meals. **Drink water throughout the day and AVOID "all" liquids 1/2 hour before, during, and one hour after meals.**

Failure to drink enough water throughout the day creates a shortfall of digestive juices which "limits" digestion. Drinking liquids with meals is extremely destructive. We do NOT want liquids in the stomach at mealtime because they "dilute" digestive juices that contain enzymes and acids.

Cold liquids are hard on the body in general, and the stomach and digestive organs in particular. When cold fluids are taken with a meal, they retard and even STOP digestion. Correct temperature is one of the necessary prerequisites for chemical reactions—like those in the stomach and intestinal tract—to occur. Low digestive temperatures promote degenerative dis-ease. Where indigestion, gas, or bloating are a problem, DiSorb Aid™, R/HCl™ and Yucca Blend™ save the day! R/HCl™ breaks parasitic peptide bonds in the stomach, while DiSorb Aid™ reaches the duodenum untouched in viable form and finishes the job on other food nutrient molecules. Yucca Blend™ acts as an emulsifier. Note: indigestion in women is very much linked to hormonal imbalance. **In other words, as goes the ovaries, so goes the liver which explains why 10 women for every man will have gallbladder surgery.**

Digestive juices are powerful "right-spin" energy fields. Liquid taken with meals dilute them and stress the system. Correct body hydration levels speeds the flow of digestive juices and greatly improves digestion. The liver and pancreas secrete their juices through ducts directly into the intestinal duodenum immediately below the stomach. Hydrochloric acid is secrete directly into the stomach from cells on the interior lining. These cells cease their function as we grow older.

Dr. Franz Morell said *"[saliva's] purpose is to coat and protect food enzymes so they will neither be damaged by nor do damage to the stomach and GI tract. Exposure to digestive juices at the wrong time during digestion derails biochemical catalysts.*

Nature designed things such that it takes 5-10 minutes to eat an apple, but only 5 seconds to drink the juice." Juices are two edged swords. Use them conservatively!

Hormones & Hydration

The **"ductless"** glands secrete hormones directly into the blood for transport throughout the body. In addition, low hydration levels in the tissues restricts hormonal activity.

Hormones—control aging and vitality. As we age, we experience a SLOW-DOWN in hormonal activity. In time, the ductless glands go into **shut-down**. Somewhere along the way, the doctor provides a diagnosis.

The aging scenario is a combination of waste accumulation, inadequate hydration, low hormonal activity, and a liver that is in trouble. Excess waste slows vital organ function and leads to an early grave. **SIGNS of aging seen on the outside of the body indicate trouble on the *inside.***

We are hormone driven creatures. At conception, hormones dictate male or female. Growth and development is also hormone controlled. Hormones bring on phenomenonal change at puberty and again at menopause and andropause. Hormones are central to aging and rejuvenation and involve the TOTAL body and all of its systems. Regular use of racemized™ hormone precursors will keep you in control of your hormones.

Racemized™ Precursors

A *precursor* is something that precedes something else. For example, we eat carrots to obtain *beta carotene* which is a natural plant food precursor to vitamin A. Dioscoria Macho Stachya is very unique plant hormone precursor. The body converts it into various corticosteroid hormones, especially when in racemized™ form. Precursors do NOT carry any of the dangers or risks that accompany the use of "hormones." In **racemized**™ form hormone precursors produce *fantastic* results for women and men. Three *different* racemized™ precursors are used. THREE "precursors" are necessary to maintain balance and support the sytstem. **NEVER, EVER** use "actual" hormones or you are playing God—including birth control pills and estrogen supplementation. Women use different precursors than do men! Men are concerned with the prostate, sex drive, impotence, and balding. **People who use racemized™ precursor creme attest to its effectiveness and appreciate how it restores their bodies and zest for life—be they teenagers, middle age, menopausal, or senior citizens.**

Racemized™ Nugestrine II transdermal creme (for

women) and Totally Male™ transdermal creme (for men) is used topically to clear hormonal receptor sites and rid the body of excess estrogen in women, and excess testosterone in men, and estrogen **analogs** in both. Hormonal EXCESSES drive aging and cancer in both sexes.

Wild yam creams have been around for many years. Most are a waste of money. Some help a little. Restoration of hormonal balance calls for racemization™ of biologically active ingredients to protect the liver from rogue corticosteroids prior to their oxidation from the body. **AVOID** over the counter DHEA and melatonin. They have been outlawed in Europe, Canada and Australia. **They are dangerous.** The glowing reports don't tell you these substances are **analogous** molecules. Consider them no different than anabolic steroids used by athletes or birth control pills used by women in ignorance.

Stress • Food • Pavlov's Dog

Stress or unpleasant circumstances grossly affect hormone production and digestion/absorption. Sitting down to a *quiet* meal and allowing enough time for casual, pleasant conversation is *vital* to good health. Unfortunately, few people eat this way anymore. Fast track meals are the rule and mealtime circumstances rarely resemble the ideal. People eat too fast, barely chewing, and guzzle **cold** liquids amidst noise and confusion. **The effects of "hit & run eating" on health are *DEADLY* even if you eat the very best food.**

Pavlov experimented on dogs. Dogs are known for their ability to *gobble* their food. Pavlov discovered that the dog's digestive enzymes flowed the moment he rang the dinner bell. So do people's! And since digestion is stressful to the body, when your dinner bell rings, prepare yourself. A meal should be a *celebration* of physical, mental, and spiritual forces.

Digestion requires the body to expend energy in an effort to get more energy in return. Bio-junk food creates an energy deficit. Undigested food produces gas and bloating. Lack of viable enzymes and hormones make things worse.

Undigested food *converts* to left-spin energy. In a constipated, anaerobic gut and colon, yeast convert undigested food into **gas** and **deadly** toxic by-products that give rise to degenerative dis-ease. **Mealtime atmosphere, digestive enzymes, food quality, and hormones CONTROL health.**

Gas

Gas—particularly *foul* gas—is a GOOD indicator of an out of balance condition in the vital organs and digestive tract.

The fouler the gas, the more we should be concerned that things are NOT right. Foul or excess gas is a sign of systemic (whole body) overload and should be considered ABNORMAL! Spoiled animal flesh (carrion) is *necrotic* flesh. Meat is dead flesh, but it is not necrotic. In a constipated, airless environment, meat, fish, fowl, and cheese become the equivalent of carrion and produce highly toxic by-products and foul gas. High stress meal time environments encourage **anaerobic** conditions and accentuate the production of foul *gas.* An anaerobic environment is a cancer environment! **The evening breeze between your knees should NOT smell like cheese!**

Otto Warburg, twice Nobel Laureate, was awarded the Nobel Prize in 1931—over sixty years ago— for documenting a vital factor behind the rise of cancer. He said, *"Cancer has one prime cause...and that is the replacement of oxygen [aerobic] respiration of body cells by anaerobic cellular respiration."*

Dr. Max Gerson, whom we mentioned earlier, went on to determine the role of sodium (main ingredient of table salt) in cancer. Both Warburg and Gerson agreed that the growth of cancer cells initiates in a low oxygen, high free radical environment. Cancer does not manifest in an oxygen-rich environment! Mild aerobic exercise followed by lymphatic self-massage with a "lymph roller" can do wonders for sick bodies.

Table Salt

It is *impossible* to avoid sodium because it is ubiquitous. It is in almost all prepared foods, and it is certainly in municipal water supplies. If you crave salt, you suffer from "salt syndrome." This condition is remedied with ionic sea minerals and BEV™ water. A body that craves salt is a body that is deficient in minerals ions. A complete detoxification program, which includes purging stones from your liver, is most helpful in reestablishing ionic balance to the tissues.

Table salt must NOT be used to meet salt cravings. It must be avoided because it is **deadly** to the body's cells and to the bacteria (mitochondria) that produce our ATP energy molecules. Thirst after meals indicates *under* hydration and/or *over* salted food, and/or pancreatic/adrenal stress. Table salt should be avoided. I use kelp, dulce, herbal combinations along with racemized™ sea mineral sprayed on my food.

The Water Molecule

The primary function of water is to act as a solvent and as a source of 'free' electrons—as measured by the oxidation/

reduction potential (ORP)—of the water.

Water **MUST** carry *energy* INTO the cells, and it **MUST** carry toxic *end products* of metabolism OUT of the body. When we drink low ORP, biologically unfriendly water—like distilled, tap, reverse osmosis, ozonated and common filtered waters for example—we DENY the body the ability to stay healthy and we create conditions of **excess** that eventually manifest as so-called "deficiency" dis-eases. **BEV™ water is conception point water. Medical grade ionized water is therapeutic water.**

BEV™ water is the foundation water used to create medical grade ionized water. Here the H_2O molecule is reduce in size, surface tension is lowered, while pH is raised as the all IMPORTANT "ORP" potential is driven up on both ends of the pH scale. These qualities create water with an energy *signature* that promotes peak health and heals sick bodies.

Below is a drawing of water molecules with their respective bonds. Look at the shape of these "bent" or "polar" water molecules.

Notice that the two hydrogen atoms on each molecule are off to one side giving each molecule a lopsided appearance. The solid lines indicate "bond" points and (+) and (-) charged atoms. The box contains one water molecule. The oxygen atom has a (-) charge, the two hydrogens have a (+) charge. The dotted line going from the hydrogen atom in the box to the oxygen to the right of the box is a **hydrogen bond** connecting one molecule to the other. The lines inside the box are **molecular** bonds "within" the water molecule.

The strength of the bonds that holds water together is determined by its load of 'free' electrons. The higher the ORP and the purer the water, the easier the water can enter our cells and fuel the production of ATP. Bond angle, electron load (ORP), and pH is what separates BEV™ water and medical grade ionized water from the rest. pH is NOT where it's at. Lastly, conventional understanding of water along with so-called testing standards—are useless yardsticks and MOOT when we enter the arena of BEV™ and medical grade water.

Why BEV Water

BEV water is biologically friendly drinking water. It's made in your own home from common tap water. While most water processing units on the market remove some (50-90%) of the toxic wastes in water, BEV™ equipment approaches 99.5% removal of all life forms, radioactivity, and toxic organic chemicals. Moreover, the process manipulates bond angles while elevating the ORP and returning the water to the point of conception—where the egg and sperm were when they joined. In other words, the 'life force' factor is elevated.

BEV™ water is highly charged and structured for living systems. It is **different** than other waters and it is very reactive in the body. By "reactive" we mean it acts like a *magnet* due its strong *right-spin* electrical charge and resonant frequency. A vibration chain, pendulum, or aurameter confirm BEV water's spin and charge intensity. The best test, of course, is to feel it in your body.

Other waters do not possess the characteristics of BEV™ water. BEV™ water hydrates the tissues and energizes the cells while removing wastes from the system. Wonderful things happen to people who drink this strange and wonderful water. BEV water is both a 3rd and 4th dimension energy substance (we will develop these concepts as we go along).

Live Food

Home grown food is the poor person's least expensive path to good health. The wealthy can benefit likewise.

If you do not have a yard or space is limited, grow vegetables in pots, plastic buckets and so on. It is amazing how much fresh food can be grown this way. Besides the pleasure of growing it, real food offsets poor choices in lifestyle.

Consider joining an organic gardening club. Many of them offer garden space for rent where the soil is rich and mellow from other gardeners before you. Or, hire someone to grow food for you and your family. Many older people have the time and would love to grow food for hire. These people are usually gardening pros. Pay them well. Gardening is hard work. They deserve the money and you need the food.

Gardening involves hard *load-bearing* work and is a good way to keep fit. Hard work is good for the body. I suggest a long handled spading fork instead of a tiller. Hand tools are inexpensive, they always start, and they don't burn gas.

For people who cannot garden, fresh live food can be purchased at health food stores and co-ops. Some organic farmers even deliver or have drop points in cities. Food co-ops are also excellent sources as are some health food stores.

Composting • Gardening

If you are going to get into gardening, you will want to learn how to compost organic matter. Proper composting technique *controls* the break-down process so you end up with a high energy product. Aerobic conditions create *right-spin* energy compost.

Aerobic compost catalyses healthy energy reactions in garden soil. Controlled breakdown of grass clippings, weeds, leaves, manure, and the like will not generate foul odors **unless** the pile becomes *anaerobic*. An anaerobic condition is what produces foul gas in the compost pile and the human gut!

Always use some liquified chicken or cow manure starter to get the pile going. Compost is MORE than old dead things that have turned brown. It is a source of "life force" for your garden. Several wonderful books on biodynamic gardening are available (see Source Page).

Gardening is superb therapy for the body, mind, and spirit. Use it to simplify your life and focus your energies on healthful habits. Once you become hooked on gardening, you will be a gardener forever! **Fresh food—and biologically friendly water—are your *passport* to agelessness!**

Devitalized food is so common in most people's diet that some form of supplementation is needed. Biogenic™ enhanced PAC⁵, Harmonic™ pollen, Klammath™ Algae, Taoist™ SUPER foods and predigested Biogenic™ organic liver are ideal 'whole foods' upon which I personally rely. As for vitamins, if you want to replace twenty different bottles with one, use VitaLight™ tablets. This product does NOT tax the liver and create secondary problems for the body to cope with. Super foods provide "real" vitamins. VitaLight™ provides racemized™ minerals.

To become *Young Again!*

- Eat organic food
- Grow a garden
- Avoid table salt & MSG
- Use racemic sea minerals
- Get plenty of exercise
- Avoid alcohol & soft drinks
- Eat RAW vegetables
- Avoid all processed food
- Drink plenty of BEV™ water
- Get plenty of sleep
- Avoid liquids with meals
- Avoid soy and canola
- *"Chew your liquids and chew your solids until they are liquid!"*

It's what you do 90% of the time that counts. Aging reversal requires focus and commitment because the body is OLD and *SLOW* and you are not young—YET! Follow the points we have outlined so far and absorb and apply the information in the balance of this book and you will become *Young Again!*

PREVIEW: *Our next chapter explains WHY people snack and WHY they become fat and WHAT happens to your body when you eat too much or too often!*

Harmonic™ Silver Water & Soc™

Few injuries equal the trauma and pain burn patients suffer. From a medical viewpoint, the issue is infection. From a social viewpoint, the issue is scar tissue formation. Infection and scars are both ENERGY issues.

To ease pain and prevent infection—even in the case of 3rd degree burns—use Harmonic™ Silver Water.

Harmonic™ Silver Water has a vibrational signature & energy footprint that is body friendly. When misted onto burned tissue or taken orally, the *energy* signature of the solution is **transferred** to the body. Healing involves energy **resonance** and **transference.**

People are told the more parts per million (PPM) of colloidal silver in a solution the better. This is NOT true! We want to keep silver ion levels to LESS than 1 PPM because metal stresses the body. Harmonic™ Silver Water uses silver's vibtrational "frequency" as a homeopathic.

For burn victims , use Soc™ lotion and Nugest II™ or Totally Male™ hormone precursor creme to promote beautiful "pain" free skin. These products rebuild and replace damaged connective tissue. They work equally well on facial wrinkles and acne blemishes. *I know a man who reduced 65 feet of 20 year old burn scars to less than 2 inches!*

When SOC™ is taken in capsule form, the body automatically begins dissolving <u>internal</u> scar tissue, and replaces it with "live" healthy tissue. SOC™ helped my body become as limber and pain free as a 10 years old. SOC™ also removes heavy metals from the body's tisues—and especially from the brain and nerve tissues.

The 90/10 Rule Of Health
Strive to live your life doing things 90% correct and enjoy your sins (the other 10%) to the fullest—and without guilt!

"Balance in all things is the foundation of health."

9

Satiety Blues

"Everything in Moderation."
Diane DeFelice

Fullness beyond desire! A primal drive fulfilled! Who can conjure a better feeling than a full stomach after a superb meal? Surely, food is one of the true pleasures of life. Aroma! Appearance! Taste! These are the things for which we live! Yet, in our drive to fulfill a basic physiologic need, we sow the seeds of old age and death.

Food requires a certain amount of time for complete digestion. When we eat too much food or too soon after a previous meal, the body suffers *overload* shock. Shock of any type puts stress on the vital organs (liver, thyroid, adrenals, kidneys, parathyroid, pancreas, pituitary, and testes). Dietary shock deserves our attention because it accelerates aging.

Snacks & Food Related Stress

People love to snack. They snack because they are hungry or because it is the thing to do—part habit, part social custom. The *experts* tell us it is good to eat every few hours. They tell us small meals taken more often are less stressful to the system and better for our health. They tell us small meals taken often maintain blood sugar levels and keep us on an even keel. They even tell us that multiple small meals increase productivity.

Unfortunately, the experts are WRONG! These things are NOT true. They NEVER were true. Let's stop and analyze what happens to the body when we eat too much or too often, which includes snacking. Snacks are simply small meals!

Food creates stress because it involves digestion. Digestion creates stress by drawing on the body's energy reserves. Food energy molecules must be broken down, transported, and reassembled into usable energy forms. Substances that do not promote health must be dumped or stored.

When we eat, we borrow from our energy reserve account. It takes energy to get the process going, and if the energy generated from food does not repay the loan, we suffer an energy deficit that is reflected in loss of health and vitality in the vital organs.

The vital organs have *limited* capacity and resilience. They require rest BETWEEN meals. When they are denied adequate and regular rest, they come under severe stress. Eating between meals and eating more often than every four hours causes the organs and glands to LOSE their resiliency.

Food related stress results in organ *burn-out*. Burn-out means LOSS of function. The organs age TOGETHER, each following the other. The effect compounds itself in chain reaction style. This scenario can occur even if the food is positive energy and nutritious. *Quality, quantity,* and *frequency* are some of the controlling factors.

If snacks and meals are composed of *left-spin* substances, organ stress is greatly increased. When combined with meals that are spaced too close together, the body is left with NO alternative but to shift into OVERDRIVE in an attempt to use, neutralize, dump, or store food energy fields.

Food imposed stress creates an 'involuntary' series of reactions in the body because the body has NO choice but to process what it has been given—even to its own detriment. The body acts as much out of duty as need when it is fed too much, too often, or when it is forced to process bio-junk food.

Snacking, like bio-junk food, overloads the VITAL organs with "waste", upsets hormone balance, destroys vitality, corrupts enzyme and ATP production, and promotes aging. Mental stress is, of course, another powerful energy force. **Stress energy is never lost, it merely changes form. In this case, youth gives way to old age.**

Trophy & Diabetes

Food related stress brings about *trophy* in the vital organs. *Trophy* means change related to nutrition. If we apply the prefix *hyper* or *hypo*, we are referring to a change in physiologic activity that is above or below the norm. Both hyper and hypo conditions lead to organ burn out or dysfunction.

For instance, *hypoglycemia* refers to a condition commonly known as *low blood sugar*. Dissected, the word means *hypo*-a low activity condition. *glyc*-sweet. *emia*-pertaining to the blood.

The body's organ system is *interdependent*, and whatever affects one gland affects all of them. Health conditions are **always** multiple in nature. Dis-ease is NEVER singular.

Dis-ease is always symptomatic —a secondary condition that points to stressed vital organs, hormonal imbalances and the presence of **excesses** in the system.

Deficiency Dis-eases & Conditions

We hear a lot about deficiency dis-eases and deficiency conditions, but there is NO such thing. The entire concept is but a carry over from the early days of allopathic medicine and the influence of Justus von Liebig's infamous agricultural theory called the *"Law of the minimum."*

Justus von Liebig developed his theory around 1830. He is regarded as the father of the synthetic fertilizer industry and the destructive practices of present day agriculture. His law says, *"the nutrient that is in the **minimum** controls."* To von Leibig, soil was nothing but dirt. He believed that there are only three *essential* nutrient salts needed by plants—nitrogen, phosphorous and potassium—commonly referred to as NPK.

Pasteur and von Liebig were contemporaries, and like Pasteur's equally incorrect Germ Theory of Disease, medical science adopted von Liebig's erroneous theory on nutrition. Clinical nutritionists perpetuate von Liebig's erroneous theory when they promote the idea that DEFICIENCIES give birth to dis-ease. The *experts* in the medical arena are wrong—and so are those in the alternative area who perpetuate the lie.

Dis-ease is exactly the *opposite* of what is popularly believed and taught. Dis-ease is nothing but the manifestation of conditions of **EXCESS** within the system. Excesses always manifest themselves as deficiencies. Excesses are energy field imbalances that *alter* health at the subtle energy level.

"Deficiency" conditions appear when excesses of toxic energy EXCEED the body's ability to handle it. For example, medical science teaches that the diabetic suffers from a "deficiency" of the hormone *insulin*. They also classify diabetics as either glucose intolerant or insulin resistant. In actuality, the diabetic suffers from **excess** toxic wastes in the body's tissues and fluids. The diabetic's body, however, keeps "carbon" sugars circulating in the blood to BUFFER acid wastes circulating in the system. *Sugar is a carbon based molecule $(C_6H_{12}O_6)$. Carbon acts as a BUFFER, moderating all life on planet Earth. To understand more about carbon's role, I highly recommend The Carbon Connection and The Carbon Cycle. (See Source Page).*

In other words, the diabetic's problem is related to **excess** waste and hormone problems. In women (and older men), the TRIGGER that sets off the diabetes is "always" hormone driven due to **unopposed estrogen dominance** and receptor site lockup—a "cumulative" condition resulting from estrogen ANALOGS (see glossary for definitions) found in meat, milk, cheese, plastics that wrap foods and poisons that are sprayed on crops. **Diabetic normalcy is easy to achieve with full cooperation of the suffering person and a strong desire to return to peak health.**

Type 1 *early* childhood diabetics problems are LINGKED to super antigens delivered via polio and DPT vaccines. A huge body of medical research is available that documents the dangers of immunizations (call **New Atlantean Books** (505) 983-1856 or write P.O. Box 9638, Santa Fe, NM 87504 USA.

The fact is, 75% of children with diabetes and hearing loss suffer from mutant pathogenic viruses, bacteria, foreign serum proteins (these ARE "energy fields") introduced into healthy children's bodies by mad men! **DEBLOCKING of neuro and hormonal receptor sites allows the body to heal and is MUST therapy for all sick people (see Source Page).**

Instead of worrying about microbial "boogie men" getting your child, detox their little bodies, flip their sensory switches and feed them Biogenic™ SUPER FOODS—all of which BOOST their immune systems and transforms their TERRAIN so no dis-ease—contageous or otherwise—can find quarter. **Control of the terrain is the key! Get it?**

Fifty million people suffer with clinical/subclininical diabetes. Science's failure to understand diabetes at the subtle energy level continues the suffering. Independent action, **without** the blessings of higher authority, is a prerequisite to the return of health. **You have to THINK for yourself!.**

Let's review. There is no such thing as a deficiency disease, but there is such a thing as excesses. Moreover, aging is a cumulative *condition* and death the confirmation of **"excesses beyond control."**

The vital organs function like gyroscopes on a ship. They keep us *even-keeled* by dealing with shifts in the body's TERRAIN. They maintain optimum health IF we do not "sabotage" them with incessant snacking, bio-junk food, unfriendly water, excess waste, and hormone "analogs."

How we *feel* is NOT an accurate barometer of our true state of health. Long before the SIGNS of dis-ease become visible, negative forces are at work at the subtle energy level. The proof is all the SUBclinically sick and dying people, who "felt" just fine—*yesterday!* **The "lag" between onset and manifestation and SIGNS of dis-ease is about 20 years!**

Mental Hype • Body Abuse

Hype is taking its toll the world over. People have become skilled in the awesome power of mind over body and drug over mind. They use both to **drive** and **whip** the bio-electric body. And when asked how they feel, people usually respond "great!" At the same time, over 80% of the US population suffers from sub-clinical illness.

Hype and the unbalanced person go together. It goes with unrealistic mental euphoria. Hype drives the body *beyond* its ability to physically respond. Bio-junk food, coffee, drugs and popular "magic bullet" supplements are forms of hype. **Hype WHIPS and DRIVES the bio-electric body into the "twilight zone" of Time—a Time warp—where aging and the passing of Time accelerates.**

Symptoms of hype-driven dis-ease are not so plainly visible, but the SIGNS are easy to see if we are paying attention. When the doctor renders a diagnosis of dis-ease, it usually shatters *hype's* hold on us—but by then, we are in trouble.

Dis-ease is the *manifestation* of stress. Dis-ease is a confirmation of aging. Dis-ease is the *manifestation* of Fourth Dimension Time in man's Third Dimension world. Aging and dis-ease are the result of our failure to square our energy account. Death is energy bankruptcy, while hype is energy inflation. *Hype* is modern man's Achilles' Heel because it involves unrealistic positive thinking and an unbalanced lifestyle. **When we avoid hype and live the simple life, aging and the passing of TIME come to a halt.**

Food Digestion Tables

The following tables indicate the amount of time required for different foods to **leave** the stomach. Only *basic* foods are listed. A couple of common bio-junk foods are listed because these substances are prevalent in our society—coffee and white bread, for instance.

Please keep in mind that this information applies to the **normal, healthy** stomach without stress or known digestion shortfalls, ulcers, etc. Also note the very small amounts of food used in these examples (1/2 ounce). Large amounts of food take longer to digest. If more food is eaten too soon, undigested food is *forced* into the small intestine and colon where parasites and anaerobic conditions produce massive amounts of metabolic poisons. DiSorb Aid™, R/HCl and Yucca Blend™ speed digestion and absorption of food energy while STOPPING **incoming** parasites dead by "lysing" (breaking) their peptide bonds which renders them harmless.

One-half to Two Hours

Pure Water	Wine
Tea	Milk
Coffee	Bouillon
Beer	Soft eggs

Two to Three Hours

Coffee w/cream	Cocoa w/milk
Asparagus (steamed)	Potatoes (mashed)
Fish (broiled)	White bread
Oysters (broiled)	Butter
Eggs (scrambled, fried, hard boiled)	

Three to Four Hours

Chicken (broiled)	Bread (whole grain)
Carrots (steamed)	Spinach (boiled)
Cucumber (raw)	Apple (raw)
Beef (roasted)	Salmon (broiled)
Tuna	Ham
Lentils (boiled)	Beans (boiled)
Green beans (steamed) Lettuce (raw)	

A Story About Satiety

Dr. Carey Reams told a story that took place during the years he and his wife were raising their large family. As the story goes, the neighbors and their children were over for dinner. When the food bowls were placed on the table, the neighbors made an effort to hide their surprise as their eyes were drawn to the modest size of the various bowls of corn, peas, mashed potatoes, gravy, meat, and desserts.

Expecting just such a response, Reams—in his characteristic style—laughed and predicted that there would be food left over. As you might guess, this is exactly what happened. Everyone had a wonderful meal, a great time, and departed with their gut plum-full!

I tell this story to draw your attention to the *satiety* enjoyed by all with a limited amount of food. What happened at the Reams' home is exactly the OPPOSITE of occurs today. Today, people are starving to death on FULL stomachs!

Reams' food was alive—chuck-full of enzymes and loaded with bio-active minerals and vitamins. Today's food is

DEAD and EMPTY. It provides minimal *energy* for the body and requires people to stuff themselves in order to *feel* full because positive energy forces are absent. Almost ALL processed foods are *left-spin* energy substances. The body cannot use negative energy and must neutralize it or store it as FAT!

Did you note those last four words? I hope so, because what we are discussing and piecing together, line by line, chapter by chapter, is going to shed light on the obesity problems that are plaguing 75% of Americans.

We could surmise that what really took place at the Reams' dinner table was that everyone was courteous and took only small portions of food and all left the table hungry—faking it all the way. But Reams was not a liar. He told the story to make the point that good food, bio-active food, food with a right-spin energy *footprint* is very nourishing! You can believe that everyone at that table left *full and gratified BEYOND desire* which is the correct definition of the word *satiety.*

Few people experience real satiety these days. Instead, they know only the pseudo version. *Pseudo* satiety is experienced when the stomach is full, but the body is not nourished. In other words, we quit eating because we run out of space— NOT because we are nutritionally satisfied. **America is a nation of overweight people whose nutritional needs go unfulfilled.**

People leave the table hungry, yet too full to eat more! It is impossible to satisfy the body's energy needs with empty, left-spin energy foods that are devoid of life giving nutrients!

The Appetite

Appetite is a combination of *physical need* and *mental desire.* It is controlled by the satiety and hunger centers in the hypothalamus of the brain. It has long been established that the hunger center is ALWAYS active unless it is *inhibited.* The body uses two inhibitory mechanisms to regulate hunger: a **physically** full stomach and a **nutritionally** satisfied body.

The hunger center is a cluster of nerve cells that generate sensations that are a combination of physical need and mental desire. Snacking is a combination of BOTH. Most people meet their body's call for nutritional *energy* (true hunger) with EMPTY calories (physical hype) and cognitive satisfaction (mental hype). These are a deadly combination!

When we are **nourished,** the "I'm hungry" *satiety* center sends a message to the *hunger* center that its needs have been met. This causes the system to shut down and we lose our desire to eat. Real satiety is **nourishment** BEYOND desire!

False satiety is different, but the mechanics are similar

in that it is based on a FULL stomach which is "bogus satiety!" When the stomach is full OR when our nutrient energy needs have been met, a message is sent to the hunger center and we lose our desire for food. This is a *negative inhibition system* because one system controls the other. It is a system that works flawlessly UNLESS we *sabotage* it with poor choices!

I'm Hungry Again

Later—after the stomach partially empties—the hungry person's body DEMANDS more nourishment, the appetite returns with a vengeance and the cycle begins over again.

Hungry people in a bio-junk food society gain weight when they fail to meet their body's energy needs AND when their hormonal system gets messed up. The need for nourishment is one reason *why* people become fat. Excess toxicity is another. Hormonal imbalance a third. Weak/insufficient digestive enzymes is a another reason, as is lack of exercise and *load bearing* work.

Natural **weight control involves meeting the bodies nutritional and hormonal needs plus DETOXIFICATION of the tissues, blood, and lymph.**

The nervous system is divided into the central and peripheral systems. The stomach is controlled by the peripheral system which is divided into the sympathetic and parasympathetic systems. We have control over the sympathetic nervous system. We control it with our *mental* thoughts. We have NO control over the parasympathetic nervous system. It is involuntary. Both systems communicate with the stomach.

Load-Bearing Work

Load bearing work is just that—load-bearing! People do not do enough of it. Society has come to view **physical work** as a curse—something to be avoided at all costs! Only poor or uneducated people do this kind of work! They are wrong; the body must be worked! Since people hate the word "work," maybe we should call it **load-bearing** *exercise* which better fits the sports bent of society. Unfortunately, for most people this kind of activity takes place on the couch in front of the boob tube. So let's compromise and call it **load-bearing** *activity!*

The body responds to load-bearing activity by building new tissue and repairing old tissue. This kind of activity is called *anabolism.* When the body is "worked" on a regular basis, rejuvenation accelerates. Aerobic exercise, weight training, and garden work are just a few examples of load-bearing activity to which the body responds with new vigor.

We are supposed to build a "new" body (bones, cartilage, muscles, ligaments, tendon, skin) every 7 years. Lifestyle and hormones dictates whether your "new" body will be stronger/weaker. The process can be speeded up or slowed down depending on your lifestyle and health status.

As people age, they lose their ability and desire to do physical activity. Part of this phenomenon is the physical inability to perform; part is a lack of desire; part is a lack of energy. A sedentary lifestyle destroys the body and precipitates loss of bone and muscle mass—along with loss of mobility. LOAD BEARING activities circulate toxic metabolic wastes which explains why people who exercise and work their bodies enjoy better health. **The more sedentary we are, the faster we age. This is called the "use it or lose it rule."**

The Dowager's Hump

The dowager's hump is a classic SIGN of total systemic OSTEOPOROSIS (degeneration of the bones and connective tissues). This humped-back, bent-over appearance—as seen among older people (especally older women)—is a SIGN that is common among younger people too —again especially women whose systems are "unopposed estrogen dominant." **It is EASY to reverse and the solution is the same for young or old.**

If you could look at the older person's skeleton (see page 100), you would see that their spinal column and related connective tissues have *shrunk*. Notice, the person has lost *inches* from their maximum height—which they achieved at their *anabolic peak*. These lost inches occur mostly in the spinal column through deterioration of the vertebrae, tendons, ligaments, and discs between the vertebrae. As this occurs, the rib cage settles until it RESTS on the pelvis (hip). **This process can take up to forty years to occur.**

Settling of the spine and rib cage distorts the visceral cavity and organs. A prolapsed (kinked) colon usually goes with it. The organs are forced OUT of position and are PACKED closer together. This is WHY older people have so many problems with their bowels. Settling of the spine results in a protruding belly and the *humped* appearance. **The process begins the moment female hormones get out of kilter, which explains why most women start into osteroprosis as early as age 30, Seldom is this horrible condition diagnosed until after menopause—that is, AFTER substantial bone mass has been lost. NOTE: when a women begins to pile on the fat (regardless of age) or her hair thins and falls out or grays, or thyroid, energy, or female problems start up, she MUST stop and take action to reverse the "slide" into old**

age that won't become "official" until the doctor says, "*You are in menopause!*" (See Source Index for solutions.)

Dowager is an old English word that described a widow who held property from her deceased husband's estate AND who had the imposing appearance of a humped back and shoulders. Hence—a "dowager's hump." The condition was predominately seen among the wealthy. The poor usually died too soon in life to get the hump. The wealthy dowager did not do any load bearing work because physical work belonged to the domain of the poor.

The story of the dowager carries an IMPORTANT lesson. Here are a few things every woman (or man) can do to soth STOP and REVERSE osteoporosis and physical degeneration.

Hormone therapy is a MUST issue for anyone who wants their life under their own control! There is **NO CHOICE** here and the products needed to make it happen in YOUR life CANNOT be purchased in stores or through your doctor. Moreover, the process is very safe, incurs NO danger and can keep women (or men) young for a very, very, long time. **P.S.** Any female suffering with menstrual difficulties or menopause related conditions including fibroid tumors, sweats, hot flashes, aching joints, degenerating cartilage in knees, hips or shoulders, "walking legs" syndrome, deterioration of the myelin sheath around the nerve fibers, MS, lupis, fibromyalgia, memory loss, foggy headedness, edema, heart conditions like arrhythymias, can easily and safely rid herself of these problems. They are all hormone driven conditions.

Hanging is a simple procedure that s-t-r-e-t-c-h-e-s the spine and joints. Make a trapeze bar or hang from a rafter, or tree limb. **Do this twice daily.** Start slowly and increase each day. *Hanging* involves getting your feet off the ground, and relaxing the spinal column. which increases blood and lymph flow. Anyone with arthritis, osteoporosis, or back pain should also take SOC™ capsules to dissolve scar tissue, cause the body to lay down healthy 'new' tissue and limber the tissues.

Osteoporosis • The Dowager's Hump • Calcium

Women are told to take large amounts of elemental calcium. These include calcium carbonate (oyster shell), calcium citrate, calcium gluconate, and calcium/magnesium tablets just to name a few. Contrary to the *experts'* opinions, these substances should be AVOIDED . They do NOT solve the problem and they create additional problems. Use only minerals that have passed through the carbon cycle (more later).

Medicine's theory about osteoporosis in POST menopausal women (due to "insufficient" estrogen) is a BALD FACE

LIE! Osteoporosis is defined as diminished bone density and honeycombing of the bones due to calcium deficiency. **For your information,** calcium's primary job—both in the body and in the soil—is to buffer against toxic wastes. The osteoporotic person is TOXIC and the body is forced to mine minerals from their bones to "buffer" wastes in the blood and lymphatic fluids.

Medicine and clinical nutritionists *foolishly* promote calcium supplements in order to *prevent* and *treat* osteoporosis. They act as if *hypocalcemia* (low blood calcium) is the problem. It is not! Osteoporotic people usually have normal to HIGH calcium levels in their blood (hypercalcemia). These people don't need calcium. Instead, they need to detoxify their bodies and realize that their hormones (estrogen in women/testosterone in men) have SHUT DOWN osteoblast and osterclast activity (these are the cells responsible for renewing the bones.

If your *present* height is LESS than it was at your peak, you need to take ACTION today!

Rouleau-Dowager Hump *Connection*

Deterioration of the bones and connective tissues is **serious** business—and it plagues millions of people! But it is only a symptomatic EFFECT, as is the dowager's hump and the Rouleau effect. Pronounced *roo-low*, the condition is a forerunner of all dis-ease and is seen under the microscope as "sticky" blood, that is, red blood corpuscles clumped together that can't service the cells. Translated, Rouleau in the blood means less oxygen and nutrients reach the cells and less carbon dioxide and wastes exit the cells leading to "deterioration" of the connective tissues, hair, eyes, ears and nerves (see page 136). **Rouleau appears 5-20 years BEFORE the doctor can render a diagnosis of a life threatening condition.** Racemized™ sea mineral ions clear the Rouleau effect. Used daily, the benefits are astounding.

SUMMARY: Aging reversal is a step at a time project—in REVERSE! If you put to work what you have learned in this chapter you will be on your way to becoming *Young Again!*

PREVIEW: *Our next chapter looks at the world of "shadows" and commonly held beliefs. Jesus and the Great Pyramid of Cheops have much in common as you will see.*

Dietary Fat
Hormones are "cholesterol" based and we cannot be healthy by depriving the body of "fat." <u>AVOID</u> "fat free" diets—they kill!

A Book Worth Reading

Your Body's Many Cries For WATER details how water cures a multitude of dis-ease conditions. In fact, chronic **under hydration** fuels rheumatoid arthritis, allergies, chronic fatigue, asthma, angina and hypertension—all of which are SIGNS of hydration stress.

The author says "advanced" cultures are *trained* to ignore thirst signals, and we are *taught* to substitute coffee, soft drinks, tea, and alcoholic beverages for water, yet, it is NOT possible to meet the body's hydration needs with **liquid substitutes** that merely contain water. We take water for granted because it is inexpensive and available.

The author's findings are astounding and his research is impeccable. Yet, the man is shunned and his work ignored by the American medical "establishment!" They don't want a society of healthy people!

The implications of the findings in this book are far reaching and RESULTS oriented. (See Source Index).

Racemized™ Asparagus

Racemized™ asparagus does wonders for heart arrythmias, lung and bronchiole congestion, and stuffy sinuses. Aspar-Max™ was developed to assist older people who suffer with a multiple of problems including kidney and bladder conditions, cancer, eye problems, diabetes, male/female problems, insomnia, and nerve disorders just to mention a few. As it turned out, it also helped attention deficit and hyper active children. Use with Yucca Blend™ and Pac⁵.

Hormones, lifestyle and dietary habits control aging!

Hormones

Estrogen is the female hormone. Testosterone is the male hormone. Women experience menopause and men experience andropause. BOTH sexes must attend to their hormonal needs if they want to enjoy good health. If you want to "stay" young or "become" young once again—no matter what your age, racemized™ hormone precursors will make or keep you young. I encourage women to get a bone density test—and then watch her bone mass RETURN to that of a younger woman. PROVE it to yourself!

10

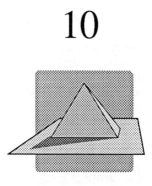

Shadow Land

"Most people would rather swallow lies than truth, especially if the liar has authority and the dis-information is soothing, like a fine liqueur."
Charles Walters

As Pontius Pilate passed by the side of Jesus at His trial, it was reported that he asked the great teacher: "What is Truth?" The Roman propounded a timely question that went unanswered, at least from the lips of Jesus. Pilate posed his question to Jesus, not as an interrogatory, but a statement about the Christ.

Socrates maintained that Truth could neither be proved nor disproved. Rather, it formed the basis of our beliefs by the reality of its existence. The Great Pyramid of Cheops is a present day TRUTH. It cannot be denied because it is THERE.

Earlier we posed the question, "Why do people like experts and expert opinions?" We also inquired, "How could anyone trust their most prized asset, their health, to the throw of medicine's dice?"

The answer to both questions is that the individual is relieved of personal responsibility when the decision process is given over to the experts. Forfeiture of responsibility gives an excuse and someone to blame if things go sour. Unfortunately, blaming others will NOT keep you young—or alive!

The "Expert" Syndrome

Medical science all too often tells us to do exactly the *opposite* of what we should do. Today, it treats its theories as gospel. Tomorrow, it casts them aside for new ones. In the process, it issues the proclamation, "magic bullet!"

An unsuspecting public buys into THEORIES that were

never true in the first place—like fluoridation of water and toothpaste, the Cholesterol Theory of Heart Disease, the Germ Theory of Disease, the idea that menopausal women are estrogen "deficient," the need for calcium to prevent osteoporosis, the benefits of soy and canola oils, vaccinations and immunizations, and so much other hogwash.

We are trained to ACCEPT and NOT THINK and IGNORE our instincts and rely on *experts* in medicine, government and industry—who are "experts" at **manipulating** us.

Mass Delusions

In 1850 MacKay wrote, *Extraordinary Mass Delusions and the Madness of Crowds.* In it, he showed how unbelievably gullible we are, and that the more desperate the circumstances, the greater is our propensity to make unsound decisions *in mass*—usually with the help of the *experts.* **People go crazy in mass, but they return to their senses one at a time.**

People seek the health care *experts* because they hope to solve their health problems. They don't know where else to turn. They're in trouble and they need a fix.

If people would learn to **read** their body's SIGNS and **listen** to the body's SYMPTOMS, they could prevent health problems and save a lot of pain, suffering, and money.

An ENDLESS supply of money—**like medical insurance**—allows the experts to keep their hooks is us. Few people escape medical science's greedy claws, expect under only two conditions: when we have no money or when were're dead! Medical "choices" should NEVER be made on the basis of "who" is paying the bill. The better your insurance, the worse it is for you. The "experts" go for the GUSTO and we get a "bone" in exchange—that is, if we are still alive when they are finished.

By definition, an expert is someone from more than fifty miles away. Our fascination with EXPERTS convinces me that this is the SAME phenomenon that makes the Law of Bureaucracy work flawlessly. This law has NO exceptions. It says: **"Regardless of the intended result, exactly the opposite will result."**

We CANNOT rely on the experts. It is the experts who have taught us to *doubt* our intuitions and ignore good sense. The experts practice tunnel vision, that is why they are called experts. **We live in a world of shadows—where most of what we see and hear only *looks like* the truth. Where the more something is believed to be true—and the greater the number of people who believe it to be so—the better are the odds that it is NOT true.**

Allopathic medicine is in trouble. So are people who

rely on it to save them from their poor decisions and bad lifestyles. Medicine's model is based on the Germ Theory of Disease. It, in turn, is based on the Scientific Method.

Consider the difference between conventional medicine's approach and vibrational medicine's approach to solving the hearing problem for the deaf.

At the age of fifteen, Dr. Patrick Flanagan invented the neurophone—a device to help the deaf hear. Flanagan sensed that the brain is a hologram and that it has different areas that are capable of performing **multiple** OR **duplicate** functions. Consequently, Flanagan used the skin as a pathway to the brain and as a hearing organ. The deaf person's "brain" could now hear.

Flanagan solved the hearing problem through visualization vs. surgical intervention. The brain is **not** hard wired as taught in the medical schools. The body can **regenerate** new brain cells. We **do** have the ability to grow new limbs, bones, cartlage, nerve fibers, skin, and connective tissues. Flanagan had **vision.** He understood the Creator's handiwork.

Cause & Effect

Earlier we referred to something called single factor analysis, which translates: For every effect there is **single** cause; for every disease there is a **single** pathogen that is responsible. This kind of academic tunnel vision has gotten us into a lot of trouble. It is unrealistic because it is NOT true. Whenever we attempt to FORCE the facts to fit a pet theory, TRUTH becomes secondary, *legitimate* science suffers, and trouble results. So it is with the hallowed "scientific method."

Charles Walters summed-up the problems inherent in the *scientific method* when he stated, *"Most of what is generally called the scientific system is not science at all, but merely a procedural aspect that calls for setting up experiments that eliminate other possibilities or it deals with making instruments that enable the investigator to find what he/she is looking for. There is a second scientific method that, although unwritten, has far greater impact on scientists and their findings. This is the reality of project funding, "peer" review, and the publishing of scientific papers."* **Walters went on to say,** *"The backbone of the scientific system has to do with asking the right questions, and a scientist can only ask the right questions after his/her life has absorbed the experiences that lead to a vision of the Creator's handiwork, hence the right question. Also,.....discovery is accomplished by the mind and soul of the whole person and cannot be reduced to a mechanical scientific (by-the-numbers) procedure. It stands to reason that you can't get the answers if* *you don't know the questions."*

The Double Helix & The Germ Theory

It was this second process that caused James D. Watson, one of the discoverers of the DNA molecule, to rock the scientific world when he disclosed the behind-the-scenes power plays, jealousy, and fights for funding in his book, *The Double Helix.* Watson also offered an antidote—the observation that scientific discovery involves human thought and vision *more* than test tubes, procedures, and microscopes.

The Germ Theory of Disease (GTD) is tremendously important to the aging process because it influences the way we perceive dis-ease. It so completely colors our thought processes that we are blind to the subtleties and cumulative effects of bad living habits and poor choice of lifestyle. Medicine does **not** understand that the battle for life and health vs. death and dis-ease is fought, won or lost, on a playing field that has absolutely **nothing** to do with the GTD. They are like **blind men** with fat egos stumbling in the dark—fearful of the light of TRUTH.

We cannot rely on medicine and science to solve our problems because they don't know what the problem is. They don't understand the phenomenon of life at the subtle energy level nor the manifestation of dis-ease. The proof for this statement is contained in the following fact.

Experts suffer from the same problems as the rest of the population. They grow old. They succumb to the same dis-eases. Their "magic bullets" do NOT save them!

The GTD is a theory, yet medical science treats it as holy writ. It is the cornerstone of the archaic medical model under which medicine labors. It is a stone around its neck! The GTD is so *accepted* that 99.99999% of the medical community own "stock" in it and live by it. Perhaps you do too. All conventional medical modalities—from diagnosis to treatment—are based on this **false** theoretical dis-ease model.

The model says we are nothing but a bundle of chemicals, proteins, fats, water, nucleic acids, flesh, and blood. It says that dis-ease results when the body is "invaded" by a bug and this causes us to come down sick. It says that dis-ease erupts out of *nowhere!* These things are not true. Loyalty to the model stands in the way of change.

Regardless of medicine's bullheadedness, we are moving into an era where the reality of the 3rd dimension *physical* body and the 4th dimension *energy* body are beginning to be recognized and brought together for total healing.

A healthy bio-electric body is a synthesis of energy fields vibrating in *concert* with Mother Earth.

Things Are Changing

Lancet and the New England Journal of Medicine are now carry "pro" alternative care articles. This is a 180° shift from the past eighty (80) years. The press is signalling the BIG "players" to position themselves for **control** over of the transition from allopathic to vibrational medicine. The driving force behind these moves are the pharmaceutical companies. They are the "forces" behind the GATT (General Agreement on Trade and Tariffs) Agreement which is already stifling competition in Europe, Canada, and Australia by hobbling the health industry via "mandatory" prescription of supplements. The FDA in the united States of America is also getting ready to implement the "CODEX" provisions of GATT.

We have a way of fighting back. It's called the **Foreign Soverign Immunity Act** *which is useful in going after any official of bureaucrat, who, with knowledge and through neglect, under color of law coerces, extorts, racketeers against, deprives, or perpetuates a FRAUD against a sovereign "Citizen." To learn how to assert yourself and defend your liberties and access to alternative health, order the 6 tape cassette package (12 hours of exciting stuff) from the Source Page.*

The movie, *The Medicine Man* is a *futuristic* movie. It was aired for a reason. It officially signaled the shift away from bogus organic chemistry and allopathic medicine to more natural modalities. Alternative medicine is growing at an exponential rate. It's no accident that our present medical and economic system is being systematically dismantled. Consider in 1994 40% of the people in the United States sought help through some form of *alternative* medicine. People are beginning to realize that conventional medicine has limits.

At the same time, *bogus* health journals and newsletters are making their debut. Natural healing is "the" thing to be into these days. Conventional doctors are authoring books and issuing newsletters that "trumpet" their charade. Few physicians can think outside the confines of their discipline and their credentials get in the way. **Do whatever you must to avoid getting caught up in it.**

The experts can ignore TRUTH, but they cannot deny it, for TRUTH is there—like the Great Pyramid of Cheops—etched in stone and timeless. Becoming *Young Again!* involves the recognition and application of TRUTH.

PREVIEW: *Our next chapter looks at HOW water functions in the bio-electric body. It is a foundation chapter in reversing the aging process. Elixir Of The Ageless provides answers to questions seldom asked.*

OSTEOPOROSIS
Affects
20 Million Americans
Kills 300,000 Yearly

Most Common – #1 and #2

❶ 33 Spinal Vertebrae

❷ Neck of Femur

Ribs

Humerus

Small bones
of hand

Small bones
of feet

**LOCATIONS IN THE BODY
WHERE PAIN AND MISERY HIT HARDEST**

Age
55 years

Age
65 years

Age
75 years

Compression fractures of thoracic vertebrae lead to loss of height and progressive thoracic
kyphosis (dowager's hump). Lower ribs eventually rest on iliac crests, and downward pressure
on viscera causes abdominal distention

Progressive Spinal Deformation In Osteoporosis

11

Elixir Of The Ageless

"In health and in sickness, pure water is one of the choicest blessings. It is the beverage given by God to quench the thirst of man and animal, and to cleanse the poisons from our system."

Byrne

At birth, the human body is over 90% water. By age 3, *average* body hydration level is 75% water. Adult hydration levels can dip to 65% in men and 52% in women. At death, hydration level can drop another 5-10%. Fat holds 55% water and muscle 75% and the brain 75-85%. These figures have meaning because they impact the aging process. They partially explain *why* we age and they **hint** at what we can do about it.

The *bio-electric* body requires water to function. When we are water deficient it is called *neglect*. When we drink contaminated water, it is called *abuse*. Most people's bodies suffer from both abuse and neglect. The *bio-electric* body can bounce back from abuse and neglect, but it can't do it without the help of *biologically friendly* water!

Water has many faces; some wet, some dry, some heavy, some structured. Water has different names. There is distilled water, reverse osmosis water, deionized water, carbon block and ceramic filtered water, hard water, soft water, tap water, ionized water, Grander water, Ludwig water, Ange water, Pi water, Egg water, Miracle water, Willard water, medical grade ionized water™, saline water, electrostatic water, and BEV™ water. Some waters are pure and wholesome, while others are the harbinger of dis-ease and death.

Water underwrites health and vitality. Water is "the" controlling dietary factor in the aging scenario.

Water Questions

Travelers sometimes experience water that is so dry that they can hardly get wet in the shower. They also experience water that is very *wet*. What qualities makes a substance as simple as water so different? Is it the well from which it was drawn or the earth through which it migrated?Is it neither?

Why does some water taste good and some not? Why does some water quench the thirst while another water satisfies so poorly that we avoid it? Why do some religions erect shrines around *certain* waters? Why are certain water holes around the world called *health* spas? Why is water used in the rite of baptism?

Why do plants grow better when it rains than when we irrigate? Is all rain water the same? Why is water used as the transport medium for fluorine and chlorine? Why is water used as the carrier for pesticides and herbicides? Why do we add poisons (like fluoride and chloramines) to drinking water? Why do people like to camp near lakes and rivers? Lastly, what does water have to do with reversing the aging process?

Water In The Body

There are TWO fluids in the body —blood and lymph— and water is the foundation of both of them. We need water to sweat, bleed, blow our nose, breathe, menstruate, spit, cough, and defecate. Without water the mucous membranes that line our air passages and gastrointestinal tract cannot function. All four excretory corridors—SKIN, LUNGS, KIDNEYS, and BOWELS—rely on water!

Water is the ONLY dietary substance over which we can exercise *complete* and *total* control.

BEV Water

Water interfaces every system in the body at the most fundamental level of human existence. 'Choice' in drinking water is the SINGLE MOST IMPORTANT health decision a person can make. My choice of "drinking water" is BEV™ water beacuse its ORP potential is close to where the egg and sperm were at conception which gives the word WATER new meaning. My choice of "therapeutic" water is high Medical Grade Ionized Water™ because if its phenomenal ORP and pH.

Experts like to talk about "pure" water, but they can't agree on exactly what *pure* water is. Chemists will tell you distilled water is pure water, but it's not so. Distilled water is purer than tap water, but it's not *pure*—and it's not healthy!

Pure water is void of ALL substances except one oxygen and two hydrogen atoms and their respective electrons. Pure water should also be FREE of the vibrational frequencies that were imposed on it by the contaminants it once contained.

BEV ™ water is extremely pure, "restructured" water that has its "memory" of toxic waste "erased." It is a right-spin energy substance that acts as a liquid magnet in the body.

Please refer to the water molecule diagram on page 79. Notice the hydrogen bonds connecting the H_2O molecule in the box to the adjoining molecules outside the box. These are *hydrogen* bonds and they cause water molecules to **stick** together. The effect is referred to as **cohesion.** The stronger the hydrogen bonds, the more cohesive will be the water. The more cohesive water is, the more ENERGY it possesses and the better people feel when they drink it. BEV™ water is VERY **cohesive.**

Water with a high energy *footprint* likes to **coat** things. The phenomenon is called **adhesion.** Again, the stronger the hydrogen bonds, the greater will be its adhesive qualities and the greater will be the water's effect on the body. BEV™ water feels and tastes wet, while its ORP gives the 'buzz' of high energy *signature* water. BUT THERE IS MORE!

The qualities discussed are further enhanced by manipulation of the *hydrogen* and *molecular* bond angles within and between water molecules.

Please refer to the drawing on page 79 and note that each hydrogen atom is connected to an oxygen atom at an **angle.** So called "normal" bonding angle is 104.5^0 at room temperature and 109^0 when frozen. The BEV™ process enhances the energy footprint and signature of water by manipulate the **angles** *within* and *between* the water molecules and drives up the ORP—giving BEV™ water more **life!**

Water that contains inorganic minerals, toxic chemicals, viruses, bacteria, radioactivity, etc., has POOR cohesion and adhesion qualities and WEAK hydrogen and molecular bonds. But contaminant removal alone isn't enough. It's memory MUST also be erased and the ORP potential elevated.

Traditional water processing units are **primitive** in comparison to the BEV™ proprietary system. People drink BEV™ water will tell you, *"This water feels different in my mouth and body and I feel good when I drink it!"*

Pollutants that hitch a ride on the H_2O molecule alter bond angles, weaken water's *magnetic* footprint and diminish its *electrical* signature. The end effect is water that has LITTLE energy to donate to the body and even LESS energy to transport wastes out of the system.

BEV™ water should **NOT** be left exposed to air or held in metal or plastic pipes. It's ORP potential causes it to "pull" contaminants from these substances and trade off its load of high energy electrons. BEV™ water is stored in its own system, in glass bottles or in inert polycarbonate containers.

It is not unusual for people who drink BEV™ water to ease years of sinus and lung congestion. For sure you feel better and have more energy. Bowel habits also change. **Non water drinkers become water lovers!**

Tap, distilled, and conventional reverse osmosis waters are NOT good for the body. They are not pure and their ORP is low. Since the body must "restructure" common processed waters BEFORE it can use them, they become energy consumers instead of energy donators.

ORP stands for oxidation/reduction potential. Translated, this means the water has extra ENERGY available in the form of "free" electrons. Oxidized water is dead water. Reduced water is "live" because it contains extra electrons that the mitochondria use to produce ATP, the body's energy molecule. pH is also high, but pH is NOT the issue here—ORP is!

Skin • Sweat • Lungs

The skin is a mechanical barrier to infection from bacteria. When we fail to drink enough water, the skin becomes stressed. Bathing in polluted, highly oxidized, low ORP tap water stresses the skin and causes it to age. Drinking it weakens the skin from the inside out and stresses the organs.

Failure to drink enough water, denies the body the opportunity to shed its wastes through sweat. When we sweat, we secrete water, toxic waste energy in our oils.

The ability to freely sweat is a good SIGN. Skin that does not freely sweat builds up wastes in the subcutaneous tissues. This closes a major waste exit portal and forces the load onto the kidneys, lungs and bowel—which are usually overloaded already. Wastes that cannot be exported from the body are stored in FAT the body *manufactures* for this purpose. Failure to drink enough water greatly accelerates aging because low hydration levels cripple the respiratory system, diminishes blood and lymph fluid volume, decreases available oxygen and raises blood pressure and pulse rate.

Water & The Lungs

The lungs also rid the body of waste energy fields. The lungs are VERY dependent on mucous secretions to protect these delicate tissues from airborne contaminants. Mucous production is dependent on water intake. Low hydration levels in the tissues cause the mucous membranes that line our mouth, throat, respiratory system and GI tract to come under severe stress. Mucous lubricates the nasal passages, airways and vaginal canal It transports airborne wastes OUT of the body. Mucous also coats and protects the lining of the stomach and intestines. Conditions like colitis, diverticulitis, and irritable bowel syndrome have their roots in poor mucous secretion. Many dis-ease symptoms vanish as water intake increases as documented in the wonderful book *Your Body's Many Cries For Water* (see Source Page).

More "Cries" For Water

The term **hypo**volemia comes to mind. It refers to a condition of low fluid (blood and lymph) volume in the body. People who are sick, immobile or bed ridden often suffer from hypovolemia because they do not drink enough water. Sexual impotent men are usually under hydrated, toxic and DEFINITELY hormonally messed up (men with "male" problems are NO different than a woman with "female" problems). Impotence, be it male or female, is a forerunner of adult diabetes Type ll, and water is a factor here.

Fluids like milk, juice, SOFT DRINKS and beer are **liquid foods.** And while these foods contain water, the water they contain creates stress because the body must dismantle and restructure the water in order to use it, a process that creates an OUTPUT of energy as well as an energy deficit.

Underhydration is a problem of EPIDEMIC proportions for much of the population and particularly among the elderly and sick—both are notorious for not drinking enough water, and their health problems are a direct reflection of it.

Prescription drug usage, when combined with tap water "laced" with toxic chemicals, is a recipe for producing sad, cranky, **depressed** seniors (depression is EASY to reverse without mood elevating drugs). Add a poor diet and **negative thinking** and you know the rest of the story. People respond quickly to racemized™ hormone precursors and BEV™ water with racemized™ sea minerals. **For certain, the elderly and the sick should AVOID TAP WATER for drinking OR bathing.** A Biogenic™, 3 stage shower and bath filter remedies the bathing problem (see Source Page).

Illness • Colon Therapy

Bile flow is dependent on water. Liver stones form and indigestion problems develop without enough water. Arthritis, fibromyalgia, gout, myasthenia gravis, systemic lupus, and dozens of other conditions all respond to the ongoing maintenance of proper hydration levels.

Colon problems manifest and multiply in people who fail to drink enough water. Colon therapy using BEV™ water is one of the BEST things a person can do to regain their health and stay on top. Unfortunately, colonics are **thoroughly** un-American. People dislike them because they "sound" strange and are a *pain in the butt.* Nevertheless, they work—especially when combined with a liver purge program simultaneously. The idea is to OPEN as many exit portals and move out as much waste as possible.

Many cleanse programs are better at stirring the system than MOVING the waste. Getting the waste OUT of the body is the goal. The programs discussed in this book do that better than anything to date—AND I can prove it to you!

Both fat AND skinny people hold large amounts of mucoid matter in their colon. I often hear people say, *"Oh! I don't need colon therapy! I go every day!"*

Regularity is NOT a reliable yardstick. Intestional build up of mucoid waste begins as early as age six and gets progressively WORSE with age. Count on it!

When the most popular cowboy in movie history died (his name was John W...), over seventy (70) pounds of **mucoid matter** was removed from his colon upon autopsy. The odor was *beyond* description! The great actor's transverse colon—the part that hangs over men's belt line—was almost **12"** in diameter! YET, the lumen (opening) through which his waste flowed was only one inch in diameter! The difference was accumulated mucoid matter, toxins, and drugs. A "healthy" colon should be about two inches in TOTAL diameter.

When you see a man's belly hanging over his beltline or filling a women's pelvic area, you are seeing a VERY engorged and prolapsed (i.e., sagging) colon—full of waste!

Colonic In A Bottle

Colon therapy is most effective especially when combined with liver purges. If you have serious or multiple health problems, a series of liver purges and colonics combined with racemized™ hormone therapy, Yucca Blend™ and the consumption of 14 day old Kombucha tea (which you make at home) will awaken the body over night by defatting the liver and increasing bile flow. Hair regrows, sex life improves, aches and pains ease, gray hair disappears and for some— *"Like me!"*— brown eyes turn green! **Wonder what I was full of?**

Deep Breathing • Aerobic Exercise

Deep breathing and aerobic exercise lead to vibrant health. These therapies are a simple and effective way maintain good health by increasing oxygen levels in the blood and tissues, stimulating the white blood cell and immune acitvity, and accelerating release of toxic energy from the lungs. Deep breathing also builds mental focus and a sense of well being.

Weak lungs do not process enough oxygen nor do they release enough toxins into the atmosphere. They are prone to infection and scar tissue formation. A weak respiratory system preceeds many dis-ease conditions—including Rouleau (sticky blood). **And don't forget, deep breathing costs nothing.**

Soft Drinks

Soft drink consumption in industrial societies is epidemic and the problems that spring from it are as SERIOUS as the effects of alcohol usage.

Soft drinks upset the body's calcium:phosphorous ratio. They are LOADED with phosphoric acid, sodium, and aluminum ions (from the can). These damage the kidney's nephrons (filters) and unbalance body pH. The sugar in soft drinks steals the body's mineral ions, and artificial sweetners like aspartame (think red and white swirl) destroy the liver. **It takes 40 glasses of high ORP medical grade alkaline ionized water to buffer the effects of just one can of soda** (more on ionized water on page 220). The nick name *"soda pop"* derives from the high amounts of sodium soft drinks contain.

Soft drinks are a socially acceptable beverage because they are considered to be safe to drink. They're not! We view them "differently" than cigarettes, coffee, drugs, and alcohol because their effects manifest over very long periods of time— NEVER in a "real time" relationship to their consumption. Soft drink junkies are addicts just like a smoker, coffee hound, druggie, or alcoholic. **The list of dis-eases related to soft drink consumption is staggering, but reversible.**

Energy Production & Water

The body uses the oxygen in water for respiration at the "cellular" level. The mitochondria in our cells use the oxygen to burn (oxidize) our glucose sugars through a process called glycolysis. This is a flameless process—a catalytic, enzymatic process involving hydrogen atom transport into the mitochondria where the *electron transport system* "frees" electrons for cellular respiration and production of the energy molecule ATP.

BEV™—and especially high ORP Medical Grade Ionized Water™—contain large numbers of free electrons. Purity, pH, ORP, and molecular size are the factors that control biological activity within the body. Some folks have to ease themselves onto these waters because they release toxins too quickly causing "healing crises."

Ionized Water

Medical Grade ionized water is being used in special Japanese clinics to heal people suffering with diabetes, cardiovascular problems, nerve, and connective tissue disorders (arthritis, fibromyalgia, myasthenia gravis, lupis, etc.) and cancer.

In Japan, it takes VERY expensive CLINICAL equipment to raise the potential of water to medical status. I am happy to report that as of January, 1996, special equipment is now available for "in home" use that can produce water that SURPASSES the water used in these special clinics.

To make this water, you must first produce BEV™ water. Next, racemized™ minerals are used to raise the resistivity level of the solution to proper levels. A "flow through" system requires a special bridge system to unite all equipment into one system. Laboratory grade "batch process" equipment is much easier to assemble and use and is now my preference over the flow through system. NOTE: I have both and the *flow through does have advantages for large families.*

The process involves shifting the electrons from the racemized™ acid elements (like sulfur and phosphorous) and super bonding them to the alkaline elements (like calcium and magnesium) which are the carriers when you drink the water. **This is water that defies all the laws of physics, chemistry and valence.**

Medical Grade 'Oxidized' & 'Reduced' Waters

Medical Grade High ORP™ water CANNOT (and should NOT) be made from tap water! Tap water is too polluted and its frequency is wrong. Ionized tap water **concentrates** and **enlivens** the pollutants—and the ORP is poor.

"pH" is a measure of acidity and alkalinity. ORP is a measure of "free" electrons in solution. When you drive up the ORP potential of water, you automatically drive up the pH.

Together, the water takes on miraculous healing powers.

We want to create **medical grade** "reduced" water with a pH between 10-12 and an ORP between (—)600-900. Without high ORP, pH is meaningless, which is a confirmation that **anyone promoting pH** as the "healing" factor doesn't know what they are talking about. But combine pH and ORP and you have something of value to share with your family and friends!

"Oxidized" acid water is for external use, with a pH between 1.5-2.4 and an ORP above (+)1200. Despite its very low pH, it does NOT burn delicate tissues like the eyes. What it does do, however, is destroy **ALL** pathogenic bacteria, viruses, yeast and fungi on contact. Nothing gets past it.

High ORP oxidized (acid) water creates beautiful skin, heals wounds and infections and promotes a youthful appearance. We have a video (and book combination) showing a Japanese man growing a new 'FOOT' with <u>water</u>! The man bathes his stub of a foot in **medical grade** high ORP acid water AND *at the same time* drinks **medical grade** high ORP alkaline water. His foot regrew over a 90 day period!

High ORP alkaline water is the exact **opposite** of high ORP acid water. Where acid water has been *oxidized* i.e., stripped of its electrons, alkaline water is highly *reduced* and is loaded with massive amounts of extra electrons.

Reduction is a organic biochemistry concept and term that indicates that a substance **GAINS** electrons and its positive valence is decreased. With the marriage of BEV™ water Medical Grade Ionized Water™ processing equipment, incredible benefits are available to anyone—right in their own home.

The ability to create this water allows you to 'UN-PLUG' from the medical system and take control of your life and health—and that of your family's.

This water does NOT cure dis-ease. Rather, it returns control of the body TERRAIN to its rightful owner—YOU! *Control of the terrain* is the guiding principle behind the development of BEV™ theory as documented in the BEV™ manuscript (see Source Page) and this book.

Let there be no mistake. If I had a degenerative disorder of any kind, I would STOP destroying my liver with medications and begin the process of detoxification and rejuvenation and prove the experts wrong. I would teach them a lesson by outliving every last one of them!

Fatigue & Water

Fatigue is a SIGN that the body has accumulated **excess** acids in the system and it's a SIGN that ATP reserves are low. When we *overdo*, when we experience muscle *soreness*, it is because acid wastes have over loaded the system. Lactate formation occurs when there is a **shortfall** of available oxygen at the cellular level which leads to **incomplete** oxidation of blood glucose sugars. Lactate is the salt of lactic acid which is the waste byproduct of **fermentation**. Lactate—like carbon monoxide from automobiles—is the result of **incomplete** oxidation. During the sleep cycle, we rid the body of lactate and other wastes. If you are always tired and require more than normal sleep, your system needs tending to. Drink high ORP Medical Grade Ionized Water™ and you will tire less easily and have more energy. Its a fact!

The new Far Infrared sauna rejuvenates the body by neutralizing acid wastes in the tissues and speeding metabolism (see pages 159, and 366).

Urine

Urine is the metabolic product of the kidneys. An examination of urine produces clues as to what is happening in the body. pH is an extremely important indicator. An alkaline (above 7.0) indicates one set of circumstances. An acid pH (below 7.0) means something altogether different.

Most people's urine pH is below 6.0. According to a nurse friend of mine, 90% of the people she checks have a pH between 5.0 - 5.5 which she says is "normal." If her patients are indicative of the rest of the population, she is prophesying a nation of people whose health is in SERIOUS jeopardy. I asked her to check my urine, the result was pH 7.2. This is good!

Low urine pH is a RED FLAG for cancer. Cancer manifests itself when urine pH drops to 4.5. Blood and saliva pH and resistivity should also be factored into the diagnosis in order for urine pH to be conclusive.

In general, body fluids with a low pH is bad news and a SIGNAL that the body is in a life and death struggle at the cellular level. Low pH signals degenerative dis-ease in both the formative and advanced stages. Our discussion thus far outlines the causes of such a condition and the Source Page and the remainder of this book will provide you with the remedy.

Water pH • Sodium

Most tap water is between pH 7-9 and is highly *oxidized*, i.e., no life force and very toxic, even though it may be classified as "potable."

For each number you move up or down the pH scale, the acidity or alkalinity is ten times greater or weaker. At a pH of 8, tap water is ten times more alkaline than at pH 7. But at pH

9, it is one thousand times more alkaline, due to its logrythym ic scale. It takes a LOT of pollutants and dissolved minerals to raise water from the ideal pH of 6.8 to a pH 8 or 9. Lime (calcium carbonate), sodium, aluminum and potassium all raise pH. Cities use all of them, but especially sodium hydroxide (lye) to manipulate pH. Sodium hydroxide (NaOH) is **extremely** alkaline (pH 12) and the sodium is toxic to the cells. People with cancer must NOT drink tap water—nor should YOU if you want to stay healthy and live a long life.

When you see tap water with a pH above 7.2, it has a huge load of contaminants attached to its molecules. The more "passengers" water carries, the less energy that is available to the body. The more waste shuttled into the body in drinking water, the less waste that can be carried OUT. Water pollutants have a left-spin and negatively impact the body.

Casts & Albumin In Urine

Casts are sometimes found in urine. They are aptly named. Casts are deposits of mineral salts (like the ones in drinking water), hyaline and plasma proteins (albumin) that have taken on the shape of the kidney's tubules.

The tubules collect urine and any wastes it may contain. Casts are a RED flag! They're indicative of: pH imbalance, degeneration, underhydration and excess mineral salts.

Albumin is a blood and lymph *plasma* protein. It does NOT belong in urine and its presence spells trouble. Albumin can be indicative of a urinary infection or worse—like problems in the kidney's nephrons (blood filters). For sure, albumin in the urine is indicative of accelerated aging.

Urine tells a story. If you drink plenty of water it should be straw colored between meals, and bright yellow after meals. The doctor usually wants a urine sample from the first urination of the day. The first urination is usually dark with strong odor and cloudy. Failure to drink enough water will give a similar effect. Too much table salt combined with a low water intake can do the same. If you sweat heavily and don't offset fluid and electrolyte loss, the same effects are seen—and urination may even be painful.

Go on a "strict" 3 day lemon juice and honey fast and the first urination on the second day will be **extremely** dark. If you collect it in a small, clear bottle and set on a shelf, it will form dark brown diamond shaped CRYSTALS of plasma protein waste byproducts such as uric acid. *Read the Miracle of Fasting* to learn more about this process. Also, the book *Your Own Perfect Medicine* (which deals with drinking your own urine for healing purposes) is also available (see Source Page).

Kidneys & Heart Connection

The blood is filtered by the kidney's nephrons at the rate of 250 gallons a day, or 1000 quarts every 24 hours. However, poor heart function equates to poor kidney function and the build up of **excess** waste in the lymphatic fluids and tissues.

When you hear someone is dying of *"congestive heart failure,"* KNOW that the heart is giving out, waste and fluids are overloading the system due to poor kidney function and the lungs are filling with fluids. Restoration of kidney function can be done with Aspar-Max™ racemized asparagus, PAC⁵ and racemized™ sea minerals. Use Yucca Blend™ and Medical Grade Ionized Water™ for the heart. A biogenic™ Lymph Roller™ will flush the plasma protiens.

The Bowel

When we are young, we experience regular bowel movements because muscle tone in the visceral organs (organs of the abdominal cavity) is good and we get adequate and regular exercise. As we grow older, the story changes—and so does our health.

Visit a doctor who thinks "basic" and one of the first questions he will ask is, *"When did you last have a bowel movement?"* Your answer tells a story.

The word *bowel* comes from the French and Latin. It means, *sausage* (intestines resemble sausage). Next time the doctor asks the same question, your response should be, "I moved my sausage,.....yesterday, a week ago, etc."

Freud said we are obsessed by defecation in our early years of development. He called it the Anal Stage. Gandhi was once described as a man who had been "over potty trained." It is reported that daily he asked each of his wives if they had moved their bowels. Perhaps great people are "anal retentive?"

Even Lawrence Welk had a thing with constipation. He always pushed a laxative on his show. The laxative company had a smart marketing team. They knew that people over forty was the perfect audience to target! Today the target audience could be people 5 years and older. The problem is very real!

Bowel problems are linked to a sick liver, poor diet, chaotic hormones, and low water consumption. Liver purges and colonics help. A roll down of the abdomen with a Biogenic™ Lymph Roller frees massive amounts of waste.

Water Therapy

Water has many uses beside drinking and bathing. It

can be used to break fevers, relieve constipation, cleanse the colon AND stimulate the flow of bile from the liver. The first thing my mother would do when we children were sick was to give us an enema to empty the lower bowel. We hated it, but the results could not be denied.

In 1983 I pushed myself too hard and became very ill with the flu. My temperature reached 106° F. I was in serious trouble. At two in the morning, all I could think of was to crawl into the bathtub and turn on the cold water. It didn't help! In desperation, I gave myself a colon irrigation and emptied my bowel. Within 15 minutes the fever dropped to 100° degrees F. I used no medication of any kind, and I recovered quickly.

Hemorrhoids • Constipation • Prostate

Hemorrhoids and appendicitis are first cousins. So are colitis and diverticulitis. Each sets up house for the other and together they make a *miserable* team. Constipation always **precedes** the other three. Constipation is serious business,.

Water keeps the stool moist and soft. Lack of water results in hard, dry stools. Dietary fiber holds water and acts as an intestinal broom and lubricant during defecation.

People claim hemorrhoids are caused from sitting on cold tree stumps, hard chairs and the like, but these things are NOT true. Truck drivers say they result from poor seats, vibration, and road bounce. These things are NOT true either. Ask a hundred medical doctors what causes hemorrhoids, constipation, and rare is the one who will mention WATER!

If you are constipated, drink 3 BIG glasses of water immediately upon rising in the morning. Thereafter, drink water every time you urininate. Throughout the day, HOLD your bladder—even if you think you're going to wet your pants! **Frequent urination robs you of your bowel movements and causes you to grow old.** A full bladder puts *pressure* on the colon, stimulates peristalsis (rhythmic movement of the intestines) and produces the gas and cramps that often go with a bowel movement. Other natural remedies are the use of Colon Prep Formula™, eating plenty of raw vegetables, apples, dried prunes, and heavy consumption of Kombucha tea.

50% of men over forty-five years of age have subclinical prostate troubles. Obesity, insufficient water intake, and poor diet are all involved. However, the major problem is SEVERE hormonal imbalances and constipation. Constipation causes the colon to swell and push against the prostate. This condition allows bacteria **to migrate** from the colon into the prostate. The inflammation and swelling is called *prostatitis.* In men, the prostate swells, where in women the thyroid swells. In men, the doctor looks for a hardened prostate, where in women the doctor looks for tissue abnormalities and hardening of the cervix. BOTH conditions are driven by hormone imblance.

Older men are known for "dribbling" their urine because their prostate is swollen and restricts flow through the uretha. In other words, these men can't make water!

When a man is young, all he thinks about is making love. In his middle years, all he thinks about is making money. When he becomes OLD, all he thinks about is making water! Become Young Again and you'll get it all!

PREVIEW: *In our next chapter you will learn how to save thousands of dollars in dental bills and how to feel good!*

Dump Those Stones!

Stones in the liver BLOCK the flow of acid wastes from exiting the body causing you to prematurely grow old.

Liver stones cause acids to accumulate throughout the body's tissues, causing wastes to settle in the joints and connective tissues producing pain, stiffness and deterioration. Waste often erupts as pimples and psoriasis because it has no where else to go and the body cannot store it because it is already overloaded with EXCESSES.

Gall stones are actually liver stones that form in the liver. They range in size from B-B's to large marbles. Occasionally, they dislodge from the liver and collect in the gallbladder. Now they are gall stones. Their accumulation eventually blocks the bile duct and often results in emergency surgery. A liver purge is simpler and safer solution.

All people—including children—have stones in their liver. The way to get them out of the liver and the body is to do a "liver purge."

All necessary preparations and instructions come as a package. Adults normally do a series of six purges, beginning the end of the third week and weekly thereafter. The process goes far beyond superficial methods that have been around the industry for over 100 years. For sure, do NOT use Epsom salts internally, as they are toxic. Preparations include Yucca Blend™, Enhanced PAC's, Biogneic™ Colon Prep Formula™, and stone softening solution. The process is safe and painless. Stones "float" on the toilet water surface in colors of green, brown, black, and red.

Everyone has stones! Your author did 13 purges and passed many hundreds of stones at age 52.

12

I Feel Good

"Stress is like a chicken. It always comes home to roost!"
John Thomas

We describe the way we feel in terms of black and white.
"I feel good!" "I'm sick!" People don't like shades of *gray* when
it comes to the way they feel.

If we substitute the word *aerobic* for good and *anaerobic*
for sick, our descriptions shift from black and white to *gray*.
Our words no longer *appear* to carry the same meaning, but
they do help us to better understand WHY we feel *good* or *sick*.

Breathing • Respiration

When we are **aerobic**, we are "with air." When we are
anaerobic, we are "without air." Both of these states of being
are influenced by the way we breathe.

Shallow breathing encourages the accumulation of
wastes in the tissues and accelerates aging, while deep breathing causes the body to shed its wastes and rejuvenate itself.

Shallow breathing creates an oxygen starved body,
windedness, low energy, and poor focus. Deep breathing
produces an oxygen surplus, endurance, high energy, and a
steely focus.

Exercise and strenuous activity promotes deep breathing and endurance. Endurance implies that a person is in the "aerobic" state—mentally and physically.

Respiration (breathing) takes place on two levels: external and internal. **External** respiration is somewhat of a mechanical process that occurs in the lungs, while **internal** respiration is more esoteric because it takes place IN the cells. **The exchange of carbon dioxide (CO_2) and oxygen (O_2) in the lungs is called *external respiration*. The exchange of CO_2 and O_2 occurs at the cellular level and is called *internal respiration.***

Glucose (blood sugar) is burned (oxidized) at the cellular level and the production of the energy molecule ATP is the result. ATP is why we eat food and drink water.

Clinical vs. Subclinical

Aging occurs at the cellular level before it appears in the mirror. And while we think of aging on the physical (Third Dimension) level, we must come to understand that aging is really an energy concept that transcends the Third Dimension where we live out our lives.

The doctor uses SIGNS to diagnose dis-ease. SIGNS are observable and ***clinical*** proof of dis-ease. Symptoms, on the other hand, are *not* observable, but they are ***subclinical*** evidence that something is amiss.

When you are clinically ill, you are usually under a a doctor's care, in the bed, or perhaps in the hospital. **Clinical illness is OFFICIAL!** "Clinical" means you are in trouble!

Subclinical illness is the "occult" or hidden stage of dis-ease. It takes place at the *subtle energy level* of our existence. It is a ***gray*** state of being, often described as "feeling a little off." People tend to ignore these *off* feelings, hoping they will go away. In time, however, symptoms take form and give way to clinical **SIGNS** and an official diagnosis from the doctor.

Most people live out their lives at the **SUBCLINICAL** level, that twilight zone **between** true health and official dis-ease. Here, ***abnormal*** is viewed as normal and black and white are lost among shades of *gray!*

Microbes

Aerobic and *anaerobic* states of being greatly influence health and dis-ease. The *aerobic* state is a right-spin condition, while the anaerobic state is a left-spin condition. These energy "states" also dictate the **type** of microbial infestation (bacterial, viral, yeast or fungal) that **develop, inhabit,** and **PROSPER** in the body of man and animal.

Pathogenic microbes LIKE an anaerobic environment. They are blamed as the cause of dis-ease, but they do NOT cause dis-ease. Instead, they are only actors fulfilling the roles that YOU & I dictate to them as a result of our chosen lifestyle and habits.

If we dissect the word pathogenic, we get: *path*-suffering, disease, *gen*-producing, giving rise to. *ic*-pertaining to.

When a condition is described as pathogenic, it is a "diagnosed" condition that displays certain **agreed upon** SIGNS. SIGNS elevate it to a "CLINICAL" condition.

Pathogenic conditions are described as *morbid* conditions, hence, the term *morbidity* as used in life insurance company morbidity tables to predict death rates among a population. A **pathologist** is a specialist in *pathology* which is the study of the nature of dis-ease, its causes, processes, effects and alterations of tissue structure and function.

Microbes

Microbes "change" form according to THEIR environment and the hosts state of health. Hence, they are referred to as being "poly or pleo" morphic because they adapt to their environment and only "appear " to be different species of organisms.

A body with a healthy energy *footprint* relies on non pathogenic aerobes to maintain peak health. **Aerobes** are usually non-pathogenic microbes that like an oxygen RICH environment. As the body's energy *footprint* becomes left-spin, aerobes mutate and become **an**aerobes (microbes that prefer *oxygenless* environments) (the prefix *an* means without), or facultative **an**aerobes (microbes that can tolerate oxygen, but don't require it). A constipated colon is an **an**aerobic environment where pathogenic microbes set up shop and do their job.

Pathogenic microbes were once "friendly" organisms that turned against the host with a vengeance. These include bacteria, viruses, yeast and fungi all of which exist and live in the blood, which is NOT a sterile medium as we have been taught. From the moment of conception, our blood caries the SEEDS of our own destruction. ***"The sins of the father shall be with us to the tenth generation [and beyond]."***

Microbes common to the human body include: *staphylococcus* —an *aerobe* that is often involved in skin infections, *clostridium* is—a facultative anaerobe that produces **enterotoxins** (*entero:* related to toxins of intestinal origin) that are responsible for deadly botulism, *E. coli* is—a VERY important facultative anaerobe that is found in the colon.

The job of pathogenic life forms is to ATTACK the host

when weak and under stress and remove it from the face of the Earth. One reason people who exercise enjoy better health is because exercise speeds blood and lymph flow, increasing oxygen levels and circulating more nutrients and waste metabolites (metabolic wastes) and CO_2 OUT of the body.

Cavities • Dental Plaque

Cavities and periodontal conditions like gingivitis, pyorrhea, and bleeding gums are indicative of microbial activity in the mouth and an out of balance body fluid pH. Bacteria that produce cavities secrete a protective substance to shield themselves from air (oxygen) while they dissolve tooth enamel. These *facultative* bacteria **create** the environment they need to do their dirty work. They can *only* do their job in a low pH saliva environment. (Periodontal problems are easily treated and solved with a bio-magnetic dental irrigator. A liver purge to "deacidfy" the saliva and raise pH finishes the job.

Low pH saliva, blood, or urine is a bell weather of trouble in the making. Body fluid pH outside the norm **translates** to sub clinical illness or clinical dis-ease.

When the hygienist removes "plaque" from the teeth, it alters the bacteria's *anaerobic* environment—but it does NOT stop new plaque from forming again. In time, you must return and have your teeth cleaned again. Some hygienists and dentists coat the teeth with plastic to discourage the bacteria from taking root on the teeth. This is helpful, but it does NOT solve the problem and it costs plenty. Coating the teeth with plastic is the dentist's version of *palliation.*

Proper dental hygiene and "terrain" management means no plaque and means no decay. Plaque, gingivitis, bleeding gums, and pyorrhea can be easily TREATED with a simple, inexpensive device called a **Bio-magnetic™ dental irrigator** that uses plain water to do the job (see page 204 & Source Page).

Instead of having your teeth cleaned twice a year, equip your home with a *bio-magnetic irrigator* and wash your problems down the drain. This simple appliance can save a family a fortune in dental bills. You can even use it to clean your dog's teeth—that is, with the animal's own cleaning tip, of course. Veterinarians charge $100 to clean an animal's teeth. My teeth are clean and bright and they haven't been cleaned in over 5 years! Here's how the dental irrigator works and why every family should have one.

Magneto-Hydro Dynamics

Plaque is a negative energy field. The coating bacteria

secrete to protect themselves has a negative (—) electrical charge on its surface. The hydrogens on the H_2O molecule have a positive (+) charge (please review diagram on page 79).

Magneto-hydro-dynamics (MHD) is the *process* used in Bio-magnetic™ irrigation. MHD uses an electromagnet to free the hydrogen ions (H+) in the water so they can react with the negative (—) surface of the plaque as they are pumped against it. Positive charged H+ protons oxidize the plaque's negatively charged protective coat by **stealing** electrons—a process referred to as **oxidation.** As the plaque loses its "protective shield" the bacteria disappear down the drain! Instead of the silly devices that squirt water at your teeth and gums, a Bio-magnetic™ irrigator converts water into a substance that really cleans the teeth and gums. This is a therapeutic device NOT be confused with common water on store shelves.

The process just described is an electrical event not unlike the rusting of iron or disappearance of aluminum window screens in a salty, ocean air environment. Transference of electrons is the name of the game. Medical Grade Ionized Water™ also involves shifting electrons.

Magneto-hydro-dynamics is a blend of vibrational medicine and technology. The process is acclaimed worldwide. The reason you have probably not heard of it is that the dental industry will suffer a huge loss of revenue once people wake up and realize that they can enjoy FEWER dental problems and save a lot of money with a bio-magnetic irrigator in their home.

I found that when I used my irrigator I could not detect the smell of decay when I flossed my teeth. The bio-magnetic irrigator is vibrational medicine's answer to dental problems!

Birds Of A Feather "FLOCK" Together

Dis-ease is an expression of negative energy dominance! Contrary to conventional thought, LIKE energy attracts LIKE energy. The sick body tends to become MORE sick unless action is taken to "create" a healthy environment and break the dis-ease cycle!

Low vitality reflects a negative energy state, and negative energy *activates* viruses and pathogenic bacteria that "FEED" on toxic energy. A toxic body CANNOT experience rejuvenation unless toxic wastes are neutralized and flushed from the system. Detoxification is as fundamental to rejuvenation as good food and water are to health. *In a polluted body, positive energy is hijacked and used to support and promote dis-ease!*

It is the terrain of the bio-electric body that ultimately determines the EFFECT an energy field will produce. It is the terrain, NOT the microbes, that determines **when, where** and **how** dis-ease will manifest itself in each of our lives. If you "tune-in" to your *bio-electric* terrain, your bio-electric clock will rewind itself while you enjoy *limitless* energy and a young body.

Stress & Attitude

Place a person under mental or physical stress and dis-ease often **erupts** onto the scene—not because of the presence of microbes and "bugs," but because stress is an energy condition that caters to the NEEDS of pathogenic life forms. In other words, **stress seeks an outlet**—and it uses the course of least resistance to express itself. Stress usually attacks an old injury or settles into an area of the body where there is a weakness. Conditions like hepatitis, chronic fatigue syndrome, asthma, arthritis, myasthenia gravis, lupis, MS, fibromyalgia are antagonized by stress and often seem to appear out of nowhere, but they have their roots in a sick body TERRAIN.

The latter four conditions are **hormone driven** *conditions involving deterioration of the myelin sheath that protects the nerve fibers as welll as disappearance of Schwann's cells located at nerve synapses along the axons. These specialized cells are responsible for keeping the receptor sites of the neurilema open and the nerve signal transferred.*

Dis-ease often appears in the wake of high stress circumstances or chronic negative thought. People often "handle" stress when they are under fire, but when the heat is off, illness appears out of nowhere ready to settle the score.

The point is this: body, mind, and spirit are irrevocably linked. Thoughts and attitude are **potent** forces in dealing with dis-ease and maintenance of good health. A good attitude, however, cannot overcome physical problems created by a toxic, underhydrated body.

Under Siege: *Fever*

There are two kinds of fever conditions: local and systemic. An infected finger is a localized condition, while a systemic condition places the WHOLE body under siege causing it to *react!* Systemic conditions bring on things like vomiting, runny bowels, phlegm, chills, fever, and horrid gas.

Fever that accompanies dis-ease is the body's reaction to the presence of a morbid condition and should NOT be considered bad. Contrary to popular belief, fever is good and serves a useful purpose. Fever is the EFFECT of an accelerated metabolic rate. Fever is a condition of **hyper** *thermogenesis* (*thermo:* heat producing; *gen:* origin of; *sis:* condition).

Mucous that accompanies colds and flu is the VEHICLE that carries toxic wastes from the body. Mucous is one way the body expels waste. Illness erupts onto the scene when toxicity levels EXCEED the body's ability to maintain homeostasis.

If fever is not allowed to go above 106⁰ degrees and the victim is FULLY hydrated, fever does a wonderful job of denaturing and destroying bacterial and viral proteins. It kills them by altering the body's "terrain". (A FIR sauna (page 60) provide similar benefits. These **therapeutic** saunas penetrate deep into the tissues, dissolve acid wastes, and kill pathogenic microbes using far infrared energy. They do NOT rely on heat or water or lights.)

Fever also destroys the microbes' "breeding" grounds—particularly in the colon (large intestine) and appendix. Fever is the body's way of ridding itself of toxic energy fields. If a fever rises too high, (above 110^0F), however, it can denature enzyme proteins in the brain and can be deadly.

Medicine and society have held strange views about the nature of fever over the years. For example, at the time of the American Revolution, people associated body lice with health. When fever got too high, the lice would leave and the person usually died. People and medicine BOTH invoked single factor analysis and came to associate the presence of lice with health. Lice=life. No lice=death. Obviously, this is wrong, but it's a good example of the problems incorrect thinking produces.

Denatured Proteins

If you drop the contents of a raw egg into boiling water, you will see the egg's proteins change form. The egg will become firm and solid. Heat denatures egg protein enzymes, alters their form, and causing the egg to harden. This is what a *febrile* (fever producing) condition does to bacteria—it destroys them by altering their protein based enzymes and structure which causes them to die. Food additives and colorings have a similar effect as do rogue analogous hormone molecules.

Muscle Tone

When body temperature becomes excessively high—as in heat stroke or a high fever—the enzymes throughout the body are altered and bed rest is required. Fever weakens protein enzymes and debits the mineral electrolytes that are responsible for maintaining **muscle tone.** Muscle tone allows us to stand, hold up our head, or maintain a position. Without tone, we would function like a jellyfish.

The muscles controlling the vital organs receive their orders through the *involuntary* parasympathetic nervous system, and loss of tone further stresses the vital organs. When high fever occurs, colon therapy and enemas are most helpful. **Colon therapy is direct, physical intervention designed to restore balance to the terrain by removing toxic wastes.**

Medications

Antibiotics, aspirin, and other drugs are forms of **chemotherapy.** All of them alter body function and accelerate aging. Despite the *apparent* positive results they produce in the short term, their long term effect on body terrain is disastrous.

Despite all the propaganda put out by the pharmaceutical companies, drugs are not safe. ALL drugs have **known** side effects. Drugs are prescribed on the same basis that is used to justify the chlorination of public water supplies and the spraying of food crops with "known" poisons. It reads like this: *"If the benefit outweighs the risk, a drug is prescribed."*

What is NEVER talked about is the long term effects of drugs on the vital organs and glands. Many older people take as many as FIFTY (50) pills a day! The short and long term side effects of these left-spin energy substances is beyond comprehension. One look at the CONTRAindications in any drug reference manual (i.e., Physicians Desk Reference) ought to be enough to cause any thinking person to opt for alternative measures in the treatment and cure of their condition.

"NEW" drugs are constantly pushed by the pharmaceutical companies to replace those drugs where patents have expired. New drugs are MORE expensive and each new generation of drugs carries an ever increasing risk.

People are taught to differentiate between "prescribed" drugs and illegal drugs. There is NO difference between them.

"How To Stay Healthy Until It Is Time To Die"

Personal survival requires that we learn to live our lives in harmony with nature so we have NO need for any drug!

Do you know anyone who has suffered from the side effects of drug therapy, or maybe someone who walked into the hospital or clinic for testing and was carried out—feet first? If you apply the lessons in this book, you will have NO need for the medical system nor will you become a medical statistic.

Drugs diminish liver function and burden the kidneys. They do violence to the kidney's nephrons which are the filters that clean the blood. Drugs destroy the liver's hepatocytes which are the functional cells that perform the thousands of *bio*chemical reactions that keep us alive and healthy.

A dis-eased body is a body that is under siege and drugs

force the vital organs to do double duty while they destroy organ function—particularly, the liver.

A healthy liver is so fundamental to health that any treatment modality—conventional or alternative—that does not make provision for restoration and maintenance of the liver is doomed from the start. We must never forget that 75% of the waste exiting the body leaves via the LIVER in the form of bile and bowel flow.

Colon Therapy

An enema is a short and quick version of a colonic. A colonic is sometimes referred to as a DEEP enema. A properly executed colonic flushes mucoid waste from the rectum, descending, transverse, and ascending colons. Mucoid is a combination of mucous, drugs, and fecal matter. It takes years to form on the colon walls and fill the cecum. When it becomes excessive, it will lock the ileocecal valve in "open" position.

The ileocecal valve is the valve that controls fecal flow between the small and large intestines. It is located in the cecum, a fist-sized pouch from which the appendix hangs (see page 46). A properly done colonic, preceded by a series of liver stone purges, reaches the cecum 6 feet in from the rectum.

The small intestine ends and the large intestine (colon) begins at the cecum. Undigested food and bile (from the liver), enter the colon by way of the *ileocecal* valve. **People with cancer usually have their ileocecal valve "locked" in the open position.** Yucca Herbal Blend™, Colon Prep Formula and enhanced PAC's clear the colon and free the ileocecal valve.

Colon therapy also stimulates peristaltic activity and causes the liver and gall bladder to dump bile. The stirring action of colon therapy sometimes causes temporary upset or general fatigue and malaise due to poisons stirred and brought into circulation.

An enema is NOT a substitute for a colonic, but its effectiveness should not be underestimated. While enemas generally purge only the lower few feet of the colon—which is six feet long—an enema is a quick and easy help when needed. Every person should own a ten dollar enema bag and take it with them whenever they travel. A women's douche bag works equally well when used with the rectal syringe that is usually supplied. Water, an enema bag and a motel bathroom are all that is needed to save a visit to the hospital for appendicitis, break a flue related fever or arrest Montezuma's revenge.

Colon equipment is more expensive than an enema bag, but it lasts a lifetime. I've had mine for 19 years! It is easy to use and nicer than lying on a towel covered floor and having to get up and down to fill the bag and **hoping** you make it to the toilet before you release your bowel.

It's especially nice to do your own "colonics" in the privacy of your own home. Clinics often charge one-hundred dollars or more per visit—IF you can find someone willing to do it. At home you have the benefit of using BEV™ water, Kombucha tea, Rene's Tea or coffee as the flushing solution.

Everyone should equip their home with colon equipment. In the case of severe illness, colonic equipment can save your life. The process may seem un-American, but I am here to testify that is a fast track to vibrant health. Begin today and you will **SHOUT** "I feel good!" as you become *Young Again!*

PREVIEW: *Our next chapter deals with the HIV virus and its alleged progeny, AIDS. There is an important connection between "weeds" and viruses.*

Dogs & Cats

Dogs and cats are people with four legs. They suffer from the same metabolic problems that humans do and their bodies respond and rejuvenate similarly.

Because animals age faster than humans, it is very easy to visually see them respond and come back to life "literally" before your very eyes.

It is hormones that bring people and animals into adulthood and it is hormones and waste "excesses" that cause us to grow old and fade away.

If you have a cat or dog that you love, all you need do is give them some Biogenic VitaLight™, Klammath™ Algae, a little Yucca Blend™, Pac's, liquid racemized™ sea minerals and rub their abdomen with racemized™ hormone precursors and your animal will come back to life in no time. I have seen this miracle over and over again—in pets and in people! Remove tisue waste, open the receptor sites and eat SUPER foods and life is a continuous miracle.

If I can practice what's in this book, so can you!

The Golden Years

The "golden years" come earlier than they used to and anyone who is honest will tell you they are NOT golden! Aging is the socially correct way of describing the ultimate dilemma, but I prefer NOT to tell stories that aren't so. Growing old is NOT my idea of a "golden" future. Instead, look forward to another 50-100 years of peak health and vitality by applying the lessons in this book.

Statistics & Palliation

It's difficult to discuss "health" with people who have been schooled in the scientific method. It's not that they are anti-health—they are not. Rather, their world is built upon medical statistics and studies. Theirs is a world of numbers—numbers that prove something is or isn't so. The *passwords* into their world are "statistics show" and "scientific proof."

Medical science sees health and dis-ease in terms of single problems that demand single answers based on "findings." Medical science demands that "health" minded people play their statistical games or suffer the ridicule of *"No scientific proof!"*

Anyone with a lick of sense knows that you must take care of yourself or good health falters and dis-ease results. Health minded people know that if you eat nourishing food, drink plenty of pure water, get enough exercise and rest, entertain positive thoughts, keep your bowels clean, and do the things we discuss, you will enjoy excellent health. **"Our" PROOF is *healthy* human beings living in accordance with nature's laws.**

Medical science sees "health" as a numbers game. Their game is designed to keep the public confused by dazzling them with skewed studies and statistical gymnastics. **"Their" PROOF is millions of subclinically sick people who *bear witness* to medicine's "findings."**

Palliation lends itself to the numbers game called "statistics." *Palliation* (see glossary) is a powerful tool of *manipulation* in the hands of medical science. *Palliation* allows science to state its case in the short run and make bogus health claims with total impunity.

Medical science **knows** the risks that accompany drug usage. However, drugs provide credibility and "scientific proof." Without the above tools of manipulation, medical science would lose its strangle hold on the people and the endless flow of cash that it derives therefrom.

Health minded people do not live in fear of medical science's statistics and studies. Rather, we **ignore** them. For us, their game is an exercise in futility. We ACHIEVE health and vitality and we try our best to live according to nature's way. Nature rewards our efforts with PEAK health instead of statistics and illness. **We measure results in years YOUNG. My goal is 250 years YOUNG! And you?**

BEV™ Water

BEV™ took its name in honor of French Professor Louis-Claude Vincent who developed the theoretical standards for **biologically friendly** drinking water for the body.
Consider these points about BEV™ water:
•BEV™ water promotes cellular metabolism. Its molecules cause the body to "dump" cellular waste and fuels mitochondrial production of the high energy molecule "ATP" within the electron transport chain.
•BEV™ water is a naturally potent biological solvent of body wastes and toxins.
•BEV™ water STOPS the flow of waste minerals, trihalomethanes, bacteria, viruses, chlorine, chloramines, fluorides and toxic chemical wastes into the body.
•BEV ™water is VERY aggressive and acts as a liquid magnetic transport system to the tissues and cells.
•BEV™ water effectively hydrates the tissues due to its bonding angles, conception point "ORP" and low resistivity. It's ORP is very close to where the egg and sperm were when life was conceived.
•BEV™ water uses the homeopathic principals of *resonance* and *transference* to bring "life" into the body.
•BEV™ water processing units do not require electricity and there are no elements to clean.
•BEV water helps maintain control of body "terrain" and it is enjoyable to drink. Non water drinkers become water drinkers with their very first glass.
•BEV™ water is the ultimate biologically friendly drinking water and is the basis for the creation of Medical Grade (High ORP) Ionized Water™. (See Source Page.)

Soft drinks are loaded with 'toxic' heavy metals.

Beating Alzheimers

Beating Alzheimer's is a "must read" book. Over 50,000,000 people are expected to have this dreaded condition by year 2005.

Learn of the mercury amalgam dental filling connection to Alzheimers. Learn how SOC™ rids the body of heavy metals trapped behind the blood brain barrier— metals that bring on brain and neurological disorders. Learn of the hormone connection (see Source Page).

13

Viruses & Weeds

"There is no difference between plant and animal."
Dr. Guenther Enderlein, 1898

Medical science knows little about viruses. The average person knows almost nothing about them. Most folks think a virus is like a bacterium—a "bug" that you somehow "catch!"

Antibiotics hold no power against viruses. If you are sick with a viral infection, you are usually told to stay warm and drink lots of fluids, okay advice, but there is a better answer.

The *informed* person will also perform COLON THERAPY, and take a hot Epsom salt, ginger, and hydrogen peroxide bath along with a shot of whiskey and a handful of SOC™ capsules. **The informed person does not wait to be told to clean the bowel and flush the body of its poisons and viruses.**

In college little time is spent discussing viruses. They are poorly understood by the student and often by the instructors too. NOTHING is taught about where they come from or how to deal with them.

Viruses Today

We hear a lot about AIDS, influenza, herpes, Hepatitis, Chronic Fatigue Syndrome, and mononucleosis. These are *here and now* viral conditions afflicting millions of people.

The best cure for any type of viral condition is prevention. Short of a clean, healthy life style, we MUST focus on the **conditions** under which viruses prosper. We need to understand the connection between these "fringe" life forms and the aging process from an *energy* perspective.

The virus is an anomaly, a paradox and a slave master. The virus is the point man of nature's garbage crew. Science does NOT consider viruses to be life forms—but they are NOT dead either. Viruses cannot reproduce on their own. They are **OPPORTUNISTIC** organisms—as are bacteria. When we create a suitable environment and lose control of our terrain, viruses appear, *seize* control of cellular machinery and take control of life at the subtle energy level.

Viruses are energy fields and they have an energy *footprint*. A virus is a strand of either DNA (deoxyribonucleic acid) or RNA (ribonucleic acid) that is protected by a protein capsule (energy shield), but this is an incomplete picture.

Viruses exist in the *grey* area between living and non-living things and can neither reproduce nor perform normal life functions on their own. Viruses are *entirely* dependent on energy generated INSIDE the cells of the target host's body. Viruses are classified based on their composition (DNA or RNA), origin, mode of transportation, reproduction methods and where they first manifest themselves in the host.

Viruses are so small that it used to require an electron microscope to view them, a problem overcome with a Nassens condensor microscope. Because viruses are ubiquitous, there is NO avoiding them, yet in a healthy body, viruses do NOT pose a threat to the host because the "terrain" is unsuitable for their proliferation. Consequently, viruses *cannot* access the host's cellular machinery unless we lose control of our terrain.

When we are under mental or physical stress, our energy fields are disrupted and the body's protective systems are sabataged. The immune system is one of those systems.

The immune system can overcome viral activation and restore homeostasis, but only IF we provide the environment that supports the process.

Viruses—like their cousins bacteria and fungi— have a job to do. Their job is to rid the Earth of weak life forms—be it plant, animal, or human!

HIV & AIDS

HIV (human immunodeficiency virus) is the virus that is associated with the manifestation of AIDS (Auto Immune

Deficiency Syndrome). HIV uses an enzyme called *reverse transcriptase* that allows it to infect the host in *reverse*. This is why HIV is called a **retrovirus** (*retro* means after the fact, in reverse). As the HIV virus mutates, it is given other names like HTLV 1, ll, or lll, etc. HTLV stands for human T-cell **lymphotrophic** virus. Dissected, *lymphotrophic* describes the following: **lymph**-the watery, clear fluid in the blood minus the blood corpuscles (think of the clear fluid that oozes when a wound is healing). **troph**-a change or a turning; **ic**-pertaining to. A lymphotrophic virus causes a *change* in certain cells within the lymphatic fluids.

The T-Cells

The HIV virus has an affinity for the T (helper) cells which are lympho**cytes** that originate in the *thymus* which is the center of the immune system. *Cyte* means cell. So a lymphocyte is a cell in the lymph fluid. In this case, we are speaking of the T-cells. Viruses wage war in the plasma proteins (lymph fluids) long BEFORE they appear in the blood. This explains why blood samples often test negative for the presence of HIV virus. As plasma toxins accumulate, the body's energy fields shift from right to left spin as the immune system weakens. This is the body's equivalent of the star ship Enterprise dropping its defense shields. Bio-junk food—including soy and canola—further weaken T-cell function.

AIDS Not A Virus

AIDS is not a virus. It is a **syndrome** of secondary conditions brought on by a weakened immune system. HIV is an **adeno**virus (*aden*-a cavity as in the lungs or chest). This class of viruses is OPPORTUNISTIC and usually results in death from infections of the chest cavity, as in *pneumonia*. We do not die from AIDS, but from secondary complications like pneumonia. (Actually, we die when the mitochondria within the cells fail to produce sufficient ATP to keep us alive.)

As HIV infects the system, a "syndrome" of problems called AIDS develops. Contrary to popular belief, AIDS is not a dis-ease of homosexual origin. Little of what the public has been told about AIDS is true. Most is *disinformation* purposely disseminated to keep the public confused.

NOTE: *People who "drink" Medical Grade Ionized Water™, bath in it, and douche with it can kiss their infectious diseases good bye. If you suffer with herpes, syphilis, strep throat, hepatitis, athletes foot, gangrene, pink eye, ring worm, insect bites, yeast infections, etc.. Here is a wonderful solution.*

Sabotage

Retroviruses—like HIV—sabotage the cell's genetic information base (DNA or RNA), then siphon away the ATP energy produced by cellular mitochondria and take control of the body's energy reserves while they multiply exponentially.

The process just described is predictable and should be expected in a toxic body terrain. The virus' job is to kill the host and rid the Earth of weak organisms. **Viruses are NOT the enemy!** They and their cousins—the bacteria, fungi, and yeasts—are present the moment the egg and sperm join. They are polymorphic "mutant" life forms that ONLY manifest when we LOSE control of our terrain.

Viral proliferation is a *confirmation* that things are not right and should cause the THINKING person to deduce that their terrain must be *"au fait"* (favorable) or the viruses would not manifest and stir up trouble.

Viruses only attack people who are toxic; people who eat dead, adulterated food; people who are not digesting and absorbing their food; and who are constipated, and anaerobic. **The consumption of high ORP water, DiSorb™ Aid, liver purges, and colon therapy goes a long way toward returning the body's terrain to peak health.**

Blood NOT Sterile

Contrary to medical teachings, the blood is NOT a sterile medium. Medical science has perpetuated this gross mistruth in the face of irrefutable evidence to the contrary, as discovered by Dr. Guenther Enderlein and Gaston Nassens and documented in *Hidden Killers* and *The Prosecution and Trial Of Gaston Nassens* (see Source Page).

"All life contains the seeds of its own destruction within its own fluids." That is what Dr. Enderlein meant when he said, *"There is NO difference between plants and animals."* He discovered that when control of the energy balance of the TERRAIN is lost, the microbes **automatically** break out of their "healthy" 3 stage CLOSED loop into a 21 stage path that leads directly to the grave yard.

The pharmaceutical companies and the medical system stand to lose trillions of dollars if the above information was taught in medical schools. **Recognition that the blood is NOT sterile is tantamount to open refutation of the Germ Theory of Disease and allopathic medicine as we know it.**

Pride and greed prevent medical science from refuting its false theories. Millions of people have suffered and died needlessly because medicine labors under the shadow of many other big lies and withheld information. As Christ said in Luke, *"Woe be unto you lawyers, scribes, Pharasies. You hold the keys of knowledge. You yourself will not enter AND you prevent those who would enter from entering."* Life was meant to be a celebration, not a requiem. Unfortunately, as Hosea said, *"My people perish for lack of KNOWLEDGE."*

Cell Electrical Charge

Strong, positively charged cells and tissues are not affected by viruses. Tissues that are waste stressed and anaerobic are taken over by viruses. A compromised body has weak enzyme function and insufficient oxygen. It is under these conditions that viruses take over the cell's machinery and reproduce themselves.

Rogue viruses *steal* the body's production of ATP and use this energy to multiply and form cancers. Cancer tumors and masses are HUGE fields of *negative* energy that control all metabolism within their sphere of influence. **Cancer viruses proliferate in a body that is anaerobic AND whose cells are loaded with sodium.**

An *anaerobic* body is an OLD body. Old bodies are unable to rejuvenate for lack of sufficient ATP. Dis-eases are energy wars and the bullets they shoot are negative energy bullets. Conventional medicine's "magic bullets" are worthless in the cancer arena. The PROOF is all the dead and dying people! The solution is a healthy lifestyle, immediate detoxification of the tissues, and restoration of hormone imbalances.

Useful Oxygen Forms

Hydrogen peroxide (H_2O_2) and ozone (triatomic oxygen, or O_3) are useful products. Their effectiveness is related to the amount of available oxygen present and their molecular instability. Instability allows them to give up oxygen atoms freely. Oxygen is a highly magnetic element, which accounts for the bent shape of the water molecules on page 79.

Oxygen therapy can be useful in the treatment of cancer **masses** and **tumors.** Skilled healers sometimes inject H_2O_2 or O_3 directly into cancer masses with good results. Given intravenously or by water infusion in the rectum or vagina, ozone therapy can be effective.

In the home, a "medical grade" ozone generator purifies the air and eases respiratory problems. Emphysema patients respond well to ozone therapy, partly due to oxidation of "in house" environmental pollutants, but also due to the elimination of microbial breeding grounds such as carpets and drapes.

Medical grade ozone destroys pathogenic molds, fungi, yeasts, dust mites and viruses and oxidizes (burns up) the food supply that these organisms feed on. Cigarette odor disappears from your clothes, house, and car, AND they are GOOD protection against winter illness. Every home should have one.

Ozone equipment is easy to use. However, only a very few pieces of ozone equipment on the market can produce "medical grade" ozone. Please UNDERSTAND that ozone in the WRONG form irritates the mucous membranes of the sinus cavity and lungs. So, get the right type of equipment. The unit I use in my home doubles as an ion generator and is self cleaning. It can also be used in the car to offset noxious fumes when in traffic (see Source Page).

Exercise & Viruses

Aerobic exercise is crucial to long term good health. Exercise increases lymph and blood fluid circulation and raises plasma and cellular oxygen levels. Exercise helps revitalize the organs and glands and speeds detoxification of the system. **People who exercise regularly experience less sickness.**

Much has been written on the benefits of aerobic exercise. Recently, however, the press is parroting the idea that we don't really need aerobic exercise. A recent article read, *"The benefits of aerobic exercise have been overstated. People can get all the exercise they need cleaning the house, or walking out to dump the trash."*

Nothing could be further from the truth! This is a *disinformation* campaign at the expense of the public parroted by "experts." If people buy into the NO aerobic exercise idea, they will suffer and grow OLD! Equally bad are those who promote *hyper* aerobic exercise. Ignore them all. Instead, seek *moderation* and *balance* in your exercise program. ***Extreme* anything translates: *abuse!*** Good circulation is a prerequisite to good health. Blood and lymph movement reduces waste build-up in the system and creates an environment that is hostile to pathogens. A "rebounder" and a "lymph roller" greatly improve fluid and waste circulation in a toxic body.

Rebounding

A rebounder (see page 367) is a mini trampoline. It is one of THE most important piece of health equipment you can own. A rebounder is about 36" in diameter and stands about six inches off the floor. The correct way to use a rebounder is to stand flat footed on the mat, gently swing the arms **together** both to the front and then the rear as you develop a slight pulse sensation in your head. You fee should NEVER leave the mat. The "pulse" sensation is produced by the movement of extracellular fluids BETWEEN the cells. The body depends on MOVEMENT to circulate these fluids, where blood is moved by the heart (pump). Hence, a sluggish lifestyle is part and parcel to illness and disease. I rebound morning and evening followed by a VIGOROUS" lymphatic roll down."

Both of these procedure are helpful in restoring hair, hearing, eyesight, and improving skin tone. They also prevent stagnation of plasma protein wastes, particularly in the legs. Edema (water retenstion) is a SIGN of fluid stagnation. Do NOT ignore it! Edema is also hormone driven, which is why so many women "puff" prior to their period—NOT a good sign!

The head receives 40% of the blood and wastes leaving the heart. In time, the VERY fine capillaries of the scalp, eyes, and ears become clogged followed by the SIGNS of old age— balding, gray and thinning hair, wrinkles, deafness, and eye problems—"appear." Most problems can be reversed with the use of Yucca Blend™, Aspar-Max™, PAC^s, and recemized™ hormone precursors. For sure, AVOID soy and canola.

Rebounding should be immediately followed by lymphatic rolling to stimulate subcutaneous lymph activity and move wastes into circulation so the liver can flush them from the body via bile secretions. Lots of 14 day old Kombucha Tea (30-48 ounces) greatly accelerates the clean up process.

Viruses & Molds On Foods

Have you noticed the vegetables and fruits in the grocery store are growing strange molds and fungi that spoil the food? Molds tell a story. They are the lowest level of parasitic growth. Their color indicates the toxicity level of the substance it is growing on. White represents the least toxic; red the most toxic; green, gray, and black are in between. Fuzzy, smooth, and shiny fungi tell a similar story.

The *experts* have been in charge of our food supply for a very long time. They have convinced the farmer to use hard chemical fertilizers, pesticides, and herbicides—the latter two containing VERY potent hormone "analogs" that foul the planet and create horrible "hormone" complications for women and men alike (read *Our Stolen Future;* see source page).

The *experts* have upset nature's balance and in so doing have brought marginal health and dis-ease upon us all. We are aging faster and dying sooner because we are eating what the experts "call" food! These are the same *experts* whom Rachel Carson vilified in her 1959 blockbuster book, *Silent Spring.* The book is must reading if you want to better understand the nature of the dilemma we face. Silent Spring is more pertinent today than when it first appeared.

The fruit in the stores has no flavor and mineral levels are almost non existant. The *experts* tell the farmers to use chemicals to ward off the bugs and weeds. The more they use, the stronger they come back! Nature will NOT be mocked, and mankind is paying the price.

Weeds & Aging

Look at the weeds! They proliferate in the face of voluminous amounts of herbicides. Each year, the weeds grow bigger. They are **mutating!** They have a job to do. They are getting ready.

Leonard Ridzon is a farmer. He is close to the Earth. He is a living Wizard and one of the most original thinkers I know. He authored *The Carbon Connection* and *The Carbon Cycle*. Both are must reading.

Ridzon has recorded ragweed over forty feet tall! Weeds are to the soil what pathogenic life forms are to the body. They proliferate and take over. They only appear to be the problem, but they are only reacting to changes in the terrain— the soil and air in this case. Their job is to protect Mother Earth and to reclaim abused soil and air with the help of the microbes. The weed's job to **absorb** the toxic energy fields in our atmosphere and soil and make them available so the microbes can break them down and return the soil and air to a healthy state.

Weeds are not plants out of place. The proliferation of noxious weeds is no more an accident than the molds and fungi on our food or the viruses in our body. They are SIGNS. Signs give rise to the diagnosis of dis-ease. Dis-ease unchecked amounts to a death warrant. Dis-ease at the sub-clinical level means a population of sick people and escalating violence.

Answers

Asking a question implies that there is an answer. But incorrect questions generate incorrect answers. There are plenty of CORRECT answers to the questions we have raised thus far, but you will not find them in the press, scientific literature or college texts. You will only find pieces—and incomplete answers. Science asks piecemeal questions—usually the wrong questions—and *pontificates* piecemeal answers.

Overview

When we use poisons against the Earth, we wage war!

When we poison plants that God put on this earth and foul our air, we wage war! We are at war with every living thing on this planet—including ourselves—and we are paying the price!

Rachel Carson, author of *Silent Spring*, died shortly after her book was released—saving her from immense hatred by those who came to hate her. She came from *within* science's camp and science proclaimed her a witch. They burned her at the stake for the TRUTH she heralded. They are still trying to burn her memory from our consciousness, but TRUTH does not go away. Like the Great Pyramid, it is there!

Anyone with a lick of sense knows that things are not right. The hole in the ozone layer is no accident. The hurricanes are not accidents. The floods, crop circles, and crop disasters are not accidents. These things are the direct result of science and money turned to EVIL purposes—and all of the inhabitants of the Earth are paying the price.

Mother Earth Is Vomiting

Mother Earth is deathly sick! She is vomiting her guts out. She is fighting back the only way she knows how—with viruses and bacteria, abnormal weather patterns, floods, and weeds. She will overcome the arrogance of our attacks.

The abnormal pressure created by negative energy forces cause the Ozone Layer to periodically open and close. In this way, deadly energy is released into space before every living thing on the planet dies. Industrialization as we know it is incompatible with Earth. Man's toxic energy fields alter life at the *subtle* energy level of our existence. These abnormal energies produce mutations in our children. **Earth and Her inhabitants CRY OUT—*"Dear God, we're sick!"***

A Word from the Author... The aging process has many pieces. Camouflaged pieces. Odd pieces. Pieces found in odd places. Pieces that fit together so precisely that when we come to understand HOW we become old, it may appear to be oversimplification.

Not so! TRUTH is simple. It is a straight and narrow path. Few people find the path—**especially** the "experts" in the fields of science, nutrition, and medicine. It is a straight and narrow path that leads to a place where dis-ease and old age are not. Seek that path and you will become *Young Again!*

PREVIEW: *The next chapter deals with the transfer of energy. Laying on of hands. Microwave ovens. Carpal Tunnel Syndrome, radiation, and irradiation of food.*

Before

After

Elimination of *Rouleau* from *live* blood one hour after drinking water with liquid ionic sea minerals. "Sticky" blood looks like rolls of pennies stacked together. The effect is due to negative energy wastes in the blood. Healthy blood does not stick together and is free to access the fine capillaries of the body and deliver oxygen and nutrients and remove toxic wastes. Photos are of "live" red blood corpuscles (red blood cells without a nucleus). Magnets and magnetic products produce a similar effect on body fluids which accounts for their therapeutic effects. Taken on a Nikon Opti that microscope with a 100 watt lamp and a Naessens condenser at 15,000 magnification.

Water Comparison

Medical Grade Ionized Water™: Uses BEV™ water as foundation water; ORP potential **far beyond** conception point; *oxidized* type water used in Japan to treat/prevent topical skin infections; eradicates venereal infections (syphilis, herpes, warts); *reduced* type water used in Japan to reverse arthritis, diabetes, heart attack/stroke, and cancer; fuels the production of mitochondrial ATP; costly to set up; cheap to operate; long term health implications beyond description; documentation available; a good investment.

BEV™ Water: Biologically friendly to body; extremely pure water (up to 99.5% contaminant removal, including parasites, viruses, bacteria, heavy metals, radioactivity, toxic organic chemicals); flushes contaminants as it works; superb flavor; feels "silky" in mouth; conception point ORP; energizes body; uses principle of *resonance* to raise ORP potential; and principle of *transference* to raise body metabolism; hydrogen and molecular bond angle restructuring; cost per gallon approx. 5-10¢. No electricity needed.

Distilled Water: Biologically dead water; partial purification; water unfriendly to body; concentrates volatile gases (PCB^s, THM^s, TCE^s, chlorines, chloramines); microbe growth problems; consumes lots of electricity; very slow; requires continuous maintenance; flat taste; negative ORP potential; water structure destroyed; diminishes body vibratory rate; zero carbon exposure time; cost per gallon approximately 50-80 cents; high parts replacement cost.

Reverse Osmosis: Partial purification (75-90%); quality and flavor better than distilled water; incomplete removal of bacteria, viruses, and parasites; does not provide BEV™ restructuring; okay taste; *resonance* and *transference* zero to poor; limited carbon exposure time; cost per gallon approx. 15-20 cents; ORP below conception point of BEV™; wide variation in quality of water produced.

Carbon Block/Ceramic Cartridge: Purification fair; not self-cleaning; microbe & toxic waste build up; cost per gallon approx. 15-40 cents. **Ceramic Cartridge:** Marginal purification; fair taste; not self cleaning; cartridge subject to fracture and leakage; expensive; poor ORP.

Bottled Water: Questionable purity; expensive to use.

"Water is MORE than wet! Water is FOOD!"

Hormone "Analogs"

Radiomimetic chemicals are everywhere around us. Pesticides and herbicides are good examples—as are the hormones prescribed by the doctor. **Analogous** hormones act like the real thing, but they are NOT the real thing. And once they attach to the body's receptor sites you become a prisoner unto yourself—unable to monitor and regulate your own system.

Radiomimetic chemicals *mimic* nuclear radiation. DDT is a good example of a radiomimetic free radical chemical. Chemical analogs raise holy hell in the body. and the ONLY way to free yourself and become whole again is to "polish" the receptor sites and oxidize these horrible chemicals from the body with racemized™ hormone precursors.

Liver purging greatly accelerates the clean up process. It takes 90 days to open the receptor sites and clear the body of analogous hormone molecules. After that, you have your life back under your control. The process restores function in women, men and animals.

180⁰ Off Course

We are told to stay out of the sun because it causes cancer, that soy and canola are good for us, to take aspirin, that liquid foods are acceptable substitutes for water, that science's version of a balanced diet is good for us, that routine work from house cleaning to dumping the trash is as good as aerobic exercise, not to eat butter, to avoid eggs, that there is no difference between "synthesized" vitamins and those in real food, that tobacco and second hand smoke are behind the proliferation of lung cancer, that alcohol in moderation is good for us, to take calcium supplements to avoid osteoporosis, that red meat is bad for us, that chicken is good for us, to eat fish in lieu of both, that healthy processed foods are just as good as fresh food, that dis-ease is the product of microbial invasion, and that genetics controls all.

None of these things are true. Follow the expert's advice and you will grow old fast and die early. All of the above is *disinformation* and *misinformation* emanating from the halls of science, medicine, and the media.

If you want proof that what I am saying is **true**, and what *they* are saying is **false**, take a good look at the "experts." They are old and sick because they live the **LIE!**

14

One Day At A Time

"The highest [energy] form of hostile organisms are fungi that are always present in the tissues of a corpse, and often in the tissues of sick patients."
Dr. Guenther Enderlein 1916

We live in a physical world and we perceive dis-ease to be a "physical" process because we can *see* and *feel* and *measure* dis-ease's EFFECT on the "physical" body. We know that the bio-electric body is a *composite* body—part physical, part energy. We know that dis-ease is the *manifestation* of conflicting energy fields where left-spin energy has dominance.

The conflict between energy fields occurs in the invisible world—a world that we do NOT see even though it is there. The process we call aging occurs in that invisible world. It occurs one day at a time.

Laying On Of Hands

An example of *positive* energy flow between the visible and invisible is the practice of **Laying On Of Hands.** Most religions have some version of their own.

Laying On Of Hands (LOH) couples the power of prayer with the physical body. It involves the *transfer* of positive energy from *healthy* people to the body of the sick person. It is a practice that demands tremendous focus.

Laying On Of Hands can spontaneously heal the sick person. Although it is not a science, it is a religious healing **modality** that involves the transfer of energy!

LOH often fails to produce positive change in the sick person. No results sometimes elicits skepticism and mockery when the event should be recognized for what it is—people with good intentions trying to help an ailing fellow traveler. Few participants understand the electrical phenomena involved, but they devoutly care about their friend or loved one.

LOH is a phenomenon that involves the **manipulation** of electrical ENERGY. The principles involved are no different than those used when dowsing for water or using a pendulum to determine left vs. right-spin substances or measuring energy fields with an aurameter—except that it takes place in a religious environment which also involves energy and intense focus and love. Positive results are called *miracles.*

In the religious arena, people accept healing at face value and without explanation because the end result is beneficial to them. We must also learn to accept the benefits that derive from other energy manipulations because they, too, can be beneficial to us.

If we could heal with a **black box** that had bells and flashing lights, no one would question it. We need the same objectivity when we discuss energy phenomena and para-normal healing that involves the manipulation of energy fields, positive thinking and intense focus. When we combine mental focus with physical touch—as in LOH, good things happen, be it in church, a hospital, or in the presence of a healer.

Therapeutic Touch

Nursing makes use of the phenomenon known as *therapeutic touch.* This involves the use of *touch* when caring for the sick—like laying on of hands. It is not always effective, but is effective enough that it is taught in advanced nursing schools and used in daily practice by cutting edge nurses.

At birth, touch is our most highly developed sense. Babies acknowledge the touch of another human being. When touch is combined with loving care, the nurse can "open" congested energy centers in the body and redirect the flow of ATP energy to promote healing.

First, the nurse assesses the person's energy state using *gut* instinct and by "reading" energy auras. The nurse then opens the body's energy meridians so **Chi** can flow. Chi is what the Chinese call the energy of life. It is also spelled Qi. Therapeutic Touch heals! Think of someone in whose presence you feel loved and whose touch—a hand, a hug—can make you feel safe, healed and free of fear. Both parties must "focus" their mental and spiritual energies for healing to occur. Disbelief, negative thinking, contempt can BLOCK energy flow.

We are talking about the use of ENERGY manipulation in healing. Science pronounces it quackery. Nevertheless, it is of practical value to vibrational healers. Therapeutic touch, dowsing, LOH, use of a pendulum or vibration chain, magnetic therapy and muscle testing are facets of the phenomena.

Reversing the aging process involves the production of "chi" energy (ATP) and learning the wisdom and techniques of when, where, and how to use it.

Energy Abuse

The proliferation of *negative* electrical energy pollution is a serious problem. Electrical pollution has subtle effects and disastrous consequences on people's health.

Consider the microwave oven. It is very popular throughout the USA and the industrialized world. I remember when it first appeared on the scene. A lot of fluff and excitement accompanied its introduction to an unsuspecting public. It was touted as *the* answer for the mother on the run and the conservation of energy. We were told of its "health" benefits!

Oh, how I remember the power companies making their case for the marvelous benefits of *microwave age* cooking. Where I lived, they even assigned an "expert" to assist people in the transition from the old way of cooking to the new. Microwave recipes appeared in the *food tips* bulletin that accompanied the power bill.

Few People Questioned

Few people questioned the idea of the microwave oven—except the usual "cranks" and everyone already knew they were nuts. Objections were ignored.

Microwave ovens initially made their way into the schools and government operations in the name of *efficiency*. They soon appeared in restaurants across the country. Owners and cooks alike loved them because they were so *people-friendly*. Food and plates would be piping hot when served. Preparation became easier too.

Today, you are considered in the stone age if you do not own and use a microwave oven. These *electrical* appliances are now considered a necessity for people on the run. People love them because they equate nourishment with a hot meal.

Microwave cooked food is neither alive nor life supporting. It should be avoided because of its NEGATIVE effects on the body's energy fields. Its effects are exactly the OPPOSITE of homeopathic remedies used to heal sick bodies. Avoiding the use of a microwave oven is something over which we have TOTAL control—if we choose to exercise it!

Effects Of The Microwave

Microwave ovens produce left-spinning energy frequencies. They are dangerous to people and children who are in the same room. They ZAP the immune system. They are DEADLY to your nutritional health!

Microwave energy destroys food enzymes by altering their molecular structure. These devices produce energy frequencies that are *anti-life* and incompatible with living things. When healthy organisms (people) are exposed to freak energy frequencies, they become *sub-clinically* ill and suffer with symptoms often described as "syndromes." In effect, they accelerate the aging process by altering the body's enzymes.

Enzymes make life possible! In their natural state, food enzymes are right-spin energy. The body uses them to build and repair tissue (anabolism). But when microwaves *zap* these living molecules, they become scrambled and useless. As a result, biochemical reactions FAIL to occur and we age a little more each day. Scrambled enzymes cannot support life and their effect is *catabolic! (Racemized™ enzymes like DiSorb Aid™ and R/HCl™ (along with a tablespoon of Yucca Blend™) are unbeatable!)*

Two Seconds

Food cooked in a microwave oven for as little as two seconds takes on the pall of death. When eaten, the body is forced to process and neutralize these **freak** energy molecules before it can get on with the business of life and health which we call *anabolism.*

All microwave ovens leak energy despite opinions to the contrary from the "experts." Microwave energy is, of course, *invisible* and it alters body frequency in the *invisible* realm. When you eat microwaved food—and water—the homeopathic principles of *resonance* and *transference* drive down the ORP potential to such a low energy state that the "food" actually draws down our energy reserves and weakens us.

Microwaved Blood

Microwave ENERGY destroys the structure of the water molecule—turning what should be a life giving substance into something antagonist to life. Microwaved water denatures enzymes in the blood since blood is 90% water. It also stresses the immune system via the lymphatic fluids.

It was reported that in a hospital in Oklahoma, a nurse used a microwave oven to warm blood. When the blood was given to the patient—he died! Blood is a living substance. As little as two seconds in a microwave is all it takes to destroy the life force in blood. I doubt any "expert" will use microwaved blood to prove this statement wrong!

Police • Carpal Tunnel Syndrome

Lawsuits have been filed throughout the country by policemen who used RADAR guns for traffic control. No one told them of the cancer causing effects of *microwave* energy fields. Eye cataract formation and joint and connective tissue disorders are a predictable outcome of microwave exposure. Microwave created degenerative dis-ease has MANY faces that take form in the invisible realm—quietly and slowly.

Do not expect the courts to protect people from microwave devices. Doing so means biting the hand of powerful interests. Faceless experts with **credentials** *can always be brought forth to testify that there is "no scientific evidence!"*

Carpal Tunnel Syndrome (CTS) is a big problem for tens of thousands of people. Repetitive activity is often blamed as the controlling factor. Yet, whenever microwave radiation is present the problem becomes exaggerated. That is why CTS is especially prevalent among supermarket checkers and computer operators—people that are exposed to small but continuous amounts of microwave energy.

Microwaves antagonize the nerve fibers and connective tissues (ligaments, tendons, muscles and cartilage). Some people are affected more than others, and some get "syndromes" yet to be given a name. We are concerned with the LONG TERM effects of microwave energy. Short term effects are hard to measure and provide the *experts* with a cover.

Computer Terminals

We hear little about computer induced health problems—except for eye strain. But have you noticed how you feel after several hours in front of one? Tired! Drained is a better word. Computer operators often have carpal tunnel syndrome and immune system problems. Did you know you can protect your immune system by wearing a Super Magnet over the thymus gland while operating a computer?

Super Magnets protect you from 110v, 60 cycle alternating energy frequencies. These rare earth magnets are 12,000 gauss "permanent" fields of DC energy that neutralize the insidious effects of 110 volt, 60 cycle radiation coming from fluorescent lights, TV, and computer terminals. Screen filters help with glare and screen radiation, **but they do NOT block the energy field itself!**

Like microwave radiation, not everyone experiences the same problems from exposure to alternating current energy fields—at least not in the beginning. For most people, the effects are *subtle* and *slow* to manifest. When the bio-electric body can't take any more, SIGNS of dis-ease magically appear out of nowhere and the doctor provides the diagnosis.

Symptoms of electromagnetic pollution are usually *sub*clinical. Degeneration occurs quietly and slowly—under cover—until dis-ease announces itself. In the meantime, the vital organ activity fades. Medical grade magnetic products can offset and neutralize these radiation hazards.

[I am wearing a Super Magnet to protect my vital organs and immune system while I process these words. I sleep on a medical grade magnetic mattress pad and use a magnetic pillow. Women use Super Magnets to ease menstrual pain by taping them over the ovaries (front and rear). Cancer and Alzheimers patients sleep better. Sinus problems and head cold congestion also respond well (see Source Page)].

FOOD: Radiation & *Irradiation*

The word "radiation" paints the picture of energy radiating outward from a central point—like light from a light bulb, but it also describes energy as a "substance" and as a condition or state of being.

Fission energy is *radiation* that comes from nuclear devices or their radioactive wastes. This type of fission energy does violence to living tissues and speeds the aging process.

People are afraid of fission (nuclear) energy for good reason. Fission energy *ionizes* living molecules. Another word for ionization is *scramble*. *Scrambling* of living molecules makes life impossible and produces suffering.

Irradiation is another term being touted in the media. It describes the *act* of applying *ionizing* radiation to living things. It also infers that energy has "substance" and for sure it leaves its "footprint" behind. In the case of food irradiation, negative ionizing energy is used to scramble food energy molecules and makes them worthless. Eat irradiated food and you will grow old and die early. Radioactive isotopes and waste products from the nuclear industry are the source of the *fission* energy that is used to "irradiate" America's food supply.

The word "irradiation" is a *bastard* term. It has little meaning and it confuses people who are not wise in the ways of crafty wordsmiths. It is a *quasi-scientific* term used to disguise a lie and distort TRUTH.

Irradiation focuses on the *act* involved, rather than on the *effect* the *act* produces. People think nuclear when they hear **radiation.** When they hear **irradiation** they don't know what to think. In the public eye, *irradiation* does NOT mean the same thing as *radiation.* The word irradiation is neither black nor white. Rather, it is *grey!*

The wise person avoids microwave radiation, refuses to eat "freak" food, and avoids subjecting their body to the effects of 110 volt, 60 cycle alternating current energy radiating from computer terminals and fluorescent lights. There are several ways to neutralize the effects of negative energy radiation. One of the best ways is to wear a Super Magnet over your thymus gland. The book *Vibrations* (see Source Page) offers many other tricks. Every person should take a **defensive** posture on this subject if they want to live a long and healthy life.

Irradiated food has NOTHING to offer the *bio-electric* body. For certain, it diminishes vital force, so why eat something that amounts to slow suicide.

Radiation • Irradiation • Genetically Engineered Food

The term "genetically engineered" is a **new** synonym for irradiation. It is acceptable to the public because it sounds scientific and does not hint of "radiation." In future chapters on hair loss, balding and blindness, you will learn that genetically engineered food is no different than irradiated food. Both are FREAK energy substances.

The experts talk of the wonders of food preservation through *irradiation.* They talk of bacterial contamination of food and water from microbes like E. coli 0158.H7 and Cryptosporidium and scare us with bogie man stories. What they forget to mention are the *real* reasons behind the drive to irradiate America's food. They *know* that chemically grown food has poor shelf life and must be *treated* to keep it from spoiling on the store shelves—so they give us the "industry's" version of a **forever** shelf life. Eat their processed food and you will experience the **graveyard** version of forever.

So, irradiated food has a "forever" shelf life. Its *living* enzyme molecules have been destroyed. The bugs and microbes will NOT eat food whose molecules have been *scrambled.* They "read" the energy signals given off by left spinning foodstuffs. They are smart and they follow their instincts.

Don't buy irradiated food. Don't eat microwaved

food. **Learn to use a pendulum, vibration chain, and brix meter to check the food BEFORE you eat it! The development of these skills should be considered "survival" training. Your life depends on it (see Source Page)!**

Measuring Energy Fields

It is easy to verify the presence of stray energy fields emanating from electrical appliances and equipment. The following method measures *SOME* negative energy frequencies, but there are many.

To check it, connect a radio to a long extension cord and locate a spot on the dial *between* two stations that is *silent*. Next, turn-up the volume to maximum, and with the radio held in front of you, approach your computer monitor, TV or microwave oven. When the radio begins to buzz, you have entered that device's *field of electrical influence*. Remember, you are only measuring SOME of the stray frequencies. Our concern is the *length* of time spent in the negative energy force field as well as the *strength* of the field.

When using 110v alternating current electrical devices like a computer, stay **beyond** its "field" and wear a Super Magnet. The EFFECTS of these anti-life energy fields are subtle—like the effects of microwaved food on health. Their short term effects go unnoticed, but they do rob us of LONG TERM health and vitality and ultimately our life!

Alternating current energy fields have a "presence" that far exceeds nuclear radiation.

A two inch thick slab of LEAD can block nuclear radiation, YET it **cannot** stop 110v energy fields from damaging the body. *Never* use an electric blanket. If you are cold, solve the problem with aerobic exercise, rebounding, hormonal precursors, and ETVC (more later).

Medicine & Radiation

Radiation therapy and *radioactive chemo*therapy used in the treatment of cancer are devastating to the body. The public believes allopathic medicine's propaganda and forms a line at the medical clinic. People are confused and fail to differentiate between diagnostic X-rays and the overkill effect of radiation therapy. Radiation is not a "therapy" because it is anti life. It is **palliative** (treatment of signs and symptoms without cure of the underlying dis-ease). Patients are taught to focus on HOPE of cure instead being told of the violence *ionizing* radiation inflicts upon the body. We are being TRAINED to "welcome" irradiation of our food, instead of being told of the plethora of symptomatic illnesses, dis-eases, and death that will surely follow.

Ask The Experts

If the things we are discussing regarding microwave radiation, irradiated food, and genetic engineering are true, why are the *experts* not telling you about it?

The answer is because these areas of risk are NOT being funded for study by the *experts*. The corporate and government GRANT SYSTEM is not about to study anything that might quash the two biggest monopolies in history: electrical power generation and the pharmaceutical industry of which allopathic medicine is a part. **It is up to you to protect yourself.**

Ignorance is a lame excuse and it most certainly will NOT keep you young. Aging is the TOTAL of all the *negative* influences in your life. You become young the opposite way that you grow old. You become *Young Again!* one day at a time.

PREVIEW: *Our next chapter looks at wrinkled skin—WHY it occurs and WHAT you can do about it. It also discusses body odor as it relates to aging.*

Sex Drive

Loss of sex drive indicates deterioration and atrophy of the internal vital organs. The problem is systemic and goes *beyond* just sexual malaise.

Loss of sexual interest is indicative of malfunction in the ovaries and testicles, prostate and uterus, thyroid, adrenals, thymus, pancreas, and liver.

Conditions like obesity, skin disorders, thinning (and balding) hair, weak nails and hair, yeast infections, bowel disorders, diminished muscle mass and wrinkles are first cousins to low sex drive. Impotence in men is a dead give away that **undetected diabetes** will one day announce itself. Behind all of these health issues is hormones!

To reclaim lost sex drive in men or women, your MUST clear your hormone and neuro receptor sites and reduce hormone excesses in your system. Once done, the miracle of life begins anew. Patience, focus, mental attitude and the **willingness** to do whatever is required are prerequisites that precede the return of sex drive, and with it, the wonder of a youthful, healthy, and vibrant life.

Incontinence need NOT be a problem for women!

Understanding Diabetes

Diabetes plagues millions of people in industrial societies. Yet, in third world countries—where people are on native diets—the incidence of diabetes is very low.

Medical science blames genetics for the rise in diabetes. They are wrong. The problem is fourfold and **genetics is NOT one of them.**

Diabetes is the product of toxic **excesses** within the system, loss of the gallbladder, hormonal imbalances, and auto immune problems resulting from IMMUNIZATIONS.

Diabetes is **proof** of vital organ slowdown and hormone imbalances. DHEA production drops off beginning at age 24 and is soon followed by a drop in progesterone production. As hormone production slows, metabolism slows and **excesses** accumulate in the system.

Type II diabetes is the most common type. It occurs between ages 35 and 55. **These are the years** when women AND men *ease* their way into old age and the window that **opened** at puberty begins to CLOSE. The hair thins, energy diminishes, sex drive slips, fat accumulates, cancers manifest, thyroid problems appear, nerve degenerative conditions proliferate, skin wrinkles, and muscle turns to flab.

Type I diabetes (AKA juvenile diabetes) is a *severe* condition where the child's immune system attacks the pancreas cells responsible for insulin production. It is an *"autoimmune"* condition brought on by the introduction of **SUPER antigens** into the body. A superantigen is a foreign protein that makes the immune system go crazy.

DPT (diphtheria, pertussis, tetanus) and polio vaccines contain **SUPER antigens** that bring on Type 1 diabetes and deafness. 75% of children with these problems suffer because of *mutant* SUPER antigens in their system.

Associated Press recently confirmed that *attenuated* strains of the polio virus *"can and do mutate once inside the body!"* And so do hepatitis B, DPT, and flu vaccines! AVOID VACCINATIONS AT ALL COSTS!

Loss of the gall bladder is a 99% guarantee of diabetes within 20 years—**unless** the person takes protective measures against it. Worse, 10 women to every man suffers gallbladder surgery. Racemized™ hormone precursors and liver purges STOP these things from happening.

Medical Grade Ionized Water™ also produces miracles for diabetics. Many children "become" diabetics at puberty due to hormone imbalances. Homeovitic remedies "erase" the sick frequencies vaccinations carry.

Biogenic™ Skin & Body Toner

Look in the mirror. Do you see sagging skin hanging from your arms and jaw line? Are you sporting "Howdie Doodie" lines from the corners of your mouth to the sides of your chin? Are those tell tale lines forming on your upper lip? And do you see crows feet around your eyes?

And what about your torso? Does it bear excess fat or cellulite? Has muscle mass given way to flab? Do you have a pot belly or saddle bags on your hips? Drooping breasts? Do you remember when your body was younger?

When you were developing in your mother's womb, you were in the presence of "antegenic" proteins and balanced hormones. Antegenic protein is very special stuff that normally is only available to the unborn. The body uses it to grow and differentiate cells and tissues in the various special organs—like heart, brain, bones, etc.

When racemized™ antigenic protein is supplied to aging adults, their bodies begin to transform into a more youthful appearance—like when they were young!

The combined effects of Biogenic™ Skin & Body Toner™, Biogenic™ hGH and racemized™ hormone precursors can be rather dramatic. As always, a healthy liver and clean tissues respond even better. To learn more, call and order the Source Packet (see Source Page).

Prostatitis & Impotence

Prostatitis or BPH (benign prostatic hyperplasia) is horomone driven. Use Totally Male™ hormone precursor to reverse the problem. **In men,** the prostate swells and hardens, while in **women,** the cervix loses its elasticity and the thyroid swells. **The problem is one in the same!** Never let a doctor do a "stab" or go in to *"Have a look!"* Liver purges are most helpful in lifting the waste load from the body.

Bleeding Gums • Periodontal Disease

Use a Bio-Magnetic™ dental irrigator to solve problems like gingivitis, bleeding gums, and other periodontal dis-eases. This simple appliance **transforms** tap water into a *powerful* substance that stops plaque and cavity formation. Decay odor when you floss means decay! (See Source Page.)

The Healthy Colon
How To "Read" Your Stool

Floaters—stools that float in the toilet. Indicative of excessive fat intake and/or poor fat metabolism; a liver in trouble; hormone imbalance.

Stringers—stringy stools that are narrow-fat. Indicative of a congested colon, kinked colon, involuntary tightening of the muscles that serve the colon due to nervous tension, high stress, negative thinking.

Pelleted Stool—Pellets are indicate slow transit time from mouth to toilet, under-hydration, inadequate roughage, and/or lack of rhythmicity (see glossary).

Pale Colored Stools—Indicative of liver malfunction, viral infection (white stools are seen with hepatitis). Stools should be medium brown.

Bloody Stools—Indicative of hemorrhoids or ulcers, lack of exercise and roughage, colitis, under hydration, lack of rhythmicity, bacterial infection, stress.

Dark Colored Stools—Indicative of sluggish gut, old blood from ulcer, colitis, under-hydration, dietary influence from eating dried prunes, raw beets, and greens.

Fat Headed Stools w/Tapered End—Indicative of "pooling" at rectum, under-hydration, ignoring nature's call, lack of roughage and exercise, incomplete evacuation.

Normal Stools—medium brown color, easy passage, little taper, blunt end, transit time under 12 hours.

Complete Stool Evacuation—characteristics of normal stool with nothing "held back." Bowel movement often ends with distinctive pocket of gas.

NOTE: Drink at least 3-4 quarts of water every day and most the above descriptions will dramatically improve. Always drink **at least** 2 BIG glasses of water immediately upon rising and follow with another each time you urinate. Add one tablespoon of Yucca Blend™ to each meal. Eat fresh veggies and fruit. Get some exercise.

15

Grandma's Lye Soap

"Oh, little Herman and brother Therman,
Had an aversion to washing their ears.
Grandma scrubbed them with lye soap,
And they haven't heard a word in years."
Dr. Roger Lent

The Integument (skin) is the largest organ of the body in surface area. It includes the **hair** and **nails**, and it is one of FOUR exit portals for the elimination of toxic wastes.

Like its siblings—the bowel, kidneys, and lungs—a functioning integument helps prevent the build-up of toxic wastes that would otherwise take the form of acne, psoriasis, wrinkles, skin ulcers and boils—just to name a few. The skin is the body's first line of defense against dis-ease. When the skin becomes stressed, regardless of the underlying cause, disease soon follows in the wake.

The skin functions much like the lungs. It breathes. It absorbs. **It releases wastes through perspiration, secretion of oil and fats, and the growth of hair and nails.** The blood and extracellular fluids *between* the cells provide the moisture given off as sweat. Sebaceous (oil producing) glands secrete oil and fat based toxins.

Wastes that cannot escape from the body become

trapped in the **dermis** (surface layers of skin) and **subcutaneous** tissues (below the dermis) and eventually erupt as pimples, boils or lead to wrinkled skin.

Wastes deposited in the "soft" connective tissues cause them to calcify, lose their elasticity and break down as in the case of wrinkled skin which is composed of collagen, elastic, and reticular fibers. Sagging skin and sagging breasts are good examples of *breakdown* of the connective tissues. The hard "connective tissues" are cartilage and bone. These tissues show their age through pain, inflammation (arthritis and gout).

Collagen comprises about 30% of the connective tissues (skin, bones, ligaments, muscles, tendons, and cartilage) which, in turn, comprise about 90% of the body. The matrix of the bones are collagen protein skeletons filled with minerals. **Healthy connective tissues are formed with *racemized*™ carbon and sulphur "sulfhydryls" as found in SOC™. SOC™ is also is useful in dissolving "scar tissue."**

Accumulation of acidic body wastes promotes **calcification** of the soft tissues. Arthritis involves calcification of the joints; tuberculosis involves calcification of the lungs; cancer tumors often become calcified as the body's way of isolating highly toxic energy.

Aging involves the build up of toxic wastes in the fluids that circulate BETWEEN the cells within the soft tissues. These **extracellular** fluids are called "lymph" when they are picked up by the lymph capillaries for return to the blood. **Extra**cellular fluid is not the same as **intra**cellular fluid which is found **inside** the cells. We will discuss both in more detail later.

Hormonal Shifts & Slowdown

DHEA is one of the "magic bullet" **hormone analogs** available over the counter. No one tell the public that there is **"NO"** difference between analogous DHEA, anabolic steroids, birth control pills, and estrogen replacements. All of them are VERY dangerous because they "lock up" the receptor sites in the body and prevent regulatory centers in the brain (hypothalamus, pituitary, and pineal) from keeping the body's hormones "balanced" and maintaining the body's "terrain." Worse, analogs have a "forever" life and don't break down. Marketing claims of "natural" DHEA are **bogus!** Crafty chemists have moved the —R group on the organic molecule so they can "patent" it. The real stuff can't be patented and anything "natural" isn't profitable for the industry.

REAL DHEA is made in the body by the adrenals and production slows beginning at age 24 followed by other hormones like progesterone and melatonin. Stay away from these popular drugs. They are NOT safe. Once they attach to your receptor sites, your will become a prisoner in your own body. I use RACEMIZED™ hormone "precursors" (male version) because they allow the body to make its own hormones AND because they "polish" the receptor sites in men and women and free them from bondage safely.

The following conditions are hormone related RED FLAGS for women: thyroid, fat, thinning hair, yeast/ bladder infections, depression, diminished sex drive.

Skin & Scar Tissue

There are only TWO classes of tissue: Healthy **functional** tissue and **scar** tissue. The body builds scar tissue in response to trauma and the inability to produce new, healthy tissue. Scar tissue can be internal and/or external. When biologically active carbon and sulphur are in short supply, the body is unable to build strong, healthy tissue. This is why SOC™ capsules—which are VERY rich in racemized™ carbon and sulfur—produce such dramatic results in people who suffer from arthritis, weak joints, and heavy metal toxicity.

Wrinkled skin, thinning/graying hair, and arthritic joints are hardly signs of youth and vitality. These represent deterioration and slowdown in metabolic activity, build up of wastes, and a shortfall in the production of ATP.

Wrinkles bother people who want to look young. They are a SIGN of trouble. The beauty industry tries the "mud against the wall" approach by putting collagen in their products, but topical collagen is NOT the answer. What is the answer and works marvelously well is a combination of SOC™ lotion, Nugest II™ precursor creme, Biogenic™ Skin & Body Toner™, and professional grade glycolic acid.

Movie Stars • Glycolic Acid • SOC™ • GH$_3$

As we age, outer skin layers become tightly bonded, stiff, and leathery. Cracking and bleeding occurs on the chafe points as conditions worsen—especially with the elderly.

Movie stars resort to face lifts to remedy their wrinkles. They understand that a young face pulls better at the box office. The stars also understand that the younger you look and feel, the longer you will be a movie star and be able to enjoy that life.

Society is strongly biased AGAINST the aged. People who look and feel young enjoy a big advantage!

Face lifts help, but they are very expensive and they do NOT solve the problem. Dermatologists also use **premium** glycolic acid—the **smallest** of the alpha hydroxy acids.

Professional grade gylcolic acid combines with dry, outer skin layers (the stratum corneum) causing dead skin to loosen, fluff, and slough so it will wash away. SOC™ stimulates the formation of NEW collagen in the dermal (true skin) layers. The dermis anchors the outer skin layers (epidermis) to the subcutaneous membranes.

When SOC™ lotion and Nugest II (for women) or Totally Male (for men) are used, the skin becomes unbelievably soft, wrinkles fade, and the skin takes on a very healthy glow that people love. These things are foods for the skin—NOT cosmetics. I use them religiously and my skin is 53 years YOUNG. *Another one of my personal secrets for no gray, full color, thick hair is Kombucha tea and Gh_3+.*

SOC™ lotion also does wonders for acne blemishes, acne and burn scars—to **permanently** fade away. SOC™ capsules are taken orally. Their combined effect is **awesome!**

Urine & Your Face

The term **acid** is a chemical term. An acid is a hydrogen donor. Natural vinegar contains natural organic acids that taste sour. Natural acids like those in raw apple cider vinegar and Kombucha tea rejuvenate the body.

Natural acids heal. Urine contains acids that beautify the skin. Some Scandinavian women wash their face in their urine because the **uric acid** in it keeps the skin smooth and young looking. Many people drink their urine to rid themselves of cancer and heal their bodies of dis-ease. [Read *Your Own Perfect Medicine, The Apple Cider vinegar Book* and the *Kombucha books* to learn more on these natural foods (see Source Index)].

Because our ability to produce STRONG digestive and absorptive enzymes diminishes rapidly after age 30, protein metabolites increase in the urine. Also, when we grow old we cannibalize our own tissues "auto" digestion of the body's tissues as a way to meet its protein needs. Cancer patients and starving people are classic examples of this sad condition.

In time the waste byproducts like uric acid show up in the urine. Elevated uric acid levels are a RED FLAG!. Worse, poorly digested food fuels the parasites in the gut, poisons the vital organs, and accelerates aging. There are many digestive products on the market, but NONE of them measuring up to a combination of DiSorb Aid™, R/HCI,™ and Yucca Blend™ .

For older folks, digestive enzymes are absolutely CRUCIAL. Digestion of proteins—via breaking of the peptide bonds—must occur in the stomachs HIGHLY acidic environment. The balance of digestion—and all absorption—occurs in the small intestine. This is a tough order for any digestive product to fill, but Disorb™ and R/HCL™ and Yucca Blend™ deliver. The **ultimate test,** however, is the cancer patient who is literally starving to death and in this arena these products shine.

Rich Man's Dis-ease

People who eat too much animal protein and who have poor digestive systems, often suffer with gout. Historically, gout was known as a **rich man's dis-ease.** The rich suffered with inflammation of the feet, toes, and hands because they overloaded their systems with too much animal protein which produced excess uric acid waste. Waste stresses the system and causes the **liver** to form STONES which block the flow of bile. Bile is both a fat emulsifier and THE vehicle by which the body rids itself of 75% of its wastes.

Purging stones from the liver and gall bladder is painless and safe "providing" you prepare your body and follow instructions precisely (more later).

Social pressure makes it difficult for people to maintain a healthy lifestyle, and the wealthier you are the more difficult it is. Alcohol, late evening meals, and fancy cuts of meat bring on gout. Eating HIGH on the hog is a carryover *cliche* from centuries past. Rich food overloads the body with **purines** (protein waste molecules from nitrogen rich meat, fish, and fowl) and overworks the kidneys causing a sharp rise in blood and tissue uric acid levels.

Excess uric acid in the blood and lymph combines with alkaline mineral bases like calcium and forms salt crystals. Waste crystals settle in the joints of the toes and extremities and cause inflammation and misery. Gout is a classic SIGN of old age. Gout medications treat only the symptoms and fail to to address the issues behind the manifestation of gout! Palliation is the word that best describes science's approach to gout. No one tells the patient that gout medication destroys the liver. **Patients are often more concerned about who is paying the bill (insurance) than long term loss of their health. Dumb!**

In the past, gout was not a problem for middle class and poor people who traditionally did hard, physical, load-bearing work. A sedentary lifestyle belonged to the domain of the wealthy. Today with the advent of the "service" society and the computer, **sedentary** life styles are epidemic. Wealth and opulence are no longer gout's domain. The middle class and poor now share the misery of gout.

Precipitates like uric acid crystals, gall, liver and kidney stones, and bone spurs are ABNORMAL. They are SIGNS of aging. The body does not handle *precipitates* well. It expresses its dissatisfaction with *inflammation* and *pain.*

In the case of stones, death occurs if they block a duct and are not removed withing 24 hours maximum. If a liver/gall stone blocks the common bile duct leading to the small intestine, systemic shock soon follows and the body goes into "toxemia" (*tox*-toxic. *emia*-of the blood) Toxemia is the pregnant woman's ultimate threat!

Poor quality drinking water compounds the problems elucidated thus far. Tap water is full of toxic chemicals and useless minerals.

[Grandma mixed and heated animal fats with lye (sodium hydroxide) and got lye soap through the process of **saponification**. *But when her soap was used in* **hard mineral tap water,** *she got soap scum in the tub. The scum comes from a reaction between the soap and the hard minerals in the water. This is called "precipitation." The scum settles-out of the solution. Precipitation of dietary oils like soy and canola oils mixed with waste similar effects in the blood and lymph.]*

Clogged and hardened arteries (atherosclerosis and arteriosclerosis) are filled with "plaques" like the scum in grandma's tub. Plaques are a combination of chlorine, fluorine, chlor*amines*, oils and fats, body wastes, and minerals.

Plaque formation in the arteries is a SIGN of impending trouble. It's also the product of a careless lifestyle and poor dietary choices. Soy and canola oils play a crucial role in plaque formation and clogging of the fine capillaries. We will discuss these devilish oils in great detail in future chapters.

Calcium & Fats

Despite medical opinions to the contrary, elemental mineral pill supplements, taken for arthritis and osteoporosis, are **worthless!** They fail to solve the problem and they create new and different ones in the process. Doctors prescribe elemental calcium carbonate (oyster shell) and citric acid calcium compounds because they "think" calcium is deficient. They try to to FORCE the body to accept minerals in elemental form, that is, minerals that have not gone through the carbon cycle (more later). These "elementals" precipitate OUT of body fluids and join with other metabolic wastes to form plaque and bone spurs. Worse yet, they are often taken with meals thereby totally upsetting the stomach environment and shutting down the digestion of proteins. Proteins MUST have their peptide bonds "broken" or they cannot be processed and assimilated. Unprocessed proteins rot in the gut and poison the body and feed the parasites. Elemental calcium and magnesium buffer stomach acids responsible for protein digestion. Avoid them!

Loss of bone mass is called osteoporosis. It is particularly prevalent among WOMEN. **It is considered a problem for post menopausal women, but ACTUAL onset begins in the "pre" menopause years (25-40).**

For women (and men), the ONSET of early menopausal SIGNS: fat/cellulite, thyroid troubles, low energy, depression, mood swings, PMS, painful periods, swelling,/bloating, gas after meals, bowel problems, mental confusion, yeast/bladder infections, arthritis, female cancer, tender breasts, vaginal infections (venereal or otherwise), loss of sex drive, fibroid tumors, thinning/graying hair, etc.

In other words, these SIGNS signal that the window that opened at puberty and changed a little girl into a woman is beginning to close, but this process isn't "medically" acknowledged until menopause manifests. In the meantime, women go through HELL and see their life, and their beauty and their joy slip away. **This process is easy to STOP. I have discovered HOW to stop the process and how to REVESE it. The window that opened at puberty can be kept open as long as a woman (or man) desires.** In other words, our middle years between puberty and menopause can be extended indefinitely. For now, set your biases aside and understand that you do NOT have to grow old or stay old—unless you choose. Moreover, I have learned how to REMOVE the threat of female and male cancer and osteoporosis. **Do what I ask, and you can live a long life "free" of fear!**

Body Odor

Body odor (BO) is a SIGN of a *polluted* body. BO is only experienced when toxic wastes build up to the point that they spill over into the subcutaneous tissues and feed the bacteria that live on those wastes. BO is more than socially offensive. It is the **shadow** of old age. When you smell BO, you are smelling toxic aromatic molecules evaporating from the body.

We first become aware of body odor at puberty. It is usually related to hormonal activity and increased secretion of toxic waste. In adults—and sometimes children and teens—BO is closely related to slow down in vital organ function and hormonal imbalance. The stronger the BO, the more toxic the person. **Strong BO is a SIGN that should not be ignored!**

You do NOT have to be old to have foul body odor. If you are *old in body* and *young in years*, you will have strong BO. If you are old in years and old in body, the odor will overpower the best of deodorants. A healthy, clean body has little, if any, BO.

Children have a good sense of smell. They are quick to detect toxins escaping from their grandpa's or grandma's body. They are smelling old age! Take note of older people's skin, color, pallor, and lack of vitality. These things paint an unfortunate and sorry picture as to why BO is often strong among them. Children smell sweet and fresh because they are YOUNG—usually in years; for sure in body. Body odor is ABNORMAL, despite that it is common. It is symptomatic of internal aging and *catabolic* activity.

People with potent BO can shower five times a day with grandma's lye soap, use the best of deodorants and get zero results. BO "oozes" from the body as fast as it is washed off. *The problem is internal.*

The quickest way I know to rid a body of BO is through a series of liver purges coupled with colon therapy. The focal point of a liver purge only **"appears"** to be the *liver* and the *stones*. This process causes the body to **safely** release the acid wastes locked up in the cellular spaces and fat throughout the ENTIRE body. Every cell in the body is affected by this process. It is one of two **fundamental** steps a person can take to reverse aging and heal a sick body/mind. The second is hormonal.

As the terrain of the body changes, so do the life forms that inhabit it. Everything we have discussed thus far in this book relates to CONTROL of the body "terrain."

Deodorants & Menstruation

Anti-perspirant deodorants should NEVER be used. They BLOCK the sweat glands, load the body with heavy metals and strangle the flow of wastes in the lymphatic system. Most antiperspirants contain toxic ALUMINUM ions that are involved in degenerative conditions like *Alzheimers*.

Please note the areas of the body where sweat is heaviest. They are areas of high lymph node concentration—like the groin, arm pits, breasts, neck, and head. Limited ability to freely sweat is indicative of a sluggish lymphatic system which is **crucial** to good health. Cancer originates in and travels the lymphatic system. Moreover, it is impossible to rid a body of cancer if the lymphatic system is in trouble.

Medical Grade Ionized Water™ has the ability to rid the body of BO and cancer. It does NOT cure cancer, but it does alter the "terrain" sufficiently to cause it to "disappear."

Hormones affect body odor. A good example of hormonal influence on body odor is menstruation. When the female body is flushing itself, hormonal shifts accelerate the escape of aromatic molecules. Humans don't detect subtle odor changes, but animals like the bear can. They have attacked women who are menstruating.

Men also experience a monthly hormonal shift in body odor. They obviously don't have a menstrual cycle, but they do have a monthly hormone cycle and their equivalent of meno-pause is called **andropause** (*andro*-refers to androgens which are **male** hormones. *pause*-cessation of).

Menopause and *andropause* follow loss of function in the vital organs, and especially in the testicles and ovaries. They are correctly named "the change." Racemized™ hormone precursors level hormonal shifts experienced by both sexes and extend the middle years indefinitely. Older people can use them to "reopen" the window that has already closed.

At the turn of the century, menopause was called "the climactic" because it is the "official" SIGN of approaching old age. **Menopause** (and andropause) are "paste tense" terms. These are *past tense'*terms because they began 15-20 years previous. The good news is that the "effects" of menopause can be REVERSED. Women no longer have to grow—or look—old.

We should get a "new" body every 7 years. Whether your new body is stronger or weaker than the one being replaced depends on the path YOU "choose."

No Sweat

People sweat. Some people sweat profusely. Other people hardly sweat at all. Sweat is a good indicator of how efficiently the skin is functioning as a waste portal.

If you sweat heavily, it's a very good sign, providing you keep the body adequately supplied with plenty of water and ionic minerals. If you do not sweat easily, you must ASSIST your body to do so.

I don't sweat easily. My solution is to spend time each day on an aerobic exerciser and in a FIR sauna. If you don't sweat easily, you must ASSIST your body or suffer the conse-quences. The body was made to be worked and used. Failure to do so means you will forfeit you life.

Far Infrared Sauna Is Here!

Steam baths and mineral hot springs are a wonderful ways to cleanse the system. So are hot tubs, but they have many limitations including space, lack of portability, and the high cost of operation. A Far Infrared sauna has **ALL** of the benefits and **NONE** of the problems. Water is not needed. Cost to operate: 15¢/day. This new technology rids the body of massive amounts of acid waste. A FIR sauna is made of beautiful wood and is portable. People who have invested in them "love them." Older people and anyone with arthritic problems or degenerative nerve conditions find wonderful relief from regular use of a Far InfraRed sauna (see Source Page).

Skin: A Two Way Door

In Dr. Dan Skow's book *Mainline Farming for Century 21*, he mentions a question that was once asked in the medical literature. *"Given two quarts of water that is contaminated with a volatile chemical at 7 parts per 'billion,' would it be better to bathe in it for fifteen minutes or to drink it?"*

The experts answered, *"Drink it because four times more chemicals will enter the body by taking a bath in it than from drinking it."*

There is no question that we absorb large amounts of poisons via the skin. Yet, the mucous membranes that line the mouth, throat, and GI tract have a combined surface area that is 600 times greater than the skin AND they absorb more efficiently, too. **The experts were wrong!** (Frankly, it was a dumb question because two quarts isn't enough water to bathe in anyway. Response options should have included "neither.")

The skin is bidirectional. It vents and absorbs. Topical medications are easily absorbed through the skin. (Nugestrine II™ and Totally Male™ hormone precursor creams are "transdermals" and are absorbed via the skin directly into the blood—however, they are NOT drugs!)

Few people realize the massive amounts of environmental poisons that access the body through the swinging door called *skin*, which includes the lining of the bronchioles and lungs. *[Please recall, the body breathes by way of the lungs (called external respiration)* **and** *by way of the cells (called internal respiration).*

Most man-made chemicals are toxic to living things—including the body. Ask a beautician if it is possible to become toxic through the skin and lungs. Many grow old and suffer dearly due to chemical exposure. Soon, however, women (and men) will have access to "safe" beauty products as a new line of them is in the works as of July '97. (See Source Page.)

If chemical toxicity is severe enough, the body will break out in a rash, hives, develop asthma or degenerative dis-ease. The body was not meant to deal with the barrage of poisons that bathe it daily—particularly environmental estrogen analogs.

Because toxic exposure is unavoidable no matter how hard you try, the use of NugestrineII™ and Totally Male™ to keep your nerve and hormone receptors "polished" and open. REMEMBER, hormones open the window at puberty, and recemized™ hormone precursors can KEEP it open despite ongoing exposure via food, water, beauty products and air.

The body has but three options when it comes to dealing with toxic chemicals: flush them from the system;

bury them in body fat; or deposit them in the membranes of the skin, arteries and joints—or all of the above!

Time Bombs

Absent the use of racemized™ hormone products, a body that is overloaded with toxic wastes must opt for a combination of options two and three (above). Unfortunately, these options only postpone our day of reckoning. **When that day arrives,** you notice a lump in your breast, abnormal discomfort, sore bones, or bleeding from the vagina or rectum, and the doctor says, "YOU HAVE CANCER!"

And all you can think about is "Why me? What did I do to deserve this? This is not possible. I'm NOT old enough to have cancer. Surely, the diagnosis is wrong."

BUT, you did have a hand in this story, didn't you? Don't bother with excuses. They don't count! Claims of ignorance won't ease the hell you face! Wouldn't it have been better to have AVOIDED cancer?

Imprint these thoughts in your memory and LIVE by them. Prevention is far better than a cure. Neither government nor science can protect you. In matters of health, never blame others. You alone are responsible.

The "health care" industry is a financially healthy oxymoron. It protects its own health and economic interests. Learn to protect YOUR health and economic interests by taking care of yourself. Be willing to do whatever is called for in your drive for good health and longevity. **Becoming *Young Again!* is a matter of choice!**

PREVIEW: *Our next chapter is about "wildcats." It was one of the favorites of those who reviewed this book prior to publication.*

Prostate trouble? Totally Male™ solves the problem.

Deadly "Word" Games
Hydrolyzed vegetable protein (HVP) is used in hundreds of foods—including health foods! HVP is a *trade name* for MSG (monosodium glutamate). MSG contains glutamate + aspartate + cytoic acid—known poisons. Aspartame is the chemical name for a popular sweetener with the red, white and blue swirl. These **SOY** derived **excitotoxins** destroy nerve/brain cells. Public outrage ended use of MSG in baby food, so they changed the name to HVP and added a pretty little swirl—but still deadly!

HAIR: What To Do About It!

Fourteen day old Kombucha tea is a very powerful body rejuvenator that has the ability to clear toxic wastes from the system, ease aching joints, and improve bowel activity. But where Kombucha really shines is in helping people grow hair and regain their "natural" hair color.

Loss of hair color and thinning and balding are SIGNS that the body's terrain is in **trouble**. Hair problems are a SIGN of aging—never youth!

We "gray" from the top down and we lose body hair from the top down. If you are fifty or older and your axillary (arm pit) hair or pubic hair is gray, realize that loss of body hair is the next step. Medical science ignores the importance of hair, but hair has purpose!

Hair draws off toxic energy wastes from the tissues below the skin and removes them from the body. Fast growing hair is a good SIGN. Hair that comes back to full natural color or returns after years of absence is a good SIGN—and Kombucha tea and GH_3+ and racemized™ hormone precursors are the surest way to make it happen.

I drink 3-4 gallons of 14 day old Kombucha tea each week (3-4 mugs a day). I also take one capsule of GH^3+ two times daily. These are my personal secrets for "jet black" hair at calendar age 53. Racemized™ hormone precursors, liver and tissue purges and SUPER foods are a few more.

Kombucha tea is VERY **inexpensive** to make at home—so no one can complain they can't afford it! To enjoy the benefits Kombucha, "brew" your tea for 14 days to peak glucoronic acid levels.

Once you set up to make your own Kombucha tea, you are set forever because the Kombucha organism reproduces itself perpetually with a little care.

I began with a "certified" disease free start and have been going strong for over four years. Best of all, I can make a gallon for fifty cents verses store bought, inferior stuff at 40^{00}—and mine is far superior!

If you want hair or natural full color hair, Kombucha tea, GH^3+ and racemized™ hormone precursors can make it happen for you—and you will rejuvenate your ENTIRE body at the same time. You can make it happen in your life if you wish it so (See Source Page)!

Hormones OPEN and CLOSE the window called the "middle" years. KEEP your window OPEN perpetually by applying the principals discussed in this book!

Colon Therapy

Fifty years of hands on experience in colon therapy and forty colored pictures is what the tissue and colon cleansing book is about.

This book should be read by anyone who is serious about health and longevity. If you are new to the subject, or *uneasy* about the idea of colon therapy, this book will help you understand how to set up and do "colonics." Colon therapy lifts the burden of waste from the body and speeds recovery time. Nothing else compares to it!

Ileocecal Valve & Cancer

Six feet up from the anus is the beginning of the colon (large intestine) and the end of the small intestine, (the ileum). Between the large and small intestines is the ileocecal valve that **controls** waste movement and nutrient absorption in the intestinal tract. People with cancer almost **always** have their ileocecal valve "locked" open by old mucoid matter that has collected in their colon. This condition causes cancer victims to **starve to death.**

Colon therapy "clears" the ileocecal valve and re-stores normal function to this most critical area of the body. A clean colon goes part and parcel with a healthy life.

People as young as 5 years have colon lining build up. Anyone over 35 years is loaded. If you're 50 years or more, your colon condition is **beyond** description!

Enhanced "PAC^S"

Enhanced PAC^{S}™ are an awesome complement of biologically acitve phytofactors—all in racemized™ form.

Pac's are used to buffer the body from acid wastes during the liver purge process. Taken on a daily basis Pac's strip the arteries and veins of plaque, lower blood pressure, help reverse heart and stroke problems and ease eye problems and aches and pains—all toxicity conditions.

Enhanced PAC^{S}™ are **both** "fat" and water soluble racemized™ antioxidants. Solvent extraction is **NOT** part of the proprietary process used to formulate the ingredients. **Pac^{s}™ are the MOST economical product available with 24,660 activity units per bottle** and a racemic™ footprint of 10/10 and a biological activity rating of 10/10—both unheard of in the industry (see Source Page).

Aluminum Poisoning

Aluminum is a heavy metal that is extremely toxic to the body. It—along with mercury and lead—accumulates in brain tissue and short circuit neuron function and eventually manifest as "Alzheimers."

Aluminum contains fluoride. Heavy metal ions leach from aluminum cookware and foil when we cook with them. "Pitted" cookware is proof positive of leaching. Aluminum cookware that is coated with non stick resins creates additional problems. Avoid it!

As long ago as 1920, Dr. Jethro Kloss documented the toxic affects of aluminum cookware in his book, *Back To Eden* (see Source Page). The aluminum industry and the AMA reacted violently to Kloss' writings.

The GREATEST sources of dietary aluminum are tap water, baking powder, and soft drinks. **Cities use massive amounts of ALUM to treat drinking water.** Do not buy baked goods that contain baking powder. Soft drinks—because of their ubiquitous nature and social acceptability—do MORE damage than alcohol.

Quick breads/pastries are loaded with aluminum (get aluminum free baking powder at health food stores). Alum is an approved food additive that is on the FDA's "gras" list (stands for: *generally recognized as safe*). Never rely on so called "watch dog" government agencies to protect you and your family. Take responsibility for yourself by thinking defensively.

In the body, aluminum reacts with toxic waste and attacks the *nervous system* and provotes *degenerative* conditions like MS, myelinoma, neuropathy, cerebral palsy, fibromyalgia, myasthenia gravis, etc.

Avoid "colloidal" minerals because they are LOADED with heavy metals. Heavy metal detoxification is accomplished with SOC™, Pac's, Yucca Blend™ and super foods like Klammath algae. Medical Grade Water™ definitely speeds their release from the tissues.

Female Cancer

Female cancer is NOT genetic, but it has everything to with lifestyle, hormones, birth control pills and estrogen replacements. Use racemized™ hormone precursors and you can remove the word "cancer" from your vocabulary.

16

Wildcats

"The skin is to the body, what the soil is to the Earth."

John Thomas

The halogens are known as the "wildcats" of the earth's elements. They are gases and chemically speaking they are *extremely* reactive. The term *halogen* can be dissected: *hals-* Greek for salt; *gen-*to produce. When a halogen atom (acid) combines with a alkaline metal atom —like sodium, calcium or magnesium—it forms a salt like sodium chloride. When a **halo**gen combines with **hydro**gen it forms an acid, like the fluoride in tooth paste.

The halogens are IMPORTANT to the aging story.

When the halogens are part of a naturally occurring mix of mineral ions—as found in sea water or soil—they do not pose a health problem because they are in balance.

But when man isolates the halogens and uses them to create out of balance products, aging dramatically accelerates. Consider rock salt (halite) which is sodium chloride (table salt). Nature isolates this compound and stores it in the earth. Man comes along, mines it, puts it on the dinner table in defiance of nature's dietary laws.

Chlorine and fluorine are HALOGENS. They are also gases. When these gasses are dissolved in water, they change their nature by binding with the metal ions and contaminants in the water. **Chlor**ine becomes chlor**ide**. **Fluor**ine becomes fluoride. They have become salts in solution.

Halogen gases are **extremely** unstable and VERY chemically active because they need only one electron in their outer valence shell. To counter halogen instability, industry stores them as salt "solids."

In LIVING systems, fluorine gas goes CRAZY once its chemical bonds are broken by hydrolysis (*hydro*-water. *lysis*-to cleave or break). Fluorine bonds to constituents in the blood and lymph and forms new, **unpredictable** compounds that are hostile to delicate life processes. Fluoridated water and tooth paste are deadly and the experts know it. Yet, "corporate" cities, counties, and states throughout America continue to force it upon citizens under the "bogus" yellow fringe" flag (more later).

Chlorine

Chlorine is a bactericidal. It indiscriminately kills bacteria and is very effective as a disinfectant (for instance, as used during laundering). Chlorine is also used to treat public water supplies. It is VERY toxic to the liver.

Use of chlorine in public water supplies is justified on the basis of what medical science calls the "benefit to risk" ratio. Applied to the population, this means the benefit to the population as a whole outweighs and justifies the damage done to individuals within the whole (vaccines are promoted on the same basis). *This type of thinking keeps the hospital stalls full! It's your job to avoid this trap!*

Chlorine's carcinogenic characteristics are well known and are expressed in the body in many subtle ways. "Subtle" is the word, since no one dies from drinking chlorinated water.

For instance, chloroform is a byproduct of chlorinated drinking water. Chloroform is extremely toxic. It is a broad spectrum poison that indiscriminately kills both good and bad bacteria in the gut and tissues. Chloroform replaced ether as a general anesthetic in surgery rooms at the turn of the century. Both are deadly. Both have been replaced by other "less toxic" substances.

There is a strong relationship between chlorine's introduction and use in public water supplies (1908) and the statistical emergence of heart attacks and cardiovascular disease. The relationship is more than happenstance.

Prior to 1920, coronary heart disease was not a statistically recognized problem in the United States. *Atherosclerosis* (build-up of plaque in the arteries) is directly linked to chlorination of public water supplies.

Chlorine's initial popularity must be understood in the wake of the epidemic of waterborne dis-eases that ravaged the

United States between 1910 and 1920—infecting or killing tens of thousands of people. In those days, there were few alternatives, but this is no longer the case.

No one wants to drink water that is contaminated with pathogenic microbes. At the same time, those of us who are concerned with health and longevity dare not rely on officialdom to protect us. Most people in the USA rely on municipal water as their primary water source. More and more people are buying bottled water, but this is NOT the answer to the dilemma. The correct response is to "make" and drink BEV™ and Medical Grade Ionized Water™. In other words, "unplug" form the system and take charge of your life!

Due to recent outbreaks of pathogenic *E. coli* and *cryptosporidium* bacteria in public water supplies, the Federal Government is squeezing "corporate" governments and water districts to use more toxic chemicals like the *chloramines.*

Chlor**amines** are extremely toxic to the liver. The BEV™ system removes these as well as fluoride, flagulates that trigger amoebic outbreaks, viruses and bacteria, radiactivity and junk minerals. Once done, the vibrational memory of these contaminants is "erased" and the water is restructured. When all this is finished, you have "biologically friendly" DRINKING water.

For showering and bathing, I use a 3 stage oxidation/reduction filter. These are unlike consumer shower filters that are small, low capacity, and low flow. The filters to which I refer writing have lasted OVER 4 1/2 years.

When I travel, I often carry a wrench and one of these shower filters to avoid bathing in toxic water.

Sodium Hypochloride

Chlorine is dissolved into public water supplies from a salt block. A salt is more stable than a gas or a liquid. The reason chlorine is used in salt form has to do with pH, which we will discuss momentarily.

From previous discussions, we know that a salt is a combination of a halogen (acid) and a metal (base). Water treatment protocol calls for the use of sodium hypo chloride. Sodium is an alkaline metal **base** and hypochlorite is an extremely **acid** form of chlorine. Together they form a solid—a salt compound called **sodium hypochloride.**

When the Jekyll and Hyde sodium hypochloride compound is dissolved in water, it separates. The chlorine kills the bacteria and the hydroxide raises the pH so the water will be palatable. The pH of most tap water is between pH 8-9. Biologically friendly drinking water—like BEV™—is a combination of Ph, reactivity and ORP potential. These are the things that heal sick bodies and return control of the "terrain."

Terrain Problems

Toxic chemicals enter the body **bonded** to *waste* mineral ions. In the body, acidic chlorine and fluorine bond with metabolic wastes and oils (like soy and canola) and form *hybrid* toxins that ALTER the terrain. The change that follows appears in the electrical "state" of the blood as "Rouleau." Rouleau manifests as clumped red corpuscles and is a "marker" condition, a red flag of dis-ease in the making and a confirmation that the "terrain" is in trouble. **The word "aging" hints at the problem. The word "degeneration" says it all.**

Sodium is a player in the above scenario. High sodium levels in the tissues often manifests as hypertension. As excess sodium invades **interstitial** fluids BETWEEN the cells, it upsets the sodium/potassium balance in the body which in turn sets the stage for cancer.

The body requires a **constant** supply of organic potassium to maintain sodium/potassium balance. Fresh home grown, organic green leafy vegetables are the very best source of organic potassium. If dietary shortfalls occur, the body *steals* potassium from the cells and sodium **invades** and replaces it. Sodium invasion slows mitochondrial activity and converts an aerobic (with air) environment to an anaerobic (without air) one. Aerobic bacteria—like the mitochondria—cannot function in a high sodium environment.

Chlorinated tap water that is high in sodium is weakening the entire population. There are better and safer alternatives, but powerful industrial interests support chlorination. Our situation today is not unlike the outbreaks of Childbirth Fever in Dr. Semmelweis' time. Chlorine, fluoride, and chloramines are good for business. They keep the cattle lines at the clinics and hospitals "full."

"Corporate" government is an ILLEGAL foreign "state" operating under the "yellow fringe flag". It has a vested interest in keeping people sick. Sick and dead people are good for litigation, probate, estate taxes and other legal mewings.

Think of the effects that safe, biologically friendly food and drinking water would have on organized medicine, the legal system, society, and the government school system.

Public Mentality

Fluoride is an American Institution, second only to hot

dogs and apple pie. Americans have a love affair going with their sweetheart "halogen" fluorine (fluoride is its salt form). The question is WHY? This book provides the answers for those who care to displace ignorance with KNOWLEDGE.

Industry, medicine, dentistry, and the pharmaceutical companies have done a magnificent job of *brainwashing* Americans on the benefits of fluoride.

Fluorine is THE wildcat of the halogens. It is numero uno—**number one**—on the list of atomic elements for reactivity. God put fluoride under lock and key by isolating it in underground water and mineral deposits. When man discovered fluoride's industrial uses, he opened a Pandora's Box.

Fluorine is toxic to all living things. Fluoride poisoning (fluorosis) of the tissues manifests itself as hundreds of symptoms. Because it is a "systemic" poison that takes *years* to manifest, fluoride escapes blame—along with the fools that promote it. Medical science's challenge of "no scientific proof" is an effective cover for the industrial poisoning of America's population. **Fluoridated water is a crime!**

HARD (Teeth-Bones-Skin) HEADS

Fluoride hardens the teeth—and the head. The experts forget to mention the toxic side effects—effects that grossly outweigh any conjured benefit. Fluoride has a subduing effect. It "slows" the brain and makes us docile—and easier to manipulate. Fluoride is easily absorbed through the skin and mucous membranes of the mouth, respiratory system and intestines. Fluoride is a perpetual money machine for the medical system.

Good medical insurance creates the "illusion" of security. Reliance on it causes people to forfeit personal responsibility for their health.

A certain toothpaste introduced in the late 1950's received the endorsement of the American Dental Association. It uses fluoride in stannous form. Stannous fluoride is a tin-containing compound. Tin is a mineral and a metal. When you mix an acid (fluorine gas) with an alkaline metal ion (tin) you get a SALT—a crystal. We know that stannous fluoride is a salt because of the -ide on the end of the word. When you convert stannous fluoride—a waste product—from the status of waste to the status of a medically endorsed and publicly accepted drug, you have really accomplished something. The profits to be made in a deal like this are beyond the dreams of avarice.

Fluor**ine** is widely used in thousands of industrial processes. Fluor**ide** is the industrial spin-off. Stannous fluoride is the waste product of the tin industry. Fluorine-containing compounds are VERY powerful left-spin energy fields. Their signature and footprint is anti life and very biologically active.

In a living system, fluoride **dis**associates and becomes EXTREMELY unstable. It looks for something to bond to—like our *protein enzymes*. It bonds with the proteins in the bones and the minerals in the body and slows metabolism.

One of fluoride's favorite habits is to attack the collagenous protein fibers that give the bones, skin, muscles and ligaments their *resiliency*. Wrinkled skin is a good example of the side effects of fluoride and the acidification of body tissues. Breakdown of the tissues sums it up nicely.

People are concerned about wrinkled skin, brittle bones, and failing hair. Yet, most American's use fluoridated water and toothpaste. The just don't get it!

If you dissolve a bone in an acid, the minerals will go into solution and leave a rubbery like substance that resembles a piece of spaghetti. This substance is the protein collagen matrix into which the osteoblasts deposit minerals.

Fluoride acts similarly to the hormones in birth control pills, estrogen replacements, and chemical analogs in food and water. Where the later interfere with the oster**blasts** (bone building cells) and osteo**clasts** (bone dissolving cells) and STOP the production of new bones and connective tissues, fluoride causes these collagen proteins to turn **hard and brittle.** The bones should NOT be hard and brittle. They need to be rigid and flexible—like a healthy tree.

Over a period of years, people who use fluoridated water and toothpaste buildup **excesses** of fluoride in their tissues. and serious degeneration manifests. The *experts* blame osteoporosis, scleroderma, lupus, and exposure to the sun. *Connective tissue syndrome* is the latest "in" label. Broken bones AND weak joints are common among adolescents and older people. Why? Something has changed! One of the somethings is fluoridated water, toothpaste and that innocent little cup of poison from the school nurse and the dental hygienist.

Racemized™ hormone precursors, SOC™ capsules, Biogenic™ Skin & Body Toner™, PAC^s™, BEV™ water, Yucca Herbal Blend™ and all of the SUPER FOODS mentioned herein can reverse the effects of fluoride and synthetic hormones.

Medical science has endorsed the use of fluoride and is too stubborn and proud to admit its mistake. Please consider what Sir Arthur Edington once said about the scientific mind. *"Verily, it is easier for a camel to pass through the eye of a needle, than for a scientific man to walk through an open door."*

The public does not know that the famous fluoride study about natural fluoride in well water and the absence of dental caries (cavities) was bogus. What the experts fail to mention is that man-made *sodium* and *stannous* fluorides are FAR more reactive and hostile to living tissues than is naturally occurring fluoride. "Living" systems are DYNAMIC. People are unlike sterile, laboratory test tubes. Fluoride **reacts** when heat, pesticides, food additives, soy and canola oils and metabolic wastes are present in the body.

Powerful interests in dentistry, medicine, and the pharmaceutical houses influence public policy in regard to issues like fluoridation of drinking water supplies. The insidious *"grant system"* decides WHO gets public monies and WHAT projects science will study—money dictates!

These same powerful interests determine what is taught in the medical and dental school curriculums and see to it that text books are heavily biased. Private interests use "corporate" government and the "yellow fringe flag" courts to shield them while they foist their deadly industrial wastes—like sodium and stannous fluoride—onto a trusting and unsuspecting public. **Expert** **act as rubber stamps, providing degenerative dis-ease new labels to keep the public confused—and new drugs to treat them.**

Synergy • Synthesis

Synergy is a term we need to understand. It refers to the "combined" action of two or more chemical agents. Synergy can produce positive OR negative consequences for human beings.

Synthesis is a closely related term. It refers to the structuring of molecules and the locating of the "—R group" which identifies the molecule and its effect on living systems.

A healthy, youthful body is the result of *anabolic synthesis* (positive *bio*chemical synergy). Organically grown food, BEV™ water and racemized™ SUPER FOODS are examples of things that fuel positive biochemical synthesis.

Fluorides, chlorines, vaccines, pesticides, mercury, toxic air, food dyes and additives, soy and canola oils, chloramines and some forms of oxygen "trigger" chain reactions in the body. If the immune, digestive or hormonal systems are stressed, negative synthesis reactions destroy cells and produce waste byproducts in the form of toxic ACID wastes.

Free Radicals • Antioxidants • Organic Food

Toxic substances are "free radicals." Free radicals trigger uncontrolled oxidation of the cells and tissues. The actions of free radicals can be HAULTED by the use of potent racemized™ **antioxidants** called Enhanced PAC's™. PAC^s "stop" uncontrolled oxidation. Oxidation involves the addition or loss of electrons between molecular substances. Uncontrolled oxidation is catabolic activity that kills cells. **Catabolic activity involves free radicals and self cannibalization.**

Pesticides are another example of free radicals. They are man-made **organic** chemicals—a term that is a misnomer. I prefer to call them poisons! Pesticides—are organic by definition. The word **organic** is used to describe them because these deadly molecules contain CARBON (atomic element #12). Carbon is the essence of life on Earth. Industry's immorally uses the word *organic* as a cover up to confuse the public.

Crafty wordsmiths and bogus science jumble terms so that their **poisons** will APPEAR to be to friendly to Earth and Her inhabitants. Confusion is the tool. *Unholy* profit is the goal. Sick people, animals, and plants are the result! This is why I keep reminding the reader to ignore the recommendations of the "experts." **Their advice will seal your grave!**

When the term *organic* is applied to food, the implication is that poisons are not present and that the food was raised using natural fertilizers as opposed to commercial, NPK salt fertilizers. Organic food is generally better than non-organic food, but home grown food is the very best!

Everyone should grow some fresh vegetables—be it in pots or a section of the yard. Even small amounts of "live" food have a powerful effect on health.

Doctors & Dentists

The entrenched scientific, medical, and pharmaceutical establishment is at odds with personal health and longevity. They have a vested interest in keeping things status quo so they can bilk the people of their money and freedom.

Professional people often suffer from **professional myopia.** Most are the product of their training and few think outside if it. At the same time, professional people are **"watched"** by their licensing boards i.e., the state. Those who step out of line or put the patient's best interest first are at odds with their fellow practitioners! Doctors and dentists who act on TRUTH must be very careful and keep a very low public profile.

It's good to know an alternative health care professionals in your area. But remember, healthy people have little need for medical care.

Recently, I moved from a city that had over two-hundred dentists. All of them—except two—use fluoride and mercury amalgam. That's TWO out of two-hundred! The rest claim ignorance. They quote chapter and verse from the medical literature in their defense. They refuse to seek alternative training and to learn to care for people in a humane manner. Most REFUSE to think or act outside of the "accepted" protocols of their profession—even when they know better! They are caught between profits, insurance companies, an ignorant public, and the medical review boards.

Many medical insurance carriers often decline to insure people who work in dental offices because of the inordinately high incidence of sickness and dis-ease. The mercury and fluoride they use are Trojan Horses in their own camp—and they pay with their health and lives—just like their patients.

Mercury • Fluoride • BEV™

Heavy metals—like mercury, cadmium, and lead are serious business. They interfere with brain and nerve activity and are MUST be purged from the tissues. SOC™, Klammath™ algae and Yucca Blend™ will remove them from the tissues.

The West—and the USA in particular—are experiencing huge increases in neurological BRAIN disorders like Alzheimers, myelinoma, multiple sclerosis, and tumors—conditions that were unknown or seldom seen thirty years ago. Today they are common and you better believe that fluoride, heavy metals and hormone analogs are at the root of them!

Fluoride hardens the cell membranes and the sulfhydryl links that compose protein based connective tissues. When fluoride combines with mercury residues, the immune system collapses. As the Schwann cells of the *neurilemma* die, scar tissue forms. **HELL on earth is now a reality!**

Mining and smelting operations are notorious for pouring fluoride dusts into the air. Third world countries suffer miserably from the uncontrolled use of industrial fluorides. The faces of the people are OLD! **Fluoride is a systemic poison. Ingestion of fluoride is in conflict with the desire to stay young or become** *Young Again!*

PREVIEW: In our next chapter, you will discover WHY sex hormone production shifts as the bio-electric body ages.

"If you think health is expensive, wait until you try disease!"
                                                    Merlyn Anderberg

---

Source Information Packet
For more information call (800) 659-1882 or (509) 465-4154 or write: Young Again! P.O. Box 1240 Mead Washington 99021-1240 USA, fax (509) 466-8103.

Think!

Did the cancer patient *always* have cancer? No! Was the diabetic *always* a diabetic? No! And did the lady with arthritis *always* have arthritis? No! These people LOST CONTROL of their body "terrain" due to:

- Failure to understand the "basics."
- Failure to remove wastes from the body's tissues.
- Failure to balance the hormones
- Failure to drink biologically friendly water.
- Failure to eat right-spin, high energy food.
- Failure to live a disciplined life.

FAILURE to make correct choices dictates health and longevity. Failure is a "self imposed" CHOICE!

Mind & Body

Never underestimate the power of the mind. Daily, I talk with people who **cannot** be helped because they **refuse** to control their thoughts.

There are many good books written about the power of the mind. Let's summarize a few points.

1. Negative, unhappy, critical, angry, fearful, depressed thoughts—and words—affect the production of brain chemicals, hormones, depress the immune system and bring on dis-ease. **Thoughts and words are energy bullets!**

2. The aura diminishes in size when we "think" negative thoughts. **Dis-ease is "thought" in the flesh.**

3. A positive outlook promotes healing. A poor emotional/mental attitude hinders healing—no matter how good our food or lifestyles. **Guard your thoughts.**

4. Bowel and liver function are affected by our emotions and thoughts. **Good thoughts are better than laxatives.**

5. Positive image visualization brings good results. **What we think, we experience. What we voice, we create.**

6. Beliefs about oneself, life, the future, and others affect us and those around us. **Refuse to harbor bad thoughts.**

7. Exercise is as good for the mind as it is for the body. **Exercise daily. Walk. Pump iron. Do calisthenics.**

8. Good thoughts, kindness to others, and self love all speed the process of becoming *Young Again!*

Read: *Your Body Believes Every Word You Say*
(see Source Page)

17

Diagnosis Or Post Mortems?

"The organs of the body can be likened to towns on a map, each being a unit unto itself, yet each is connected to the other and ultimately to the composite body."

Dr. Arnold Lorand

The Golden Age of Medicine extended from approximately 1840 to 1930. It was a period that saw an explosion of new knowledge in all fields of science.

The clinical observations of the doctors of this period are of particular interest to us because of their impact on the aging process. Their observations *precede* the advent of modern man's environmental mistakes.

The Golden Age of Medicine was a period of "low tech" drugless medicine. Doctors relied on astute observation to guide the patient. They also spent more time with patients, often getting to know them better than they knew themselves.

Uncommon good sense was the guiding rule. There was no place to shift the blame if the chosen modality (therapy) failed to cure the patient. The patient was viewed *in camera*—as a unit—rather than as separate parts. The word "syndrome" was not in fashion. Cause and effect, diagnosis, and prognosis were anchored in observation, rather than endless tests.

Modern Medicine

Present day medical technology is a mixed blessing. It excels in diagnosis "after the fact," organ transplants, and in emergency medicine. Beyond this, it is a never ending process that produces *isolated snap-shots* of the process we call dis-ease—each picture but a *glimpse* of the suffering patient.

High-tech modern medicine suffers from severe short-coming because doctors and nurses are **NOT** trained to diag-nose **sub-clinical** illness. Observations of yesteryear are considered to be "dated"—even primitive—for lack of hype and high tech smoke and mirrors.

Allopathic medicine has an *unholy* reliance on high tech gadgets and high powered, left-spin chemical drugs. It views us as a flesh and blood machine composed of "parts." Medicine doesn't understand ENERGY at the "invisible" level where vitality is lost before dis-ease is seen in the "visible" realm. They don't see us as *energy* dynamic beings and they don't under-stand that ours is a world of dynamic energy forces that interface the vital organs and **dictate** body terrain.

Diagnosis Or Post Mortems?

If it were possible to examine the vital organs of the body, particularly the ductless glands—the pituitary, thyroid, parathyroid, adrenals, thymus, pancreas, and gonads (testes and ovaries)—the effects of our living habits would be plainly evident. But we cannot make such an examination and must therefore learn HOW to assist the *bio-electric* body through a healthy lifestyle and common sense.

Dr. William Albrech, a brilliant professor of soils at the University of Missouri, once commented that we no longer know what healthy animal organs look like because we see only *abnormal* organs. That's the way it is in medicine today.

There was a time when the physician could examine both healthy and *pathogenic* organs and compare them. By knowing what healthy organs looked like, the doctor could identify dis-ease in its "formative" stages and if a good observer, pick up on *subclinical* symptoms before they became SIGNS. Subclinically sick people are now the norm and the vast majority of medical science's efforts goes towards "naming" the dis-ease. What we want and need is to "cure" the problem.

Strange Meanings

To compensate for the universality of a subclinically sick population, the medical schools have rewritten the STAN-DARDS by which they define health and dis-ease. This is similar to what is occurring in "government" schools, where today's "A" is yesterday's "C."

For example, BOGUS holistic medicine, as taught in

"traditional" medical schools, defines **illness** as an abnormal condition where the present level of function has declined compared to a *previous* level. By this definition, *neither* the present level nor the previous level of function meets any defined STANDARD. Traditional definitions have become moot. They no longer define illness as the absence of health and health the absence of dis-ease. **Illness is neutral!**

Today, bogus definitions of health and illness are defined in terms of the individual's *personal perception* of their state of being. In other words, how one *feels* about oneself. Trying to make sense out of all of this reminds me of the Chinese journalist who exclaimed, *"Explain please, strange words and meanings."*

Approximately 85% of the population suffers with Rouleau in their blood. Rouleau is the harbinger of dis-ease in the formative stage.

Reversing the aging process requires that we become enlightened as to WHY we age. We must not assign responsibility for good health to a medical "model" that ignores the root causes of illness, dis-ease, and aging.

The Endocrine System

To further understand the aging process, we must look at the endocrine system of the body. This system is one of two regulatory and communication systems that transmit and coordinate messages to various parts of the body. The other is the nervous system. *(Medical science ignores the lymphatic system which is the body's protein "communication" system because it involves the movement or stagnation of the plasma proteins that "leak" from the capillary walls into the spaces between the cells to provide nourishment.)*

The *nervous* and *endocrine* systems are *irrevocably* linked to each other, but they function differently. The nervous system transmits electrical impulses (energy) that originate in the neuron's cell body and are relayed via dendritic fibers that are composed of axons. The signal is transmitted in milliseconds (thousandths of a second)—faster than the speed of light—moving along the axon from synapse to synapse by specialized cells called Schwann cells which boost and pass on the electrical signal. Schwann cells are critical to the neurilemma and are **absent** in nerve degenerative conditions.

As we age, the neurilemma that covers the nerve fibers (also called the myelin sheath) deteriorates and eventually manifests as degenerative conditions like Alzheimers dis-ease, MS, myelinoma, neuropathy, burning feet/legs, and lupis.

Once nerve degeneration progresses enough for the

doctor to diagnose it, the person is in deep water.

Nevertheless, give the body the opportunity and help it with racemized™ hormone precursors and it will regenerate an entirely new and functional nervous system. It can regenerate missing limbs, grow hair on bald heads, trade in fat for muscle, grow new cartilage in the joints. But to perform these miracles, it needs a functioning endocrine system.

The endocrine system makes its wishes known using chemical **and** hormonal messengers. Chemical messengers are chemical *energy* that causes a *fast* response in the body.

Hormone messengers are *different.* They often take hours to produce a response. Hormone response, however, can last for hours, days or weeks. *(Think of the effects experienced in the aftermath of an emergency situation where large amounts of adrenalin were produced to help you cope with the situation. You are wired for hours afterwords!)*

Hormones control our *internal* environment by assuring normal body function and energy balance. Hormone production and balance is ABSOLUTELY vital to the aging reversal process **and it is now available for anyone who wants it.**

Exocrine & Endocrine Glands

Most exocrine glands secrete into *ducts* which in turn flow into body cavities like the stomach or intestines. Some exocrine glands, however, like the sudoriferous (sweat) and sebaceous (oil) glands, secrete to the skin's surface.

The *ductless* glands of the endocrine system secrete their hormones directly into the extracellular spaces around and between the secreting cells, instead of into ducts. The extracellular spaces—between the cells—are filled with extracellular fluid and house the blood and lymph capillaries.

Some hormones are transported *by the blood* to their destination(s), which may also be another gland. Hence, the ductless glands depend on each other and act in *concert* with the entire body terrain via the "receptors." If the receptor sites "lock up" as in the case of women who have EVER used birth control pills. talen estrogen supplementation, or used anabolic steroids including DHEA or melatonin, the person LOSES the ability to monitor their system and they become a prisoner in their own bodies. Synthetic hormones do NOT release from the receptor on their own, It takes Nugestrine II or Totally Male creme to clear the receptor sites of these damnable molecules.

When one gland becomes stressed, the effect is compounded **throughout** the system as in the case of women with thyroid problems. The real issue is hormonal imbalance in the form of "unopposed" estrogen dominance!

Some endocrine glands are both duct and ductless glands. Examples are the pancreas, ovaries, testes, kidneys, stomach, small intestine, skin, heart, and placenta.

Hormones maintain health by changing the *rate of activity* in the body. The amount of hormones released into circulation is based on need, the gland's ability to produce them and the body's ability to utilize them. **Hormonal excesses manifest themselves as deficiency conditions.**

Some hormones are carried "free" form in the blood. Others require blood plasma *carrier proteins* to bind and transport them—for example, insulin. Blood plasma carrier proteins are made by the liver, hence, a stressed liver creates additional stress on the other organs and glands.

When the receptors on the target cells respond to a hormone, a message is relayed back to the gland that produced the hormones to STOP production. Excess hormones are then degraded and disposed of by either the target cells themselves or by the liver and **removed from circulation** by the liver and/or kidneys.

Old Age Symptoms In The Young

Some of the SIGNS of early senescence (aging) as seen in young adults are obesity, graying/thinning hair, balding, wrinkles, gas/bloating, and lethargy.

Symptoms that serve as **markers** of poor health are amenorrhea (irregular menstruation), low sex drive, impotence, accelerated pulse, cold in the extremities, a tendency to constipation, edema, fading memory, mental depression, excess albumin or the presence of casts in the urine.

Albumin is a blood protein that has escaped through the capillaries of the kidney's glomeruli (filters). Albumin in the urine is a SERIOUS indication of loss of kidney function. Since the kidneys are one of the PRIMARY waste organs of the body, the presence of albumin spells trouble.

Casts are composed of salt, hyaline, protein, and chemical and mineral wastes. These wastes take the shape of the kidney's tubules. Their presence indicates *catabolic* activity and degeneration. Weak kidneys are a *prerequisite* to cancer and viral infections. Weak kidneys allow the establishment of clandestine outposts throughout the body and cold war maneuvers by viruses and bacteria fueled by the build up of acidic wastes in the system. Acidic wastes are left-spin energy.

Cold in the extremities indicates thyroid disfunction stressed ovaries and hormonal excesses. All of these are linked to a stressed liver—the body's furnace. An accelerated pulse indicates a systemic condition where the body is overworking to make up for shortfalls or excesses in the system.

Constipation is a systemic condition that influences ALL body functions. The so-called acid stomach is a symptomatic condition experienced after a meal. It is NOT an acid condition at all, but a short fall in the production of digestive enzymes. A tablespoon of Yucca Blend™ some DiSorb Aid™ and R/HCl™ provide instant relief!

Complete digestion and absorption allow people to enjoy their favorite foods. Allergies fade away. The flow of fully digested food into the small intestine deprives yeast and parasites of the food energy they need—gas and bloating being one effect. Complete digestion and absorption also prevents edema and further acidification of the tissues because of the accumulation of toxic plasma proteins in the tissue spaces.

Edema (water retention in the tissues) is linked to **excess** plasma proteins in the fluids that surround and bath the cells. **Edema is a sign of serious toxicity** and is usually involved in loss of body hair.

As people age, body hair is lost and the nails become thick, yellow, and troublesome. Drugs and protein wastes settle in the legs of older people further compounding swelling.

Oxidation/Reduction

As early as 1903, it was demonstrated that the **ductless** glands control **ALL** the processes of oxidation and that the diseases of metabolism like diabetes, obesity, gout, arthritis, heart dis-ease, etc., are the direct consequence of *alterations* in the function of these important glands.

Oxidation is another word for aging and breakdown of the tissues. Oxidation is the opposite of "reduction." In a broad sense, oxidation amounts to a slow down in the production and storage of the energy molecule ATP.

Hormones play a key role in glandular metabolism and are a driving force in the production of ATP. The adrenals, pancreas, and ovaries stress-out whenever the body is UNABLE to rid itself of **excess** waste due to a shortfall in liver activity. *Myxedema* of the thyroid gland (goiter)—as well as low energy and a cold body —indicate diminished thyroid activity and slow down in the secretion of the thyroid hormones T_3 and T_4. Central to all dis-ease is the liver and linked to the liver are the ovaries and testicles, adrenals, pancreas, and hormone receptor sites throughout the body.

Women who are dependent upon thyroid medications often return to normal with the use of the racemized™ hormone precursor Nugestrine II and liver detoxification.

Stroma & Parenchyma Cells

When functional (parenchyma) cells die, their tissue is replaced by dysfunctional (stroma) cells which form scar tissue. In the liver, the parenchyma cells are called hepatocytes (*hepat*-liver; *cyte*-cell). **Stroma cells cover and protect the liver. As the hepatocytes die, the stroma cells invade the dead spaces and form scar tissue.**

Alcohol • Cirrhosis • Liver Test

Alcohol is a POISON! It kills the hepatocytes in the liver. That is why a drunk person is said to be in**tox**icated. **Tox**—as in **tox**in—means poison. When you drink alcohol you are **poisoning** yourself. If you want to REVERSE aging, you are going to need a healthy functioning liver. Avoid the use of alcohol if you want to see your wish fulfilled.

For your information, the alcohol industry (like the dairy and ice cream industry) is not required to list the toxic ingredients it adds to its brew—ingredients like sulfites (wine) and urea (beer). If you insist on drinking beer and wine, make it yourself!

If you know someone who drinks, perform this liver test on them. First, have the person lie on their back on the floor and raise their knees to relax their stomach. Then, gently but deeply, push down on the person's right side, just below the rib cage. You will feel a *firm to hard* mass—the LIVER! Be careful, it may be very tender and massaging it harshly can cause the person to become ill! The liver should be soft and somewhat hidden under the ribs.

People with hepatitis, mononucleosis, or chronic fatigue syndrome usually have a distended, swollen liver. These *conditions* HEAVILY stress this vital organ as do problems in the adrenals, gonads, and pancreas.

Here is another test. Have the alcoholic person stand and extend their right arm. Next, gently pull down on the arm while your other hand touches the liver region. People with limited liver function will lose their strength and their arm will fall. Some people become **nauseated** and have to lie down because of the *surge* of electrical energy into their sick liver.

Atrophy Of Sex Glands & Obesity

Atrophy (deterioration) of the sex glands goes hand in hand with systemic toxicity, obesity, thyroid, and liver problems. Obesity is a SIGN of metabolic slow down and hormonal imbalance. Atrophy of the ovaries (which includes the ova and follicles from which the egg springs) and testicles takes years to manifest. Loss of the ovaries (female castration) causes immediate slow down in metabolic activity. Many doctors think nothing of removing a woman's female organs (uterus and ovaries). **Removal of a woman's ovaries is the equivalent of castration for a man. How many men have you seen standing in line to be castrated lately?**

Women MUST learn HOW to stay healthy if they expect to avoid female problems. Racemized™ hormone precursors are wonderful aids for both sexes. Women should NOT wait until there are problems to start. Remember, a problem avoided is a problem SOLVED.

Detoxification of the tissues goes a long way in keeping a woman young and vibrant and provides the foundation for effective prevention or treatment of female problems. Women MUST learn to manage their own health and not depend on medical "experts." Sadly, OBGY physicians—even female ones—do NOT have any answers for most women other than the usual estrogen hormone analog approach which not only does NOT work, but almost guarantees that a woman will develop uterine or breast cancer *(read contraindications in a reference)*.

Amenorrhea (skipped menstrual periods) and obesity are NOT normal and are proof positive of an unopposed estrogen dominance situation. Women with PMS difficulties need not suffer and can ease their lives and avoid loss of their female organs with the use of **racemized**™ hormone precursors. It really is that simple!

It is now possible to cause older men and women with a dowager's hump to become erect and regain normal posture. This is also accomplished with the products and procedures mentioned. If you would like PROOF, find a person in need and watch it happen. A bone density scan will document the internal miracle as the bones become more and more dense and NEW cartilage forms.

Obesity is a SIGN of hormone imbalance, poor digestion, and a slow metabolism. Obesity is defined as being 20% over standard height and weight tables. If, for example, your maximum desirable weight is 130 pounds, you would NOT be considered obese until you reached 156 pounds according to conventional wisdom.

In good health, you would probably be near the bottom of your table or 118 pounds. The difference here between obesity and ideal weight is 156 less 118 or 38 pounds overweight. Please notice, 38 pounds is 32% overweight!

Obesity is a SIGN that is easy to verify, It is a "marker" condition and should be considered a red flag by women and men alike.

Osteoporosis

Osteoporosis or **honeycombing of the bones** involves vascularization (invasion) of the bones by the blood vessels. The blood vessels are the body's front line troops. Their presence precedes bone formation as well as bone *dismantling*. Osteoporosis is a symptomatic EFFECT. It is not the cause of loss of bone mass, but it is related to hormonal imbalance and **excess** toxicity in the form of acid waste build up within the system AND reduced bone formation by the osteo**blasts** which are responsible for building new bone and cartilage. Osteoporosis is common in older people—and especially in post menopausal women due to the INABILITY to ovulate since available follicles have been used or have atrophied. Osteoporosis is easily prevented and treated, and has EVERYTHING to do with "unopposed" estrogen dominance and **NOTHING** to do with the need for increased intake of calcium compounds.

Tissue Types

Connective tissue is one of the four basic types of tissue in the body. It performs the functions of binding, supporting, and interfacing other tissues. It consists of relatively few cells in a sea of "intercellular substance."

The four basic types of tissue are **Connective** *(elastic, collagenous, reticular)*, **epithelial** *(skin)*, **muscular** *(muscle)* *and* **nerve** *tissue.*

Beautiful Skin

The last two words of the definition of connective tissue (intercellular substance) are of particular importance to aging. *Intercellular substance* is the material between the cells.

If we are speaking of the skin, we are talking about the dermal and sub-cutaneous layers which are composed of CONNECTIVE tissue. This area is served by the blood and lymph capillary systems. It is here, in the basement membranes of the skin, that the body dumps excess acid wastes, mineral salts, and FATS. These wastes are deposited by the blood capillaries and lodge in the spaces "between" the cells.

When the tissues become overloaded with waste and can no longer function normally, the connective tissues of the skin break down and wrinkles make their debut. Metabolic wastes **below** the skin break down the connective tissues that bind the skin layers together, and cause *hardening* and *thickening* of the outer skin with LOSS of *elasticity* and resiliency.

Glycolic acid skin cream (mentioned earlier) *fluffs* and *loosens* the dead outer horny layers of the skin. SOC™ lotion softens topical scar tissue while SOC™ capsules dissolves internal scar tissue and encourages new tissue formation **from the inside out.** Waste movement is accomplished with Yucca Blend™ and Enhanced PAC™ and again SOC™ capsules. When these products are used with Medical Grade Ionized Water™, the effects are often DRAMATIC! **An old body is nothing to be ashamed of UNLESS you refuse to apply the knowledge imparted herein.**

Venereal Disease • Sexual Excess

Sexually infectious dis-ease is on the rise. The increase transcends promiscuity and reflects the poor health of people.

Few people reach adult age as virgins. These days contraction of one or more venereal (*venus*-love; *al*-pertaining to) dis-eases (VD) is very common—and for good reason.

A healthy body is immune to VD just like measles, hepatitis, flu, and dozens more. Venereal infections can only occur when the body's "terrain" is ripe for infection. Conditions from genital herpes and vaginal warts to syphilis and gonorrhea RESPOND to Medical Grade (acid) Ionized Water™ via douching and topical application. (I had a buddy in the army who visited brothels regularly. When I asked him how many times he had contracted VD, he responded, *"Never! I always take a fresh lemon and wash down immediately afterwords!* The principle here is that men and women can do the same thing to protect and heal themselves using this special "water."

Sexual excess alters thyroid function as noted by the ancient Hebrews. They examined the neck of the newly married bride the morning following the wedding night. If the neck was swollen, this was a sign that the marriage had been consummated and a SIGN of heavy sexual activity. Young adults who sexually abuse their bodies lose their youthful appearance early and grow old much faster—especially females—because of the stress they place on their ovaries.

A man's inability to get an erection or frigidity in women is hormone DRIVEN and is tied to poor blood flow, low fluid levels, thyroid/hormone problems, borderline diabetes, a stressed liver, and/or *atrophy* of the ovaries and testicles.

Soy and canola oils play a part in sexual function. In fact, I have a fax on my desk that says a test lab found that canola oil caused sterility in rabbits. In the current bood ('97), *Our Stolen Future*, the soy myth is exposed for the damage it does to BOTH sexes by loading the body with estrogen "analogs" that skew the system. **Some "soy miracle!"**

VD is a "terrain" issue and Medical Grade Ionized Water™ is useful here to cleanse the system and fuel the production of the ATP energy molecule, reduce acid wastes in the tissues, and restore balance—all of which are necessary ingredients. And don't under estimate the value of racemized™ hormone precursors for "polishing" receptor sites and restoring lost nerve function—a common VD side effect. They also help women who are prone to miscarrage during the first trimester of pregnancy.

Too frequent pregnancies, prolonged lactation accompanied by a poor diet can precipitate **goiter** in women. The female body needs at LEAST two years of rest and nourishment between each child. Over stress of the liver also fuels menstrual and ovarian disorders, obesity and thyroid problems. Coldness in the feet and hands, low energy, the inability to get going in the morning and obesity are all hormone driven conditions and all are linked to blood sugar management and low energy. ETVC™ and racemized™ hormone precursors work wonders and will keep you young and energetic. I use BOTH.

Diabetes

Diabetes and obesity are first cousins. Adult onset diabetes (TYPE ll) is the most common type.

There is no question that buildup of metabolic waste and slow-down in organ function precipitates the development of adult diabetes. When waste energy levels EXCEED the body's ability to cope, blood sugar levels go ballistic.

As for juvenile diabetics (type l), there is NO question that polio and DPT vaccines mutate and bring on at least 75% of the cases. Hearing loss in children is closely linked to vaccinations. However, the deaf can "hear again" with a Neurophone™ using the skin as the conduit to the brain. This wonderful device is now available (see Source Page).

Rene's™ tea and Yucca Blend™ are used in mainland China for the treatment of diabetes and degenerative dis-ease via by IV drip—and with great success! It also works orally, knocking out blood viruses. ETVC™ helps diabetics with glucose intolerance and insulin resistance. Again, racemized™ hormone precursors should be considered a MUST!

Sugar is a **carbon** molecule. The diabetic uses carbon sugars to BUFFER acid wastes. (The soil uses carbon and calcium for the same purpose.) This is why colon therapy and liver purges do wonders for the diabetic. Get rid of the acid wastes, balance the hormones and diabetes often disappears. **The goal of diabetes therapy should not be to RETURN the diabetic (or any other suffering person) to NORMAL!**

Iodine

Iodine supplementation is the traditional treatment for hypo (low) thyroid conditions, along with synthetic and glandular thyroid products. And although iodine is a vital element, it is also a powerful *stimulant* to the thyroid, often making matters worse, not better. **When iodine is given to a person suffering from dietary imbalances, it can cause goiter and exhaustion of the thyroid gland.** Stimulation of the thyroid in the face of dietary insufficiency is futile. So is the *chronic* use of all thyroid supplements because thay are *palliative* in nature and fail to restore normal function. A series of liver purges combined with racemized™ hormones and a diet of SUPER FOODS usually does the trick in short order.

Let's Review

The organs become stressed from over activity, waste buildup, and malnutrition. Stress *alters* vital organ function and brings on symptoms of dis-ease that manifest as "deficiencies" when the real problem is "excesses" in the terrain.

When the body becomes stressed, it experiences a NEGATIVE energy shift and dis-ease proliferates. Reversing this process requires commitment and patience—**two qualities few people have enough of!**

The healing "crises" experienced during detoxification are a direct reflection of the person's toxicity level. Detoxification is not fun, but it is a necessary step that lays the foundation for long term aging reversal. **Healing "crises" are the price you must pay for your sins. I can assure you the price is little compared to growing old and suffering!**

The body s a DYNAMIC living energy field that succumbs to the process we call aging through our own mistakes. We cannot escape death, but we can keep the window that opened at puberty open for a very long time. **Post-mortem examination is a poor way to discover that your "chosen" lifestyle and belief system were fraudulent.** When you assist your body—instead of sabotaging it—you become *Young Again!*

PREVIEW: *Our next chapter discusses HOW the body "manufactures" what it needs by way of the bacteria and how mineral energy fuels our life processes.*

Source Information Packet
For more information call (800) 659-1882 or (509) 465-4154 or write: Young Again! P.O. Box 1240 Mead Washington 99021-1240 USA, fax (509) 466-8103.

Take Back "Your" Life!

If you suffer from low energy, depression, or obesity, here are some of products that will help you get your life back under your control. They are: ETVC™, DiSorb Aid™, Yucca Blend™, and R/HCI. These products help manage blood sugar which is central to weight control, aging, muscle mass, energy, and tissue regeneration. They work by improving digestion and absorption of the food we eat.

ETVC™ is taken with breakfast or lunch and raises **energy** levels all day. Excess body fat fades away and is replaced by lean muscle mass. Blood sugar problems—like diabetes and hypoglycemia—ease or disappear. Sexual interest improves, mental "fog" and depresion disappear. ETVC™ helps people feel and look better by opening their metabolic pathways.

DiSorb Aid™ and R/HCI work with ETVC™ to extract maximum energy from food, and also stoparticular undigested food from "putrifying" in the gut and fueling parasitic related problems like bloating and gas.

These products are a boon for diabetics because they help with insulin dependence, glucose intolerance, insulin resistance.

And don't forget, all of the problems mentioned above are closely linked to your hormones and liver—especially in women. Racemized™ homone precursors are unequaled in polishing the receptors sites and restoring CONTROL of the body's terrain (see Source Page).

PAC' have 24, 660 antioxidant units per bottle!

Take Care of Your TEETH

The VERY best way to take care of your teeth and gums is with a Biomagnetic Dental Irrigator™. This device "converts" tap water into a very powerful cleaner by manipulating the hydrogens ions on the water molecule so the plaque and calculus are "oxidized" from the tooth's surface and washed down the drain.

Please **do not confuse** a vibrating tooth brush or squirt gun type tooth irrigator with this device! There is NO COMPARISON. My teeth are beautiful and my gums are healthy and I haven't had my teeth cleaned in **over 5 years!** No plaque means NO decay and NO gum disease (refer to pages 79, 204, and Source Page).

False Readings

Positive energy can *stir* the system to the point of illness. This type of reaction is called a "healing crisis." It often occurs in people who are very toxic.

The body has *innate* intelligence. It **knows** and can **anticipate** the effect a positive energy substance will produce. Hence, the bio-electric body often rejects therapy or food or supplements that it actually needs. Sometimes it "rejects" because it **knows** know what it is going to have to go through to heal. Some it rejects because it knows the person does NOT truly desire to be healed or is unwilling to bear the misery that accompanies true healing.

The body occasionally "tricks" its owner by giving *false* muscle tests or false pendulum or vibration chain responses. To be useful, many dowsing practices require the novice and professional alike to sharpen their skills and **clear** their minds and operate on gut instinct.

Muscle testing is NOT accurate in the presence of heavy metal contamination in the tissues. Heavy metals impinge on the autonomic nervous system and interfere with test readings.

People go through the **motions** and issue **proclamations** based on "false" readings—including many practitioners. False responses and incorrect interpretations lead people astray. False readings are common when testing racemized™ products because of their very high biological activity when released into the body. After a short time, most people's systems settle down and heal.

The Pendulum

Learning to **effectively** use a pendulum is a MUST in this day and age. Learning to use a pendulum requires discipline and focus.

I recommend the books *The Pendulum Kit* and *Vibrations* because they have proven to be the best and least expensive way to teach people how to plug into the *invisible* world of energy fields that surround us.

The Pendulum Kit comes complete with a nice bronze pendulum and a beautifully illustrated book, while *Vibrations* comes with a vibration chain.

"Dowsing" is a phenomenon and a GOD given gift that's available to anyone who desires to come to grips with the reality of life on planet Earth (see the Source Page).

18

Biological Alchemy

"Since Einstein, Physics has been relegated to Mathematics, the former having lost all contact with reality. Your magnificent discovery of weak energy transmutations should have marked a scientific turning point, (but instead it) encountered a wall of stupidity."

Ren de Puymorin

...speaking of the work of Professor C. Louis Kervran and his discovery that the motion of life derives from the continuous transformation of one mineral into another or—"transmutation."

"Alchemy! Impossible! This is a good example of just plain old BAD science!" So ended my official inquiry at the college level—but it did NOT end my inquiry.

What sparked the explosive outburst was the trigger word "transmutation" which means **alchemy**. The *attacker* was a superb college chemistry instructor who did not like the implications of the questions I was raising, questions like... *"How* do you explain food plants that contain minerals not present in the soil? *How* does the cow produce milk that contains minerals far in excess of her dietary intake? *Where* does the hen get the minerals for her egg shells when they are not in her diet? *Why* does horsetail herb thicken and harden the nails, yet we derive NO such benefit from calcium supplements? *How* can organic manganese produce an increase in blood serum iron levels when it's not iron? *How* is it that a dried prune has more minerals than a fresh one? How, indeed? The answers to these questions derive from unrecognized genius (WIZARDS) and compromise ignored and forgotten knowledge.

Asking these type of questions is like proclaiming the invention of a perpetual motion machine. They can get a person in a lot of trouble, especially when put to the wrong person.

In our world of neatly packaged chemicals and defined LAWS of chemistry and physics, these questions have no answers. But, make no mistake, these ARE valid questions—just the kind Professor Kervran liked to ask. The problem isn't the questions posed, but the implications they suggest.

Some people of science are intimidated by questions for which they have no answers. Daring to ask them is an assault on DOGMA and enough to get a person branded *"science heretic!"*—and instant burning at the stake!

Mineral Energy

The life work of Professor C. Louis Kervran (1899-1990) has startling implications for reversing the aging process.

Kervran surmised that the energy *phenomena* we call LIFE is related to the transformation of one mineral into another. He called this process *"transmutation."* Science calls it alchemy. We will refer to it as biological alchemy.

Alter the energy forces within an element and a new and different element results. In the process, energy is released. Kervran believed this energy fueled metabolic processes and was the "life force" upon which life manifests. Transmutation, as he described it, would require a change in elemental structure at atomic and subatomic levels and the rearrangement of **an**ions and **cat**ions. In other words, COLD fusion!

Kervran's discoveries came from inside Science's camp. Kervran was a member of both the French and American National Academy of Sciences, the most prestigious watering holes of modern science.

Professor Kervran *dared* to ask the right questions. He *sinned* against Science and dogma when he offered God's answer to his fellow man. He broke the rules because he failed to submit his findings for "peer" review. Great Wizards have NO peers! They see visions of God's handiwork and proclaim the great news—while science curses them in contempt!

Like Copernicus, Kervran's peers *attacked* and *ridiculed* him as they have done to so many other Wizards before him. They tried to ignore him, but they could NOT deny the TRUTH he heralded. When a vessel of TRUTH is opened, it can NEVER be closed again. Truth is a Pandora's Box for those who live in ignorance and who are afraid of it—**especially those who egotistically "bask" in degrees and credentials.**

Visions

Kervran suspected that minerals contained concentrated energy fields within their bonds. His vision of the Creator's handiwork was not unlike that of his contemporary, Dr. Carey Reams. These great men of science never met. Each developed his own vision independently. Each talked about the same phenomena from their own perspective and interpretation of the phenomena they observed.

Reams called his vision, *The Biological Theory of Ionization*. Kervran called his, *The Theory of Biological Transmutation*. Both spoke of energy forces that grant permission for life. Both spoke of energy as a "footprint" or signature, the same phenomenon described by Vincent and incorporated in BEV™ and Medical Grade MikroIonized Water™.

Reams talked of positive energy ions called **an**ions, and negative energy ions called **cat**ions. Kervran spoke of the rearrangement of energy forces and the fusion of these forces at the atomic and *sub*atomic levels.

Reams spoke of left and right-spin energy and the release of cosmic forces trapped in mineral bonds (ionic bonds). Kervran talked of mineral **transmutation** in the gut of animals and in the skin and lymph of the Earth—soil and water.

The Sun was a central fixture for both men. They saw plants, animals, and microbes as mediators between Sun and Earth. Both men sought the answer to the "Why?" of life that we raised in chapter two—the mystery of life and death, health and illness. God answered both men with living examples of the importance of biologically "live" food, high ORP water, and disciplined lifestyles. He answered Reams in English and Kervran in French. Our version will be a translation of both.

Plants • Animals • Microbes

The plant is the link between the Sun and the animal world to which man's body belongs. The plant converts solar energy into carbon sugar molecules with the help of the microbe. Plants bring life and energy INTO the Earth.

The animals—with the help of the microbes—process plant tissue and live off the electron energy released during the digestion process. Animal waste becomes part of the Earth's "skin" and provides a catalyst for new life—both plant, animal, and microbe.

To Kervran, mineral energy fields in a living system were forever dynamic—shifting and changing one into the other. For example, in HEALTHY multiple stomached animals (called ruminants), calcium limestone is "transmutated" by bacteria in order to meet the animals needs. Humans have but one stomach. To be effective, man's minerals must be in the most biologically active form—"racemized" ionic form!

Kervran saw "life" energy flowing from a potpourri of mineral elements. To him, health was a manifestation of a microbial *fiesta* in the gut and liver of man and animal! In order for Kervran's *fiesta* to occur in man's body , the "terrain" must be electrically balanced. The microbe is at the center of the *alchemy* process we call *fusion.* Cold fusion allows life to express and maintain itself. It involves the transmutation of one energy field into another. **Transmutation of mineral energy fields slows aging and maintains peak health.**

Cows & People

The cow utilizes the transmutation process. She eats plants (compounds of carbon, hydrogen, sulphur, nitrogen, sugars, fats, proteins, and minerals) and converts them into NEW and DIFFERENT energy forms—like muscle and bone.

The cow does this by way of the enzymes and microbes in her liver and GI tract. The bacteria that share her system have a *symbiotic* relationship with her. She provides them room and board; they provide her with energy and vitality. Without the microbes and enzymes, the fantastic biochemical reactions Kervran called *transmutations* CANNOT take place. Without the microbes, the cow is unable to nourish herself. Without the microbes, man grows old and dies early.

The microbe is man's passport to a continued presence on the Earth. However, man's disobedience is causing the microbe to turn against him.

Sick cows have much in common with sick **people**. Both are UNABLE to effectively use the transmutation process. Health and vitality in man is a reflection of the **terrain** and the processes Kervran and Reams called transmutation and ionization. The requirements for a healthy life are nutritious, right-spin, high energy food, ionic minerals, biologically friendly high ORP water, exercise, and a clean *internal* environment.

When the cow drinks chlorinated water, the chemicals create an energy imbalance that causes the microbes to mutate into *pathogenic* life forms. The result of this energy shift is a slow-down in metabolic activity in the gut and liver and loss of vitality and health.

Antibiotics cause a similar effect. They upset the balance of intestinal flora by changing the **terrain** of the body. So called "good" microbes live off right-spin energy, while pathogenic microbes live off left-spin energy present in a toxic environment. Anaerobic environments are left-spin environments. Aerobes (friendly bacteria) cannot live in an anaerobic environment and they **forfeit** their "terrain" whenever such a condition develops. A sick cow—or a human being—is the reflection of a sick internal environment.

Fusion & Fission

Life is a tug of war between opposing energy forces. Transmutation and ionization are involved in both positive and negative biological energy shifts—fusion and fission.

Fusion involves the joining of atoms to form larger molecules. Under normal biological circumstances, it is a positive energy activity and represents the buildup process we call *anabolism.* Fusion occurs on the surface of the *Sun,* in the *soil,* in plants and in the gut and liver of man and animal.

An example of *abnormal* biological fusion would be cancer. Cancer results from toxic waste buildup, hormonal imbalance, the introduction of *radiomimetic* substances that produce or mimic the physiological effects of nuclear radiation. Examples would be additives, preservatives, drugs, microwaved food, etc. These things cause oxidation of the tissues and the formation of free radicals. Uncontrolled oxidation is nothing but aging in FAST FORWARD—a condition where Enhanced PAСˢᵀᴹ, Yucca Blend™ and DiSorb Aid™ can save the day.

"Fission" breaks down molecules and atoms. Normal, biological fission activity is good. But once we lose control, the fission process becomes *catabolic* in nature. Examples of destructive fission reactions are nuclear reactions, irradiated food, radiation therapy, microwave cooking, etc. Fission reactions orchestrated by **friendly** microbes are beneficial. But, when we lose control of the *terrain* (acidification of the tissues) we usher in negative fission reactions and dis-ease orchestrated by mutant pathogenic microbes.

Skin • Dirt • Soil • Lymph

The Earth has skin. Her skin is called soil. Some folks call soil "dirt." Dirt, however, is *dead* unless it is *energized* with microbes, organic matter, and carbon. The microbes *transform* dirt into soil. Soil is biologically *alive.* Soil has *life.*

Water is the essence of life. Water is the Earth's lymphatic fluid and it is capable of transporting massive amounts of energy. Soil energy and soil depth is controlled by carbon. Carbon underwrites Mother Earth's aura.

When the Earth becomes stressed, her skin forms boils, her lymph becomes toxic, the plants become weak, the animals suffer and man experiences dis-ease. The condition of Earth's skin and lymph dictates the quality of life AND which life forms live or die. Fundamentally, life is a microbial affair that involves transmutation and ionization of mineral energy. **The microbes and the minerals are man's ticket to longevity —if he has the wisdom to recognize their importance and follow nature's rules.**

Synchronization

Synchronization can be the end result of a chemical reaction—like mixing vinegar with baking soda—one acid, the other alkaline. When the reaction has run its course, two things have occurred. Energy has been released (heat) and synchronization has occurred between the original reactants. If the reaction stopped because of a shortage of ingredients, *potential* energy remains in synchronized form.

Energy management in the body is similar, but here, it's the body's ability or inability to "digest" food and break the bonds that hold food energy intact that must be addressed. With SUPER FOODS like Klammath™ algae, Harmonic™ pollen and Synergy, Biogenic™ liver, and Taoist™ products, desynchronization of energy is less of an issue because they. However, where an *anaerobic* gut and a toxic liver are involved, **even right-spin energy foods can synchronize or convert to a left-spin energy state.** Colon therapy, DiSorb Aid™, Yucca Blend™ and enhanced PACs™ usually remedy an anaerobic "state" causing health to rebound and energy to take off.

An anaerobic gut is the perfect terrain for a negative energy takeover—like cancer.

Synchronized energy is energy that is on hold. It is energy that is NOT available to the body. People in poor health are in energy **gridlock.** They are both unable to neutralize *negative* energy fields and too weak to free potential positive food energy. Negative energy neutralizes positive energy. Sick bodies produce lots of negative energy. Dis-ease is the end product of a left-spin *anaerobic* take over—a *catabolic* state.

Liver detoxification and high ORP Medical grade Ionized Water™ can break a gridlocked, intestinal environment and drastically bosst vitality. Try it!

When the bio-electric body suffers *systemic* synchronization, OLD AGE goes into FAST FORWARD and life becomes impossible! As we approach total synchronization, we lose our "radiance." The aura diminishes and dwindles until it ceases to be and the physical body dies. The ghost is gone! Yet, synchronized energy remains in the form of a cadaver which Earth reclaims. Ashes to ashes! Dust to dust! **Energy is never lost, but it does change form and recycles again.**

Energy Takeover

When the chemical bonds holding synchronized energy under lock and key are broken, energy can go EITHER way. If the bonds are broken in a predominantly *anaerobic* environment, the energy can become a negative force—even if it was originally positive in nature. This is what I meant earlier when I said right-spin energy entering a left-spin environment can be diverted and used to promote dis-ease. A clean terrain is key. **Cancer lives on the negative energy available in a sick, anaerobic body. Learn HOW to manage your TERRAIN and cancer will never be a threat.**

A person suffering with constipation is under stress—*anaerobic stress.* Constipation SLOWS ionization and transmutation of mineral energy and promotes the appearance of **parasites** that feed on toxic energy. Gas and bloating are PROOF of incomplete digestion and DiSorb Aid™ rids the body of these problems.

Cancer follows in the wake of years of personal abuse. It likes an anaerobic environment where it can divert positive energy to negative purposes—like the growth of a "mass." People with cancer should NEVER be given large amounts of high protein foods—be it meat, fish, fowl or beans unless DiSorb Aid™, Yucca Blend™ and R/HCl are present. I prefer to obtain my proteins from Klammath™ algae, Biogenic™ liver, tablets, Harmonic™ pollen, Taoist Rice Polish™ and Harmonic Synergy™ because all of them are ZERO stress SUPER foods.

Cancer—A Different Set Of Rules

The rules of life are different once a person is under cancer's pall because cancer is a *catabolic* state and the cancerous person is very fragile.

Alternative approaches often fail because the doctor/patient fail to understand that the rules have changed. Clinical nutrition doesn't work here—the rules are NOT the same! Cancer hijacks the body's energy. Cancer masses are **viral black holes** that draw-in and subvert all available energy and then EXPORT it to outlying colonies. Cancer also uses biological alchemy to BREAK **synchronized** bonds to fuel its growth.

There will NEVER be a "magic bullet" cure for cancer. Cancer defies the rules and complies with none of the LAWS of normal health. Cancer has but one purpose: to kill the host and rid the Earth of weak organisms. **Cancer is NOT the enemy, but it is the perfect double agent. First it kills the host. Then it kills itself. SYNCHRONIZATION!**

When you control your body terrain, YOU are in control

of your life and the magical processes that Kervran and Reams described so eloquently.

Medical Grade Ionized Water™ **is a very powerful way of restoring TOTAL control over your body terrain and those of your loved ones,** To learn more, order the BEV™ and Japanese manuscripts, the water video and the water book that goes with it (see Source Page).

Health and vitality are the EFFECTS of the process we call *biological alchemy.* The process depends on our microbial friends and the internal environment we provide for them.

Kervran and Reams discovered a vital piece of the process we call aging. Their life's work points the way to total body rejuvenation and good health if we understand the rules of the game and are willing to take personal responsibility for ourselves. Only then can we become *Young Again!*

PREVIEW: *Our next chapter is about the gut (small intestine) and the E. coli bacteria infections that killed many people and children during 1993. You will also learn what's behind Montezuma's revenge.*

Ozonate Your Home & Your Car

Ozone has many forms. **Medical Grade** ozone is very beneficial to your health. Use it to clear lung and bronchiole congestion, ease asthma, oxidize odors, viruses, molds, and pathogenic bacteria in air, carpets, and drapes.

An ozone/ion generator is a wonderful way to stay healthy and hold down microbial outbreaks that fuel colds and flu. Older folks find medical grade ozone very beneficial, particularly in the winter. Respiratory patients see often see their ailments ease in a matter of days.

Protect yourself, family and pet from airborne pollutants—both external and in house off gasses released by construction materials, furniture and chemicals. Environmentally sensitive people discover wonderful releif.

Never Use "TAP" Water To Make...

"Tap" water is NOT suitable for use in a "microwater" machine because it concentrates and activates the POISONS and chemicals in the water creating serious problems for the body. The production of Medical Grade Ionized Water™ requires two pieces of equipment plus racemized™ sea minerals to create safe, high ORP water. Never use "tap" water in a "microwater" machine. Never!

Cancer "Craps!"

Conventional cancer therapy has more than a little resemblance to the game of "craps."

You have stakes—your life. You have rules—*house* rules. You have the dealer—a *house* dealer that wears a white robe and who is controlled by the licensing boards and pharmaceutical industry. You have the *house* support team—they wear uniforms and they have licenses and are trained to do as they have been trained or are told. You have the other players—who appear to be winning enough to justify your joining the game. You have chips—called insurance, life savings, a farm, a house. You have dice—weighted in the *house's* favor. You have liquor—called radiation and chemotherapy. You have the *house* bouncer—his name is Fear. You have the *house* preacher—his name is Hope. You have odds—the **75%** the house *dealer* gave you during your "consultations" prior to joining the game.

All games have an end. When you play cancer craps, the game automatically ends when you run out of money, or when you die—whichever comes first.

The *house* always wins when people play *their* game, on *their* turf, by *their* rules. Is there a solution? You bet! **Don't play!**

Instead, clean up your body. **LAUGH!** Don't cry "poor me!" Don't dwell on hate, anger, and fear. Use your mind to create a new body. Never entertain the negative thoughts. Got it?

What you say your body believes! What you think, you get! It took me fifty years to get this straight and I am here to tell you that your mind has the ability to create or to destroy! Use it to create a better life and world.

Celebrate! You're *ALIVE* and if you do what you need to do, you will continue to celebrate life and see your great, great grand children mature and you will get to experience the many wonders the future holds for those who love life MORE than those who fear death.

A Life Of Cancer Craps Is A <u>Crappy</u> Life!

Infections

Medical Grade Ionized **"Water"** can rids the body of things like genital herpes and warts and yeast and bladder infections. Use if for douching, pink eye, nail funguses, athlete's foot, intestineal flu, and cuts and wounds.

Young Again! Pyramid

Life is a scrapbook of lessons—never mistakes!

pH Scale

19

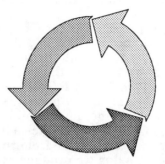

A Tube Within A Tube

Dr. Spot: *"There's always scissors!"*

Earlier we described some of the characteristics of the integumentary system (skin) as it relates to health. Now, we will consider our "inner" skin and see what part it plays in the process we call aging.

Man's body is a tube within a tube. The skin is our *outer* tube and the mucous membranes form the *inner* tube. The mucous membranes are the soft tissues that line the mouth, nasal passages, respiratory tract, stomach, gut, colon (and vagina). They begin in the mouth and end at the anus. The mucous membranes have tremendous significance to the story of aging and dis-ease.

The tissues lining the mouth, nasal passages, respiratory system, and mucous membranes are classified as *stratified epithelium* and their primary job is to protect underlying tissues, secrete fluids, and to transport waste.

The remainder of the inner tube is the GI tract. Its membranes are made up of *simple epithelium* whose job is to ABSORB nutrients, protect underlying tissues, SECRETE mucous and enzymes, and transport food and waste.

Our outer tube, the skin, has a combined surface area

of about 30,000 square inches. The pores (openings) of the skin are called *stoma* and there are as many as 3,000 of them per square inch. By comparison to the skin, the mucous membranes have an approximate surface area of 18,000,000 (million) square inches or 600 times greater. One inch on the outside equals 600 inches on the inside or a ratio of 1:600. THIS IS IMPORTANT!

In healthy people, eating induces digestion, absorption, and elimination. But beyond age 24, digestive/absorptive capability diminishes exponentially because food and drinking water imposes HEAVY stress on the body. The purposes of DiSorb Aid™, Yucca Blend™ and R/HCI™ is to eliminate food imposed stress and to eliminate the parasite's food supply. This single move increases energy, helps normalize body weight, prevents gas and bloating and promotes a healthy colon.

The longer the transit time from the dinner table to the toilet, the more toxins we produce and absorb.

The mucous membranes are a favorite conduit for drug chemotherapy. Medications in the form of suppositories, sublinguals, and aerosols are easily absorbed through the membranes of the rectum, vagina, and respiratory system. A doctor dares not prescribe the same amount of medication to be administered via the mucous membranes as would be given orally or by subcutaneous or intramuscular injection.

E. coli & The Gut

Most nutrient absorption takes place in the intestinal mucosa. This is the body's most vulnerable and most important terrain. An infection in the gut—salmonella, typhus, pathogenic E. coli— causes the natural sloughing action of the mucosa to increase. Normal sloughing occurs at the rate of approximately twenty million cells a day. These cells provide an important source of intestinal enzymes (the enzymes are contained in the sloughed-off cells) which act as the vehicle of delivery. *Pathogenic* infection increases sloughing to such an extent that digestion and absorption of nutrients and fluids fails to occur resulting in diarrhea and malnutrition. **Medical Grade Ionized (acid) Water™ can clear these infections.**

The infamous E. coli 0157.H7 bacteria that contaminated hamburger in the USA in early 1993 produce severe sloughing of the intestinal mucosa and "bloody" diarrhea followed by dehydration, starvation, and electrolytic shock.

E. coli 0157.H7 produces an **exotoxin** *(exo*-to export; *toxin*-poison) that severely STRESSES the functional tissues of the liver and kidneys. Dead (necrotic) cells MUST be removed immediately or their acid wastes will putrify and produce systemic toxemia and even gangrene. A dead body left unattended, swells like a balloon due to the gasses produced by gangrene; hence "gas gangrene."

Such a condition of heavy waste removal overloads the kidneys, thus forcing the need for kidney dialysis (artificial filtering of the blood) is required to prevent systemic (whole body) toxemia (*tox*-poison; *emia*-blood).

Old & Young

Elderly people are grossly affected by E. coli infections because their organs and glands are weak and their metabolism is sluggish. Moreover, their ATP energy reserves are low and toxicity levels are high. Their bodies are catabolic and usually anaerobic. Lack of resiliency is their Achilles' heel.

Children are at the other end of the continuum. They have high resiliency, but are often malnourished and toxic because they eat the *usual and customary* American diet. Poor bowel habits, bad diet, **marginal** digestive/absorptive capability, and oxidized and biologically DEAD, low ORP water are at the root of toxicity-driven illness in children and adults. A stressed body terrain is a **made-to-order** environment for bacterial infections like E. coli 0157.H7. (Not all E. coli are alike! Life is IMPOSSIBLE without the friendly strains of E. coli that inhabit the intestine.)

Not Everyone Died

Over a million pounds of E. coli contaminated beef found its way into fast food restaurants, yet only a few hundred people became sick and only 6 died. The question is WHY? The answer has to do with the vibrational frequency of the "terrain" of the sick and dead people.

Pathogenic organisms "feed" on negative energy fields produced in a TOXIC environment which explains why, in a family with three children—all of whom ate contaminated beef—only one child died. NO mystery is involved here. **The body's energy field—the TERRAIN—dictates sickness and death or health and vitality.**

The contagious dis-eases that plagued mankind throughout history—bubonic plague, smallpox, typhoid, typhus, etc.—did NOT kill everyone. Fact is, most people did NOT die. Those who did die had stressed TERRAINS. and were anaerobic, toxic, under-hydrated, and malnourished.

These points raise serious questions about the absurdity of immunizing against dis-ease—a **sacred cow** in the USA. A healthy terrain is a smarter answer. Medical Grade Ionized

Water™ can make the body impregnable against infection and makes MOOT the issue of "contagious" dis-ease.

The panic seen in the recent movie Outbreak is understandable in light of the general level of ignorance regarding contagious dis-ease. Clean up your act and Ebola plague, Hanta virus, Cryptosporidium bacteria, necrotizing facitis (flesh eating bug), and their likes will bass you by.

A clean body is equivalent to the blood on the lintel stone over the doorway of the Israelites. Death passes by.

Lack Of Understanding

People of science have difficulty understanding discussions like this because of their training. Scientific thought embraces the "scientific method" and the Germ Theory. Our discussion does NOT fit their "model" or their false theories and conflicts with their pusillanimous mewings.

Whenever the phone rings and the caller asks, "What are your credentials?" I know I have an "expert" on my hands, or someone who wants to defend something. Credentials are for the ego and the licensing boards. The modest professionals have their ego and prejudices in tow and don't care about credentials which are only proof that you know how to regurgitate and not think. Credentials are nice—IF they don't get in the way. Got it?

Vibrational medicine asks square questions and it provides square answers. It approaches health related problems from an ENERGY vantage point. It is not hindered by the Germ Theory of Disease and other theoretical artifacts.

Remember, healthy bodies are nourished bodies. Healthy bodies are clean bodies. Healthy bodies are bodies in good physical condition. Healthy bodies produce and store massive amounts of ATP energy. The healthy body will not support proliferation of pathogenic microbes.

It's The Pits

The small intestine is lined with convoluted folds called the *plicae circularis*. These folds are lined with *villi* (little fingers) and *microvilli* (hair-like structures) that increase the surface area of the intestine to 600 times that of the outer skin. The microvilli contain the cells that absorb and transport food nutrient energy. The spaces *between* the villi are known as the Crypts of Lieberkuhn. The Crypts are lined with cells that secrete our digestive enzymes and mucous.

As we age, the valleys that make up the intestinal *pits* become shallow. The villi and microvilli atrophy. The transit time of food—from mouth to anus—slows. Constipation manifests. Parasites appear. As these alterations occur, the pits, villi and microvilli become smothered in slow moving fecal matter, mucoid substances and metabolic wastes.

Anaerobic conditions in the colon produce serious changes in the chemical make up of the fecal matter interfacing the intestinal walls. Fecal matter transforms into a semi-hard, rubber-like, mucoid material that *smothers* the intestinal wall. Over a period of years, this *stuff* thickens and narrows the opening (lumen) leaving a narrow tube—like an occluded water pipe—through which the body's wastes must pass.

Earlier I mentioned that the colon of a very famous Hollywood cowboy had grown to almost twelve inches in diameter at the time of his death, yet the lumen (opening) for waste movement was only 1 inch. The rest was mucoid waste.

Fully 85% of the population needs colon therapy to get their house in order. The Rouleau effect seen in the blood of 85% of the people is no coincidence.

The combined effect of limited digestive and absorptive capability, poor liver function, and congested skin means the average person **forfeits** over 75% of their waste processing capacity! The waste exit portals that remain—lungs and kidneys—are NOT capable of handling the load. Toxic overload of the entire *bio-electric* body and accelerated aging result.

A CLEAN bowel and healthy liver are the difference between youth and vitality vs. old age and death.

Colon therapy may be unAmerican, but it should NOT be dismissed. For people with a history of sickness and obesity, colon therapy is the FAST TRACK to good health. This was the path I took many years ago. Yet, a series of liver purges produced over 1600 stones from my body, despite 18 years of colon therapy. And following the stones, a massive dumping of colon lining took place again at age 52.

A great book on the subject of colon therapy is *Tissue Cleansing & Bowel Management.* I highly recommend this book because it shows the reader —in forty full color pictures—how to set up and perform colon therapy (see Source Page).

My Story

By 1977 I had reached a plateau in my personal health. I visited a lady who had been trained by Dr. Reams in the Biological Theory of Ionization. Dolly took saliva and urine readings and read the sclera (whites) of my eyes—which is quite different than reading the iris of the eyes (Iridology).

The results showed I had mucoid buildup in my colon. Subsequent colon therapy confirmed this as I saw hard, compacted fecal material exit my body. The event caused my health to reach NEW heights, as my body immediately **surged backward** to more youthful days. **Without colon therapy, I could never have achieved the results described.**

Colon therapy can be done at home and is safe. In times of severe medical illness, colonics can save your life.

UNPLUG from the medical system, follow the path outlined in this book, and you will enjoy a wonderful life. That's what this book is about. I did it! And so can you!

A *live testimony* from your author, and you can believe it, for I am *Young Again!*

PREVIEW: *Our next chapter is about YOUR aura. Why do people climb rock mountains? HOW could Jesus pass through the wall of the temple?*

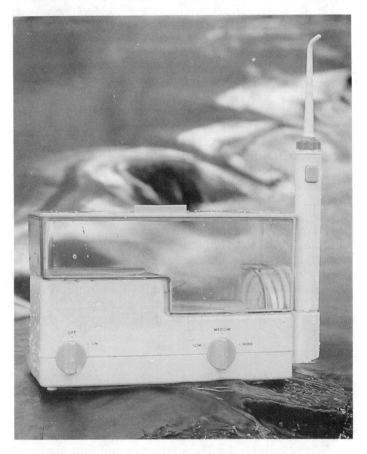

The Bio-Manetic Dental Irrigator™

Oxidation = Aging

Enhanced PAC's prevent uncontrolled cellular oxidation better than any product available because they are racemized™ to increase their metabolic activity rate. Uncontrolled oxidation causes the body to cannibalize itself. **Oxidation is another word for aging.**
As we age, the tissues oxidize faster and faster. An example of extreme oxidation is a massive heart attack where heart muscle disintegrates almost instantaneously. Doctors sometimes refer to the heart as a "mass of mush" in the aftermath of a massive coronary.

A *free radical scavenger* is a chemical compound that **bonds** to free radicals which are highly reactive chemicals that are short or long on electrons. PAC's prevent the rapid oxidation and destructive chain reactions that free radicals produce.

We ingest massive amounts of free radicals every day. They come from air, water, and food. The body also *manufactures* them in the process *metabolism.*

Once toxic substances enter the body, they change their chemical form and become even more toxic. Examples would be food additives, fluorides and chlor**amines** in tap water, soy and canola oils, pesticides, microwaved food, vaccination induced viruses and bacteria, and animal serum proteins that transport them.

Enhanced PAC's stabilize wastes released into circulation during detoxification and liver stone purges. They prevent acid wastes from being reabsorbed as they worm their way down 20 feet of intestine on their way to the toilet.

All dis-ease conditions respond favorably when PAC's are incorporated into the diet. And if you consume Medical Grade Ionized Water™ at the same time, their combned effect is truly awesome. Other beneficial adjuncts are Yucca Blend™, Aspar-Max™, racemized™ hormone precursors™ and the SUPER foods.

Enhanced Pac's have 24, 660 antioxidant units per bottle and TOTALLY eliminate the need for common antioxidants like vitamins A, E, C and zinc which get in the way and produce secondary problems of their own.

Aging reversal is a very BIG order and the older or sicker you are, the bigger is the request. Thanks to the racemization™ process, most any condition can be reversed or at least eased. Try some and find our for yourself (see Source Page).

Vital Organ Flow Chart

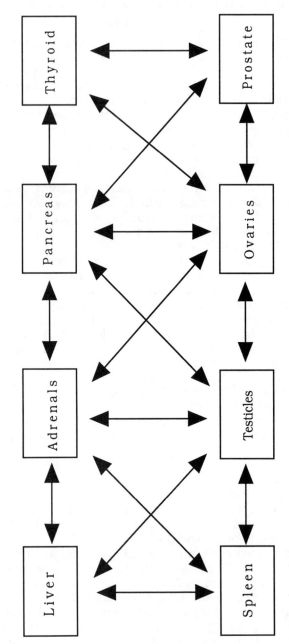

As goes one vital organ, so goes the others. Each organ triggers another producing a cascade of symptoms and illnesses that manifest as dozens of conditions and SIGNS (for instance, the ovaries affect the liver/thyroid/adrenals). To return the body to a state of "health," all organs and glandular systems MUST be addressed simultaneously, which explains why so many alternative and traditional approaches fail. Note: All body systems collapse together and all must be restored TOGETHER. Refer to the Triangle of Health, page #39.

20

The Aura Effect

*"Man's mind stretched to a new idea never
goes back to its original dimension."*
Oliver Wendel Holmes

The injury had occurred the night before, but Jerry was not aware of any specific damage. As Jerry and I walked into the shop and began browsing, the lady who owned the shop approached Jerry and said,

"OOOH! You must be hurting pretty bad?"

He looked at her blankly and asked what she meant.

"Oh! Your aura! You have a very BIG hole in it in your groin area. Did you injure yourself?"

Jerry was hurting. He had torn a hernia in the connective tissues of his pelvic region the night before.

What was so intriguing about the encounter was that this lady was a total stranger. She knew nothing about Jerry, yet she was able to vividly see his body aura and the hole in it. We had heard of people like this lady, but neither of us had witnessed the phenomena before.

The Glow Of Health

The body has a radiation field surrounding it. This is an established fact. Kirlian photography can capture the aura on a photographic plate—its size, shape and color in direct relation to the overall vitality of the person.

Jesus was reported to have a *glow* about Him. Whenever He is pictured, the halo or aura effect is always seen around His head. The halo and aura are right-spin energy. Many people believe the greater your aura, the more advanced human being you are. Perhaps. For certain, each of us has one, and the greater it is, the **healthier** we are!

When people suffer with dis-ease, the electrical charge of the bio-electric body shifts from one that is right-spin and healthy, to one that is left-spin and pathogenic. Whenever we notice the sickly pallor of another person, we are taking note of a diminished *aura*, though we may not recognize it as such. We also recognize when the person has returned to health—by noting their pallor and vibrant *electrical* appearance.

Energy Drain

Some people are exhausting. I am not speaking of the person who runs in *hyper drive*, but the person who drains your energy and leaves you feeling very tired. These folks are energy sinks! They may be nice people, but the *effect* of their presence is less than refreshing. A whole lot less!

Sue owned a massage therapy and iridology clinic for many years. She once commented that certain people drew so much energy from her that she could not work on them. Later, I learned that my wife had severed her friendship with one lady Sue would no longer treat. The reason was that the lady was *exhausting!*

Sue was an interesting person. She had the uncanny ability to *see* and *feel* things about people who came to her for treatments. They call people like Sue' "healer." Sue definitely was a healer. Sue was also a superb organic gardener. Sue had a green thumb and the plants produced abundantly for her. Her plants were "vibrantly" healthy and never required any form of poison to control bugs or weeds.

One day I asked her, *"Sue, what is your secret?"* She just smiled. As I came to know her, I realized that she knew how to speed up body frequency—through the laying-on of hands. In her case, it was called massage therapy. Sue could speed up the electron flow in the body of the patient to such an extent that the person walked out of her clinic TOTALLY refreshed and happy to be alive.

By accelerating the flow of energy, Sue strengthened the positive energy fields in the body and "drew off" negative energy forces. The effects were seen immediately in the patient's *aura* and vibrancy. Sue had mastered the skill of energy manipulation. She understood that **life** is a field of competing energy forces. Sometimes she would shake her hands, walk barefoot in grass or sand, or hug a tree barefooted to dissipate the negative energy she had taken on from her sick patients.

Energy & Auras

The world is composed of but one thing: energy! When energy condenses it is called matter. Matter has three states: gas, liquid, and solid—every substance is a variation of energy density and vibrational molecular frequency.

Rocks are hard and solid. Skin has texture and can be stretched. Rocks and skin are not *really* solids, we just "classify" them as solids. Solids are energy fields joined together in such a way that they take on the shape, feel, and smell of something we learn to identify as rock, skin, tomato, etc.

All things living and non-living have an aura. A rock's aura—and the effect it exerts on things near it—can be positive or negative. If the rock's energy state is positive, it will have a therapeutic effect on plants and visa versa.

If we increase the flow of electrons around the nuclei of the atoms in a rock, it will change form. For example, if we heat sulphur, it will change from a solid, to a liquid, to a gas. Water does the same—ice to liquid to steam.

Rocks & Mountains

In the Bible, rocks had particular significance in matters of health. Rocks have a sacred place in most religions. Rocks are not *live* in the animal sense, but they do possess *life*. A rock's life is expressed in its energy footprint and signature.

People like rocks. Some people like them so much they have a head full of them. People who climb rock mountains are often asked, "WHY?" The answer usually given is *"Because they are there!"* There is a more accurate reason. People climb rocks because they find it *invigorating.* Climbers absorb fantastic quantities of ENERGY from rock mineral formations. Rocks radiate ENERGY that syncs the climber with Mother Earth.

Man transmutes rock energy into fuel energy. Climbing rocks is just another way man taps into nature's energy bank. The same idea applies to swimming in sea water or walking bare foot in sand or grass or hugging a tree while barefooted. Earth energy is "transferred" to the body and it makes us feel good!

Jesus & The Wall

It is recorded that when Jesus was about to be stoned in the Temple, He passed through the wall and disappeared to the frustration of his enemies. As a child, I accepted this story, but I never believed it because anyone with a lick of sense knows that you cannot walk through a wall.

Today, this story delivers a different message—one that is both factual and explanatory. Christ possessed the knowledge and ability to accelerate the flow of electrons in His body. In so doing, He was able to pass through the wall of the temple. By speeding up His electrons to the point of disintegration (think of ice becoming steam), He squeezed between the atoms of the stone wall and vanished. Neither He nor the wall were solids! Both were made up of energy "particles." Christ did not violate natural law, rather He knew how to manipulate it.

Life is a STATEMENT of positive (+) and negative (–) energy forces. Man gives them different names and classifies them in ways that are more easily understood. For example: good and evil, light and dark, right and wrong, left and right, YOUNG and OLD and so on. Regardless, we are referring to the phenomena we call ENERGY!

Reflections

The body's aura is a reflection of our inner state of health. We can measure our aura with a pendulum, vibration chain, or aurameter and it's easy to do but it does require the dowser to focus his/her thoughts. **(The Pendulum Kit, Vibrations, and Map Dowsing is a trilogy of books to teach you how to effectively dowse.)**

A pendulum is nothing but an antenna that sends and receives electrical energy. Our mind receives the information and "interprets" it. Measuring your body aura establishes a **reference point** that we can use to measure change or determine the effect a substance is likely to have on the body. The hitch involves learning to clear you mind and ask valid questions. What will be the immediate effect of this product? The long term effect? Can I expect a healing crisis? And so on.

Use a pendulum or aurameter to check food substances. Identify left-spin or right-spin apples, carrots, etc. Whatever is being measured is like a radio station that is sending out ENERGY signals. In this case, the pendulum is the receiving antenna. It can also be used to transmit signals.

We send and receive electrical signals when we sense with our intuition, which is a kind of sixth sense. We will discuss these Fourth Dimension concepts in a future chapter.

As you reverse the aging process, your aura expands and your physical VITALITY increases. When your aura has returned to the level it was before you began the descent into old age, you have returned to your *anabolic* PEAK. In the process of getting there, the passage of Time slows until it STOPS altogether. When this occurs, you have achieved agelessness and you are *Young Again!*

PREVIEW: *Our next chapter deals with energy and numbers. Did you know that big can mean small, and weak can mean strong?*

Do YOU Show Signs of PREMATURE Aging?

Is everything you do
a big effort?
•
Have you started to lose
your skin-tone?
Muscle-tone?
•
Do small things irritate you?
Are you forgetful?
Confused?
•
Have voices begun to fade?
•
Has your vision started to dim?
•
Do you wobble a little
when you walk?
•
Do you get out of breath
when you climb stairs?
•
How limber is your back?
•
Do your joints creak?
•
How well do you adjust
to cold and heat?
•
Ask yourself this important question:
Do I seem to be slipping and
not quite like myself anymore?
If the answer to this question is "Yes"
You had better do something about it.

START TODAY...
It's the first Day
of the Rest of
Your Life!

Hormone "Driven" Conditions

1. Asthma/emphysema
2. Excess fat/poor figure
3. Thyroid problems
4. Hearing loss
5. Menstrual PMS
6. Prostate troubles
7. Thinning hair
8. Gray hair
9. Cold body/feet/hands
10. Low energy/drive
11. Impotence
12. Bladder/yeast infections
13. Sagging cheeks/neck
14. Skin wrinkles
15. Joint pain/stiff body
16. Female/male cancers
17. Osteoporosis
18. Spontaneous abortion
19. Inability to conceive
20. Ovarian cysts
21. Loss of physical height
22. Knee/hip problems
23. Low sex drive
24. Painful sex (females)
25. Edema in legs/hands
26. Loss of muscle mass
27. Cellulite (hips/thighs)
28. Irregular menstruation
29. Painful periods
30. Fibroid tumors
31. Painful breasts
32. Endometriosis
33. Depression/gloominess
34. Body painful to touch
35. Nights sweats/hot flashes
36. Body painful when touched
37. Arthritis/rheumatism
38. Allergies/sinusitis
39. Fibrcystic breasts
40. Gas/bloating after meals
41. Low back pain w/period
42. Menstrual crankiness
43. "Out of control" feeling
44. Constipation/bowel prob's
45. Thinning vaginal walls
46. Dowager Hump/stooped over
47. Nerve diseases (Multiple sclerosis/lupis/fibromyalgia/myasthenia gravis)
48. Foggy Headedness/memory
49. Eyes (macular degeneration/retinitis/glaucoma)
50. Attention deficit/hyper activity in children

The common denominator to ALL of the above SIGNS and symptoms is "hormones." Follow the suggestions in this book and use racemized™ hormone precursors (Nugest II™ for women; Totally Male™ for men) and these problems moderate and "go away" (read *Our Stolen Future*).

Shower & Bath

Bathe in safe, biologically friendly water with a three stage oxidation/reduction filter that goes far BEYOND common shower/bath filters. A redox shower filter keeps your skin, and hair look healthier, protects your liver, and keeps you healthy. These units "full flow" and are VERY long lasting devices (so far they are in operation over 4 years without any problems). Best of all, they are inexpensive to purchase and easy to install (see page 383).

21

Carbon
12.01115

C

6

Avogadro's Number

*"The health of the people is the foundation
upon which their happiness depends."*
Benjamin Disraeli

It was a hot August day in 1975—the mercury had
reached 95⁰ Fahrenheit. Out of nowhere came what looked to
be a hippie carrying a clip board. He said, *"I'm from the City of
Madison and I'm checking all buildings for proper placement of
address numbers and you don't seem to have any!"*

"Do too!" I retorted.

*"Well, I looked and I didn't see any and I want to know
what you are going to do about it?"* he rattled as he flashed a
copy of the local business ordinance in my face —expecting to
cement his authority and intimidate me.

"Do too!" I said again, *"And I can prove it!"*

As we proceeded to the front of the building, I motioned
to Dale to follow my new found acquaintance and me.

There we stood, the three of us, facing a 4x4 'blank' post
that formed the door jam, and I said;

*"Dale, this fine gentlemen is here from city hall and he
says that we are not in compliance with city ordinances regarding having our building properly posted with our street address."*

"Right there!" I said. *"See! It says, 505 S. Main. What's
wrong with that?"*

The man looked at me and said with a strange look on

his face, *"There is no address there! It's blank!"*

"Hmmm!" I buzzed, as I turned to Dale and said,

"Dale, do you see 505 S. Main posted here on this post?"
Dale look at me and fired back, *"Sure do! Right there on the post!"*

With that, the man looked at me, then at Dale, shook his head—unsure WHO was crazy—gave up and just *walked away.*

Things Not What They Seem

Things are not always what they seem. Sometimes nothing can be something. Something small may actually be big. Something weak can be strong. We cannot always trust our eyes and sometimes logic does not make sense of conflicting circumstances or experiences. Sometimes we must follow our instincts or we lose our direction, go insane or just *walk away.*

The man in our story knew when to *walk away.* Science does not. Instead, science tries to make natural energy phenomena comply with its LAWS and in the process, it misses nature's lessons.

In homeopathy, something weak is actually strong. Something that should not exist actually does exist. Something that is nothing can be made into something.

These *apparent* "contradictions" cause science and medicine to ridicule instead of open mindedly inquirie. They demand *scientific* proof backed by a body of "literature" when they should be interested in RESULTS. They get caught up in theory and method and forget that their **double blind "studies"** and discoveries are **riddled** with contradictions.

Phenomena

Here are a few examples of electrical phenomena. Let's see if they shed light on the aging process.

Biodynamic agricultural practices *transmute* raw cow manure into a potent, yet *different* substance. It mixes a "pinch" of the *potentized* substance in twenty gallons of high energy water and *transfers* the energy from the new substance to the water through convoluted stirring procedures that elevate and concentrate energy. Applied to hundreds of acres of dead soil, the *energized* solution creates an energy *explosion* in the soil and life bursts forth. *Science cannot explain this phenomenon because it does not fit its model.* Science wants proof, when it should be interested in results.

Homeopathic medicine uses the principle of *dilution, succussion, resonance,* and *transference* to create energy substances (called remedies) that effectively treat dis-ease in the Fourth dimension energy level.

If you were to add one drop of black paint to one gallon of white paint, you would have a MIX of both colors. The black paint would, of course, be very diluted and would exert little influence on the white paint. The more white paint added, the less influence the black paint has. However, black paint is still there, albeit in smaller amounts each time more white paint is added. This is a "physical" dilution, and this example deals with the **physical** influence of the black paint on the white paint.

Homeopathic medicine is concerned with the influence of invisible energy fields upon each other, rather than the physical influence in our paint example above.

Potentiation

Remedies work on the basis of "similars." Homeopathy starts with a substance that has a *similar* vibrational frequency as the dis-ease energy field. The substance is then **diluted.** At each dilution, the remedy is pounded (succussed) so that it will absorb various frequencies (10x, 20x, 50x, 100x, 200x, etc.). This process is called **potentiation** and the remedy is referred to as a "potentized" solution.

The idea is to create multiple dilutions of different vibrational requencies that, when taken into the body, will "cancel" the dis-ease's frequency. A *potentized* remedy treats the patient at a Fourth Dimension energy level. In homeopathy, dilution and succussion add power, where in our paint example, the black paint became less influential each time we added more white paint.

Homeopathic dilutions are different than physical dilutions. They are electrical phenomena instead. Remedies are CONCENTRATED energy fields that are derived from the vibrational frequencies of "physical" substances. The more the remedy is *diluted* and the more it is *succussed,* the more energy the remedy contains and the more effective it becomes. Logic says a remedy should NOT exert any influence because the original substance is weaker—almost non existent. Energy transference through *succussion* pushes the "scientific" mind too far. Logic, however, is faulty here because it is based on Third Dimension physics instead of Fourth Dimension acceptance of natural energy phenomena. Homeopathy **manipulates** and **transfers** the electrical **signature** (frequency) of one substance to that of another, hence, *resonance* and *transferance.* In homeopathy, something that should not exist, DOES exist. *Science cannot explain this phenomenon because it does not fit* *its model, so they ridicule and express contempt!*

MORA is a spin off from homeopathy, just like the word processor is a spin off from the typewriter. MORA electronically duplicates energy *signatures* and electronically *transfers* them to the patient INSTEAD of using the actual *remedy* itself.

The *remedy* is placed into an scanning "well" where its frequency is *duplicated*—much like a computer scanner reads a typed page and converts it to codes and signals so the computer can work with it. The **duplicated** frequency is then *transferred* to the sick person's body and the desired healing takes place. The process can be repeated over and over without consuming the remedy itself. In homeopathy, something that doesn't appear to exist does exist and does work.

Whether or not a healing modality "fits" accepted medical theory, models, dogma, or the LAWS of science doesn't matter. The only thing that counts is results!

It's In The Numbers

Amedeo Avogadro (1776-1856) was the Italian chemist who saw big numbers in small things. He developed a method to estimate the number of atoms that exist in a substance by comparing it to a known reference substance whose number of atoms were known—at least in theory. This reference number is called Avogadro's number or [N], in his honor. Like Reams, Pauling, Caisse, Semmelweis, Carson and Gerson; Avogadro was ridiculed by his "peers" for his vision and the TRUTH to which he bore witness. *(Avogadro was a wizard, and wizards don't have peers. Often, they are surrounded by copy cats who want to put their name on someone else's discovery.)*

Avogadro's reference substance was 12 grams of carbon-12. The carbon atom is extremely small. The number of atoms in 12 grams of carbon-12 is *extremely* large! It is estimated to be approximately 602, 000, 000, 000, 000, 000, 000, 000 atoms!

In homeopathy the most powerful remedy is one where a substance has been **diluted** and **potentized** to a point that NONE of the original substance remains. Physically, a substance no longer exists once it goes *beyond* Avogadro's number or *twenty-two places*. Logic says that when the original substance ceases to exist—you have reached NOTHING! Yet, a homeopathic remedy has an enormous energy "footprint" for something that supposedly doesn't exist.

A 9x remedy equals 1 part per **billion** (ppb); at 30x it's beyond Avogadro's number with 30 zeros, and so on. Homeovitic remedies are **combinations** of 9x, 20x, 30x, 100x, 200x and provide broad spectrum bioresonance to meet a sick body's changing electromagnetic requirements.

Aging & Avogadro's Number

Avogadro's number is VERY important to the aging process. If the positive energy contained in a highly diluted homeopathic remedy can cause MASSIVE change for the "good," then the negative energy **transference** of a poor lifestyle, bad food, and dead water should be equally DISAS-TROUS to health and longevity. The same reasoning holds true for **negative** *actions* **and** *thoughts* that produce effects millions of times greater than the actual event. Like ripples that are created when a rock is tossed into a pond—each negative thought and action creates an exponential reverse effect on health that manifests with negative consequences.

Dr. Samuel Hahnemann

Samuel Hahnemann (1755-1843) is considered the father of "modern" homeopathic medicine. He was a brilliant German physician. The electrical phenomenon he discovered is known as the medicine of **"similars"** or homeopathy.

Let's compare homeopathic medicine to allopathic medicine and see if a contrast of the concepts involved can help us to understand the aging process.

Allopathic medicine (conventional medicine) attempts to treat dis-ease with drugs and chemicals that are *antagonistic* to the symptoms being treated. Drugs induce a **pathologic** reaction that stresses the system with an **"opposite cures opposite"** approach. A pathologic reaction is one where pathology (dis-ease) is "induced!" Drugs are prescribed based on the benefit : risk factor we discussed earlier. Pharmacology recognizes that all drugs carry **RISK** and all drugs **DAMAGE** the vital organs. Allopathic medicine thinks short term by attempting to *overpower* dis-ease with drugs that SHOCK the body into a condition of *subclinical* illness. Allopathic medicine uses powerful, *left-spin* energy fields (drugs) and shoots their negative energy bullets—magic bullets—into the vital organs, tissues and glands. Allopathy is the medicine of "opposites."

Homeopathy is the exact opposite of allopathy. It is the medicine of *similars* and it uses energy fields with *similar* vibrational frequencies to CANCEL offending disease energy frequencies. Homeopathy is "legitimate" holistic medicine that relies on **like cures like** reactions that don't offend the body.

How Homeopathy Was Discovered

Hahnemann was extremely disillusioned with conventional medicine. While treating patients for yellow fever, he discovered that if he gave a healthy person—who did NOT have Yellow Fever—a tea of cinchona bark—which was known to be effective against the fever—intermittent fevers would spontaneously develop as if the person actually had the condition.

Hahnemann further discovered that a *diluted* substance is more powerful than a *concentration* of the same substance. He further refined his new method of treatment and eventually included the physical, emotional, and mental disturbances of the patient. Remedies were developed by *trial and error* based on their ability to *produce* a response similar to the sick person. If a trial remedy produced a **similar** reaction, it was further tested on a sick person to see if it would produce a healing. *(Present day homeopathic remedies do NOT bring on actual illness or dis-ease in a healthy person. They can **only** cancel offending energy fields that **exist** in the patient and they produce NO side effects.)*

Hahnemann experienced much success applying his *remedies*, but noticed that their effectiveness increased in direct proportion to **dilution** and **potentiation**. In other words, the MORE he *diluted* and *succussed* the remedy, the more effective it was on the patient! His findings were in serious CONFLICT with the orthodox medical dogma of his day. The conflict continues to this day!

Dosage-related effects—as practiced in modern pharmacokinetics (the study of the dynamics of chemical drugs in the body) looks at the action of drugs on body metabolism with emphasis on the time required for absorption, duration of action, distribution in the system, and method of excretion from the body. These things determine the activity level—the saturation level of the drug in the blood and tissues.

Allopathic medicine is acutely aware of the problems brought on by drug usage. It walks a tight rope between short term benefits and short term damage to the vital organs. Long term damage is NOT an issue because it cannot be proven. Long term effects are given "new" names as dis-ases are "coined."

Hahnemann got wonderful results using remedies that *exceeded* Avogadro's number. His findings conflict with Newtonian physics which states, *"where there is an action, there is an equal and opposite reaction."* Newtonian LAWS are the basis of modern drug chemotherapy mentality. Pharmacology and medicine as we know them, rely on HUGE quantities of drugs to produce an **activity level** that can be MEASURED. Medical science uses a sledge hammer approach based on

opposites; homeopathy uses *gentle* remedies based on *similars.*
**Allopathic medicine loads you up with drugs to a
point BEYOND the ability of the kidneys, liver, lungs and
skin to excrete them.** The cells and tissues are forced to
accept drugs by default! Damage to the *bio-electric* body varies
with the *type* and *quantity* of drugs used and the *duration* of
time they remain in the system.

Homeopathy is the modality of **preference** for patients
and physicians who are interested in "healing." Remedies
interface the subtle energy level where dis-ease has its roots.

Homeopathy & Agriculture

Modern agriculture uses SUPER *potentized* poisons to
try to stop insects and weeds. Until recently, large amounts of
poison was called for. Now, VERY small amounts of poison is
mixed with huge amounts of water. The principles involved
here are homeopathic, but the effect is the exact opposite.

Agricultural and pharmaceutical companies have cloned
Hahnemann's principles of *dilution, potentiation,* and *transference* and have turned them to **EVIL** purposes. The *experts* are
at war with Earth and her inhabitants.

This is why I encourage the reader to plant a garden and
grow some food. Home grown food makes up for a plethora of
poor choices and mistakes in personal lifestyle. Live, fresh food
is a gift from God. It causes the cells to resonate "healthy!"

Think Small

Americans like to think big—big cars, big houses, big
meals, big surgeries, big bottles of pills! In fact, the "big"
syndrome is so prevalent that people complain and feel cheated
when they pay a lot of money for a small bottle of pills!

In health related matters, we must LEARN to think
small as in terms of the HUGE side effects created by the
negative energy substances we put into our bodies. We must
understand that the body is altered by both positive and
negative energy forces and that "tiny" amounts of a toxic
substance exerts massive **long term** effects on health.

We are surrounded with toxic chemicals everywhere.
The prudent person who thinks in terms of Avogadro's number
has the best chance of becoming *Young Again!*

PREVIEW: *Our next chapter looks at our multi-dimensional
body. It looks at the "terrain" of the bio-electric body and
reconsiders Pasteur's obsession with "bugs" and the Germ
Theory of Dis-ease.*

Medical Grade Ionized Water™

This is a special class of *therapeutic* water used in special Japanese clinics to treat everything from diabetes and nerve disorders, to cancer, heart/stroke problems.

In Japan, this special water is made with very expensive equipment designed for **clinical** settings. In the USA, where tap water pollutant levels are gross, the BEV™ process is used to create "conception point" water with a biologically friendly ORP potential and a "clear" memory.

Medical Grade Ionized Water™ is then made from BEV™ water and racemized™ liquid minerals. Raw tap water is **NEVER** used. It is vitally important the reader understand that pH (acidity/alkalinity) of this special water is **NOT** what does the healing. Rather, it is the "ORP" potential which is a measurement of electron availability for mitochondrial production of our energy molecule, ATP.

The benefits of high ORP water derive from a combination of purity, ORP, resistivity and pH. Highly *reduced* acid water and highly *oxidized* alkaline waters have pH values of 1.5-2.4 and 10.5-12 respecitively, and ORP potentials of -900 and +1200 respectively.

High ORP water is composed of tiny water molecules that easily cross cell membranes so the **reduced** water can deliver its load of electrons to the mitochondria for increased ATP production and tissue rejuvenation.

Dis-ease has its roots at the cellular level which is where high ORP Medical Grade Water™ does its job.

Oxidized water is used externally to heal infections, for douches, treatment of genital herpes and for beautiful skin. **Reduced** water is taken orally at the rate of 3/4 to 1 gallon a day, thereby pumping the body with energy while neutralizing acid wastes similarly to the way a *Far InfraRed™* sauna deacidifies the soft tissues WITHOUT the use of heat, steam or lights.

Medical grade Ionized Water™ is one of the biggest health advances in medical history, second only to recent work on racemized™ hormone precursors that are freeing women and men from their personal "prison"—meaning sick bodies whose receptor sites are "locked up.":

It took over 3 years to find the formula to make water in the home that far exceeds that being made in Japanese clinics. **Order the water video and water book to learn more.** BEV™ systems can be retrofitted, or you can set up to make Medical Grade Ionized Water™.

(See pages 107-110 and Source Page)

22

Change The Terrain

"No tree has branches foolish enough to fight among themselves."
"Watashi Wa"

The great French bacteriologist, Pasteur, said, *"Le microbe c'est tout! The microbe is everything!"* A contemporary, Claude Bernard retorted, *"Le microbe c'est rien. Le terrain c'est tout! The microbe, that's nothing! It is the terrain that's everything!"*

When we look *beyond* the microbe, we see that they are only participants in a grand scheme. Microbes take their cues from the body's "terrain." Microbes cannot prosper unless the *terrain* is conducive to their growth. **Microbes include bacteria, virus, fungi, yeast, and parasites.**

It is the *terrain* that must concern us. The terrain is the doorway through which dis-ease appears and old age expresses itself. Body terrain is multidimensional and goes BEYOND the Third Dimension world in which we live.

Multi-Dimensional Body

Humans are *multi-dimensional* creatures that experience life on mental, physical and spiritual planes—but life goes beyond these. We learn early to perceive and interpret our world in physical terms and geometric concepts we call length,

width and height—the First, Second, and Third Dimensions,.
But there are other dimensions—higher dimensions—that we
experience from time to time like intuition, telepathy, dowsing,
and maybe even the ability to see holes in another person's
aura—things that belong to the 4th dimension and beyond.

Aging & The Fourth Dimension

These higher dimensions are *invisible* for all but a few.
Aging occurs in higher realms before it is experienced in our
Third Dimension world—before it is seen in the mirror. Vitality
and health are controlled by the electrical energy forces of the
Fourth Dimension. Anything that impacts the Fourth Dimension electric body affects the Third Dimension physical body
and visa-versa.

**Health and dis-ease are expressions of the "energy"
tug-of-war constantly going on in the *invisible* world of the
Fourth Dimension.**

When we die, the tug-of-war is over. The negative
energy forces won! Simultaneous with death, vital force (spirit)
leaves the body. We *"give up the ghost!"* The spirit returns from
whence it came. It returns to a *higher* energy level, perhaps the
Fourth Dimension. Maybe higher. No one knows for sure. Call
it heaven, hell, hereafter. Suit yourself.

The Fourth Dimension body goes by different names
like—**subtle energy** body, **soul, astral** body, **spirit, invisible**
body, **bio-electric** body, **etheric** body, **Chi, Qi, Prana.** They all
refer to the same thing, depending on your belief system.

Our Fourth Dimension existence is generally invisible,
but it is there nonetheless. Some folks try to deny its existence,
but doing so does NOT change the reality of it or alter its
influence on our earthly journey.

When we attempt to heal the physical body, but ignore
the spirit body, healing is marginal. If we allow the electric body
to become old, the physical body follows suit. If we experience
death in the physical realm, but maintain our hold on our
spirit, we are NOT really dead and we return to our physical
world with tales of *after death* experiences. If death occurs in
the Fourth Dimension realm—where our spirit body resides—
we experience physical death and life on Earth ceases.

Vantage Point

**The electric body should be viewed as an *extension*
of the physical body, and the physical body as the *expression* of the electric body. The multi-dimensional body
interfaces dis-ease and health, life and death.**

Try to become comfortable with the above concepts. Understanding them will help us to understand our earthly dilemma. (Read *The Holographic Universe*)

Long before dis-ease manifests itself in the physical realm, the electric body is undergoing *vibrational* changes that set the course for the physical recognition of illness. This is what Bernard meant when he said, *"The terrain is everything!"*

Before we can learn how to *manipulate* the energy forces that interface the physical AND electric body terrains, we must adopt a **vibrational** view of health and dis-ease.

In order to understand the forces of aging, one must understand the idea of an "invisible" world of *antagonistic* energy fields. We feel the influence of these invisible forces when they appear in our physical, *visible* world in the form of SIGNS confirmed by the doctor's diagnosis.

The *invisible* world is poorly understood. Yet, this is the arena where the war for health and dis-ease is fought. We are concerned with the terrain of BOTH worlds—the *visible* and the *invisible*—and the energy force fields that influence and govern them. Examples of these energy fields are bio-junk food, low ORP water, negative thoughts and words, drugs, and bad living habits and their effects.

Food Plants & Insects

Chinese Taoism teaches that humans are a reflection of the universe and that **all life** is of the spirit of the creator. Man has much in common with plants and insects. They can help us to better understand our *dual* existence because they too have a *dual* existence.

Plants have many functions. Two functions are the production of food energy and the infusion of solar energy into the soil. In the process of synthesizing food molecules, plants take CARBON from the atmosphere and *infuse* it into Mother Earth's dermal *skin* layer—the soil through their roots.

The plant is the mediator of solar energy. Plants capture it and use it to form complex organic food molecules. Organic food molecules contain carbon, oxygen, nitrogen, hydrogen, sulphur, and other "ionic" minerals. These molecules are biologically active and they participate in anabolic activities we call *growth and repair.*

The body needs sulphur and carbon in sulfhydryl form. When sulfonyls are present in sufficient quantity, the body automatically dissolves scar tissue and restores elasticity to unhealthy tissues. SOC™ capsules supply massive amounts of sulfonyls so healing can occur.

Mediators

As mediators of energy, plants receive solar and cosmic energy and convert them into new and different energy forms—like food and wood. **Energy is never lost, it merely changes form!**

Plants are live ANTENNAS. They receive energy constantly—by day from the Sun and by night from the cosmos. By day, plants convert solar energy into hydrocarbon sugars (*hydro*-water. *carbon*-atomic element #12.) with the help of mineral ions and enzymes supplied by the soil bacteria. At night, plants use the sugar molecules and earth minerals for growth. The "dew point" is the **peak** of the plant feeding period when sufficient sugar is burned and heat is given off to cause the formation and condensation of sweet "dew."

Early Viking adventurers who landed in New England reported tasting early morning "sweet" dew from the blades of grass.

Plants CANNOT create by themselves. They need the trillions of unpaid workers in the soil—the microbes—to perform the miracle of **photosynthesis** which is the **same** as metabolism in humans. All higher life forms—be they plant, animal or man—require help from the microbes for their continued existence.

The microbes live on cosmic energy as well. They consume the carbon sugars that plants manufacture. Their roots eat the energy released in the breaking of covalent bonds when carbon based cellulose (carbonaceous matter, like leaves, stems, manure, etc.) is broken down in the soil.

It is the microbes that are responsible for breaking the bonds that hold earth minerals and rocks together. Plants and animals live on that energy and so do humans.

Plants submit their order for nutrient energy at the *root level*. The bacteria receive and fill the order IF the soil is in a POSITIVE energy state. Unfulfilled orders **stress** the plant and cause an energy shift to the left. Stress related changes in the plant's "terrain" lower its vibrational frequency which causes the plant to TRANSMIT negative energy signals to nature's garbage crew—the insects and viruses.

The health minded person must learn to MANAGE "stress" if he or she expects to enjoy good health and endless vitality. Techniques like yoga, deep breathing, prayer, Qi Gong, Tai Chi, walking barefoot in sand or on grass, sleeping under the stars, exercise, laughing, meditation, positive thoughts, etc.—ALL neutralize stress.

NEVER forget, *stress* seeks an outlet, just as electricity seeks ground. Be alert and PROVIDE a safe outlet for it to dissipate. When you fail to dissipate stress energy, it will take physical form. Neck and spine problems are good examples.

The Carbon Connection

The body is built of proteins. **Sulfonyls** are amino acid proteins that contain sulphur and carbon in their structure. These are organic molecules by definition because they contain carbon. Carbon is number 12 on the chart of atomic elements.

Carbon is UNIQUE because it can *bond* with so many different elements and *participate* in millions of different reactions—all of them *unique* unto themselves. It is this characteristic that allows toxic **organic** poisons to *hitch* a ride on the carbon atom. The R-group (stands for reactive group, usually desiganted —R on a molecular diagram) and its location on a carbon molecule determines whether something is DDT, malathion, or dioxin. All are **organic** poisons!

Toxic organic chemicals are POTENT left-spin substances. When used on plants, the health of the plant suffers greatly. Animals and humans that eat poisoned food suffer too. In only a few decades, man-made organic poisons have spoiled life on Earth. Poisons rate high on science's bogus agenda (which is a front for the "yellow fringe flag" interestes of the "corporate" state)—an agenda which says *"cheap food at politically popular prices is desirable."* **There is an implied threat in the words, *"Cheap food is better than no food."***

Plants are more than green things. They are living miracles. The *experts* tell us plants only need NPK (nitrogen, phosphorous and potassium) to produce food that will sustain life. This is NOT true! It is a covert effort to mislead and confuse while keeping the "misery" line at the clinics full.

Agricultural practices control nations. A gut full of poisoned, empty calories CANNOT produce or maintain a healthy human being or a happy nation. When we eat left-spin food, violent crime soars. Violent people suffer from toxic excesses, hormonal imbalances and slowdown of the vital organs. Eventually, these changes are confirmed upon post mortem examination. **Too soon old, too late smart is a sorry excuse for a premature death.**

Explosions

Carey Reams did most of his life's work in the agricultural arena. He believed that plants and animals live on the energy released from the breaking of mineral bonds. He referred to these reactions as "explosions!"

Explosions occur when WATER reacts with soil—especially rain water! Rain greatly accelerates plant growth—grass leaps; the corn jumps! Rain water is biologically active water. It reacts with the soil minerals and acids and releases energy so plants can grow. **High ORP Medical Grade Ionized Water**™ **also provides lots of electrons for growth and healing.**

The roots of plants secrete carbonic acid (carbon + hydrogen) which dissolves and frees mineral ions from rock with the help of water. The bacteria absorb the minerals into their bodies, digest them, and then hold them in solution or secrete them mixed with sugars as a kind of glue-like substance. It is this sugary secretion that gives organic soil its crumbly texture and causes it to flocculate and hold together.

Carbon-rich soil is **young** soil, **active** soil, that is **anabolic** in nature. It's *alive* because it is high in what Leonard Ridzon calls "biogenic carbon" in his book *the Carbon Connection.* Soil that is rich in biogenic carbon will NOT leach. It holds minerals and nutrients in **colloidal** form [charged (+) (–) ions] for the plants and earthworms. Ionic mineral ions are held in colloidal form until the plant places an order for them. If the plant orders ions that are *different* than what is on hand, the bacteria use the *alchemy/transmutation* process we described earlier to **transmute** them into the element(s) the plants needs. This process can be best described as "cold" fusion.

Carbon acts as a bridge in cold fusion reactions—be it in the soil or in the gut and liver of man or animal. Carbon underwrites health and aging. It is the basis of all life.

Transmitters & Receivers

Plants grown as nature intended have a healthy aura which radiates "healthy" energy signals. Plants grown with commercial fertilizers and poison sprays radiate signals in the *"I'm sick, Come and eat me!"* **band.**

Phil Callahan discovered how insects use their antenna to pick up these distress signals and navigate by them—like an enemy war plane homing in on the target. Insects eat **sick** plants, but they do NOT wage war. The garden and fields are not a war zone. Insects comply with nature's mandate to remove weak organisms from the Earth.

In the human arena, acid waste buildup stresses the bio-electric body and weakens vital organ function. Microbes detect stress in humans. They operate like insects by tuning into our *"I'm sick, come and do away with me!"* **signals.**

Insects have antenna on their heads and cilia (tiny hair like projections) on their body. Both structures are tuned to vibrate in the "sick" band—where stressed crops broadcast their signals.

Insects know exactly which plants represent a meal and which ones do not. Different insects are tuned to different frequencies. You won't find Colorado Potato Beetles eating sweet corn. Nature tunes each insect's antenna to its own *"I'm sick, come and eat me!"* frequency. Signals are transmitted in the near and **far infrared** spectrum of light which are neither audible nor visible to man.

White light contains all visible color frequencies and is part of our Third dimension experience and world. Light is electrical in nature which means anything electrical in nature is related to light. Color therapy, cold laser therapy, and ultrasound are applications and variations of **therapeutic** light frequencies that stimulate healing. Microwaves and radar are also light, but they are anti-life energy frequencies. **Disease belongs to the world of invisible energy frequencies.**

When a plant is sick and stressed, you will see the insects gorging themselves. When farmers have to spray insecticides to produce a crop, you can bet the food crop is a reverse homeopathic and that it will *sicken* whatever eats it. This can be measured with a pendulum, vibration chain, or brix meter..

Any crop that requires poisons to keep the insects at bay is sick food. Eat it and absorb its freak energy frequencies and you, too, will become sick.

Organic Poisons

Organic poisons are **potent** negative energy fields. They work like a homeopathic remedy, only in REVERSE and their effect on the body of man or animal is beyond instant comprehension.

Organic poisons are a band-aid approach to food production. Their use is NO different than medical science's insistence on mass immunization of the population. Healthy crops don't require poisons for their production. Healthy people don't need—and should NOT have—immunizations.

Medical Grade Ionized Water™ safely replaces BOTH immunizations and insecticides. If you would like to see documented PROOF, order the water video (see Source Page).

The Refractometer & The Terrain

If sick plants attract predatory insects, viruses, and molds, can we assume that healthy plants repel them? The answer is a big YES! The same rules apply to the bio-electric body. A positive energy **terrain** repels dis-ease, but negative energy attracts more of the same UNLESS a concerted effort is made to break the cycle and take control over the body terrain.

Dr. Carey Reams discovered a unique way to determine the health and nourishment level of food plants. **He discovered that healthy plants have a high level of dissolved mineral solids in their juices.** He determined this with a refractometer, which is a simple, hand held device that refracts light and measures the *brix* level of natural sucrose sugars in plant juice.

The higher the "brix" level (brix is a unit of measure—like a foot or a pound), the higher the mineral content of the juices. The higher the level of sugar and minerals, the healthier the plant and the more the food satisfies you. *(Do you remember the story earlier in chapter nine about satiety and Dr. Reams' dinner party for his neighbors?)*

When sugar levels are high, plants do NOT radiate negative energy in the *"I'm sick, come and eat me!"* band. Moreover, if an occasional insect stops by to have a bite, it promptly dies because high sugar levels—which the insect is not equipped to handle—quickly turn to alcohol in the bug's system and it dies! **Instant and fatal intoxication!**

Alcohol is a toxin (POISON) to living systems. Yet, when sick, it is often helpful to take a hot bath containing 2 C. of Epsom salt, 1 qt. of 3% hydrogen peroxide and a pulverized fresh ginger root, followed by a shot of whiskey before going to bed. The alcohol kills multiplying organisms and SHOCKS the system. The alcohol serves as a drug and the effect is palliative, but it often brings relief. A better solution is colon therapy, followed by the above bath water mix and a shot of Harmonic Silver Water or Medical Grade (acid) Ionized Water™.

Plants grown in highly mineralized high carbon soil that is loaded with microbes will have high brix readings—brix levels are a "marker" of the level of dissolved minerals in the plant's juices. The higher the brix readings, the MORE nutritious the food and the greater is its "life force." Protein level is another way of gauging life force, but this method fails to account for the footprint and signature (SPIN) of the proteins, fats or carbohydrates—as with soy and canola.

The refractometer scale is 0-32 brix, '0' is the bottom and 32 the top of the scale. **The lower the number, the more insect infestation and plant dis-ease that will be seen.** In the case of sweet corn, nature's garbage crew back-off at 18 brix and will cease to be a problem above 24 brix. The insects will not be seen at maximum brix levels. High brix means NO disease and food that is extremely nourishing for man and animal. Crops raised by conventional means will be **low brix** and insect infested. The "experts" and the chemical companies—and their yellow fringe flag interests—don't like the simplicity of this.

99% of the crops grown in the USA are low brix, low vitality food that spoils easily. Low vitality food breeds violence in children and adults. **This is the perfect food for perpetuating a militaristic society that will do as it is told by the forces behind the yellow fringe flag.** Sick food, weak minds, and violence are part of our obsession with sports. Rome took a similar path—that is, AFTER desecrating its flag and flag poles with an "adornment" similar to the yellow fringe, ball, eagle and/or spear that has imposed foreign state "corporate jurisdiction over Citizens of all countries worldwide today.

"In a nation whose legions once commanded the known world, the people cry but for two things; bread and more games."   Pliny

Civilizations deteriorate because nature's dietary laws are ignored with reckless abandon. Poor nutrition manifests itself in a plethora of ways. Populations under nutritional stress are weak. Sick food and water spawns social EXCESS, not the other way around. Birth defects are also part of the "terrain" story. Birth defects are linked to poisoned food and water. Pregnant women labor under severe liver stress. These problems are easy to offset with racemized™ hormone precursors like Nugestrine II™ and Totally Male™.

Eat Your Vaccinations, Dear!

Inferior food with a short shelf life is behind the drive to *irradiate* America's food supply. Ditto for the genetic manipulation of food crops. Did you know that **madmen** scientists have begun gene splicing Hepatitis B and dozens of other disease organisms into fruit and vegetable DNA.

If historical myth has any substance, I would remind the reader that Atlantis and its people were destroyed for genetic cruelties and cross breeding of life forms. Genesis says, *"Kind* (is supposed to) *beget kind in the order of things."*

I <u>predict</u> that people who eat genetically manipulated food will sicken faster, suffer miserably, and die early. Furthermore, their offspring will experience gross pathologies with no hope of cure. Darwin's "survival of the fittest" will take on new meaning (see page 369).

We are breaking the rules when we cross species lines. Like with like. Kind begets kind. Cross breeding of species produces offspring whose vibrational *signatures* and DNA are "freak" beyond comprehension.

We are making another horrible mistake by classifying animal fats and liquid oils together just because they have similar characteristics. The difference between them is more than just a matter of liquid, solid, saturated, unsaturated, short chain, long chain fatty acids, omega this and that, etc.

Vegetarians and meat eaters alike MUST strive for MORE balance in their diets or their body's will break down. Real, homegrown food offsets dietary mistakes. **For those who can't grow their own food, I highly recommend the use of Klammath algae, Biogenic™ predigested liver, Harmonic™ pollen and Taoist™ food herbs (see Source Page).**

Parenteral Nutrition

The food we eat is metabolized in to glucose. Glucose fuels the electron transport chain in cellular mitochondria which produce the ATP energy molecule that keeps us alive. Glucose is stored in the liver and muscles: glucose is called glycogen. We need glucose, but we cannot live on it alone.

*It is now standard medical procedure to add a few minerals and vitamins to glucose solutions if a person is on any form of parenteral nutrition in the hospital for more than a few days. Parenteral nutrition is **any** form of nutrition administered other than by way of the mouth. For example, intravenous feeding or the use of a feed tube inserted directly into the small intestine.*

Parenteral nutrition is a band-aid measure and a crummy way to keep someone alive. It's a **glimpse of life to come** for those who think they can eat bio-junk food and soft drinks, consume toxic water and IGNORE nature's laws!

The Terrain Of Weeds

Weeds are a yardstick of soil fertility. They tell a story AND their presence holds meaning in the scheme of things. For sure, weeds don't have to be a curse to the farmer or gardener.

The popular definition of a weed is "something growing out of place." This definition is based on ignorance. Weeds grow where they choose because they have a job to do. Their job is to *absorb* negative energy from both the soil and the atmosphere for the benefit of all life. Their job is to *rejuvenate* the soil. **Weeds—like bacteria and viruses—only grow where the "TERRAIN" is to their liking!**

We bought a home with a 1/4 acre garden space that was infested with quack grass. The neighbors laughed when we told them we would be rid of the quack grass and have a nice garden the following year. They stopped laughing when we gave them beautiful vegetables. All we did was change the soil TERRAIN—and no more quack grass!

Quack grass grows on soil is low organic matter soil with a high in pH, an unbalanced decay system, and an excess of aluminum. The solution was simple. We "hand" dug, shook and piled the quack grass. We then built four or five compost piles around the garden site using organic matter of all types —including quack grass, leaves, fresh manure, grass clippings— plus chicken manure for a starter, granite dust, gypsum, soft rock phosphate, and red wigglers (worms). We turned the piles biweekly. After two months, we spread the finished compost and dug it into the top four inches of soil.

After this process, we could NOT get quack grass to grow. The reason? We changed the TERRAIN of the soil. We helped Mother Earth energize her skin. Every weed has a place and a time. If you change the environment, that weed will cease to be a problem because you have altered the terrain. Some weeds grow where food plants cannot grow. Some weeds also grow along side food crops. Their job is to maintain energy balance.

I remember a story an acquaintance of mine told me about how the pioneers abused the soil as they came west. They found virgin soils high in life giving energy and nutrients. They would move on as soon as the soil had "burned itself out." Later, after the deserted farm had sat for eight or ten years, Tex's father would come along and buy the farm up for next to nothing and presto, the soil produced! Tex's father understood that weeds play a very important part in life on this planet. Weeds ONLY proliferate when the *terrain* dictates their presence. **Weeds, insects, bacteria and viruses are our friends. Understand them and you will enjoy a better life.**

The food supply is sick because the soil is sick. We should not be surprised that man, who eats sick food and drinks sick water is also sick!

Hybrid Food

The advent of the hybrid seed has particular significance for the health minded person. The hybrid was heralded as a wonderful thing. Bigger crops, sweeter corn, better germination, and more control at harvest. Some of these things are true, but there are serious trade-offs—like unbalanced enzymes and vitamins, freak proteins, and poor mineral uptake.

It should be noted that hybrid crops better withstand hard salt fertilizers and poisons used to force food crops to produce on sick soils.

Hybrid seeds came into "fashion" because seed companies can *patent* them. The farmer—ever dependent on bank loans—was *persuaded and often strong armed*, to use these new seeds. **The ag schools and government "experts" said, "Hybrids are the wave of the future!" And a poor**

future it has turned out to be. In the words of one farmer, *"We traded open-pollinated seed left over from the past harvest— which was a FREE gift from God—for these damnable hybrids that we have to buy every year!"* Powerful interests took control of people's food supply as we exchanged high vitality food produced on healthy soils, for empty calories and poisoned crops grown on sick soils. **The Earth and her inhabitants are now paying the price.**

Native Wisdom

We live in a world beset with conflict. The four corners of the square are at odds with each other. Philosophy, science, law and religion have lost their moorings. The people gyrate from pole to pole—confused, mad, frustrated, depressed, violent—at odds with their world and themselves. They need wisdom and guidance.

My friend comes from the Lakota nation of American indians. His native name is *Watashi Wa* which translates *"I am here!"* I am glad he is.

Watashi Wa offered some Lakota wisdom that health-minded people need to understand and incorporate into their lives. ***"No tree has branches that fight among themselves."***

We cannot enjoy good health and longevity when we are at odds with the world and ourselves. We cannot fulfill our destinies when we eat food and drink water that is *anti-life*.

Hybrid Inferiority

When we eat food grown from hybrid seeds we are eating food that is genetically weak. Hybrids do not reproduce true to their own kind. They *defy* the ultimate test of viability for any living thing: offspring that duplicate the parents.

Hybrid seeds are the freak offspring of controlled breeding techniques. They are *inbred* and they are inferior. Their energy spin is LEFT! **Hybrid food is INFERIOR food.**

Food crops grown from hybrid seed play into the hands of the yellow fringe flag "devils" who CONTROL commodity prices and markets—and the food supply of the whole world.

Remember these points when *experts* in the "media" **hype** the wonders of genetically engineered crops and irradiated food. Behind the rhetoric, you will find sick food and GROSS human suffering.

Food is a gift from God. It was NOT meant to be a plaything. Eat good food and drink high ORP biologically friendly water. Do these things and you will enjoy health and vitality as you become *Young Again!*

PREVIEW: *Our next chapter is about "OBESITY." Learn the "real" reason for obesity. Whether you are thin or not, the chapter contains VALUABLE information that you will need to understand the remainder of this book.*

Magnetic Health

Depolarization of body tissues occurs when people are exposed to extraneous microwave radiation and chemical pollutants everywhere present in the world we live in.

Computer usage is the greatest source of ionizing radiation. Microwave cellular phone transmitters and dishes also account for MASSIVE amounts of ELF (extreme low frequency) energy that corrupts cellular balance.

Super Magnets™ "kindle" cellular activity by stimulating mitochondrial activity and the production of ATP—the body's energy molecule—used to "heal" sick bodies and carry on daily metabolic activity. Super magnets also **BOOST immune activity**—a key ingredient in health. They are helpful for **carpel tunnel** syndrome, **sleep** irregularities, and HELP in **emergencies** like a bad fall, a mashed finger, broken bones, head injuries, etc. by slowing histamine response and accelerating blood and lymph flow.

There are ONLY a few magnetic products that are practicable for people to incorporate into their lives. The **Super Magnet**™ **pendant** is suspended from the neck directly over the thymus area (upper chest) and is used to neutralize energy radiation and boost immune activity. A **medical grade** mattress pad "REpolarizes" body tissues. **Shoe inserts** stimulate reflex points in the feet.

Medical grade mattress pads MUST possess six characteristics to be of any benefit. They are: the # of magnets, gauss rating, placement, thickness, surface area and field direction. **Biogenic**™ **Super Matress Pads are constructed to meet ALL six requirements.**

Modern medicine classifies magnetics as *witchcraft*, but users of Biogenic™ products will tell you they work. (See diagram on page 293.)

Source Information Packet
For more information call (800) 659-1882 or (509) 465-4154 or write: Young Again! P.O. Box 1240 Mead Washington 99021-1240 USA, fax (509) 466-8103.

Colon Therapy

Colon therapy speeds the removal of waste and accelerates detoxification of body tissues and fluids. The process is about as basic as you can get to turning around a sick, polluted body terrain.

The colon book contains forty colored pictures of body waste and colon related conditions. It shows you how to set up and perform your own colonics at home, in the privacy of your own home for little cost.

Many people are *squeamish* on this subject, but those who make the effort "see" their lives transformed. Simultaneous use of Parasite Purge™ and the liver and tissue flush programs produces wonderful results.

Order *"The Tissue Cleansing Book "*

Parasites In "YOUR" Body

Parasites are a monumental problem, but they are **NOT** the enemy! Rather, they merely reflect loss of control over the body's "terrain"—and I can assure you that your are **loaded** with parasites. How do I know? Because every time food or water enters your mouth, parasite eggs and adults come along for the ride.

"IF" your digestive system is working at peak capacity—and very few are—the *peptide bonds* on the proteins that form the parasites are broken and the parasites and their eggs are "digested."

To solve the problem of INCOMING parasites and their eggs, Yucca Blend™, DiSorb Aid™ and race-mized™ hydrogen chloride are taken with each meal. This combination is so powerful that travelers to India and Mexico swear by it! No sickness. No diarrhea.

Parasite Purge™ drives parasites from the brain, heart, lungs, spleen, and other "vital" organs. Intestional parasites are also driven out of the body. It takes 90 days to "clear" your vital organs of parasites. Parasite Purge™ goes far **beyond** common parasite products because it is a racemized™ formulation. Try some.

23

Fat Falstaff

Shakespeare's Prince Hall to grossly overweight Falstaff:

"Leave gormandizing; Know the grave doth gape?
For thee thrice wider than four other men!"
Shakespeare

Obesity is the **curse** of the industrialized world! We eat the wrong things instead of the right things. We live to eat, when we should eat to live. We eat much when we could eat little. We dig our grave with our teeth.

Obesity is an EFFECT. It has little to do with inheritance and everything to do with incorrect living habits. We are concerned with the causes of obesity and its influence on the aging process.

Obesity is dis-ease. It is a forerunner of more serious conditions! Lifestyles that precipitate obesity involve *under activity* (not enough body movement) and *over activity* in the vital organs. Metabolic over-activity stresses the vital organs, causing them to exhaust themselves, while lack of movement weakens the connective tissues and leads to degeneration.

Obesity has its own rules—like cancer. Fat bodies respond *differently* once they are fat. Traditional dietary approachs to obesity don't work well. **I prefer liver flushing, ETVC, racemized™ hormone precursors, SUPER foods, exercise, rebounding, and biologically friendly water.**

Obesity is confirmation of metabolic "slow down" and loss of vitality in the body "terrain." Obesity is the most obvious SIGN of aging. It is **not** something that just happens to people— it is a self-imposed condition brought on by ignorance, lack of self-love, and poor choices. **Obesity is maintained through ignorance, reliance on conventional beliefs, and "experts" who perpetuate the problem.**

Factors That Contribute To Obesity

Excess food intake contributes to obesity, but hormonal imbalance, incomplete digestion, and bio-junk food are worse. Bio-junk food is the equivalent of "sabotage." Hormonal imbalance slows the system and poor digestion provides a steady flow of putrified food and poisonous byproducts.

As body fat increases, vitality and organ function slow. Fat does not *cause* the body to slow down, but it is a confirmation that slowdown is in progress. Obesity gives way to diabetes, hypertension, gout, poor self-image, frustration and a wardrobe full of unusable clothes.

As waste levels increase, the aura dims. The aura can be compared to the defense shields on the Star Ship *Enterprise*. A *vibrant* aura works like a defense shield—nothing can penetrate it. If it is weak, dis-ease manifests.

A fat body has LIMITED electrical capacity which is reflected in low energy and drive. As body fat increases, the fat person's body slows down even more. Hence, the fat person gets fatter and the path to a youthful existence becomes ever more difficult and further out of reach.

Obesity is a vicious cycle. Sluggish blood and lymph flow slows cellular respiration (mitochondrial production of ATP) and movement of waste to the liver where bile wastes are carried to the intestines and eventually to the toilet.

The obese person often fails to understand that because they are obese, they will have to go the extra mile to get their health back. Colon therapy is STRONGLY recommended.

Detoxification of the fat person's body produces **many** healing crises. Healing crises occur when toxic waste energy fields are released into the **blood, lymph,** and **intestines**. These wastes must be quickly flushed from the system or headaches, gas, cold sweats, dizziness, etc., often result. Hormone therapy and liver purges are HIGHLY recommended with colon therapy. The former "turns on" the body, while the latter moves the waste. **This combination works!**

The liver dumps its bile wastes just 3 inches below the stomach's outlet—or about twenty feet UP from the anus. If waste mucoid and fecal matter impedes the flow of bile from the

body, healing crises occur as these poisons are "reabsorbed."
Wastes must LEAVE the body for healing to occur.

As toxic waste exits the fat person's body, a roller
coaster effect is often encountered because all of the body
systems that have been on hold or barely functioning must
come to life quickly. ETVC™ raises energy and burns fat,
PAC™ buffer the waste, Yucca Herbal Blend™ keeps the waste
in solution and gets it to the liver, Colon Prep Formula™ moves
massive amounts of old fecal matter and VitaLight™ tablets
supply needed mineral energy. The SUPER foods provide super
nutrition and DiSorb Aid™ and R/HCl™ take care of digestion.

Eat Less • Live Longer

Little food is required to maintain good health if high
vitality foods are consumed in place of the usual low vitality
diet. The SUPER foods are: Harmonic™ pollen, Klammath™
algae, and Biogenic™ predigested organic liver, Taoist Rice
Polish™, Harmonic Synergy™ and Taoist™ Five Elements and
High Performance. These foods, along with fresh fruit comprise
my breakfast. A salad or fresh vegetables are often my dinner
along with the above. People who follow my regimen NEVER
hurt for energy and feel fantastic—and the fat disappears!

Avoid over cooked food. Eat one third of your food RAW!
Foods like kale, collards, beets, apples, carrots, and fruit are
excellent choices.

It has been demonstrated over and over again that
animals live longer when their food intake is reduced to
approximately 75% of their optimum intake level. In order to be
able to reduce your food intake and not feel hungry, your must
meet your body's nutrient needs.

It is impossible to reduce body fat and restore balance
by reduction of food intake alone. All of the things I have
mentioned thus far should be included in your program.

Try to grow some food. NOTHING can equal fresh, "live"
food. A small garden, some planter beds, some large pots or
plastic 5 gallon buckets on the patio or deck can produce a lot
of good food.

FAT MUST be understood in terms of energy management and in terms of what, when, and how much we eat.
Nutritious food and body friendly water are steps that help
here. Hormone balancing and liver stone purges finish the job.

Sabotage & Body Instinct

Bio-junk food and unfriendly water stand in the way of
a healthy lifestyle. They short circuit fat burning enzymes and

shut-down fat burning pathways and block mitochondrial oxidation. Once the body slows, it has difficulty getting going again. A fat body *resists* movement!

Body fat contains massive amounts of toxic waste. But before the body will burn its fat, it MUST be assured that the wastes left behind will be flushed from the system.

The body has *innate intelligence.* It is intuitively smart. It knows what to do to keep itself alive—like placing toxic wastes OUT and AWAY FROM the vital organs. The body can withstand horrendous abuse—and survive—but it can't do it forever. Eventually, we overload the system and we die.

Turning on the body's fat burning pathways requires MASSIVE amounts of energy. The body cannot heal and rejuvenate without energy any more than you can get across town in your car without gasoline in your tank.

YET, in a fat body even the most nutritious food can become a *liability.* Anaerobic, left-spin environments like those found in a fat body convert positive energy to fat. **Fat bodies are sick bodies and sick bodies REJECT the very nutrients they need.** Sometimes the body REBELS and become sicker in the presence of nourishing food unless all body tissues are detoxified and the wastes are moved OUT of the system symultaneously.

It's not that the fat body has forgotten how to handle nourishing food. It's that it instinctively "knows" that food in the face of accumulated waste only makes matters worse. The body's inability to process and metabolize right-spin nutrient energy is linked to EXCESSES in the system.

Obesity and constipation always go hand in hand. Just because a person has regular bowel movements doesn't mean that their colon is fine. Obesity is often accompanied by diverticulitis, colitis, and irritable bowel syndrome.

Kindling Wood & Fat

Once liver purging is under way, the body will accept high quality proteins, **complex** carbohydrates, and fresh green leafy vegetables. Complex carbohydrates are "long-burn" food molecules—like those in multi grain cereals and whole grain breads made with *blackstrap* molasses.

Complex carbohydrates can sustain a person for four to six hours. Greens are extremely nourishing and provide the very best type of bulk for a healthy bowel. They are loaded with chlorophyll—the plant's "blood!" Comfrey leaves are very delicious when lightly steamed and dressed with a little olive oil and apple cider vinegar. Kale and collard greens are also excellent choices. Fresh, grated beets on a salad are great too.

People confuse complex carbohydrates with worthless starches and sugars found in processed foods. Complex carbohydrates do not make people fat. In fact, the body needs them to oxidize fat. **Complex carbohydrates are to fat burning what kindling wood is to a wood fire.**

In other words, the body can't "burn" fat unless you have something to kindle it and keep it going. Body fat is the **LAST** energy source the body will use to fuel its energy needs because fat is synchronized energy. The body draws on muscle tissue protein BEFORE it will draw on body fat reserves. The body is reluctant to release fat bound toxicity unless it knows that the waste can be safely moved OUT of the system. That is the purpose of the liver purge. This program provides the foundation that is needed for the body to clean itself and get the mitochondrial power generators going in the cells.

Oxidation Of Fat

Aerobic exercise activates fat-burning enzymes. Exercise should demand 60—80% of the maximum heart rate (MHR) for a minimum of twelve minutes causing the **liver** to produce enzymes that oxidize small amounts of fat during exercise and LARGE amounts throughout the day.

The more exercise you do, the more fat you will burn, NOT because exercise burns fat (it only burns a little), but because exercise increases enzyme and metabolic activity. Exercise stimulates metabolic activity as well as increases the rate of circulation of body fluids (blood and lymph).

Exercise should NEVER be used to offset poor choices in food, water, and lifestyle. Obesity ceases to be a problem when people adhere to a healthy lifestyle. For the fat person, that means you MUST cooperate if you want your life back.

Basal Metabolism

Basal metabolism refers to the *minimum* energy requirements necessary to keep us alive. Basal metabolic rate is usually measured upon waking which is twelve hours after eating, before pulse and temperature rise or the emotions become stirred. Nutritional needs—as reflected in charts and graphs dealing with height, weight, and activity—are based on this rate. Unfortunately, "caloric" intake greatly misleads and

For example, I am 5' 11" and weigh 160 pounds. According to the nutrition folks, my body needs approximately 2200 Kcalories (a Kcalorie is 1000 calories) a day to meet my minimum requirements based on my *activity* level. This is my total daily energy requirement. Kcalorie energy units should be derived from ALL food sources (carbohydrates, proteins, fats; vegetables, fruits, meat, fish, milk).

Of the 2200 Kcalories I need, over 80% are used to meet my **minimum** physiologic energy needs—heart beat, body heat, breathing, peristalsis, mental processes, etc. If I add twenty minutes of brisk aerobic exercise to my daily routine, I raise my energy needs by **only** 300 Kcalories—which is very little. If I do NOT add those Kcalories to my dietary intake, my body will **withdraw** them from fat reserves **providing** that my diet is nutritionally sound and toxicity problems are not a threat to my system. Acid waste management is CENTRAL to weight control as well as aging reversal. Manage waste and you hold the keys to a long and healthy life.

Another reason fat people stay fat is that their body is "programmed" NOT to lose weight. In other words, you will need patience because losing weight and restoration of health are one day at a time projects. The fat person needs the same focus and patience as the cancer patient. This is where mental control, meditation, and DETOXIFICATION come into play. The body *anticipates.* It has a *sixth* sense. It has *innate* intelligence. Detoxification precedes fat reduction. Fat reduction by any other means produces transient results at best. **The fat person MUST pay attention to the basics!**

Exercise NOT to burn fat, but to form fat burning enzymes, circulate blood and lymph, and become aerobic. Exercise reduces the appetite and frees up energy as EXCESSES are moved out of the system. DO NOT FORGET IT!

Thermogenic Supplements

Thermogenic supplements (*thermo*-heat; *gen*-production of; *ic*-pertaining to) help the body to burn fat. Certain herbs like MaHuang (Ephedra), however, are dangerous because they WHIP the body. Others like Guarana and Capsicum are fine when "complexed" with a full array of other ingredients. Poorly complexed or isolated thermogenics **hype** the system and are just as damaging as synthesized drugs.

Thermogenic supplements (like ETCV) work best when used with food and with hormone precursors. The idea is to balance the system while burning excess fat. ETVC™ burns fat on both men and women while boosting energy.

Enhanced PAC'sᵀᴹ assist thermogenic supplementation. So does 14 day old Kombucha tea and Yucca Herbal Blend™. The flushing of stones from the liver and gall bladder ushers in dramatic change in metabolic activity. Water intake must be tended to. Water is CENTRAL to everything in this book. Men should try to drink 1 gal/day; women 3/4 gal/day.

Include 5 drops of racemized™ sea minerals per glass of BEV™ water. Medical Grade Ionized Water™ requires the use of the liquid minerals also.

Oxygen • Exercise • Salt

Fat will NOT burn unless oxygen is present. No oxygen, means no oxidation. High ORP water, aerobic exercise, and medical grade ozone supply lots of oxygen to the mitochondria in the cells so they can burn body fat.

If you are obese, exercise may be difficult for you. Obese people find it difficult to get their body *moving*—especially aerobically. Use aerobic exercise equipment that does not jar the joints. Start slow. Each day increase your time a few minutes. Push yourself until you reach twenty minutes duration. Exercise to move waste, NOT burn fat.

Next, get OFF the salt. Get OFF all prepared foods. Stop eating restaurant food. Avoid seasonings that contain MSG (monosodium glutamate) and hydrolized vegetable protein (aspartate + glutamate). Get your mineral electrolytes from **racemized** sea mineral complexes like VitaLight™ tablets. If you insist on using granular salt, use Celtic™ salt.

Common table salt and sea salt contain 98% sodium chloride. Celtic™ salt contains 35% sodium. I chose to use neither. Both upset body chemistry, however, Celtic™ salt contains more minerals than common sea salt. Liquid racemized™ sea minerals are 99.5% trace minerals with under 1/2% sodium. **RACEMIZED™ sea minerals clear Rouleau from the blood and boost energy.**

Obēsity and sodium toxicity go together. When waste proteins overload and stagnate in the extracellular fluids due to lack of exercise and movement, water accumulates. Obese people are **endematous** (water retensive). Exercise and liver stone detoxification move massive amounts of waste into the blood for transport to the liver where bile carries it to the small intestine and finally to the toilet. PAC$^{s™}$ and the Yucca Herbal blend™ serve as emulsifiers and buffers in the process.

Cleansing the fluids and cells of sodium occurs naturally PROVIDING plenty of *organic potassium* is available. Fresh green leafy vegetables and limited amounts of juices are excellent sources. Pill supplements will suffice.

As the cells **give up** sodium for potassium, cellular mitochondria multiply and produce more energy. Simultaneously, the hepatocytes in the liver convert body fat into usable energy that is used to make ATP. **The body needs ATP to POWER the transformation to a slim, healthy body.**

Obesity ceases to be a problem when the liver is healthy

lymphatic fluids circulate more freely and health improves.

Fats • Proteins • Allergies

Fats and fatty acids are extremely important to normal body metabolism. They should make up 20% of the diet. Do not be afraid of naturally saturated fats like coconut oil and animal fats. They will not hurt you. Butter, olive oil, flax, sesame, sunflower, and nut oils are also excellent choices.

NEVER use margarine, soy, or canola oils. Ignore claims by the experts that they are good for us. They are not. Always do the *opposite* of whatever the "experts" tell you.

NEVER eliminate all oils and fats from the diet—the body needs them! In John Noble's wonderful classic *I was A Slave In Russia*, Noble told how, when he was in the Soviet gulag prison system (1945-1954), the human slaves were given a thimble full of sunflower oil each day. Without it, the prisoners would die! **Up to 40% of the body's energy needs come from dietary fats, and without sufficient fats in the system, many pathways shut down.**

For instance, without sufficient fat availability and healthy liver and adrenal glands, corticosteroid hormonal production ceases. Fat free diets are killing people!

Proteins should be carefully scrutinized as to quality, quantity, and source. Go easy on meat and avoid cheeses if possible. NEVER eat artificial junk proteins like TVP (textured vegetable protein). When you get to the hereafter and you look in God's recipe book for healthy living, you are NOT going to find any recipes calling for TVP, soy, or canola. Manipulated proteins CANNOT sustain life. Lentils, beans, and legumes (except soy) are just fine IF some of the SUPER foods are included.

Food allergies are a good indicator that the body is **TOXIC** and that serious liver clean up is needed. Allergies and asthma are hormone driven conditions, so don't be too quick to condemn good foods or racemized™ products that "stir" the system as they heal the sick or obese person.

Bias has NO place in vibrational testing! Too many people (professional and lay alike) fail to recognize that muscle testing is TOTALLY misleading with checking racemized™ products. Some patients LOOK for excuses not to get well and others allow their mind to control body response. Good questions from a properly "cleared" mind can provide valuable insight and information. **Poor technique is worse than none at all.** Learn to use the speedometer chart on page 368. It is one of the best tests I know of and it provides clear, definitive answers if the procedure is followed. I often use it to dowse sick people over the phone! All that is needed is a pen and a piece of paper. I can perform it in my mind without either and determine the path someone needs to follow or quickly differentiate between a healing crisis or a serious problem.

Klammath™ Algae & Harmonic™ Pollen

Klammath™ algae is a superb FOOD product that greatly enhances fat reduction. It is one of most powerful, naturally occurring, right-spin food substances on the planet. Harmonic™ pollen is another. I eat both.

Klammath™ algae is indigenous to Upper Klamath Lake, Oregon. Harmonic™ pollen comes from the wilds of northern British Columbia. Both are pure, raw, and wild. They are "low stress" foods because they require very little digestion.

The vitamin B-12 in Klammath™ algae is easily assimilated. This is an important issue for vegetarians. The minerals and enzymes in Harmonic™ pollen are nothing short of impressive. A couple of algae tablets, a spoonful of pollen, and an apple makes a very good **low** stress, **high** energy, **no** let-down lunch. Both foods are very complete proteins!

The electrical *signature* of Klammath™ algae corresponds energetically with—and has an affinity for—the lymph more than for the blood, which explains its role in detoxification. When used together, Klammath™ algae and Harmonic™ pollen enhance the immune system and play KEY roles in fat metabolism. In other words, algae burns fat!

Klammath™ algae serves as janitor and free radical scavenger while fine tuning and regulating the entire metabolism. It is particularly effective in balancing the obese person's metabolism and easing hunger cravings. A good combination is algae, pollen, and Taoist Rice Polish™.

These are NOT hybrid foods nor have they been genetically *manipulated.* They contain large amounts of chlorophyll, biologically active minerals and enzymes that fuel cold fusion reactions in the liver and gut of humans and pets alike.

When you eat foods with a high vibratory *signature* and racemic energy *footprint* the fat person experiences a new dimension in health.

Raw Milk • Real Food • Obesity

Raw, unpasteurized milk is a wonderful food and a good source of nutrients and enzymes. Few people raise milk cows or milk goats, but they can buy raw milk from someone who has these animals. Older people, especially, benefit from drinking raw milk. It is a very good food. *(Raw milk is neither pasteurized nor homogenized. Both processes destroy this wonderful food.)*

Don't be frightened by the **scare tactics** of the "corporate state" yellow fringe flag bureaucrats who are doing their best to end public access to raw milk. I think it most convenient that outbreaks of E. coli, cryptosporidium, etc., occur just when they are needed to scare the public into submission.

Bureaucrats like to *regurgitate!* They quote *chapter and verse* to justify enforcement of their programs. They may not be privy to the manipulations of America's food supply or medical agendas, but they ARE are acting in a "official" capacity under the yellow fringe flag in direct violation of their oath and affirmation in violation of Title 42, USC 1986 for "knowledge" and "neglect" of the law.

Obesity and good health don't go together. Behind obesity is hunger and behind hunger is dis-ease.

Water & Obesity

Water is important to the obesity story because water is CENTRAL to all metabolic function. The three variables of water consumption are: quantity consumed, frequency of consumption, and the nature of the water consumed.

For the obese person, these variables are critical because their body is under so much load and stress that the rules of the game for normal body types don't apply.

Metabolically, all systems in the obese body are operating at maximum. Energy is lacking. The joints are strained. The heart is overworked. Movement of lymphatic fluids is poor. Intercellular waste is beyond description. Fat stores hold huge amounts of toxic poisons.

The path to youth and vitality can be difficult even for normal body types. For the obese, we have to take an alternate route for reasons of safety as well as compassion. All body systems age together and the obese body is advanced and overloaded.

High ORP water provides needed intercellular energy and acts as the waste "carrier." High ORP water denatures acid wastes due to its incredible free radical scavenging ability. Yucca Herbal Blend™ and PAC^s dislodge and stabilize the wastes. ETVC™ accelerates the burning of fat and the building of muscle while managing blood sugar levels within safe limits. Diabetes is always a concern and potential threat when working with obese people.

VitaLight™ is a racemic product used primarily for its heavy load of racemized™ minerals that are so very helpful in fueling metabolic reactions in unhealthy and healthy people alike. VitaLight™ replaces dozens of supplements that get in the way and overload the liver. This one product replaces vitamins A, B, C, D, E, zinc, calcium/magnesium, various herbs, etc. It is the ONLY such supplement I have used for over 15 years! People notice a response almost immediately.

Both BEV™ and Mikrowater™ are made in home from tap water. BEV™ units come in counter top and under counter models. Special self contained (6, 12, 24, 110, 220 volt and solar) models for emergency situations and for 3rd world country use are also available. All models make 2 gallons per hour at standard household pressure of 60 psi. In home models do NOT require electricity. There are no boiler elements to clean (as in distillers). Filters are long lasting under normal circumstances. A "conductivity meter" is used to monitor water quality and determine when it's time to change the filters.

BEV™ units are made in the USA and the technology behind them is **"proprietary."** They are shipped to the end user ONLY after each unit is **individually** bench tested to ensure it exceeds BEV™ standards. Extremely strict quality control insures customer satisfaction.

BEV water is strange stuff! It's ORP potential is near "conception point" and therefore must be kept in its own tank or in glass or polycarbonate bottles—away from atmospheric contaminants so the water will NOT draw pollutants and lower its ORP. Glass and polycarbonate are the only substances that do not react with this water. Polycarbonate bottles are available in pint, 1/2, 1, 3, and 5 gallon sizes.

Magnetic Sponge

BEV™ and high ORP waters act like a magnetic sponge in liquid form. When they come into contact with body toxins, they bond to them and carry them OUT of the system. In the process they create positive energy vortexes that EXCITE cell chemistry and stimulate metabolism through the increased production of ATP in every cell of the body. Atherosclerotic plaques in the arteries dissolve. Capillaries in the posterior eye, ears and scalp respond. **Body fat diminishes.**

BEV™ is a *proprietary* water processing system that can stand on its own or provide the foundation water for the creation of Medical Grade Ionized (high ORP) Water™. While purity is very important, it's the biological activity of BEV™ water that makes it *unique.* Traditional water processing systems don't even come close. At this time, 100% of my water consumption is high ORP water.

Avoid distilled water! It is biologically unfriendly water. Toxic volatiles *concentrate* in distilled water, It tastes flat and it is a breeding ground for viruses and it's expensive to make.

Fat & Chain Reactions

Metabolism occurs through a continuous series of biochemical reactions. These reactions stall out if the body is missing the raw materials it needs OR if it labors under **systemic excesses.**

When metabolism slows, aging accelerates. The body has but three choices in processing toxic food and water. It can try to dismantle (oxidize) the toxic molecules, expel them from the system, or store the them in NEW body fat made for this purpose.

Bio-junk food and water contain **radiomimetic** chemicals that "mimic" hormones. They are so potent that the body often has to isolate and store them in FAT to protect itself. A WEAK liver cannot process these freak molecules for lack of needed catalysts, enzymes, hormones, and energy.

Besides, most livers are so loaded with **stones** that bile flow is limited. Parasites in the liver (flukes) live on these toxic energy fields, reproduce, and spread throughout the body. These poisons are too "hot" for the kidneys. DiSorb Aid™, Kombucha tea, and liver flushing lifts the load from these organs and helps the body to dismantle wastes and burn excess body fat.

Blood & Lymph Circulation

As body fat increases, blood, and lymph circulation slows. Insurance companies use height and weight as the basis for their rates. They *know* that obesity is an excellent *indicator* of trouble in the making. They know the slim person is healthier. **The way to beat the insurance companies at their game is to be slim, healthy, and never file a claim!**

Feel Worse <u>First</u>!

During the early stages of detoxification, expect to feel worse BEFORE you will feel better. It's called two steps forward, one step backwards. Action of any type indicates things are happening! Colonics and enemas provide quick relief by sending wastes down the toilet. You feel better fast!

Liver stone purges are simple to do. Three weeks of preparation is needed, during which time you lead a normal life and eat a normal diet. The purge itself is done at night and the stones exit via the bowels over the next 24 hours. The second and subsequent purges are done weekly thereafter. Green stones come first, followed by brown, black, then red. The process is unique, safe, and pain free—and it works!

Over one hundred problems are simultaneously dealt within the liver purge program. Over 75% of the benefits that accrue take place during the **preparation** for each purge.

Diuretics

NEVER use diuretics (water pills) to reduce weight! Diuretics upset electrolyte balance, especially potassium. Potassium pills do NOT replenish lost potassium. Potassium loss promotes sodium invasion of the cells, shut down of mitochondria production of ATP. **Potassium drives OUT sodium if the potassium is from live foods.** Edema is confirmation of EXCESS intercellular plasma proteins. Obese people don't need diuretics once they restore balance to their systems.

When the obese person becomes thin, no one needs to tell him or her that they **ARE** *Young Again!*

PREVIEW: *Our next chapter deals with the relationship between lightning, energy, vitality, and BROWN FAT!*

Breast Implants: Silicone or Soy?

Thousands of women suffer from the toxic side effects of silicone breast implants because they trusted the "experts" who told them they were "safe."

ALL of them leak—no exceptions! Silicone is THIXOTROPHIC (the silicone migrates via intercellular plasma proteins in the lymphatic system) and severely stresses the immune system. **NEVER** attempt to boost the immune system if you have breasts implants.

The latest **scam** in "safe" breast implants is "soy oil." Soy oil is an industrial oil. Avoid it in your food and don't be foolish enough to implant it into your breasts.

The silicone dilemma can be safely handled, but action is mandatory! SOC™ capsules **scavenges** stray silicone as well as heavy metals and removes them from the tissues while dissolving scar tissue and creating a pain free limber body. See Source Page.

People Getting Fatter

Over **half** the population is obese. Hormones **control** metabolism—and hormones **drive** obesity. Toxic waste overload makes matters worse. If you are fat and want to be slim, call and ask for help.

GH_3 + & Kombucha Tea

We are "supposed" to regenerate a **NEW** body every 7 years. But as we age, the process slows and in subclinically sick people it can take 12 years to get a "new body" which is often worse than the one they traded in.

If you would like your new body to be *younger, stronger,* and *better* than the one you are in the process of trading in, implement the ideas in this book—along with some GH_3+ and Kombucha tea while you are at it.

GH_3+ is a cell stimulator that is used in conjunction with 14 day old Kombucha tea specifically for hair regrowth and restoration of natural hair color.

GH_3+ rejuvenates the tissues with NO side effects of any kind. The jaw line regains a youthful appearance (as people age their jaw changes). Liver spots disappear from the skin—especially if racemized™ hormone precursor creme (for men and women) is used regularly. The skin takes on a youthful appearance, and white and gray hair returns to its natural color (at 53 years my hair is jet black!

If you want to enjoy a *youthful* appearance as seen on the faces of movie stars, use GH_3+ and make and drink 14 day old Kombucha tea.

A youthful appearance is PRICELESS! It translates into a good job, respect, and high self esteem.

Hearing & Learning Problems

Do you know anyone who is deaf? A newly patented device allows deaf people to **"hear" through their SKIN.** The device has even been used to communicate with dolphins. It helps hyper/attn. deficit children learn and it is now available. Send $5^{00} and SASE to obtain documentation.

A dashed line resembles a nerve fiber axon. Schwann cells reside at and "polish" the synapses (gaps) in healthy nerve tissue, passing on the signal along the axon. Aging and disease causes Schwann cell acitivty to falter and the myelin sheath that protects the nerve to deteriorate. All nerve related conditions like MS, Lupus, fibromyalgia, mysathenia gravis, and shingles are "HORMONE" driven!

"The difference between an old man and an old *gentleman* is the way he dresses and <u>looks</u>."

The Vaccination Dilemma

Vaccinations are part of life in the Western World. In fact, they are so **pervasive** that health-minded people had best "tune in" to the Jeckyl and Hyde nature of vaccines if they hope to enjoy a long and healthy life.

Vaccines are supposed to encourage the body to build antibodies against future exposure to contagious diseases. The process involves the introduction of **pathogenic** life forms into the body in a serum of **foreign** proteins.

Immunity and antibodies are desirable, but the long term effects of vaccinations are not. Immune system response to vaccinations is an act of *self-preservation* that does NOT lend itself to tampering by medical madmen.

Natural, cell mediated immunity is *different* than vaccination *induced* attempts to *force* antibody formation and immunity. Vaccinations set up "resident" enemy troops throughout the body. Later, when we are weak or old, these foreign troops bring about insurrection from **within!**

Vaccines create electrical *static* because their **signature** is *foreign* to the body. Their vibrational frequency interferes with health and longevity by creating "disharmony" at the *subtle energy* level of our being.

If you have been vaccinated, it's VERY important that you REVERSE the process and eliminate the foreign protein energy fields from your system. If these substances are not **neutralized** and **driven** from the body, they will eventually manifest as chronic degenerative dis-ease.

The best way to deal with vaccination-induced foreign proteins is to **"erase"** their *signatures* from the body. This is accomplished with the use of *biogenic*, full spectrum, homeovitic remedies in mixed, multiple potencies of 9x, 20x, 30x, 100x, and 200x. **The process does NOT reverse existing immunity or antibodies present.**

The goals of immunization is admirable, but the side effects can be heart breaking—especially in young children whose immune systems are undeveloped. Always **buffer** vaccinations to avoid DEATH, hearing loss or the development of Type 1 diabetes in your child.

Request the Homeovitic packet to learn how to protect yourself or your child (see Source Page). For **documentation** on the dangers of immunizations and how to "legally" avoid them and protect your children, call (505) 983-1856, or contact the National Vaccine Information center, 512 Maple Ave. West #206, Vienna, VA 22180. USA (703) 938-0342. **Knowledge dispels ignorance and fear!**

Homeopathy & Homeovitics

"Homeopathy is wholly capable of satisfying the therapeutic demands of this age better than any other system or school of medicine."
Charles F. Menninger, M.D.

Homeovitic detoxification is a *crucial* step in the treatment of dis-ease and chronic health conditions.

Homeopathy teaches that *symptoms* of disease are a *natural* part of the healing process and that their expression should be **encouraged** rather than suppressed.

Recent advances in homeopathic formulation have led to the enhancement of *traditional* remedies with *biogenic* and nutritional support (homeovitic+bio+nutritional). Enhanced support intensifies the *innate* healing ability of the body through *vitalization.*

Vitalization enhances the energy *footprint* of a substance by a stepwise series of dilutions + succussions designed to increase **resonance** (vibrational frequency) so energy can be transferred from the "vitalized" substance to a less active substance or system—as in a sick body!

Transfer of resonance to toxins occurs when the vitalized substance (vitic) is similar (homeo) to the less active one. Thus, all vitalized substances obey the law of similars (homeovitic) which says *"like is cured by like."*

The cause is the cure is even more specific. For instance, the use of mercury in its *vitalized* form removes mercury residues from the body through *resonance* and *transference.*

Transference of energy from the *vitalized* substance to offending toxin(s) speeds healing and eases stress on the body's vital energy reserves.

Enhanced homeovitic remedies in a "single solution" of MIXED *multiple* potencies of 9x, 20x, 30x, 100x, 200x provides *bio*genic support and cellular rejuvenation by dealing with **underlying** health problems at the **subtle energy level.** (Ask for the homeovitic packet.)

Homeovitic remedies are NOT available in stores, but can ordered by mail and are very effective against:

Alcohol	Allergens	Tobacco	Bacteria
Viruses	Chemicals	Dentals	Yeast
Fungi	Metals	Parasites	Radiation
Stress	Spider Bites	Additives	Nematodes
Acute Stress	Sys. Support	System Clearing	

"Enhanced" Homeovitic Remedies Work!

24

Brown Fat

"Where I am, death is not. Where death is, I am not."
Epicurus

In 1976, Peking, China (now Beijing), suffered a massive man-made earthquake that killed 650,000 people. The events prior to its occurrence were exactly in line with the predictions of the electrical wizard, Nicola Tesla (1865-1942). Tesla said earthquakes could be *created* by manipulating massive amounts of electrical ENERGY!

Tesla predicted a highly charged ionic atmosphere would be exhibited. Buildings and objects may have an iridescent blue green glow about them. Multi-colored lightning—red, blue, and gold—may be seen in the early morning sky around the epicenter for hours prior to the event. The earthquake would be the EFFECT of a massive electrical energy shift, NOT the cause.

The lightning we see in the sky and the electrical phenomenon of the *bio-electric* body have much in common. BOTH are *expressions* of electrical energy. Both are electrical phenomena.

The *physical* body is **condensed** energy (i.e., frozen light) that we can see and touch. It belongs to our Third Dimension world. The *electric* body, however, belongs to the world of the Fourth Dimension—an electrical world that is *invisible*, but is there nonetheless.

Our aura also belongs to the Fourth Dimension world. It is a "generated" energy field that radiates from the physical body. Energy that is *generated* must have a source—something that is producing it. We are interested in the body's source of its generated energy because **energy** DEFINES the aging process in terms of *rate* and *ability* or *inability* to control aging. *Bio-electric energy* is the body's version of *lightning!*

Bio-electric Lightning!

Animals produce electrical discharges similar to lightning. For example, electric eels and electric rays— creatures of the ocean—release enough electricity to light the dark at night or even kill a man.

The Portuguese Man o' War—a jelly fish—is but a mass of transparent protoplasm, yet it can kill any living thing that comes within the grasp of its umbrella of tentacles. It kills with a MASSIVE discharge of bio-electric *lightning.*

Consider the electrical spectacular that occurs when the human sperm enters the ovum at fertilization. At that instant, over 480,000 volts of electricity (Yes! 480,000 volts) are released!

The discharge of electricity coagulates the outer surface of the ovum and prevents penetration by other sperm. The event is the beginning of a new organism. It is an *electrical* event of massive proportions that *generates* a new life! Death is a similar—but opposite—electrical event where "spirit" energy returns from whence it came and metabolism synchronizes.

While we are on this earth, it would behoove us to understand the SOURCE of *lightning* that keeps us alive. Understanding it is the key to becoming *Young Again!*

The Body Electric

The body is a flesh and blood electrical storage battery and power generation system in one. Peak health depends on the bio-electric body's ability to generate and store electrical ENERGY! We are dependent on a source of *fuel,* a storage system, a *transmission system* to distribute our energy and a method to *control* the ebb and flow of that energy. Energy is a **two way bridge** between youth and old age.

We draw on our electrical energy reserves as needed and we replenish them through rest, detoxification, and nourishment. When we fail to restore electrical balance, we lapse into partial or total energy synchronization. A *decomposed* corpse is an example of total energy synchronization. Aging is the abbreviated version—the *crock-pot* version! Aging confirms a LOSS of electrical vitality. Aging is *slow* death. **Once we lose control of the body "terrain," vital organ function and ATP energy production slow and eventually cease.**

The Mitochondria

The mitochondria are bacteria that inhabit the cells of all animals. They were first observed through the microscope around the year 1800. However, they were not officially identified as "living" organisms—capable of independent existence and given a name until approximately 1935.

The *mitochondria* derive their name from the Greek *mitos*—a thread, and *chondros*—a grain. These root words describe their shape, NOT their function. Originally, the mitochondria were thought to be artifacts (waste) or organelles (tiny bodies) found within the cells. Eventually it was discovered that they are our SOURCE of *bio-electric lightning!*

Life is **impossible** without the mitochondria. They process our glucose sugars and produce the energy molecule **adenosine triphosphate (ATP).** ATP energy *is* our *life force.* Glucose is our sugar fuel. It is stored in the liver and muscles as glycogen. When energy is needed, the cells convert glycogen to glucose and the mitochondria oxidize the glucose sugar through a process called **glycolysis** and produce ATP.

Conversion of body fat to energy takes place in the liver. Aerobic exercise helps the liver's functional cells (the hepatocytes) to produce enzymes that CONVERT body fat into usable **glucose fuel** that the mitochondria can burn. The mitochondria CONTROL aerobic cellular respiration which is also called *internal* respiration because it occurs inside the cells as opposed to *external* respiration, which occurs in the lungs.

Mitochondria Control Aging

The mitochondria are BOTH power generators and storage batteries. They convert food energy into metabolic electricity. They are referred to as the **power house** of the cell.

The mitochondria replicate (reproduce) on their own. This is important! They are **NOT** dependent on the host even though they reside in our cells and are influenced by the body environment. They have their own DNA code. (Think of DNA as cellular programming *software*, genetic instructions, *ability to make their own hormones*, and a road map all in one.)

Mitochondrial activity is what *drives* anabolism— the process of build-up and repair of body tissue. Anabolism is a youthful condition and the opposite of catabolism.

As we age, anabolism gives way to catabolism. When we reach our *anabolic peak*, growth and repair of body tissue slows. Energy production slows. Hormone production slows. Health and vitality diminishes and old age becomes a reality.

Mitochondrial ATP is right-spin, positive energy. It keeps us **alive.** When mitochondrial function becomes limited, the effects are seen in the mirror. When energy production falls short of our minimum requirements, life ceases.

Growth Plates

Medical science's *dividing line* between youth and old age is based on long bone extension. When the growth plates between the diaphysis (shank of the long bones) and the epiphysis (end of the long bones) "close," science says we cross the threshold into that *twilight zone* between youth and old age. Whatever growth or lack thereof that has occurred is a done deal. We have officially *stopped* growing. This event usually occurs between ages 18 and 22. Science's definition of aging focuses on the extension of long bones. It is incomplete.

Our definition of aging focuses on the body's *shift* from anabolism to catabolism, which can be accelerated or reversed at will. Our focus is on **perpetual growth and repair** of body tissues, instead of long bone extension. We are NOT concerned with closure of the epiphyseal plates.

When the mitochondria cannot produce enough ATP to meet the body's needs for growth and repair, we age. Aging and the passing of bio-electric TIME are one and the same. Our friends, the mitochondria, control TIME.

We must learn HOW to assist the mitochondria if we want to reverse aging and stop the passing of Time.

The Sweat Zones

The sweat zones of the body are areas of heat production and waste energy release. Concentrations of mitochondria in the sweat zones confirm the relationship between mitochondrial function and waste ENERGY release. These zones experience heavy lymphatic fluid movement (lymph is our non-blood body fluid). Good lymph flow is crucial to good health.

The lymphatic system is cancer's electrical highway. The lymph nodes are the power stations. The lymph nodes are most plentiful in the sweat zones of the body.

The lymphatic system's job is multiple in nature. It includes toxic waste management and recirculation of extracellular fluids. Most importantly, the lymphatic system is the body's primary *protein* communication system. The lymph nodes **hold** toxic energy fields and release them only when the body can handle them. Swollen tonsils are a good example of this.

Body hair is found in areas of high toxicity—like the

groin, arm pits, scalp, face, and legs. Hair siphons off and releases toxic energy.

Hair Analysis

Hair analysis measures the EXCESSES **leaving** the body. It is NOT a measure of *deficiencies* within the body because we do NOT suffer from deficiencies, only **excesses**. Hair analysis but a window into the body, but in the PAST TENSE.

Let's say hair is analyzed and found to contain mercury. The metal may be coming from the amalgam fillings in the teeth or from the diet. Whatever the source, the person IS excreting mercury —via the hair. That's good! We know that the body is releasing the mercury.

But let's say hair analysis shows NO mercury even though there are amalgams in the teeth? What does this mean? It means the personss's skin (and hair, hair being an extension of the skin) isn't working efficiently and dangerous levels of mercury are building in the tissues. Remember, there is NO such thing as deficiencies! The only thing deficient in this example is the limited and backward thinking by **alternative** practitioners when using hair analysis and live blood cell microscopy to "prescribe." **Hair analysis and live blood cell analysis are tools of observation ONLY and should NEVER be used to prescribe.**

Unfortunately, live blood cell microscopy is commonly used to prescribe **in direct conflict** with Dr. Guenther Enderlein's ground breaking microscopic work a century ago. The misuse of a potentially helpful tool is based on the FALSE premise that we suffer from deficiencies which simply isn't so. **Deficiencies and magic bullet mentality go together!**

Healthy hair, fast growing hair, a full head of hair, and a head of natural full colored hair is what we want to possess. We make it happen with SOC™, kombucha tea, GH₃™, PACˢ™, VitaLight™ tablets, Yucca Herbal Blend™ and all of the basics we have discussed thus far. Like exercise, lots of high ORP water, a clean bowel, a purged liver and tissues, and regular use of a rebounder and Biogenic™ Lymphatic Roler.

Healthy hair is related to your level of BROWN fat and the activity level of the mitochondria in your scalp.

Insects • Birds • Sperm

Insects and birds have heavy concentrations of mitochondria in the muscles that are responsible for flight because that is where the ATP energy is needed, stored, and used.

The sperm makes the long trip into the woman's fallopian tubes to fertilize the ovum with *power* generated by the mitochondria. The base of the sperm's tail is saturated with mitochondria. When the sperm fertilizes the egg (ovam; ova plural) the electrical discharge of 480,000 volts of electricity comes from both the sperm and the ovum. Both are energy bodies—one is huge, the other is tiny.

The electrical discharge of the ovum generates only .19 volts. The discharge by the sperm is 25,263,157 times GREATER than that of the ovum—a huge difference!

Moreover, there is a massive difference in physical size between the sperm and ovum. The volume of the ovum is $1,760,000^2$ microns. The volume of the sperm is only 21^2 microns. When we divide the size of the ovum by the size of the sperm, we find that the egg is 83,809 times greater! These differences in physical size and electrical potential fuels the release of the 480,000 volts we call *bio-electric lightning!*

At Birth

Mitochondrial numbers and their activity level at birth is very high. So is the level of BROWN FAT (which we will discuss shortly). This is why children and "young" people are warm blooded and **prematurely** aging people—like women in their early 30ˢ through menopause suffer from internal coldness. Anyone experiencing "coldness" needs to understand that behind the condition is a serious HORMONE condition.

The mitochondria produce the huge amounts of energy a child requires to grow to adulthood in a few short years and be able to stay warm even when subjected to cold conditions.

As we grow, we experience the ebb and flow of energy called health and sickness. By the time we reach adulthood, the growth plates in the long bones have closed and we reach our maximum height. When we cross the threshold of our anabolic peak, we experience an energy shift and we begin our descent into old age—UNLESS we are willing to **take control of our life** and **responsibility for our condition and begin the rejuvenatory process.**

As the *bio-electric* body becomes toxic and hormonally unbalanced, mitochondrial production of ATP falls. Next, mitochondiral replication (multiplication) falls. Then, ATP reserves diminish as BROWN fat disappears from the system causing dis-ease to manifest and the doctor an opportunity to provide a diagnosis.

So aging is really just loss of function in the vital organs, hormonal imbalances, and toxicity of the tissues . **It does NOT have to be this way! Aging is easy to prevent and reverse.**

Rest • Detoxification • Illness

Rest is a part of the rejuvenation process. Rest allows the *bio-electric* body to heal. It *frees* and *redirects* ATP energy so critical metabolic processes can rebound.

Illnesses ARE healing crises. When someone suffers with the flu, hepatitis, cancer, etc.—there is NOT enough available energy to both heal the body and carry on normal activities—so we must seek rest!

Young people and sick people need lots of rest because their bodies are under load.

When we force the body to work under conditions of high stress—be it a *diagnosed* illness or mental stress—we "squander" mitochondrial ATP that should be used for detoxification and healing.

To restore energy and vitality, the mitochondria NEED our assistance. They automatically increase their numbers and activity if we do our job by flushing the system of EXCESS metabolic wastes, balancing our hormones, and eating SUPER FOODS.

Mitochondrial replication involves the doubling of DNA and genetic material —so two bacteria are created out of one. This process is called *mitosis*. As the mitochondria increase their numbers, ATP production increases also.

When the mitochondria FAIL to return to former activity levels, we break through a Time "barrier" and experience aging. All of us have seen our parents and friends jerk and slip their way *down* the catabolic side of the pyramid. Metabolic slowdown results in a *plateau* effect. **Aging accelerates in direct relationship to slowing of cellular respiration, loss of mitochondrial activity, build up of acid wastes in the tissues, hormonal shortfalls, and blockage of bile flow due to stones in the liver.**

Sodium & Waste

Aging, toxicity, and catabolism are peas in a pod, and where you find one, you will find the others. Toxic substances come in many forms. Sodium chloride is one of them.

Sodium chloride (table salt) is of particular importance to our discussion of the mitochondria. Sodium in excess is a *poison.* Sodium is also a *preservative.* Sodium is an electrolyte. Sodium conducts electricity in a solution—like the *inter*cellular fluids in the spaces between the cells as well as in the blood. Intercellular (interstitial) fluid is composed of blood plasma proteins and is found between the cells while blood SOLIDS circulate in the blood vessels. These fluids are NOT sterile as commonly taught in medical schools. They are dynamic, live *organism-bearing* body fluids whose energy profiles are *easily* altered by diet and stress. The elimination of the Rouleau effect (see page 136) from the blood is accomplished with racemized™ sea minerals.

Soft drinks dramatically alter blood and lympnatic fluid pH and should be considered as toxic as alcohol.

I have a strong hunch that deterioration of the brain neurons and nerve fibers throughout the body is DIRECTLY linked to consumption of soft drinks, heavy metal (mercury) accumulation, and buildup of acid wastes in the system. In the case of Alzheimers, add brain inactivity from too much TV and too little reading AND MOST IMPORTANT, hormonal excesses that grossly affect the Schwann's cells and the myelin sheath that protect the nerve fibers. To learn more, read Beating Alzheimers, Reverse Aging (see Source Index).

In our society, it is impossible to get too little sodium. Many people, however, do suffer with symptoms associated with low electrolytes. Conventional medical *protocol* calls for increased sodium intake. This approach is wrong because it fails to address the issue of EXCESS toxicity and a broad based electrolytic foundation. Racemically activated ionic sea minerals are a better answer to electrolytic short falls.

Under **normal** conditions all but a fraction of sodium remains OUTSIDE the cell membranes—out in the **extra**cellular fluid—**between** the cells.

Potassium is sodium's twin. Potassium remains within the cell membrane (i.e., in the cytoplasm (cyt-cell. plasm-fluid.). A healthy body maintains a balanced ratio of sodium to potassium. When we eat devitalized and processed foods, we ingest EXCESS sodium and insufficient potassium and we upset the balance between these "twins." The more sodium we consume and the more acid waste we accumulate, the greater is the loss of potassium from the cells. Excess sodium brings on death. *The word death is mostly "eat."*

STOP The Salt

Under normal conditions, few sodium ions (Na^+) are allowed inside the cells. Excess sodium ions gain entrance to the cells as potassium ions (K^+) are given up by the cells for use elsewhere in the body. This *one for one* trade occurs in the face of sodium **excess.** As each K^+ ion leaves the cell, it is replaced by one Na^+ ion. A poor diet FORCES the body to *steal* potassium from the cells to sustain itself.

The body depends on the process we call *biological alchemy* to meet its dietary needs. It can make what it needs **if** all systems are functional, but the alchemy process fails under conditions of **excess**. Sodium also affects hormone balance. **Sodium plays an important part in the menstrual cycle.** Sodium and potassium ions BOTH carry a (+) charge and are close in size, hence, EXCESS sodium drives out potassium. When Na^+ ions invade the cells, mitochondrial activity comes to a HALT, vitality wanes, and dis-ease follows as metabolic waste accumulates. It is under these conditions that auto digestion (self cannibalism) of muscle proteins occurs.

Older people and people suffering with degenerative dis-eases build up **MASSIVE** amounts of toxic wastes in their tissues. To repeat, conditions of EXCESS, as in edema, appears as turgor is lost (turgor is resistance of the skin to deformation). This *waterlogged* condition is common in the extremities (hands, legs, ankles, and feet).

Edema is **more** than water retention. It is a SIGN of excess waste plasma proteins in the tissues, diminished heart function, and kidney slowdown. NEVER use diuretics for edema! Instead, detoxify the tissues, use racemized™ sea minerals, PAC^s, and racemized™ asparagus (Aspar-Max™).

Allopathic medicine relies on diuretics (water pills) to force EXCESS fluids from the tissues. In the process, potassium is lost and the body is forced to cannibalize its muscle proteins and fats as alternate fuel sources. When it runs out of reserves, the person's weight **collapses** overnight—leaving skin and bones—an extremely serious condition.

As waste and toxicity increase, body hair decreases. Again, this is very common among older folks who become "bald" all over their body, especially the legs. Fungus under the toe nails and feet irregularities are also SIGNS. **When body hair is lost, the system is on its way down. Hair is crucial to detoxification of the skin and body and will regrow over the entire body if the procedures outlined are followed.**

STOP the use of table salt at the dinner table. Never use the salt a recipe calls for. Instead, dissolve a "pinch" in a little water and add to recipe for desired effect. Better still, use home grown food. It doesn't need salt. It is loaded with mineral ions.

Salt's effects are insidious, and cancer loves high sodium environments. Cancer tumors and masses surround themselves in a field of sodium saturated tissue. Sodium doesn't singularly cause cancer, but it is a serious player. **Cancers are strong, sodium saturated energy fields. Cancer <u>tumors</u> "import" and "condense" toxic energy. Cancer <u>masses</u> export negative energy (see page 307).**

The invasion of sodium into the cells is the equivalent of shutting off the power in Jurassic Park. When the power goes off, nature's dinosaurs—the cancer viruses—ACTIVATE and take control of the DNA and RNA software and multiply in our cells. Their proliferation rate is exponential (2, 4, 8,16, 32, 64,128, 256, etc.). Their job is to eliminate weak organisms. **Viruses ONLY gain entrance and proliferate in our cells when our electrical defenses have been sabotaged. We are our own saboteur when we include table salt in our diet!**

BEV™, Medical Grade Ionized Water™, and racemized™ sea minerals are VERY helpful in sodium detoxification because they are PERFECT *carrier* solvents due to their high ORP potentials. They transport excess sodium OUT of the cells and OUT of the body. **Sodium must be DRIVEN OUT of the cells, but the body voluntarily withdraws potassium to meet its daily needs if DAILY dietary intake is insufficient.**

As the sodium in the cells is replaced with potassium, the mitochondria come alive, multiply, and produce ATP! Cellular repolarization always precedes ATP production.

*A Chi Gong machine, ATP Inductor™, or Lymphatic Inductor™ promote polarization of the cells and activate the mitochondria. Damaged and inflamed tissue and injured joints heal quickly when mitochondrial activity is accelerated. Remember, healing requires **energy** and it is the mitochondria that produce it. These devices have successfully "settled" aching teeth, injured knees, and backs and drained sinuses.*

Pricking the finger is a good way to gauge the overall health. If you prick your finger and the blood fails to stand-up with a very distinct "pearl" and instead produces a low profile ball, or flows or oozes onto the skin, you are in trouble! Detoxification is mandatory. Blood should be BRILLIANT red, never dark red. Blood with a low *crown* and dark color is in a **pre-cancer** state and Rouleau will be present.

Brown Fat & Mitochondria

Brown fat has a great deal to do with vitality and rejuvenation. Understanding it sheds light on WHY some people are fat, skinny, thin, sick, energetic, etc.

Officially, brown fat is called *brown adipose tissue* or BAT. BAT was only recently discovered. BAT is brown because of the extremely heavy *concentrations* of mitochondria. It is very active, biologically speaking. Except for the word fat, BAT has NO resemblance in appearance or function to its shirt-tale relative, *white adipose tissue* or WAT (normal body fat).

Officially, BAT is responsible for **"non-shivering thermogenesis"**—the generation of heat in the absence of shivering. Shivering is a normal body function that is part of heat production under cold OR high stress conditions (people shiver during and after a serious accident). BAT is heavily vascularized (lots of blood vessels) compared to WAT.

Babies have much higher concentrations of BAT than do adults. People who live and work in cold climates have more BAT than people in warm climates. Japanese women skin divers have very high concentrations of BAT and are able to bear frigid ocean waters for hours at a time. They can do this because of the high concentrations of BAT in their tissues and because of a right-spin energy diet. BAT generates much ATP.

Healthy people have more BAT than do sick people. Thin people have more BAT than fat people. The more BAT you have, the leaner you will be and the more energy you will have! To understand BAT, let's review the physiological process called ***thermogenic hyperphagia.*** Dissected it looks like this: *thermo*-heat. *genic*-pertaining to the production of. *hyper*-above normal. *phagia*-that which eats.

People who are subclinically sick, or who suffer with degenerative dis-ease have low concentrations of BAT!

Obese people do not have enough BAT. Instead, they have too much WAT (white adipose tissue). As WAT increases in a person's body, BAT decreases. Obesity is the most obvious SIGN of metabolic slow down, accumulation of EXCESSES, and hormonal imbalances.

When we reach our anabolic peak, loss of BAT accelerates, obesity becomes a problem, vitality diminishes, and aging accelerates. This downward spiral normally begins in the middle twenties to early thirties.

In industrial societies like the USA, BAT loss among women (and men) is *epidemic!* Premenopausal symptoms are now appearing 20 years AHEAD of official onset of menopause. Symptoms that used to manifest in the late forties and early fifties are now RAMPANT among women in their late twenties and early thirties. **Signs and symptoms of aging develop in direct relationship to loss of BAT, development of hormonal problems, and toxic excesses in the body.**

The use of **racemized**™ hormone precursors encourages BAT formation and reverses menopausal and andropausal symptoms in BOTH sexes with NO danger of any kind. Liver flushing, aerobic exercise, rebounding, and lymph rolling are important. Subjecting the body to cold is VERY beneficial. Swim regularly in a cold pool, ocean, or lake. Never plunge in as it can cause temporarily paralysis and death due to the "gasp reflex." Do yard and garden work and take walks during the cold months dressed in only a light, short sleeved shirt to encourage BAT formation and strengthen the immune system. Finish bathing with an ICE COLD shower!

My favorite cold therapy is to do my aerobic exer-

cise OUTSIDE in nothing but boxer shorts—year around! Workouts in the "COLD" stimulate the body and train the mind to focus beyond the immediate present.

ETVC™ encourages BAT formation, warms cold bodies, and puts on muscle (muscle has more mitochondria than fat), and levels blood sugars.

Increase BAT and you will BACK your way UP the aging pyramid (see page 21) to your **former** anabolic peak. When you reach that peak, you have become *Young Again!*

PREVIEW: *Our next chapter is going to SHOCK you! You are going to learn WHY men and women are going bald—and what they can do about it! You are also going to discover the relationship between certain cooking oils and the HIV/AIDS virus.*

Look at all the sick and dying people!

Medical Studies

People rely on the advice of their practitioner. Practitioners, in turn, foolishly rely on the *credibility* of medical studies to guide them.

Unfortunately, most medical studies are flawed. For the patient, *bogus* medical studies means the difference between life and death at worst or pain and suffering at best.

In front of me is a news article captioned, *"Fraud Mars Breast Cancer Research."* Investigators uncovered more than a *decade* of fraudulent breast cancer research. And another report condemns mammograms for damaging women's breast tissues.

These reports are frightening, but the **message** is clear. Your MUST learn to think for yourself because you cannot afford to rely on scientific "studies" and "experts" to save you. Hopefully that is why you are reading this book. **And please, do NOT fall into the trap** of conjuring reasons why tried and proven techniques outlined in this book will not work for you. **If you want your life back, be willing to do what needs to be done.** Excuses do not wash. Health and longevity are gifts we experience in the wake of *personal* responsibility and informed action. So go to work and experience the miracle in YOUR life as I did in mine. It feels wonderful to be "19" at age 53.

25

Bald Heads & Oils

"Hair on my legs, hair on my chest, but no hair on my head?"
Uncle Ross

Balding is a SIGN of premature aging. So is thinning hair. Balding is *loathed* by men, yet it is accepted as inevitable if it "runs" in the family. The *experts* tell us balding is a genetic trait. They are **wrong!** Balding is neither inevitable nor genetic, nor does it have to be permanent. Balding is related to oxygen dietary and digestive short falls, reduced ATP production, EXCESS waste in scalp tissues, hormonal imbalance, and poor diet. **Hair follicles die or go dormant in a toxic scalp!**

Scalp toxicity and congestion are linked to the consumption of certain dietary oils. If you eat the oils the *experts* tell you to eat, you will likely go bald or develop thin hair as well as succumb to degenerative conditions like arthritis, gout, heart problems, stroke, and cancer.

Almost ***everything*** the public has been taught about dietary oils and fats just isn't so. We have been manipulated and lied to. It's time to wake up.

A Short History Of Oils

Beginning in the 1930's, cotton seed oil became the primary "liquid" dietary oil substitute for fats like butter and lard. During WW ll, cotton seed oil was **hydrogenated** to create a butter substitute that was SOLID at room temperature. They called it **oleo**margarine, margarine or *oleo* for short. War mentality caused the public to accept oleo and by the 50's—when I was growing up—margarine was considered an *acceptable* butter substitute. By the early 1960's, Americans experienced ANOTHER fundamental shift in the TYPE of dietary oils and fats they were eating. This time, the move was even further away from solid fats like butter, lard, and oleo to "healthy" oils and tastier margerines.

While the media and the *experts* vilified butter and lard, the Cholesterol THEORY of Cardiovascular Dis-ease became the new scientific "buzz" within the halls of academia which spilled over engulfing the populace with fear and almost total rejection of butter, lard, and eggs.

Later, more cliches and buzz words were added to the American vocabulary, such as *unsaturated* and *poly-unsaturated.* Corn and safflower oils appeared on the scene. These replaced cotton seed oil for those with finer tastes and fatter wallets. Oleo was history and margarine was in its hey-day. Fewer people were eating butter. Lard was only for the poor.

By the late 1960's, SOY BEAN oil began to appear on supermarket shelves and in thousands of *processed* foods. Cotton seed, corn, and safflower oils were still in wide use, but there was a new focus—health! Soy bean oil became synonymous with **health *and the* health food movement.**

The shift away from natural fats—like butter, lard, and and coconut oils—to liquid and semisoft *hydrogenated* margarines coupled with chlorination and fluoridation of public water supplies, caused Americans to experience a dramatic increase in degenerative heart dis-ease.

The **experts** blamed naturally occurring *saturated* fats and *cholesterol* for the rise in cardiovascular problems and the increase in degenerative dis-ease while they **ignored** the dietary alterations. They also ignored "balding" because it was considered to be a "genetic" problem, NOT a dietary one.

The experts like to razzle dazzle us with oily words like omega 3's and 6,'s phrases like long vs. short chain fatty acids, and concepts like unstaurated and polyunsaturated. These terms are meaningless to the average person. What does hold meaning are the effects of premature old age. For instance, LOOK at the huge increase in young men with balding heads! And young women with thinning hair! Ignore the fancy talk. It is designed to keep you confused.

With the advent of the new "healthy" oils and soft margarines, balding and *thinning* hair increased in both sexes, young and old. The only person who noticed that something was going on was Dr. Carey Reams, who worked in the agricultural arena. He was a voice crying in the wilderness.

Please acquaint yourself with the following terms so we may continue our story with better understanding.

Arteriosclerosis—Hardening of the walls of the arterioles (small arteries) due mainly to fibrous thickening of the connective tissues in their walls, hyalinization, and infiltration of lipids (fats) into the intima (innermost wall) of the arteriole.

Atherosclerosis—a form of simple intimal arteriosclerosis with atheromatous deposits within and beneath the intima of the arteries.

Atheromatous deposits—the fatty *degeneration* of the artery walls with infiltration of those walls by lipids (fats)—as in arteriosclerosis. Cellular debris, toxic waste, and calcium deposits are usually involved.

Intima—the innermost layer of the three layers that compose the artery wall.

Hyalin—a clear substance that has undergone amyloid degeneration; material deposited in the glomeruli filters of the kidneys.

Amyloid—abnormal hyaline deposits in the tissues during pathological state (dis-ease).

Hyalinization—normal infusion of hyaline; seen normally in the matrix of cartilage and abnormally elsewhere; any alteration within the cells or extracellular spaces which involves the deposition of hyalin.

Plaque—a cholesterol containing mass in the intima or tunica of the arteries; means *patch.*

The Soy Connection

Dr. Carey Reams often commented on the rise in balding, but it was my friend, Tom Mahoney, who provided the clue that solved the puzzle. It was an *agricultural* clue.

Tom talked of a strange family of plants known as the **Fabales**. He observed that if cows or sheep were are allowed to graze on soy for any length of time, their health would suffer and thair would **thin** and/or **fall out.**

Tom's observations were the trigger I needed to solve Dr. Carey Reams' thirty year old question. Reams was sure there was a link between the dietary soy, balding, and aging

Soy Oil & PHG

Soy bean oil and soy bean curd (tofu) contain a toxic biochemical called **phyto-hema-glutinin** or PHG for short. Dissected, the word looks like this: *phyt(e)*-that which comes from plants). *hem(e)*-blood. *glutinin*-a vegetable protein "glue." **PHG is a large protein molecule that has proven to be specific in its ability to *agglutinate* human blood.**

Agglutination means to "glue," to cause to "adhere," to combine into a "mass!" The Rouleau effect we have been referring to is a good example of agglutination. Soy oil—and soy based products—are rich in PHG and promote Rouleau.

PHG causes blood circulation to slow. It causes blood to clot. It combines with impurities in the blood and forms plaques on the walls of the arterioles and clog the fine capillaries in the posterior eye, ears, and SCALP. It magnifies the Rouleau "sticky blood" problem affecting 85% of Americans. PHG numbs the immune system's T cells and it negatively influences the central and peripheral nervous systems. It alters hormonal activity and it influences endocrine and exocrine activity while it slows vital organ function.

PHG kills rats DEAD! It is poisonous to *all* living things. As with any systemic poison, the *quantity* consumed, *length* of exposure, and *individual* predisposition are factors that hint at why the body tolerates soy oil and proteins even though they are "bad news!" **The effects of soy PHG is "cumulative."**

Soy & Digestion

Soy interferes with *normal* digestion. Soy beans produce gas and upset body chemistry. Peanuts are another *famous* member of the Fabale family of plants and many people cannot digest peanut butter. Peanuts contain little PHG in comparison to soy. More examples of the Fabale family of foods are garbanzo beans (chic peas), fava beans, lentils, and mung beans. These contain *almost* no PHG.

Two Fabale legumes that cause serious long term problems for *grazing* animals are clover and alfalfa. In the field, they can be deadly toxic and cause bloating in ruminants. Cows, horses, and sheep thrive on grasses which contain **growth energy** proteins and sugars. Grasses have a different "spin" on their molecules than do legumes like alfalfa, clover and soy.

Soy PHG reacts with circulating minerals and dissolved blood gases like chlorine, chloramine, and fluorine and forms substances that resemble bath tub scum—like that which comes from using Grandma's lye soap in hard water.

*Municipalities use chemicals like sodium hypo-chlorite (sodium hydroxide + chlorine) to treat public water supplies. Sodium hydroxide **(lye)** is what Grandma used to make her lye soap. It is extremely alkaline (pH 12). Chlorine is extremely acidic (-2 and +2 pH) and is used to kill bacteria. The hydroxide is used to drive up the pH so that the acidic water will not kill you. Halogenated (chlorinated and fluoridated) tap water reacts with dietary oils and other circulating wastes and produces plaques that are a combination of these ingredients (Please note: these plaques are NOT difficult to clear form the body using the products and programs outlined herein.)*

Lipids (oils and fats) are absorbed by the lymphatic capillaries called **lacteals**. Unlike lipids, they are NOT absorbed directly into the blood capillaries as are proteins and carbohydrates. Lacteals give way to larger ducts that join the blood at the subclavian veins which feed the subclavian veins that empty into the superior vena cava that returns the blood to the right side of the heart. The heart then pumps the blood to the lungs for oxygenation AND energy *transference* before it is returned to the left side of the heart for distribution to the body. It is only AFTER the blood has run its course that it returns to the liver for cleaning. In the meantime, precipitates form the plaques that clog the heart and starve the hair.

Forty percent (40%) of the blood leaving the heart feeds the head via the carotid arteries. Soy REACTS with blood toxins and chemicals and settles OUT of the blood. These precipitates are electrically "charged" energy fields that cling to the walls of the coronary arteries that **service** the heart, slowing blood flow and oxygen delivery. **These precipitates are called *plaque!***

Plaque formation causes the lining (intima) of the arteries to deteriorate and form clots. When a clot or piece of plaque breaks lose, it can migrate up the neck and into the brain and cause a stroke. If, on the other hand, the oxygen supply to the heart becomes severely limited due to plaque formation, a heart attack will result.

As blood enters the neck, waste sticks to the artery walls, narrowing the carotid arteries that feed the head and brain. Waste finds its way into the VERY FINE capillaries that feed the cells of the posterior eyes, ears, and scalp closing them off. Plasma proteins that escape into the extracellular spaces further clog the lymph capillaries compounding problems for the scalp, ears, eyes, hair follicles, and nerve fibers.

Balding and graying are SIGNS of deteriorioation. Removal of acid wastes from the body causes hair to grow. Kombucha tea and GH$_3$™ are two ideal remedies.

Alfalfa Sprouts

Alfalfa sprouts are a popular vegetarian delight, but there is a caveat that comes with them. Alfalfa **sprouts** contain powerful *phytotoxins* that are detrimental to people with weak immune systems. In dry leaf form, as used in food supplements—alfalfa does not pose a problem. But in "fresh" sprout form, alfalfa should be avoided like the plague!

Cancer patients should NEVER, EVER eat alfalfa sprouts. Sprouts depress the immune system and create EXCESSES that fuel cancer. Sprouts cause cancer to attack with a vengeance! (Mung bean sprouts do NOT pose a problem.)

People with immune conditions or liver problems (AIDS, hepatitis, mononucleosis, chronic fatigue, cirrhosis, etc.) should avoid alfalfa sprouts because they STRESS the liver.

Occasional sickness is good. It means that your immune system is functioning and that your body KNOWS when things are out of balance.

Eyes • Ears • Chemothrapy

Glaucoma, retinitis, and macular degeneration occur for the same reasons that drive hair loss and graying. Translated, this means *insufficient* oxygen and nutrients reach the these organs, waste overload and hormone and neuro receptor sites lock up. Nugestrine II™, Totally Male™, SOC™ capsules and liver purges flip on receptor site "switches" and remove the waste burden so the body can rejuvenate itself.

Hair follicles are heavy energy feeders. They require good blood and lymph circulation. Slow growing hair and nails are a SIGN of low metabolic activity. Thinning hair is but another version of balding. Gray hair speaks for itself.

Loss of body hair—especially leg hair—is a SERIOUS condition and a red flag. Waste accumulation brings on problems in the feet, like walking legs syndrome, corns, bunions, deformed toes, and nerve and connective tissue disorders that make the feet "burn." Behind these problems is severe EXCESSES of waste plasma proteins and hormone irregularities. These problems can be easily REVERSED.

Supplementary Information On Soybeans

Soy beans are *unlike* other beans. Soy is a *toxic* plant! It is one of two **toxic** seed oil plants grown for their "industrial" oils. Insects seldom touch soy. Soy bean plants—and canola too—thrive on toxic soil and air. Soy proteins have a powerful

left-spin and should never be consumed. Soy converts and stores toxic energies in its "oil." **Humans do likewise by entombing their toxic waste energy fields in body fat. Remember, energy is never lost, it merely changes form.**
Few people know that soy beans were genetically altered in the middle 1950's with that "harmless" process called *irradiation*. This was done to INCREASE the soy bean's oil content and to create a plant that would prosper on toxic soils.

Powerful interests made sure "corporate" government funded soy research. They are the same people who promoted vaccinations and touted the Cholesterol and Germ Theories. They needed an oil crop that would grow on negative energy soils treated with synthetic salt fertilizers and poisonous sprays. The soy cartel was not concerned about the long term effects of soy on people. **Soy oil is an "industrial" oil that is being peddled as a food oil. Soy protein is a spin off.**

Sticky Oils • Sick People

The toxic nature of soy has been known for a long time, yet, soy oil is added to THOUSANDS of processed and prepared foods (read the food labels and see). Soy is even substituted for dairy products—like milk, butter, and baby formulas. *(A good article that details the dangers of soy baby formulas is available. To obtain, send SASE with $1 postage and $5.)*
Heat olive oil, butter, or lard in a skillet and you will observe that they become "thinner." Soy and canola oils thicken and become gummy—especially after they cool. Put soy and canola oils into a 98.6°F human body and you have a recipe for dis-ease. Soy oxidizes in the body and produces free radicals. **Industrial oils do not belong in the human body.**
Peanut oil is an interesting oil. Edgar Cayce said it was a nice massage oil for the skin. But put it in the body and all hell breaks loose. It is toxic inside the body, but not outside.
The best dietary oil to use is OLIVE OIL, followed by sunflower oil. Olive oil is the product of a **fruit**—the olive! If olive oil was good enough for Jesus, it ought to be good enough for you and me! Nut oils are fine, also sesame and flax seed oil. Avoid corn, safflower, and cotton seed oils.
Tofu is a **very** popular food among vegetarians. Tofu is the curd of the soy bean. It is rich in PHG because of its high oil content (up to 52%) and is therefore toxic. If you make Tofu a regular part of your diet, long term health will suffer and you will grow OLD and see your connective tissues break down. Tofu should NEVER be eaten by recovering cancer patients! NOTE: 99% of vitamin E capsules use soy oil as the carrier. Wheat germ oil is a better choice. PAC's are even better than

vitamin E in regard to antioxidant activity.

Many people ask, *"What about soy protein?"* My answer is avoid it if you can. It is not as toxic as the the oil which contains the PHG. However, it has a left spin and it's the wrong "kind" of protein. Scientists tell us that protein is protein, but then they tell us sugar is sugar, too.

All substances have an energy "signature"—including proteins. Soy protein is extremely difficult to digest because it contains large quantities of trypsin, a harmful substance that inhibits digestion and enlarges the pancreas. Foods high in trypsin fuel cancer too!

Soy is also high in phytates, which are salts of phytic acid. Phytates cause widespread mineral imbalances because soy has the highest phytate content of any food plant **EVER** studied. Vegetarians who consume soy and tofu eventually experience degeneration of the connective tissues and the buildup of excesses in the system. Phytates deprive the body of zinc which the body uses to ward off diabetes (pancreas) and strengthen the immune system. Soy produces connective tissue disorders in laboratory mice and in children affecting bones, cartilage, muscles, tendons, ligaments, and skin, and the myelin sheath protecting the nerve fibers. Soy is trouble!

Soy baby formulas are a **synthesized** product that create serious short AND long term problems for infants. **Toxic chemical SOLVENTS are used to extract the protein isolates (and oil) from the soy bean.** High heat processing denatures soy proteins and makes them unhealthy. Heavy metal contamination in soy formula is "10 times" that of the seed making soy formula a real threat. Mothers turn to soy formulas due to infant lactose intolerance. Breast milk is the first choice, then goat milk, followed by the recepie on page 368.

Food intolerance to "real" food in children disappears when DiSorb Aid™ and a little Yucca Blend™ is used. In adults, allergies are the confirmation of poor digestion, a toxic system, and hormonal imbalance.

Debating The Issues!

I am fully aware that the contents of these pages are totally contrary to what the 'experts' are saying about the benefits of soy ingestion. A week doesn't pass that some new "study" or *"soy miracle"* marketing scheme doesn't land on my desk with a note asking me to debate the issues regarding soy. **Sorry! There is nothing to debate.** Believe whomever you like. The choice is yours. Go ahead. Believe the experts. Ignore common sense and logic. In the end, I can assure you that the scoffers will be "dead" right!

Rotenone • Fish • Insects

Rotenone is used by organic gardeners as a "natural" organic pesticide. It is also used for poisoning unwanted fish species in lakes throughout North America.

Rotenone comes from the *soy bean. Roten* is Japanese for *derris.* It means to destroy, to tear apart. Derris is the specie name for the soy bean within the family Fabale.

Home gardeners have been told by the *experts* that rotenone is great stuff. However, if you read the label you will be warned against breathing the dust.

When inhaled, rotenone is absorbed through the mucous membranes. These membranes are a direct conduit into the blood and lymph and provide easy access to the body's IMMUNE system. A breath of rotenone dust is a direct shot at the central and peripheral nervous systems. It is the **glycosides** in the rotenone that brings on paralysis of the muscles.

We can LEARN from watching an insect that has been dusted with rotenone (PHG). Insects react to rotenone in a matter of seconds with TOTAL paralysis! This **harmless** *stuff from SOY BEANS shuts down the insect's nervous system and muscles. Soy foods do the same thing to people, but it does it a day at a time over a period of years!*

In lakes, rotenone causes a complex *series* of changes in metabolism that prevent fish from extracting ENERGY from nutrients! **Rotenone can kill ALL the fish in a lake with an application as small as 1 part per million (ppm).**

One-half pound of rotenone is equivalent to 60,000 ppm. One-half pound equals 8 ounces or 7,500 ppm per ounce. The *experts* tell us that it would take **1 ounce** of rotenone to kill a 150 pound man. If 1 ppm can kill all the fish in a lake, do you think it would require a concentration that is 7,499 times greater to kill a human being?

It would appear that the *experts* calculations as to what is a "safe" amount of this **poison** that the human body can handle is off a bit. The truth of the matter is that the *experts* don't know or care what is a safe amount. These are the same "experts" Rachel Carson struggled against in her effort to warn mankind of the inherent danger of pesticides. I suggest you read *Silent Spring* and *Our Stolen Future* (see Source Index). When you eat soy oil, you are ingesting PHG—which gums up your blood and puts your IMMUNE and NERVOUS systems under severe stress. Avoid it!

Sweet Proteins

Glycine is an amino acid. It is one of approximately

twenty-three amino acids that form larger molecules called proteins. Sow peas (soy beans) are very rich in glycine containing proteins because they have been *irradiated* and *genetically engineered* to produce proteins that are high in glycine. Industry, in turn, concentrates glycine through a process called hydrolysis. The result is a glycine-max (glycocide) concentrate (*glyc*-means sweet, as in glycogen which is glucose in storage form in our muscles; *cide*-death by prevention of glycolosis). Glycolysis is the process by which the mitochondria produce our ATP energy molecules (*glyc*-sweet; *lysis*-to cleave or divide.)

Saponification (the same process Grandma used to make her lye soap) is used to concentrate glycine. A liquid glycer**ol** is produced that is extremely sweet and syrupy. These molecules have an *alcohol* molecule attached.

An -**ol** on the end of a chemical name means it is an alcohol. Alcohols are excellent *non-polar* solvents, that is, they dissolve fatty substances like those that comprise our cellular membranes. Alcohols destroy our cells and attack the myelin sheath that protects our nerve fibers.

The chemical industry likes *glycine-max* glycer**ol**. It is widely used as a *solvent* and as a **plasticizer** in the manufacture of hundreds of plastics, including PVC water pipe.

BEV water cannot be transported in common plastics of any kind or processed through a carbon block filter, because it reacts with the plasticizers and glues and dissolves them. Bottled water—especially distilled water—is loaded with plastic isolates leached from the plastic bottles. That is one of the reasons distilled water tastes so bad. Concentration of poisonous volitiles is another shortcoming of distillation.

When the soy molecule is subjected to heat in the presence of organic compounds like those in our blood, "thermoplastic" resins are formed. The result is **sticky blood** that clumps and closes off the capillaries. Keep in mind, this is a "subtle" process that occurs SLOWLY over a period of years! The body cannot tolerate these resins, so it stores them in the soft tissues and fat. Blood vessel degeneration and plaque formation are part of this scenario.

Glycosides • Opium • Morphine • Atropine

Glycosides (rotenone) from soybeans causes physiologic reactions in humans and animals. *Morphine* and *atropine* are examples of drugs that contain high concentrations of glycosides. Morphine comes from opium and skews the **central nervous system**. It affects muscle control, pupil dilation, and is extremely reactive in the body. *Atropine* comes from the belladonna family of plants. It alters response to electrical signals and causes paralysis of the **parasympathetic nervous system,** the part of our nervous system over which we have NO direct control—like the heart muscle, breathing muscles, and intestinal muscles. *Digitalis* is a glycoside that comes from Foxglove. **Morphine, atropine,** and **digitalis** are "legally" controlled substances that have been *isolated* and *concentrated.* **Synthetic** glycosides are openly substituted for the real thing with serious side effects for patients. The experts tell us there is no difference between *real* and *synthesized.* Really?

Soy & Dog Food

In front of me is a label from a can of a well known brand of dog food. You will find it on your supermarket shelves. It says "Soy FREE • Highly Digestible."

The implications of the words on the label and those on TV ads (January 6, 1994) indicate that there is a serious problem with soy protein in dog food. Some dog food manufactures tout *digestibility* because they have removed the soy. At the same time, they are very closed mouthed about the **long term** *degenerative* effects of soy on dogs. They are afraid of retaliation by the soy cartel and other *yellow fringe flag* types.

The dog food and grazing animal connection confirms the problem of soy oil and soy protein in HUMAN metabolism. Soy causes serious degenerative problems in humans, but it is NOT being taken out of our food. Instead, it is being **promoted** by *expert after expert* as the "perfect" food. The miracles of soy are now the subject of a recent book.

This book is behind the introduction of a soy "miracle" product—complete with the usual multilevel hype and an army of experts!

If food that contains soy is toxic to dogs **(carnivores),** and grazing animals **(herbivores),** what do you think it will do to human beings **(omnivores)** who are a little of both?

Maybe people should decide what dog pedigree they would like to be so they can qualify for *soy free, highly digestible food—arf, arf!* Avoid foods that contain soy oil, soy protein solids, and tofu—period!

Note: Private soy interests—via government—recently strong armed the largest hamburger chain in the world (guess who) from going back to using animal fats for their french fries. It appears that soy cartel interests "control" government.

Conclusion

We know the cumulative effects of soy bean oil, canola oil, tofu, and alfalfa sprouts on humans and animals. We know their effects on the blood, the central and peripheral nervous systems, the immune system, and how they "block" hormonal receptor sites and foul the environment. **The evidence is obvious for those with eyes to see!**

Please **do not** call the publisher making demands for "documentation." There is more than enough information contained in this book for those who can think without the blessings of higher authority. **Ignore the experts and you stand a much better chance of becoming** *Young Again!*

PREVIEW: *In our next chapter, you will learn about the connection between blindness, glaucoma, and canola oil!*

"Women should get a bone density test every year!"

The Gulf War Connection

Gulf War veterans were <u>ordered</u> to take a drug called Pyridostigmine Bromide (PB) every day. This drug interferes with *acetylcholinesterase*—an enzyme that is critical to nerve synapse function (nerve signal transmission). **The side effects were known & predictable!**

PB produces the symptoms being experienced by Gulf War veterans. The question is WHO ordered its use and WHY? The answer is "the experts!" The same experts that tell us to eat soy and canola oil and promote birth control pills, estrogen replacements and "harmless" organophosphate poisons like malathion.

Anyone who is taking or who has taken **ANY** of the above mentioned drugs can now "clear" those analogous molecules from their body's neuro and hormonal receptor sites by using racemized™ hormone precursors, Yucca Herbal Blend™ and PAC's.

Noticeable biological activity is experienced by most people within 24-72 hours of usage. Nerve signal function and rebuilding of the myelin sheath on the nerve fibers precedes the formation of new bone and cartilage, muscles, ligaments and tendons.

These products work equally well for veterans, osteoporotic women and hyper active or attention deficit children—all of which have receptor site "lock up."

Women with SIGNS of premature aging, or menstrual difficulties, experience a rebirth, while men with prostate problems get to stop worrying.

War In The Marketplace

It takes twenty years to create a market for a product. Early on, consumers fight back IF an enemy can be identified. In time, fight gives way to resistance. After twenty years, fatigue sets in, memory fades, and the metamorphosis is complete.

The rules for *creating* a bogus market are the same as for waging war. I refer the reader to Sun Tzu's 6th century B.C. book *The Art Of War*, summarized as follows.

Outline an agenda, disseminate disinformation and misinformation, create confusion and dissension, raise an army of experts, use subversion, quote statistics, and finally create fear. Fear leads to panic, and panic to victory.

Perhaps now you can see how the soy and canola oil cartel(s) developed antipathy towards butter, coconut oil, and lard while creating a high demand, consumer-friendly market for **industrial** oils like soy and canola.

Sun Tzu was correct! The game is called **divide and conquer!** It's simple. It works. His book was the official training manual in the rise of the Soviet empire.

Hear what the experts preach. *See* which way the masses are moving. *Tune-in* to what the media is pushing. **Now! Go the other way as you spread the word!**

The '250' Club

The "250" Club is for anyone who would like to live to the age of 250 vibrant, healthy, years *young!*

Please do not dismiss such a goal as impossible or ridiculous. It's within the reach of anyone who truly desires to see it become a reality in their life.

Society needs goals and role models. Think of the good things that would spin-off from a core of people who have healthfully lived five generations? Instead of each generation starting over every fifty years losing wisdom and experience, the "250" Club would act as a *transition* team to help other humans worldwide to learn to live in harmony with Nature and each other as GOD intended.

Think of the suffering and strife that could be eliminated through the transfer of correct living to our g...r...e...a...t grand children. Life on Earth would become a joy. So clean up your body, use racemized™ hormone precursors, and eat SUPER FOODS, and "250" will happen for you.

The "250" Club is a testimony to the world.

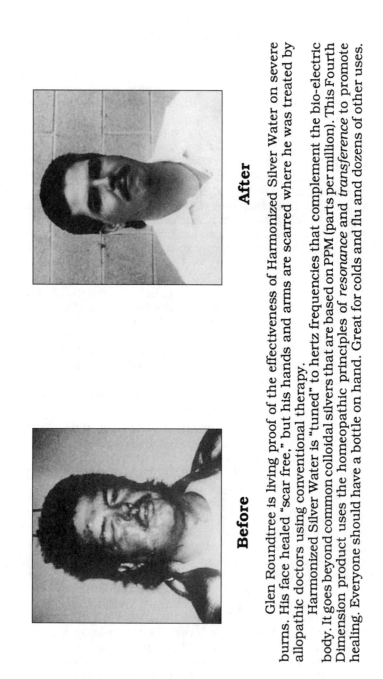

Before

After

Glen Roundtree is living proof of the effectiveness of Harmonized Silver Water on severe burns. His face healed "scar free," but his hands and arms are scarred where he was treated by allopathic doctors using conventional therapy.

Harmonized Silver Water is "tuned" to hertz frequencies that complement the bio-electric body. It goes beyond common colloidal silvers that are based on PPM (parts per million). This Fourth Dimension product uses the homeopathic principles of *resonance* and *transference* to promote healing. Everyone should have a bottle on hand. Great for colds and flu and dozens of other uses.

26

Blindness & Oils

"Since the days of revelation, the same four corrupting errors have been made over and over again: submission to faulty and unworthy authority; submission to what was customary to believe; submission to prejudices of the mob; and worst of all, concealment of ignorance by a false show of unheld knowledge, for no other reason than pride."
Roger Bacon

Millions of people have suffered the loss of their vision from glaucoma, a dis-ease involving *atrophy* (deterioration) of the optic nerve. For years, the *experts* have been telling people that glaucoma results from fluid pressure buildup in the eye which causes the optic nerve to deteriorate. This THEORY was based on an incorrect medical model. **They were wrong!**

The *experts* now admit that these things are NOT true and have given birth to a new theory that says glaucoma is caused by a deficiency of oxygen and blood flow. Finally, they are on the right track. In the end, they will discover that glaucoma is the result of insufficient blood flow and agglutination (clumping) of red blood cells, metabolic waste buildup in **inter**cellular fluids and spaces, and hormone irregularities.

Agglutinated blood CANNOT squeeze through the extremely fine capillaries of the posterior eye (over 80 miles per eye) and, therefore, cannot deliver oxygen and nutrients to the cells and the mitochondria, nor can it remove cellular waste.

Death of the mitochondria in the cells of the *posterior* eye is due to oxygen starvation, sodium toxicity, and waste accumulation. When the cells die, the tissues of the posterior eye *atrophy* and the dead cells create acid waste. Acid waste buildup, nutrient starvation, and hormone short falls are also behind hair loss, Alzheimers, multiple sclerosis, cerebral palsy, fibromyalgia, and hearing disorders. For sure, the hormonal issue must be addressed if the body's receptor sites are to be cleared of hormone analogs. (An hormonal "analog" is a molecule that fits neuro receptors and blocks normal function.)

Rape or Canola?

The name **Canola** is a "coined" word. It is not listed in anything but the most recent reference sources. It is a word that appeared out of *nowhere.*

The flip side of the canola coin reads: RAPE! You must admit that canola sounds better than *rape*. The name *canola* masked the introduction of **rape oil** to America.

Canola oil comes from the rape seed, which is part of the Mustard family of plants. Rape is the **MOST** toxic of all food oils. Rape is a toxic plant and insects will not eat rape. It is deadly poisonous. **The oil from the rape seed is a hundred times more toxic than soy oil!**

Canola oil is a *semi-drying* oil that is used as a lubricant, fuel, soap, and synthetic rubber base, and as an illuminant for the slick color pages you see in magazines. Canola is an **industrial** oil. It does NOT belong in the body!

Canola oil (like soy) has some interesting characteristics *and* effects on living systems. For example, it forms latex-like substances that cause *agglutination* of the red blood corpuscles just like soy only MUCH more pronounced. Loss of vision is a **known** characteristic side effect of rape oil. Rape oil *antagonizes* the central and peripheral nervous systems—like soy oil, only worse. Deterioration, however, takes years.

Rape (Canola) oil causes pulmonary emphysema, respiratory distress, anemia, constipation, irritability, and blindness in the bodies of ANIMALS—and humans.

Rape oil was in widespread use in animal feeds in England and Europe between 1986 and 1991 when it was thrown out. Do you remember reading about the cows, pigs, and sheep that went **blind,** lost their minds, and attacked people? They had to be shot!

*Not long after the first edition of this book appeared, a woman called me from Chicago to tell me that she was in England at the time the Mad Cow Disease was at its peak. She told me that she witnessed a news report on television that told people not to panic if they had been using rape oil in their diet and were over 65 years of age. The "experts" added that the effects of rape oil ingestion takes **at least** ten years to manifest, and in all likelihood, most of these people would be dead by then anyway. Interesting!*

In the reports I read, the "experts" *blamed* the erratic behavior on a viral dis-ease called *scrapie*. However, when rape oil was removed from animal feed, scrapie disappeared. Now we are growing rape seed and using rape (canola) oil in the USA.

Canola oil is now *our* problem. It is widely used in thousands of processed foods—with the blessings of government watchdog agencies, of course.

Officially, canola oil is known as "LEAR" oil. The acronym stands for *low erucic acid* **rape.** The *experts* in the industry love to tell the story of how canola was developed in Canada and that it is safe to use. They admit it was developed from the rape seed, but that through *genetic engineering* (irradiation) it is no longer rape seed, but instead "canola!"

The experts love to talk about canola's "qualities"—like its unsaturated structure, omega $3's$, $6's$, and $12's$, its wonderful digestibility and its fatty acid makeup. They malign **naturally** saturated oils and fats and come to the rescue with Canola oil. They even tell us how Asia has warmly embraced Canola due to its distinctive flavor. *Isn't it wonderful how multinational oil cartels "help" third world people? Doesn't their story remind you of the introduction of microwave ovens?*

In the old west, there was an **earthy** expression that sums up the industry flim flam that accompanied the smoke and mirror introduction of rape oil into the diets of unsuspecting people world wide. It was, *"Horse Shit & Gun Smoke!"*

The term *canola* gave the perfect cover for cartel interests who wanted to make billions. The name "canola" is a warm fuzzy, but it is no longer needed. I suggest you go to the grocery store and look at the peanut butter ingredient labels. The peanut oil has been replaced with **rape** oil.

Chemical Warfare

The chemical warfare agent, MUSTARD GAS is derived from rape oil. This is the chemical agent that was responsible for blistering the lungs and skin of hundreds of thousands of solder and civilians during WW I. Recent reports from the French indicate mustard gas was used during the Gulf War.

Between 1950 and 1953, white mustard seed (rape seed) was **irradiated** in Sweden to increase seed production and oil content. *Irradiation* is the same process the *experts* want to use to make our food *safe* to eat. Genetically engineered fruits and vegetables—which will soon have innocent things like hepatitis-B spliced into their DNA—are another example of man's misuse of technology and abuse of public trust by powerful interests and "head in the sand" watchdog agencies.

Canola oil contains large amounts of **iso-thio-cyanates** which are **cyanide** containing compounds. Cyanide IN-HIBITS mitochondrial production of ATP. ATP is the chemical acronym for adenosine triphosphate, which is the energy molecule that fuels the body and keeps us healthy and *YOUNG!*

Canola Oil & Body Metabolism

Many substances can *bind* metabolic enzymes and block their activity in the body. In biochemistry, these substances are called *inhibitors.* We have spent a great deal of time talking about inhibitors, only we used terms like bio-junk food, toxic waste, negative energy, drugs, left-spin, etc.

Toxic substances in canola and soy oils encourage the formation of covalent bonds. Normally, covalent bonds are *irreversible* and CANNOT be broken by the body once they have formed. This is particularly true of hormone analogs contained in birth control pills, estrogen replacements (primarin/provera) and anabolic steroids used by athletes. Environmental hormones are so ubiquitous that they are unavoidable. **The solution to these dangerous molecules is REGULAR use of Nugestrine II™ and Totally Male™ hormone precursors.**

For example, consider the pesticide **malathion.** It binds to the active site of the enzyme *acetylcholinesterase* and stops this enzyme from doing what it is supposed to do, which is to divide acetylcholine into choline and acetate.

Malathion is the "harmless" pesticide spray used to kill the Med Fly and blanket every living thing in California a few years ago and again in February and March of 1994, and in Texas in April of 1995. Malathion is an **organophosphate.**

Nerve Function & Organophosphates

Acetycholine is critical to NERVE impulse transmission. When inhibited, nerve synapses do not function normally and the muscles do not respond.

For example, think of your garage door opener. If no signal is sent, the door does not open. In the case of the body, your hand or leg does not respond. Perhaps you have noticed the tremendous increase in disorders like systemic lupus, multiple sclerosis, cerebral palsy, myelinoma, pulmonary hypertension, and neuropathy in recent years. Soy and canola oils are players in the development of these dis-ease conditions. So are the **organophosphate** insecticides used in food production in the name of efficiency.

Acetylcholinesterase inhibitors cause paralysis of the striated (skeletal) muscles and spasms of the respiratory system.

That is why malathion is the pesticide of choice by the *experts.* It kills insects by causing **muscle paralysis**—just like *rotenone* from soy beans! It inhibits the insect's *enzymes*. It inhibits the enzymes of humans too!

Agents *orange* and *blue* that were used in Vietnam to defoliate jungle cover are organophosphorous compounds. The Vietnam Vets and the Vietnamese people know first-hand about them. Government *experts* who okayed their use and chemical companies that manufactured them have finally owned up to their toxic effects on PEOPLE and the environment. Nevertheless, present day *experts* in academia and government continue to **"abba dabba"** the public with stories of "safe" science and cheap food through the use of poisons.

Canola oil is rich in glycosides. Glycosides cause serious problems in the human body by blocking enzyme function and locking up nerve and hormone receptors.

Glycosides interfere with the biochemistry of humans and animals. Consider the effect of a rattlesnake bite. It is the glycosides in the venom that **inhibit** muscle enzymes and cause instant immobilization in the target host.

Canola Oil • HIV & AIDS

Soy and canola oil glycosides depress the immune system. They cause the **white blood cell defense system**—the T-cells—to go into a stupor and fall asleep on the job. These oils alter the body "terrain" and promote dis-ease.

The alcohols and glycosides in canola and soy oils shut down our protective grid—the immune system. Fluoride, immunizations, antibiotics, and bio-junk food play complimentary roles in immune system collapse.

An *alcohol* is a chemistry term for the "reactive" chemical group on an organic molecule. The "-R" group is what makes organic compounds work—for good and bad! Canola alcohols and glycosides are very reactive. They are just as toxic as alcoholic beverages, but their effects manifest differently. **The damage takes years to show up.** *(You may wish to review our discussion of sweet proteins in the soy chapter.)*

When the medical experts check your blood for the presence of the HIV virus, they are looking at your white blood cell count. If the numbers are normal, they will tell you that you do NOT have HIV. What they don't see is that the T-cells are in a toxic *stupor*. This *opportunistic* condition allows life forms in the blood and lymph to metamorphose and manifest as hepatitis, pneumonia, herpies, **HIV,** and to *bypass* the body's immune system defenses (the T-cells) and get a foothold. As Claude Barnard said, *"The terrain is everything!"*

Once inside the cells, HIV takes over the RNA and DNA. It uses the mitochondria to produce energy for their

own use. Quietly, the virus multiplies (replicates) and one day—BANG!—you wake up and you are dying of AIDS.

AIDS & Green Monkeys

In his earth shaking book, *AIDS The End of Civilization,* Dr. William Campball Douglass asked, *"Do you really think some Green Monkey all of a sudden bit some guy in the ass and presto, AIDS all over the world?"*

Dr. Douglass was examining the hype that the Centers for Disease Control in Atlanta was *peddling* to the public about the AIDS virus—HIV. Douglass' book tells the "whole" story of the development of HIV at the Ft. Detrick, Maryland military installation. His story is well documented and confirms the theme of the futuristic movies *Outbreak* and *The Twelve Monkeys* which I highly recommend you see.

Lorenzo's Oil

Another movie, *Lorenzo's Oil,* offers another good example of how far off course medical science has strayed and how muddled is the scientific mind. Early on in the movie, the *experts* said the problem with the dying child was not in the math (i.e., pH). They were wrong.

Had the experts determined the pH of the saliva, urine, and blood they would have *instantly* known what they were up against. That dying boy had a chronically low total body pH! So low that his body fluids were *dissolving* the myelin sheath that protects the nerve fibers. This was causing his nervous system to disintegrate. *Does this description smack of the dozens of degenerative nerve related disorders plaguing people today?*

The boy was given Lorenzo's oil to boost energy output and act as a detoxifier of metabolic poisons. The oil *shocked* his body into a LESS acid condition. Lorenzo's oil is OLIVE oil! When given in large quantities, olive oil SHOCKS the body and causes it to adjust its pH.

Shortly after Lorenzo's Oil was released, my brother witnessed a TV talk show where an expert claimed that Lorenzo's oil was rape oil. This was a lie. Give rape oil to a sick person and you will seal their doom. Here is another good example of "disinformation" in the public domain. These falsehoods should cause every thinking person to question the molding of public opinion by **yellow fringe flag** *interests behind the scenes.*

Blood & Oils

By now it should be obvious to the reader that congested blood and lymph flow negatively affects every part of the body. It should be equally obvious that there is a direct link between dis-ease, diet, and the water we drink. Moreover, the astronomical increase in the use of processed foods that contain canola oil, soy oil and soy proteins, and chemical additives CONFUSES the body and weakens the immune system.

It should also come as no surprise that anyone wanting to enjoy peak health and longevity MUST take control of their life and personal responsibility for their health. Fortunately, all of the health issues dogging people can be eases or reversed.

The "health care" industry is an oxymoron. It protects its own health and economic interests. Learn to protect YOUR health and economic interests by learning HOW to take care of yourself and acting upon that knowledge immediately.

Note: *ABC news just aired the results of a damning medical study that confirmed that soy and canola oils are definitely linked to prostate cancer in men. The report aired on February 15, 1994.* Now the *experts* are promoting soy oil breast implants for **unsuspecting** women. Amazing!

PREVIEW: *Our next chapter looks at the connection between onions, your liver, and aging.*

It's important to hang and s-t-r-e-t-c-h every day.

"Everything In Excess Is Opposed By Nature."
Hippocrates

Vibrations! And Other Books Worth Reading

Learn how to use a vibration chain to determine energy "spin," siphon away pain from an injury site or inflamed joint, and eliminate stray electrical energy fields from your home. *Vibrations* is the life work of an 87 year Wizard and the perfect member of a trilogy that includes the *Pendulum Kit* and *Map Dowsing*. *Vibrations* is more than a book. It's an experience. And if you like history, you'll fall in love with the big 8 1/2 x 11, 372 page, profusely illustrated masterpeice on the 500 year history of dowsing called *The Divining Hand* (see Source Page).

Comfrey Greens

In the good old days, before the FDA decided to save us from the evils of comfrey, it could be found in stores. Today, if you want comfrey, you have to grow it yourself or have someone grow it for you. And, if you are smart, that is exactly what you will do.

Obtain a few crowns with a few shoots, and plant each one flush with the soil surface. In a few weeks, you will see luxurious plants spring out of the ground and grow up to 5 feet high and 4 feet wide. Allow plenty of space. Pick greens and blossoms from spring to frost. Nothing bothers comfrey. The roots grow to forty feet. I often cut the plants down to force new, tender growth.

The leaves may be mixed in salads or put on sandwiches. Eaten like spinach, the leaves and blossoms are at their very best! Steam until wilted, yet bright green in color. Add a little olive oil and apple cider vinegar and you've got a highly nutritious meal.

The FDA says comfrey is dangerous. If that's true, my family and I should all be dead! We've eaten comfrey several times a week for years and love it.

Plant comfrey once, and you will have "free" food forever—food that is outside the reach of the bureaucrats! It can also be grown in pots on the patio or inside and is easy to divide and repot over and over. Pulverized comfrey root and aloe heals peptic and intestinal ulcers! Maybe that is why the pharmaceutical companies had the fed's ban it?

What Is A Precursor

A precursor is a chemical substance that precedes the formation of something else. A racemized™ precursor accelerates the speed at which this occurs.

All racemized™ products produce excellent results that far exceed store or MLM supplements.

Use them once and you will never again ask if they "really" (?) work. Besides, racemized™ products are a wonderful way to get MORE bang for your dollar.

Pesticide Free?

I recently saw a *huge* canola oil display in a store. The sign said, "Pesticide Free." What they didn't mention was that canola oil is a long term "systemic" **poison!**

27

Liver & Onions

"As goes the liver, so goes the body!"
Anon.

The liver is **THE** most abused organ of the body. It is the body's *primary* waste removal organ. A healthy liver is essential to good health and central to the aging reversal process.

The liver is a phenomenal chemical factory that is responsible for *thousands* of biochemical reactions. It is the second largest organ in the body and the ONLY organ that will *regenerate* itself on its own volition—even when only 25% remains in tact. The liver's regenerative ability is an indication of its importance. The liver's functional cells are called **hepatocytes,** (*hepat*-liver; *cyte*-cell) and are classified as *parenchyma* cells.

The liver metabolizes food, drugs, pesticides, wastes and alcohol that arrive via its **dual** blood supply. These substances impose heavy physiologic stress on the liver, and in turn, on all the other organs and glands of the body.

When the liver becomes overly toxic, the hepatocytes die. The spaces they leave behind are filled by connective "scar" tissue which is comprised of *stroma* cells that normally cover the "outside" of the liver. When the hepatocytes die, stroma tissue invades and forms scar tissue. This occurs in cirrhosis of the liver, a condition of EXCESS that often manifests as a nutritional deficiency dis-ease, when in fact it is not. Cirrhosis causes the liver to "yellow" and "harden."

The liver is **heavily** vascularized with blood vessels. It receives a DOUBLE supply of blood. *Oxygenated* blood from the heart is supplied via the hepatic artery and nutrient laden *deoxygenated* blood comes from the intestines via the hepatic portal vein. If waste accumulates on the walls of the portal vein, blood pressure rises and its called *portal hypertension.*

The Kupffer's cells that line the blood vessels of the liver are of *immense* importance to health and vitality. Kupffer's cells are both **hepatocytes** and **phagocytes** (*phag*-to eat. *cyte*-cell.) Phagocytes remove microbes, foreign matter, and worn out red and white blood cells from circulation.

The liver filters toxic waste from the blood and normally disposes of it through the bile via the intestines and bowel. Bile also acts to emulsify dietary fat for proper assimilation. Fats provide NEEDED cholesterol necessary for the forming of all of the corticosteroid hormones made by the adrenal glans (cortisone is a commonly recognized steroid).

In a sick or aged body, liver function becomes so compromised that the body instead builds fat and cellulite. When you see a fat body, you are seeing a sick body.

The liver consumes large amounts of energy in the performance of its job. If the body is under stress—mental stress (negative thinking; worrying, anger, fear, etc.) or physical stress from drugs and toxic food and water—fatigue and dis-ease eventually follow.

Toxification of the blood, lymph, joints, and soft tissues of the body ALWAYS involves a sick liver!

Hepatitis (*hepat*-liver; *itis*-inflamation of) is a liver condition. So are mononucleosis, Epstein-Barr, and Chronic Fatigue Syndrome. All of them mirror conditions of EXCESS waste overload in the system and hormonal imbalance. Practitioners blame nature's garbage crew—the viruses—for the damage inflicted on the liver, but they are wrong.

Thanks to Dr. Guenther Enderlein, we know the exact sequence of microbial metamorphosis that occurs along the trail of degenerative dis-ease. We also know what to do about it as described in *Hidden Killers* (see Source Page).

Officially, hepatitis manifests as type A, B, C, D, or E. All are currently prevalent in the USA and are **not** difficult to reverse if the person is willing to cooperate.

Rene's tea is being used intravenously in mainland China for viral blood conditions with great success and for distemper in dogs and cats by a few US veterinarians. PAC's and Yucca Herbal Blend™ are very helpful as is Kombucha tea. Detoxification, hormone precursors, exercise, good water, and rest all play an important part in healing.

Choleric Personalities

As people age, their personalities change. One personality type—the choleric—reflects the condition of a person's liver. The *choleric* has a *bitter* personality that is vile and difficult. The word *choleric* comes from *chole* which means bile in Greek. *Chole* refers to the liver's digestive juice and waste product, bile. A "bilious" person has a foul personality. Alcoholics and some older folks are notorious for being *bilious*. (The Greeks believed there were four basic personality types: choleric, melancholy, sanguine, and phlegmatic.)

Much of Western medicine's disastrous history was the result of the theories of the Greek physician and medical writer Claudius Galen (circa A.D. 130-200). He was the personal physician to the Roman Emperor, Marcus Aurelius.

Galen believed in the four basic personality types. He called them "humors." A humor is a body fluid that was believed to influence personality. Galen's theories were, for the most part, in total error. His personality types, however, are still in vogue, but under new "personality" names like type-A, type-B, etc. **Humoral** *immunity refers to circulating antibodies and antigens in the blood and lymphatic fluids.*

Hydrogen Chloride • Bile & Aging

Aging of the vital organs seriously limits our ability to process food, FLOODING the body with a never ending flow of toxic wastes. Insufficient production of hydrogen chloride by the stomach cells, LIMITS protein digestion and allows parasites and their eggs to PASS into the body. Indigestion is often blamed on too much stomach acid, but exactly the opposite is the case. Racemized™ HCl, Yucca Herbal Blend™ and DiSorb Aid™ do wonders for digestion problems, eliminating indigestion, gas, and bloating. They also relieve "hyetal" hernia pain by relieving abdominal "pressure" on the diaphragm—a **very common complaint** of women. **Hormones** and **digestion** are CLOSELY linked. Gas, bloating, indigestion, fat, cellulite, hair problems, thyroid issues and low energy should be **RED FLAGS—especially for women!**

Stomach acid has a pH as low as .8. It is so acidic that a drop of it on the skin will eat a hole in it. Healthy mucous membranes protect the stomach's walls from this powerful acid. **When the issues discussed thus far are addressed, the membranes return to health.**

Peptic ulcers occur on the stomach's walls. Duodenal ulcers occur on the walls of the small intestine. Aging, stress, and H. pylori (a bacteria) all underwrite peptic ulcers.

The liver strongly affects digestion. A sick liver does NOT discharge enough bile—and the quality is poor, and is often noticed in the evening or after a greasy meal. A healthy liver produces about **1 quart** of bile a day. Bile is a yellowish-brown or sometimes olive-green juice with very alkaline pH. Bile contains mineral ions, **chole**sterol, and bilirubin from worn-out red blood corpuscles. Bilirubin gives bile its yellow, brown, and green color. If we dissect the word **chole**sterol, we get *chole*-bile. *ster*-a fat and *ol*-alcohol.

Gall stones are CLOSELY related to digestion problems. They are very common and very serious. Due to hormonal problems, they are 10 TIMES more prevalent in women than in men! Gallstones are LIVER stones that have migrated out of the liver, hardened and settled in the gallbladder (stones range in size from lentils to golf balls). A little Yucca Blend™ with each meal does wonders for gallbladder troubles. A Liver purge erases the problem.

Partially digested food (called chyme) exits the stomach and enters the first of three sections of the small intestine which is called the *duodenum* where it is mixed with secretions from the pancreas and bile from the liver. These secretions are VERY **alkaline** and are designed to raise the pH of the chyme so carbohydrate bonds can be broken and the sugars digested. **Note: drinking fluids with meals dilutes stomach acids and digestive enzymes and creates the perfect environment for parasites—an environment of putrified food—and a steady flow of poisons that sicken and age the host.**

Micelles

Bile (and Yucca Blend™) work like dish soap. They break up and emulsify up large fat globules into pin head droplets called *micelles*. Micelles have more surface area, making it easier for the body to process and absorb.

The gallbladder stores bile secreted from the liver and digestion triggers the release of bile into the small intestines. **Bile is to digestion as detergent is to greasy dishwater.**

Without enough bile, dietary fats cannot be digested. Partial digestion robs the body of energy because up to 40% of our energy comes from the oxidation of fat. The formation of micelles is central to the absorption of the fat soluble vitamins A,D,E, and K. Poor fat metabolism results in serious health problems and low energy and its effects are similar to the disastrous effects of current "fat free" foods and programs.

Bile contains heme (organic iron). Loss of heme, which is *said to be* the oxygen carrying component of hemoglobin, results in the loss of energy and vitality. This is particularly true for menstruating women. *Iron Deficiency Anemia* is, however, NOT the result of a lack of dietary iron, but of loss of function in the vital organs due to systemic toxicity and hormonal imbalance (excesses). Iron deficiency anemia is easily treated when the basics are tended to.

Most **heme** iron is reabsorbed in the gut. It is FAR more biologically active than dietary iron. If there is a shortage of heme iron in the body, there will be a corresponding shortfall in mitochondrial oxidation of glucose (conversion of glucose into ATP, our energy molecule) and diminished capacity of the blood that supplies the mitochondria as well as the hepatocytes. Elevated blood sugar levels (diabetes) is related to low heme iron levels, hormone imbalances, and a poor diet.

Dietary iron supplements are disastrous to the body. Iron is an oxidizer and participates in the formation of free radicals. Klammath™ algae is a perfect solution for iron deficient people because it provides needed raw materials in a form the body can use to produce heme iron. Fresh, organic, green leafy vegetables are excellent.

If the liver is toxic and cannot remove bilirubin from the blood, waste backs up into the entire body. Jaundice is the result of excess bile and bilirubin in the blood and produces a yellow coloration in the whites of the eyes. People with hepatitis, cirrhosis, and mononucleosis often reflect a jaundiced appearance. Jaundice is a SIGN of serious liver malfunction.

Children often suffer from liver malfunctions. Acne, boils, jaundice, constipation, appendicitis, psoriasis, and learning difficulties are symptomatic of liver problems and systemic toxicity—all of which can be treated at home.

Lecithin is the fat emulsifier in bile that keeps cholesterol in solution. As the body ages and pH shifts, cholesterol, salts, drugs, and minerals in the bile settle out and cause gallstones to grow in size. Gallstones **originate** in the liver and **grow** to giant proportions in the gallbladder.

If gallstones BLOCK the bile duct connecting the liver and the small intestine, gangrene will set in a matter of hours. Gangrenous tissue is dead tissue that has rotted in the absence of oxygen. A gangrenous gallbladder must be removed or the person will die from toxic shock poisoning (toxemia). **Loss of the gallbladder usually results in diabetes within 20 years unless action is take to prevent it.**

Modern medicine has made quick work of gallbladder removal. However, people need to understand the CAUSES behind gallstone formation and NOT rely on "magic bullet" technology and invasive surgery to save them from death's pall. Gallstones account for some **8,000** deaths and over one BILLION dollars in medical costs in the USA every year.

Gall & tones are a confirmation that old age has arrived—no matter your calendar age!

Loss of the gallbladder equates to accelerated aging and life at the subsistence level UNLESS proper action is taken to assist the body. We can live without a gallbladder, appendix, spleen, testicles, ovaries, etc., but health and vitality are sacrificed. Remedial action to offset the loss is critical and can restore a person's quality of life and add many good years.

Do everything possible to avoid losing your gallbladder. Once removed, the liver continually drips directly into the intestine—one drip at a time, instead of in mass at meal time, creating stress similar to that imposed on the body from snacking between meals.

Liver Hygiene

People with cancer should temporarily abstain from eating meat, cheese, and fish. These are **heavy, high stress** proteins that drain the system. *(Klammath™ algae, racemized™ organic liver tablets, Taoist™ food herbs, Harmonic™ pollen, Harmonic Synergy™ are all excellent low stress SUPER foods. Disorb Aid™, Yucca Herbal™ and R/HCl™ ensure 100% digestion and restoration of health.)*

Dr. Max Gerson used fresh, organic calf liver "juice" to treat cancer patients. It is LOADED with biologically active nutrients and enzymes. In the USA, fresh liver is no longer an option due to the condition of the animals. A safer alternative is **predigested** racemized™ organic calf liver tablets. They are the equivalent of swallowing a lightning bolt without any of the problems associated with eating meat.

Fresh, raw, organic fruits and vegetables are also VERY therapeutic to the liver. "Raw" milk products like yogurt, buttermilk, and kefir are very healing. Kombucha tea and fresh lemon juice are also wonderful dietary additions.

Anatomical Location Of The Liver

The liver is located directly under the anterior right rib cage (page 46). It is above the ascending colon, below the right lung, next to the stomach and opposite the spleen which is under the left anterior rib cage.

Intestinal parasites often reach the liver via the portal vein or by migration up the primary bile duct. It is COMMON to find colon bacilli (E. coli bacteria) in an inflamed liver—a condition that goes with cirrhosis. parasites, constipation, and bowel problems. Similar infections occur in women's vaginal canal, but here HORMONE problems are behind it.

Distended Belly

A distended abdomen is a classic SIGN of a person with a liver problem and a body under siege. An enlarged belly is partly body fat and **mostly** an engorged and distended colon. This is a tell-tale SIGN that waste is accumulating. This condition goes hand in hand with colitis, diverticulitis, prostate, gout, arthritis, and heart problems—just to name a few. A congested bowel is a breeding ground for dis-ease and a fast ticket to the grave. Consider a distended belly an interim report card and a warning of trouble to come! One very recent discovery is the use of Biogenic™ Lymphatic Roller which breaks loose massive amounts of bowel waste.

All bowel problems are the result of a poor lifestyle and diet. Hopefully, the reader now understands why chewing your food, high water intake throughout the day, exercise, and good food are so crucial to the aging reversal process.

Liver Breath

Certain foods—like raw onion—cause some people to get *liver breath.* Raw onion is a potent detoxifier that produces a "metallic" odor in the breath of some people.

I once overheard my biochemistry teacher's assistant discussing her health problems with another. When she came over to help me, I got a whiff of her breath and I recognized the odor instantly. The lady had a stressed liver.

People with stressed livers get hepatitis, mononucleosis, and chronic fatigue syndrome. They are the ones who suffer with psoriasis, heavy dandruff, ringworm, impetigo, athlete's foot, dry skin, weak nails, cancer, periodontal gum dis-ease, constipation, diverticulosis, colitis, irritable bowel syndrome, parasite infestations, Alzheimers, and more.

Fully 90% of the population have stressed livers. This is why I have hammered away at YOU, the reader, to do whatever you need to do to detoxify your system, balance your hormones and ingest SUPER foods.

There are different paths a person can take to achieve super health and I support all of them. But, if your health has slipped or your are aging or dealing with dis-ease—and especially if you have been on the "health food" trail—then you need to face the facts. **I woke up at 45 and found myself in trouble. But instead of continuing on the same dead end path so popular in the health movement, I cut a NEW path and at 53 years young I got ALL of my life back. So can you!**

Mineral Baths & The Liver

Throughout history, mineral springs, hot pools, and mud holes have attracted health-minded people. As a child, I remember going with my family out to Desert Hot Springs, California where we would see people soaking in mineral water pools and taking mud baths to improve their health.

I can attest to the detoxifying effects of mud and mineral waters. Most people are invigorated by them, but they exhaust me! People with weak livers must be careful when using hot pools because they cause the body to release too much toxic waste into circulation and if you are not prepared for it, you will become exhausted. Loss of mineral electrolytes also occurs here and we will discuss them in the next chapter. Drink large quantities of water with plenty of racemized™ sea minerals when detoxing the tissues through the skin.

A **Far InfraRed™ sauna** (FIR sauna) is a wonderful way to experience the benefits of a hot spring right in your own home. This marvelous device dissolves and flushes acid wastes from the soft tissues and restores the liver. Special elements produce FIR energy. It does NOT work by using heat or lights.

A healthy liver leads the way to becoming *Young Again!*

PREVIEW: *Our next chapter deals with energy flow, limitless vitality, and the body's toll road system.*

SUPER FOODS for a SUPER LIFE

These are the racemized™ SUPER FOODS that comprise most of my diet, since I only eat once a day. Use them and your hunger will **vanish** while your energy and mental clarity skyrockets. And given a little time, your weight will normalize and your hair will grow.

Harmonic Synergy™	ETVC™ Tablets
Taoist Rice Polish™	Harmonic™ Pollen
Taoist 5 Elements™	Harmonic™ Royal Jelly
Klammath™ Algae	Biogenic™ Skin & Body
Biogenic™ Liver	Biogenic™ hGH
VitaLight™ Tablets	Racemized™ Precursors

These items are taken as a meal with perhaps an apple, mango, pear, peach or some fresh vegetables. DiSorb Aid™, Yucca Blend™, and R/HCl always accompany these items for maximum absorption and energy release.

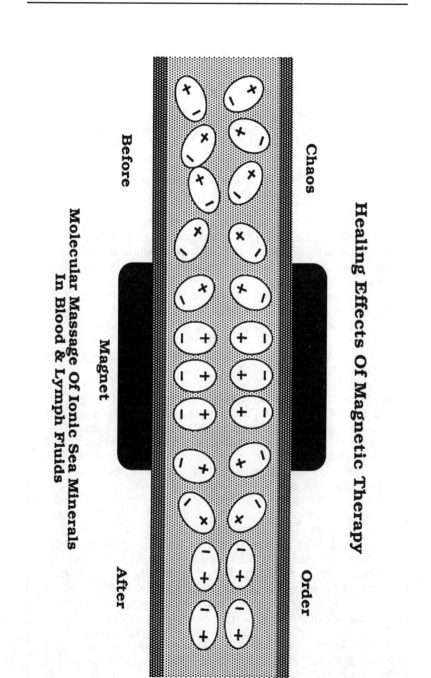

Healing Effects Of Magnetic Therapy

Chaos

Order

Before

After

Magnet

Molecular Massage Of Ionic Sea Minerals
In Blood & Lymph Fluids

Why
"Racemization™"

"Racemized™ formulas are combinations of circular, overlapping energy fields unified to achieve maximum viability and biological activity."

Because racemized™ health products are *extremely* biologically active and produce maximum benefits quickly.

The word *viability* best describes the effect **racemization™** has on high energy FOOD nutrient molecules. *Viability* refers to biological *usefulness* and *activity* rather than potency. Racemization™ greatly **enhances** nutrient energy profiles.

Racemized™ products carry a dual rating: "biological activity" and "racemic footprint." These indicate **potential** available energy and **expected** biological response. They are NOT a measure of carbohydrates, fats, proteins or calories, but they are a measure of **life force** activity in living systems.

The racemic™ scale is 0-10. All right-spin substances receive a **static** reference score of "0" keyed to their energy profiles. The racemization™ process then raises the reference score by a factor of ten times (10x). This 4 step *proprietary* process **unifies, boosts, stabilizes** and **locks** energy frequency(s) so individual and composite fields cannot revert to a lesser energy state or deteriorate for a very long time.

Racemization™ does **not** involve the use of magnetics, homeopathy, or other known processes heretofore used in the health arena, and therefore, has no historical analog. **Unification** of overlapping nutrient energy fields into a unified composite field increases the **rate** of spin and **depth** of the **composite** energy field—thus, enhancing biological activity in the body.

All Biogenic™ and Harmonic™ products carry a 10/10 reference score—which means they are ten times (10x) more **viable** in the body than in their non racemized™ state, and therefore, offer **incredible** value and results to anyone using them. Racemized™ products have NO equal in the marketplace.

28

Soil To Sea

"Man does not die, he kills himself"
Seneca

People love the seaside! The air makes them feel good. It buzzes with electricity. The **ionized** water invigorates their bodies. Barefoot, the sand siphons away the toxic energy from the reflex points in the feet. It is the *charged* ionic minerals that give the sea's air, water, and sand its healing qualities.

The sea is nature's storage battery of right-spin EN- ERGY! It is a phenomenon of tremendous importance. Under- standing the source of the sea's energy is central to the aging reversal process and health.

Mineral ions in solution are called **electrolytes**. Ions are atoms that have gained or lost electrons. Ionic compounds are two or more ions that have bonded together. Ionic com- pounds are crystals—like table salt (sodium+chloride). Salts are STABLE and maintain their crystal form UNTIL they are *hydrolyzed* (dissolved) in water.

When salts dissolve in water or body fluids, the mol- ecules disassociate (split) into and become *unstable* mineral ions, chemically speaking. If the ions come from a non living source—like table salt or calcium carbonate—they **de**stabilize the system and create conditions of **excess** in the body. In contrast, racemized™ sea mineral ions balance the system.

SOME ions are capable of conducting electricity in solution, while others cannot—an important point that can save a life if heat stroke or heat exhaustion are involved.

The blood and lymph contain electrolytes. Our nerve

fibers and cells are lined with them. Electrolytes relay electrical energy and are responsible for transferring electrical signals from one end of the body to the other via the nerve fibers with mineral ions supplied by the blood.

Toll Road

It is helpful to think of the nervous system as a toll road where a price must be paid BEFORE each "energy" signal is allowed to cross each synapse on its way to its destination—perhaps a finger or leg. *(Think of the synapses as "toll booths" along the nerve axon. The Schawnn cells keep the gate open by producing hormones that polish the receptor sites at the synapses, and the mineral ions supply the energy to BOOST the signal so it can "jumb" the gap and continue along its way.)*

The body conducts its daily affairs using electrical currency. A unit of electrical *currency* is called a mineral *ion*. As nerve impulses cross the synapses, mineral ions give up their electrons which supply the energy for the process.

The body needs a **constant** supply of ions. Minerals that are **not** in ionic form do not suffice—INCLUDING colloidal minerals. A body with enough ions enjoys health and vitality, otherwise, sickness, and lethargy rule.

Disrupted electrical signals produce spastic motions that make it difficult for a person to move and function. Cerebral palsy and multiple sclerosis (MS) are classic examples of sporadic, *uncontrolled* electrical impulses. Shingles, neuropathy, and myelinoma share some of these problems too. For sure, loss of Schwann cells at the synapses and deterioration of the myelin sheath are involved. SOC™ and biogenic™ Skin & Body Toner are very effective in restoration of this sheath. Racemized™ hormone precursors provide the hormonal activity needed to reestablish the Schwann cells.

Athletes

Electrolytes are VERY important to athletes. They associate performance, strength, and vitality with electrolytes. They know their bodies will NOT perform without them and will excel when they are in full supply.

Athletes USE large quantities of electrolytes because their bodies are under heavy *physical* stress. Regular people also use electrolytes, but unlike athletes—who burn out in a few short years—people take years to bankrupt their ionic mineral account. They do it in *slow motion*—a day at a time!

All mineral ions are NOT equal. Those that have gone through the carbon cycle and are in **racemized**™ form are FAR more active in the body. When racemized™ their activity level is unequaled. These minerals are also the basis for the creation of Medical Grade Ionized Water™.

Synchronized, ancient sea bed deposits dug out of the ground and hydrolyzed into "toddy" that contain mineral ions in colloidal form are not a good idea. Their energy signature electrical footprint is inferior to **racemized**™ sea mineral ions AND they are LOADED with toxic **heavy** metals like lead, cadmium and mercury—just to name a few. Racemic™ sea water ions keep us young and strong because they are concentrated from a biologically *active* medium—sea water—and then "enhanced" via the racemic™ process.

Table salt is composed of sodium and chlorine. Sodium is an *electrolyte* and it assists the body in the flow of electrical energy. We **need** sodium in VERY **small** amounts. Too much sodium upsets the sodium:potassium ratio in the body and sets the stage for cancer.

When the body is given NO other option, it will use sodium ions in lieu of more desirable trace mineral ions.

Sports Drinks • BEV™ • Energy

Many athletes use commercial sports drinks to meet their ionic mineral needs. Sports drinks are bad news! Their energy footprint is unfriendly to the body and their signature is incomplete. Athletes who depend on them experience rapid aging of the vital organs and connective tissues. Smart athletes make their own sports drink for pennies using concentrated **racemized**™ sea water ions and BEV™ water.

My children **voluntarily** lug their ionized BEV™ water to school each day in their polycarbonate bottles. They love it and do better in the classroom and in sports. They call it *"power water!"* All their buddies bum water from them!

BEV™ water has a "conception point" ORP. Its high energy *footprint* comes from the **restructuring** of the water molecules and erasing of the memory of the toxic contaminants that are in native water. The BEV™ process enhances hydrogen and molecular bond angles and changes the *vibratory* frequency of the water—making it biologically friendly. BEV™ water resonates (vibrates) at a "healthy" frequency. Add racemic sea minerals and you've got unequaled drinking water.

Transference of energy can be demonstrated in other ways. For instance, walking barefoot in sand or grass, or hugging a tree bare footed. These alter abnormal body frequencies and tune the body to *vibrate* with Mother Earth. Five minutes a day spent walking in this manner releases MASSIVE amounts of toxic energy and stress from the body. I have seen people with severe back pain, unable to stand up straight, walk in beach sand for 15 minutes, straighten up and return to normal! A vibration chain can be used in a similar fashion. Chiropractic acknowledges that vertebral orientation is directly related to stress in the vital organs, and walking in sand is proof that when toxic energy is drawn out of the body, pain and health problems vanish.

Electrical "current" is the movement of energy *along a metal wire*. In body fluids like blood and lymph current is carried by activated mineral ions.

$10,000 For A Bag Of Salt

Ions in solution allow electricity to pass. No electrical flow means no ions are present. Electricity flowing through a liquid creates electrolysis (*electro*-electricity, *lysis-dissolution of*).

Dr. Carry Reams was once paid $10,000 for solving a electroplating problem in a chroming shop that involved ions and electrolysis. No one—including the manufacturer of the equipment—could make the electricity flow in the processing tank. Reams came along and poured a few pounds of common table salt into the solution and bingo, the electricity flowed through the solution of water and salt and the plating process proceeded. Sodium chloride solved the electrolysis problem because sodium is an *electrolyte.*

The human body requires a **constant** supply of balanced, electrolytic mineral ions for optimum health. Substitution of table salt to supply sodium—as done in allopathic medical circles—band aids the immediate problem and leaves the cause untouched. Sodium creates conditions of EXCESS and accelerates the aging process. Sodium is poison!

Sugar

Sucrose (table sugar) is a crystal, but sucrose will NOT conduct electrical current when dissolved in water. It is a non-electrolyte because it contains no mineral ions. Sugar is a "concentrated" left-spin energy substance that lowers the body's vibratory frequency and dims the aura.

Sucrose *sabotages* the flow of energy in the body. It does this by **bonding** with our mineral ions. When ions bond with sugar, their energy is **neutralized.** When the supply of ions in the body is low, a health crisis occurs and aging accelerates.

Most people live out their lives on the edge of starvation—their diet supplying them with just enough mineral ions to exist between subsistence and dis-ease.

If you choose to eat food laced with table sugar, you will lose your vitality and grow old.

Earlier, we discussed Kombucha tea. It is important that the reader understand that the Kombucha organism has the ability to convert a left-spin substance—like white sugar—into a right-spin energy field that is loaded with enzymes, hormones, and healthful organic acids. It does this by way of biological alchemy. Kombucha is a live food product whose energy field has been reversed. The sugar is gone, but the energy remains.

The experts tell us sugar is sugar. *They* tell us there is NO difference between sucrose, maltose, dextrose, and lactose except in their molecular structures. *They* tell us that mannitol, sorbitol, and xylitol are harmless. *They* tell us **aspartame** is harmless. *They* tell us that the body does not care what sugar we feed it. *They* tell us the sugar *blues* that haunt millions of people are "imagined." The experts are wrong and they know better.

The body differentiates between sugars as it does with oils. It differentiates based on the energy SPIN.

Some sugars accelerate aging by neutralizing the body's supply of mineral ions. White and artificial sugars destroy food energy through "ionization" or scrambling of food molecules. Translated, the food molecules are altered through the gain or loss of electrons. Purified sugars (table sugar, fructose, corn syrup) and artificial sugars—like **aspartame** (better known by the red, white, and blue "swirl" on packages of processed foods) and food additives have *radiomimetic* qualities that mimic the effects of nuclear radiation on cellular DNA. These poisons "zap" body energy and are no different than eating microwaved food. They bring on graying of the hair, wrinkles, and diminished glandular activity and hormone imbalances by "locking up" the body's receptor sites. The problem can be reversed with racemized™ hormone precursors.

Foods processed with large amounts of sugar and salt do not spoil because their enzymes have been scrambled. Bugs seldom eat sugar and salt laden food. They are not stupid.

If you MUST make a choice between table sugar and aspartame or other synthesized sugars, choose white sugar! If you choose to splurge, take a few VataLight™ tablets to buffer the white sugar, but try and not make a habit of it!

Major & Minor Minerals

The body needs the **major** minerals and the minor (trace) minerals to function. Science has known about the major minerals like calcium, iron, sulphur, and phosphorous for a very long time. The TRACE minerals, like manganese, boron, iodine, molybdenum, and sixty or so others have only recently been recognized to be of any importance in human nutrition. *(Science is reluctant to acknowledge man's mineral dependence, yet they **rubber stamp** the use of soy and canola, aspartame, and genetically altered foods.)*

We KNOW minerals are crucial to good nutrition and aging. What is NOT widely known is that the "form" that the mineral is in is as important as the mineral itself. Form determines the mineral's effect on health.

Elemental mineral compounds are of little use to the body. A commonly consumed elemental compound used to supplement **misdiagnosed** calcium deficiencies (as in osteoporosis) is calcium carbonate or oyster shell which is composed of calcium and carbon. The *-ate* tells us that it is in a *salt* form—a *crystal.*

Elemental mineral compounds do NOT belong in the body. They foul our nest and create secondary health problems.

Consider the absurdity of taking calcium carbonate to get more calcium. It is the equivalent of a postpartum woman drinking milk so she can produce more milk.

Chelated minerals cause problems in the body. Chelated minerals are elemental mineral compounds bonded to a carrier—usually an amino acid. The carrier shuttles the minerals through the GI tract and into the blood. **This is NOT desirable!** These mineral compounds are unbalanced energy fields that have NOT gone through the carbon chain. They put stress on the system and create **excesses.** They "trade" one problem for several new ones. Do NOT use them.

The chelation process *tricks* the body into admitting substances into the blood that otherwise could NOT gain admittance under normal body protocol. These elemental substances are the equivalent of a *bogus* $20^{00} bill!

Biologically active mineral ions come from healthy plants, animals, and racemized™ sea mineral ions. SUPER foods like Klammath™ algae, Harmonic™ pollen, Taoist™ food herbs, Harmonic Synergy™, and Biogenic™ liver are also excellent low stress food sources.

Enzymes • Minerals • Nitrogen

Enzymes are mineral-dependent. They are protein molecules that function as **on-the-job** engineers within the body. Enzymes create *hot spots* within the body that throw the switch so blood and lymph can deliver nutrients to the areas in need.

Nitrogen plays a KEY role in the life process. All proteins and amino acids contain nitrogen. Nitrogen is NOT a mineral ion in the classical sense (it's a gas), but it can function like one.

Nitrogen (atomic symbol "N") is very important to electrical conductivity and energy *transference* in the body. Nitrogen has many forms. In its *metallic* form, it conducts electricity and "acts like" an *electrolyte*.

Life CANNOT exist without nitrogen. The atmosphere is composed of 78% nitrogen. Plants and animals require nitrogen to grow. Unfortunately, the *experts* use nitrogen to FORCE plants to grow on the premise that food is food. They *think* they can bribe Nature into building high vitality food with nitrogen based **salt** fertilizers. Nature responds with left-spin energy food that is high in "funny" proteins.

Funny Proteins

"Funny proteins" are "unavailable" proteins—that is, proteins that confuse the body—soy is a "classic" example. Food protein is measured by its nitrogen content. When you hear a nutritionist or farmer talk about a crop or a food's protein percentage (%), they are actually referring to the nitrogen content. Nitrogen is a gas. It is an extremely **acid** gas (pH 1-2). When proteins are digested and broken down into their constituent parts, nitrogen is released (think of a compost heap, a pile of fresh grass clippings, or a rotting carcass).

Nitrogen has many different forms. Funny proteins contain nitrogen in the **wrong** form. When funny proteins are turned loose in the body, they create EXCESSES. Massive amounts of calcium is required to buffer the effects of funny protein nitrogens that are released into circulation during the digestion process.

Environmental deterioration, high powered synthetic salt fertilizers, and poisonous sprays are part of the reason why more and more funny proteins are entering the food chain. As **FREAK** protein levels rise, so do degenerative dis-eases.

Look at a bag of dog or cat food. It will list total protein and crude (unavailable) protein. If you subtract one from the other, you can calculate the amount of available protein. There was a time not so many years ago when the amount of unavailable or "bastard" protein was under 1/2%. Today we are seeing unavailable protein levels as high as 2%—and more!

Each time the level of *funny* **protein doubles—say from 1/2% to 1%—the amount of calcium needed to stabilize blood pH increases by 200 times! Think about it!**

I have repeatedly stated that there is no such thing as a deficiency condition or a deficiency dis-ease. Problems and deficiencies are the result of conditions of EXCESS within the system. In the case of osteoporosis, the problem results from an "excess" of funny protein nitrogen in the blood, hormonal imbalances (unopposed estrogen dominance and blocked receptor sites), and buildup of "excess" metabolic acids.

Body tissue is comprised of nitrogen based proteins. Billions of cells die each day and if they are not promptly removed from the system, they release **nitrogen** into the blood making it ever more acidic. When you see someone aging at an accelerated rate, understand that their body is acidifying. The quickest way to reverse acidification is by drinking Medical Grade Ionized Water™ and doing a series of liver purges.

As the level of *funny* protein nitrogen rises in the blood, the body goes into a survival mode and begins withdrawing minerals from the bones to **BUFFER** the acidic condition in the blood. Medical science labels the process osteoporosis and shouts **"deficiency"** of calcium. Not true! The body has innate intelligence and it knows what to do to keep itself alive when it encounters conditions of excess.

HOWEVER, *when the neuro and hormonal receptor sites become "locked up", the body becomes confused because it is UNABLE to determine what needs to be done or is unable to get a "hand shake" from the receptor on the receiving end of the signal because hormone chemical "analogs" have the system locked up.*

Nitrogen & Plants

Nitrogen is the unit of **electrical currency** that opens the plant's toll gates so energy and mineral ions can pass on their way to enzyme created *hot spots* in the plant's tissues.

Chemical agriculture has learned how to manipulate the life process in plants and trick them into taking unwanted minerals and poisons into their tissues. The process is similar to that of chelation of elemental minerals to trick the body into ignoring its own normal protocol.

The need to chelate elemental mineral compounds or force crops to grow is based on the assumption that God and Nature are stupid, plants are stupid, the body is stupid, but the *experts* are smart. Chelation smacks of the same mentality that says genetically engineered food is just as good as *real* food, hydroponically raised crops moot the need for *real* soil, microwaved food is the same as conventionally cooked food, and synthetically fertilized crops are just as nutritious as crops raised on biodynamically enlivened soil.

Nature designed things so that the elements would have to pass through the carbon cycle before gaining legitimate status and a ticket into the human body.

The Carbon Cycle

The carbon cycle explains how earth minerals are ionized and assimilated into food molecules and sea water. **CARBON CYCLE = rain + soil + sun + microbe + plant + animal = biologically *enlivened* mineral ions.**

The carbon cycle transforms biologically inactive earth minerals into active, right-spin *energy* fields that people can use to stay or become strong and healthy.

Bacteria in the soil are the bankers for earth minerals. They are "made available" when minerals react with weak acids like carbonic acid, which is atmospheric carbon + hydrogen that is **secreted** from plant roots. The bacteria hold and modify mineral ions and live off their electrical energy until the plant withdraws them from its mineral ion account. Enzymes act as the cashiers and oversee the exchange. The mineral ions are the currency (electric money). Plants combine ionic and solar energy to produce proteins, fats, carbohydrates, vitamins and enzymes—all of which contain biologically active mineral ions.

Animals eat plants and deposit their waste on the soil. Plants grow, die, and leave their residues on the soil for the bacteria, yeast, and fungi to consume. In time, nutrient ions make their way to the sea where they become a **solution** of biologically active *ionic minerals.* Mineral ions give sea water its characteristic salty flavor and copious quantities of trace mineral ions give it ENERGY! This is same energy that causes racemized™ mineral ions to breakup Rouleau in the blood.

ALL of Earth's mineral ions are present and in a dynamic, high energy state when sea water is racemically activated. Their effect on the body is confirmation of their valence condition and energy footprint.

Sea water is a solution of *charged* mineral ions and is the *blood* and *lymph* of Mother Earth.

Vitamins

Vitamins **cannot** function unless mineral ions are present in balanced form. Vitamins are NOT well understood, but we do know that they are mineral dependent. Science has had to *shadow box* with vitamins, learning of their importance through **so called** *deficiency* conditions.

Pellagra is one of these conditions. Pellagra is a **marker** condition that supposedly indicates a niacin deficiency (vitamin B-3). This condition responds well to B vitamin therapy, quality dietary proteins, and the elimination of body excesses.

The word **vitamin** derives from "vital" meaning *necessary* and "amine" which is the chemical name for a nitrogen bearing molecule. The word *amino*—as in *amino* acid—is also related to *amine.* Aminos join and form proteins that contain nitrogen. SOC™ supplies racemized™ carbon and sulfur (not to be confused with elemental forms) so it can build the sulfhydryl bonds that link the proteins.

When SOC™ capsules are used regularly, the body AUTOMATICALLY goes to work dissolving internal and external scar tissue and replaces it with live, functional tissue proteins. The body is 90% connective tissue and the older you become the more SCAR tissue you have which is what is behind that old **STIFF** body. Soc™ makes you limber!

Amino acids, fats, and carbohydrates are organic molecules produced by anabolic activity in living things. Organic molecules contain oxygen, nitrogen, sulfur, and carbon. **Carbon** grants the title, "organic!" **Carbon**aceous matter (leaves, grass, wood, etc.) contains carbon. **Carbo**hydrates contain carbon. Life is impossible without carbon. So, a vitamin is a nitrogen containing substance that also contains **carbon** in an amine group.

*Earlier, we talked about the use of a family of chemicals called "chlor**amines**," chemicals that are used by cities throughout the USA to treat public water supplies. Here, chlorine has been combined with an organic amine group to kill bacteria in drinking water. Unfortunately, chloramines **penetrate** the skin when we bathe and destroy the liver and poison the gut.*

Your author rejects the use of all but a very few **food based** vitamin supplements because most are synthesized, even if they are labeled "natural." Man-made vitamins STRESS the liver and are toxic to the body. They **mimic** the effect of the *real* thing, but they cannot build healthy tissues. VitaLight™ tablets are the only supplement I use. *Never forget that live food grown in your own garden is a thousand times better than the best supplement—and a lot less expensive, too!*

In biochemistry and nutrition, vitamins are referred to as *cofactors* or *coenzymes.* Vitamins and mineral ions need each other to work. Please engrave the following statement into your consciousness and *never* forget it.

We DO NOT live on vitamins, minerals, and enzymes—but from the *energy* released by the chemical reactions they fuel.

The Carbon Connection

In his timeless book, *The Carbon Connection,* my friend, Leonard Ridzon defined carbon as *"The governing element that determines the vitality of food crops [and life on Earth]."*

Carbon is extremely important in the aging process. It

is THE common denominator between high vitality food and healthy soils. Carbon is the barometer of the soil's aura and magnetic field. It is the basis of all life.

Carbon can combine in **millions** of combinations because of its unique molecular form. *Bogus* science uses carbon to create organic poisons like pesticides and herbicides.

Soil that is highly magnetic is usually described as **para**magnetic (i.e. *para*-beyond). Soil that is paramagnetic grows right-spin energy food with a complete energy signature.

Devitalized soil has NO paramagnetism and the food grown on it will NOT produce healthy human beings, barnyard animals, or plants. Sick soil is LOW in carbon, low in microbial activity, and low in biologically active mineral ions.

The fastest and best way to convert sick dirt to vibrant soil is through the use of biodynamic principles. If you would like to read about this marvelous field of *esoteric* agriculture, read Biodynamics I & II by Alex Podolinsky (see Source Page).

People can now avail themselves of a biodynamic type product that is easy to use; one that can turn polluted soil into a nice garden the first year WITHOUT the use of synthetic chemicals. It is the product of a "dirt smart" American farmer (see Source Page).

The best we can hope for is to eat home grown food that's packed with life giving nutrients with a right-spin footprint. If our food doesn't contain all the minerals we need, we must get them from the next best source available—**racemized**™ sea mineral ions, as in VitaLight™.

I obtain my minerals from live fresh food, SUPER foods and VitaLight™. The liquid racemized™ minerals are used in water to break up the Rouleau in the blood.

I want to stay YOUNG for a very long time and I get *ENERGY* from racemized™ minerals. They are my electrical *currency*. They trigger my biochemical processes, prevent Rouleau in the blood, and make me feel good!

If you tend to the basics, you won't become OLD and you won't die prematurely. Each of us must take responsibility for our lives. Hopefully, this book will be **your catalyst to action** so you also can become *Young Again!*

PREVIEW: *Our next chapter is about the immune system and cancer and how to avoid things like AIDS.*

The reflex points in the feet are wired to the vital organs of the body. Walking in sand, green grass, and hugging trees makes sense when you understand the rules of the game.

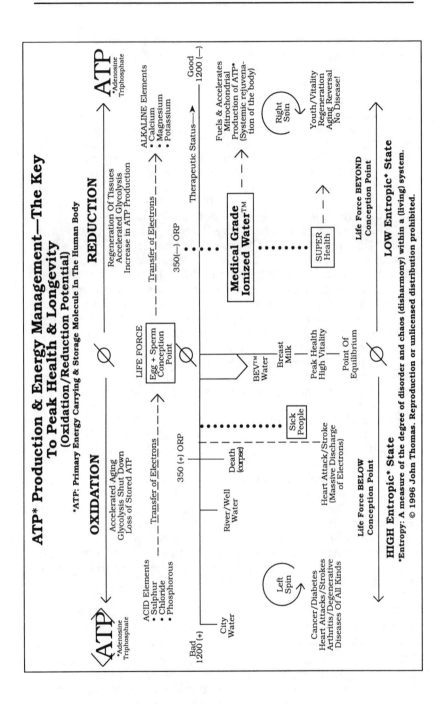

ATP* Production & Energy Management—The Key To Peak Health & Longevity
(Oxidation/Reduction Potential)
*ATP: Primary Energy Carrying & Storage Molecule In The Human Body

OXIDATION   **REDUCTION**

⟨ATP⟩
*Adenosine Triphosphate

ATP⟩
*Adenosine Triphosphate

ACID Elements
• Sulphur
• Chloride
• Phosphorous

ALKALINE Elements
• Calcium
• Magnesium
• Potassium

Accelerated Aging
Glycolysis Shut Down
Loss of Stored ATP

Regeneration Of Tissues
Accelerated Glycolysis
Increase in ATP Production

Transfer of Electrons

Transfer of Electrons

350 (+) ORP

350 (−) ORP

Bad
1200 (+)

Good
1200 (−)

Therapeutic Status

Fuels & Accelerates
Mitrochondrial
Production of ATP*
(Systemic rejuvena-
tion of the body)

Left Spin

Right Spin

Youth/Vitality
Regeneration
Aging Reversal
No Disease!

City Water

River/Well Water

LIFE FORCE
Egg + Sperm
Conception Point

Point Of Equilibrium

Medical Grade Ionized Water™

SUPER Health

Sick People

BEV™ Water

Breast Milk

Peak Health
High Vitality

Death (corpse)

Heart Attack/Stroke
(Massive Discharge
of Electrons)

Cancer/Diabetes
Heart Attacks/Strokes
Arthritis/Degenerative
Diseases Of All Kinds

Life Force BELOW
Conception Point

Life Force BEYOND
Conception Point

HIGH Entropic* State

LOW Entropic* State

*Entropy: A measure of the degree of disorder and chaos (disharmony) within a (living) system.

© 1996 John Thomas. Reproduction or unlicensed distribution prohibited.

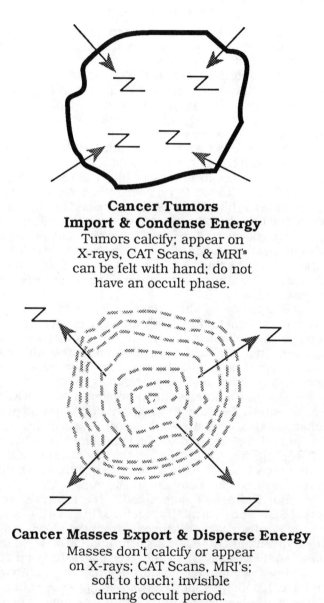

Cancer Tumors
Import & Condense Energy
Tumors calcify; appear on
X-rays, CAT Scans, & MRI's
can be felt with hand; do not
have an occult phase.

Cancer Masses Export & Disperse Energy
Masses don't calcify or appear
on X-rays; CAT Scans, MRI's;
soft to touch; invisible
during occult period.

Cancer Tumors vs. Cancer Masses
They are NOT the same!

Rouleau & SOC™

The battle for health and rejuvenation is WON or LOST at the cellular level. It is here that the very fine blood capillaries interface the cells.

Blood corpuscles "flow" IN and OUT of the fine capillaries (arterioles) in single file fashion. A corpuscle is a *nucleated* cell, that is, a blood cell *without* a nucleus. Think of a chicken's egg without a yoke. An egg is a single cell and the yoke is the nucleus.

As the cells become overloaded with acid wastes, the energy *footprint* of healthy blood shifts to the left and **sticky** blood takes form. Sticky blood is the EFFECT of what is officially known as *Rouleau.* When Rouleau sets in, the ability of the blood corpuscles to access the tissues and service the cells becomes severely compromised.

Slowdown in the *bilateral movement* of oxygen, nutrients, carbon dioxide, and waste **across** the cell membranes is called **aging.** Aging is just another word for self inflicted fouling of our own nest—and the fouler we become, the faster we age.

Stagnation of the **intra**cellular fluids inside the cells causes them to die. Conditions like cancer, arthritis, fibromyalgia, scleroderma, and hundreds of others have their roots in a combination of **stagnant** extracellular and intracellular fluids. Without question, hormonal imbalances and excesses also play a MAJOR role.

One of the interesting characteristics of SOC™ is that it softens cell membranes so nutrient and waste exchange can accelerate. As the process speeds up, aches and pains disappear and the body becomes very "limber" and free moving. SOC™ helps the body build sulfonyl bearing proteins that replaces scar tissue that it simultaneously is dissolving throughout the body.

Put 5 drops of **racemized**™ sea minerals into a glass of BEV™ or Medical Grade Ionized (high ORP) Water™ and the Rouleau effect disappears from the blood and the body rejuvenates. The effect is a combination of the water(s) and the minerals electrical spin (see pages 133 and 296).

If you want to regain your health or hold onto what you have, it's VERY important that you provide your body with a constant flow of racemized™ mineral ions. When the body is supplied a **regular** flow of water bearing these energy substances, the miracle just happens. It's called *reversing the aging process.*

29

Body Fluid Dynamics

*"When science falters, it is because no
one is asking the right questions."*
Charles Walters

Blood is central to all body metabolism. It carries
oxygen and nutrients to the cells and carbon dioxide and
wastes OUT of the cells and OUT of the system by way of the
kidneys, bowel, lungs, and skin.

Blood is systemic. It **interfaces** ALL body systems and
is, therefore, an excellent medium for testing. It is a good
barometer of present or pending dis-ease and is one of two
sources of information derived from body fluids.

The blood has a fraternal twin that performs many
similar functions. This "other" system has NO heart to act as
a pump. Its fluid color is straw to clear—not red. Unlike blood,
no one will buy it from you. If there is a medical emergency, no
one will ask you to donate any of this other fluid. This fluid is
called LYMPH and it is part of the *lymphatic* system.

Healthy lymph is central to health and vitality. It is
impossible to reverse aging without good lymph circulation. We
promote lymph circulation by vigorous walking, running,
aerobic exercise, swimming, calisthenics, deep breathing, and
load-bearing work. We do more of these activities when we are
young, and we tend to **avoid** them as we grow older.

The lymphatic system is a network of capillaries and
vessels similar to the arteries and veins with some notable

differences. Lymph capillaries begin as blind alleys, while blood capillaries are continuous. The lymphatic system has nodes where the blood circulatory system has none.

The lymphatic system is primarily a "plasma protein" communication system that is responsible for the movement of 75% of the body's liquid proteins. Its capillaries remove wastes and service the extracellular fluid in the spaces between the cells. Lymph capillary walls are *more* permeable than blood capillaries and they ONLY work in one direction. Once extracellular fluid enters a lymph capillary it cannot escape until it joins the blood at the subclavian veins near the anterior base of the neck. Blood is filtered by the kidneys and liver.

It is VERY important to recognize that the lymph "nodes" are really energy storage sites. TOXIC energy fields are stored and held there for safekeeping until the body can manage them. When you feel swollen lymph nodes under the jaw, in the armpits, under and outside the breasts, or in the groin (above and to the outside of the hairy area), you are feeling "condensed" energy. That is why they are swollen and hard. They should be soft and pliable—not swollen! The tonsils are lymph nodes. They swell and become inflamed during illness.

Rebounding and lymph rolling move toxic energy fields into circulation so the liver can rid the body of them. The process is greatly assisted by the use of Yucca Herbal Blend™, PAC's, SOC™, and Kombucha tea.

Blood is pumped where lymph is not. Blood corpuscles (red blood cells without a nucleus) are *pumped* into the arteries under pressure from the heart. 10% of the blood that leaves the heart *escapes* as **plasma** through the capillary walls into the **extracellular** spaces BETWEEN the cells. This **extra**cellular fluid is what actually services the cells and tissues.

The lymphatic system performs critical functions that the cardiovascular system cannot. The veins return 90% of blood fluid volume to the heart. The lymph ducts return the other 10% to the blood as lymphatic fluid.

Insufficient exercise and water intake lead to congested tissues and eventually dis-ease.

Lymphatics & Aging

The lymphatic system is one of the most important systems in the body. BOTH health and dis-ease have their roots in the watery fluid called lymph. If lymphatic circulation is active and body fluid pH is balanced, toxins and wastes will NOT accumulate in the tissues. Otherwise, wastes mix with organic poisons, tap water minerals, salts, and fats FOULING our tissues and shutting down vital organ function.

When the tissues are congested and the body is unable to cleanse itself, oxygen and nutrient flow slows. As wastes accumulate in the **extra**cellular fluids between the cells, body pH shifts and the sodium/potassium ratio is upset.

The body requires a constant supply of organic potassium. If it does not get it, it **STEALS** it from **inside** the cells. As potassium exits the cells, sodium invades and replaces the potassium. This ultimately shuts down mitochondrial production of the ATP molecule in the cells.

Cancer BEGINS in the lymphatic system and metastasizes (spreads) by way of the body's plasma protein highway—the lymphatic system.

The lymphatic organs of the body are the lymph nodes, thymus gland (between the heart and base of the neck), tonsils (we have three kinds), spleen, and red bone marrow. Lymphocytes and macrophages are part of the lymphatic system.

Fats & The Immune System

The lymphatic system transports dietary fats out of the intestines and INTO the blood. The **lymph**ocytes and **macro**phages in the blood and lymph fluids protect the body from invading microbes and foreign material.

Lymphocytes include the T-cells and B-cells, both of which the HIV virus infects or circumvents. B-cells originate in the bone marrow. Some of them become **plasma** cells which secrete **anti**BODIES. Antibodies concentrate and conduct their warfare in the blood and lymph.

A sluggish lymphatic system is an OLD system! Fluid retention in the legs, ankles and feet is due to the accumulation of EXCESS wastes. Where proteins are, water accumulates.

Fungus under the nails is related to poor lymph circulation, toxicity and loss of body hair. These SIGNS are **red flags** of dis-ease in the making. They are also driven by hormonal complications which must NOT be ignored.

Exercise & Lymphatics

Exercise has tremendous influence on lymph flow because lymph transfer depends on body movement and muscle contraction. The mini-trampoline, called a *rebounder*, greatly enhances lymph circulation. Women try to improve lymph drainage in the breast and chest region when they hold their arms high and move them excessively while walking. They would be **better off**, however, allowing their arms to swing as God made them to do. A swinging arm is an *exaggerated* lever.

Swinging arms exert a more influence on lymph movement than the rediculous antics prescribed by the *experts.*

Here is an interesting exercise that demonstrates the dynamics of lymph movement. First, have the person stand erect and extend their arm straight out to the side of the body level with the shoulder. Next, attempt to gently but forcefully pull down on the arm and note the amount of "resistance" the person generates. Then, have the person run in place while actively moving the arms and lifting the knees high for about 10 seconds. Now, repeat the arm deflection exercise and note the loss of resistance and strength. The loss of strength is related to lymph displacement and use of charged mineral ions (please recall that ions give up their energy in exchange for the passage of electrical signals).

Lymph • Red Bone Marrow • Fluoride

Red bone marrow is the part of the lymphatic system responsible for red blood cell production. Red bone marrow is located in the flat bones of the body AND in the epiphyses (ends) of the *long* bones. Between the *epiphyses* and diaphasis, which is the shank of the long bones, is where the growth plates are located. The growth plates give us our physical height.

Fluoride interferes with the production of red blood cells. It blocks enzyme activity and weakens bone integrity. Toothpaste and drinking water that contain fluoride suppress red blood cell production and promote *pernicious* anemia.

Anemic people have poor vitality and tire easily. Fluoride's effect on health and energy is similar to taking chemotherapy for cancer except that it occurs in SLOW MOTION! Table salt negatively affects body metabolism. When you combine sodium with fluoride, the effects spell trouble.

The Romans knew the power of table salt. When they defeated Hannibal's Carthage, they made sure that Carthage would NEVER rise again by salting her soil.

Excess sodium stresses body metabolism, while fluorides limit oxygen-carrying capacity of the blood (fewer blood cells produced by the red bone marrow means less oxygen). Together, they reduce ATP production.

The lymphatic system services the colon, which begins at the cecum (see chart). The cecum is the juncture of the lower small intestine (ileum) and the beginning of the large intestine (colon). The *appendix* dangles from the cecum. This area is the most toxic site in the body. It is loaded with lymph nodes (called Peyer's patch). Lymph nodes isolate and manage toxic waste overload and prevent death. **Appendicitis is confirmation of toxic waste overload to the point of death!**

A sluggish colon and lymphatic system are **symptomatic** conditions related to a toxic liver which, in turn, leads to bowel problems. People who experience appendicitis, diverticulitis, colitis, or irritable bowel syndrome are under **indictment** for MORE serious health problems to come unless remedial action is taken.

Acne & Scars

As lymph fluid circulation slows and acid wastes accumlate in the basement membranes of the outer facia, the skin becomes clogged, the connective tissues break down, and acne becomes a problem (adults get a little extra: wrinkles!).

Acne is nothing but an acute case of a sluggish lymphatic system in the sub-cutaneous layers of the skin and toxic waste overload. A TOXIC liver is central to this problem.

Scar formation and a congested lymphatic system go hand in hand. Scars result from damage to the *parenchyma* cells which are the ACTIVE, functional cells of an organ—like the skin. Scars are like the battlefield where armies of competing energy fields wage war. Scars are proof that the negative energy forces won. Acne scars are easily cleared with SOC™ lotion and capsules and regular use of NugestrineII™ racemized™ hormone precursor creme.

Injuries that do trauma to the *parenchyma* cells result in scars when acid waste is stressing the system. The parenchyma cells will **erase** acne scars if the tissues are cleared of its waste. Formation of new tissue requires the presence of sulfhydryl carbon and sulphur. SOC™ it the source.

An astute surgeon can tell the physical age of his patient by the amount of scar tissue in the vital organs. *Due to an accident, I had a hernia repaired when I was 48 years. My doctor was astounded because my vital organs were those of a 15 year old! We captured it on video.*

At the same time, I must tell you that my connective tissues were in poor condition, partly due to a "vegetarian" diet. (I had been a vegetarian for about eight years) and partly due to impending hormone problems

*One of the negative side effects of the vegetarian, fruitarian, and macrobiotic diet is systemic **breakdown** of the connective tissues. I have since renewed my entire body by doing the things outlined in this book and returning to a more balanced dietary approach. SOC™ has done wonders at rebuilding the joints and connective tissue and I can attest that I look and feel better at 53 years "young" than at any point in my life. I did it! **And so can you!***

Burns • Scars • New Limbs

In 1983 I suffered a *severe* burn in a welding accident. The skin and underlying tissues of the inside of my right elbow were burned and destroyed by a hunk of red hot 5,000° F steel that fell and landed in the crook of my arm.

At that time, I was age forty-three. By medical standards, I was old and should have scarred horribly. Instead, healing progressed without ANY scar formation. I did not see a doctor. Why was there no scar formation? The answer is related to vital organ function, blood/lymph circulation, and lifestyle.

The body can regenerate itself—limbs, nerve tissue, and bones. I am talking about TOTAL limb regeneration as well as total restoration of function with no evidence of scar formation. These things have been amply demonstrated by Dr. Robert Becker and Dr. Melvin Saunders and recently by the Japanese who helped a diabetic grow a missing foot using Medical Grade Ionized Water™! The Japanese video is available and is best understood with the help of the Water Book, both of which are available (see Source Page).

The miracle of "regeneration" was personally experienced by Mitchell May who made medical history by growing new skin, bone, and nerve tissue after suffering over forty breaks to his femur (thigh bone).

Medical **miracles** are closely aligned with the principles of vibrational medicine and the manipulation of subtle energy forces in the bio-electric body. True health is healing without scars and the formation of new tissues in spite of the defined laws of science and medicine.

Clogged Arteries & Lymph

Atherosclerosis (clogging of the arteries) is a major problem in the USA. Yet, **nothing** is said of the relationship of the lymphatic system or hormones to cardiovascular problems.

The two main trunks of the lymphatic system join the blood system at the origin of the subclavian veins at the base and front of the neck just below the collar bones. The subclavian veins feed into the superior vena cava vein which feeds into the right side of the heart.

The heart pumps blood to the lungs where TWO things occur: the blood is reoxygenated AND toxic energy is RELEASED into the atmosphere. The blood is then returned to the left side of the heart for distribution to the body. As the blood leaves the heart by way of the aortic artery, the left and right coronary arteries branch off and feed the heart muscle. These are the arteries that become blocked and require coronary bypass surgery.

Toxic fats like soy, canola, and hydrogenated marga-rines COMBINE with *chlorine, fluorine, and chloramines* (from tap water), and metabolic waste products in the blood. Athero-sclerotic plaque is the result.

Some people age so rapidly in their vital organs that they simply drop dead! *Angina pectoris* is a good example of chest pain that results from oxygen deficiency AND low ATP production. A reduced oxygen supply to the heart is called ischemia (*ischein*-to hold back. *hemia*-pertaining to the blood). When we suffer a heart attack, some of the heart muscle tissue dies for LACK of oxygen due to blocked arteries that feed it. This is called *myocardial infarction.* If a blood clot is involved, it is called a *coronary thrombosis.* A clot is a *thrombus.*

People & Plants

Human beings and plants have MUCH in common. They also have ONE major difference. That difference has to do with MOBILITY and fluid movement.

Humans rely on physical activity to assist the move-ment of lymph fluid, and we have the heart to pump our blood. By comparison, plants have no heart and must depend on capillary action, osmosis, enzymes, and ion energy to overcome gravity and move water and nutrients up into their tissues and back to their roots.

Humans depend on the mitochondria to produce the ATP energy that fuels body processes. Plants rely on mineral ions, photosynthesis, and solar energy to fuel their metabolic processes. Humans rely on red blood corpuscles and hemoglo-bin for their supply of oxygen. Plants rely on chlorophyll and the chloroplasts. Human body fluids are called blood and lymph. Plant fluids are called chlorophyll and sap. Human beings need movement, exercise, and load bearing work to assist in the repair and maintenance of body tissues. Plants enjoy little mobility.

Lack of exercise and load bearing work, SLOWS blood and lymph flow and leads to dis-ease. The tendency towards lack of movement is the CURSE of all people.

Blood and lymph are flip sides of the same coin. A dis-ease condition in the lymph mirrors trouble in the blood. The lymphatic system directly influences blood chemistry.

When we learn HOW to control body terrain, we control the aging process. Aging reversal requires that we assist the body in cleaning up and maintaining the lymphatic system through increased ***body fluid dynamics.*** Examples are load bearing work, rebounding, exercise, and lymph rolling.

Dis-ease "develops" in the lymph. Later, it appears in the blood. Maintain the lymphatic system and dis-ease will not be found in the body.

We *limp* our way into old age. We must *lymph* our way UP the catabolic side of the aging pyramid—back to our anabolic peak, for it is there at our former PEAK that we become *Young Again!*

PREVIEW: *Our next chapter is the "cancer" chapter! Learn HOW to avoid becoming a cancer statistic.*

Stroke Damage

If you have can think fast in a moment of crisis, long term damage that follows "stroke" can be avoided and/or reversed by placing the victim in a bathtub of 86^0 F water for 24 hours, then raise the water temperature and slowly warm the victum to 98.6^0. Presto NO damage!

Life! A Dual Perspective!

We grow old and die in the *invisible* realm of the Fourth Dimension **BEFORE** we see and experience aging in the Third Dimension where we live out our lives.

Detoxification of the body requires a **dual** perspective to be truly effective. For example, colon therapy accelerates the release of toxic metabolic wastes on the physical level, while enhanced homeopathic remedies bring about detoxification on a higher "invisible" level.

When we *erase* toxic energy conditions in the Fourth Dimension, we deal with **underlying** health issues and promote true healing in the Third Dimension.

Life is the manifestation of what we in the West refer to as *spirit, soul, grace,* and what Eastern thought calls *life force, chi, qi* and *prana.*

Good health and rejuvenation demands a dual perspective. So does spiritual enlightenment.

Howdy Doody Facial Lines

Lines from *the corners of the mouth to the sides of the chin* indicate colon/liver problems, hormonal imbalance, and a body that is in **trouble.** Liver purges, colonics and racemized™ hormone precursors reverse Howdie Doody lines.

A Typical Day

1. Wake up early the same time each day & immediately drink two BIG glasses of water and one mug of Kombucha.
2. Get on the rebounder and "rock'n roll" for a 5 minutes.
3. Do stretching exercises and calisthenics followed by a lymph roll down with the lymph roller. Drink MORE water.
4. Do pull ups (both over and under hand), pump some iron, and finally get on a good aerobic exerciser and raise heart beat to 80% of your maximum heart rate and HOLD it there for 12 minutes. Do this in cold, fresh air with a minimum of clothing using *mind over body* to stay warm.
5. Drink a mug of Kombucha tea along with some SOC™ caps and R/A catalyst, then do another lymph roll down.
6. Take a hot shower followed by a long ice cold shower.
7. Eat a healthy breakfast, preferably of SUPER FOODS with some fresh fruit. For instance, take 1 tbsp. Yucca Blend™, 1 tbsp. Harmonic Synergy™, and 1 tbsp. Taoist Rice Polish™ in a glass of juice or water and use to wash down the SUPER FOODS listed on page #292, plus 2 DiSorb Aid™ & 2 R/HCI™ tabs.
8. Each time you urinate throughout the day, drink more water. Take additional Kombucha tea "between" meals.
9. Lunch: You won't want lunch if you do the above. But if you insist, repeat the SUPER FOODS list and you will ZOOM the rest of the day. An apple or fresh veggies are always acceptable. A short walk in fresh air, some relaxing music, meditation, good conversation, breathing exercises, prayer, whatever—as long as it's uplifting is a relaxing lmakes for a nice lunch break. **P.S.** Don't buy into other people's problems and don't worry about your own.
10. Hold your bladder to promote bowel movements. Use Biogenic™ Colon Prep Formula to free colon lining and increase the number of bowel movements each day.
11. Do some load-bearing work every day. Move boxes. Lift things. Do gardening work by hand (no rototiller). Use a push lawn mower. Walk to the store. *Carry* your groceries home. Pump some iron. Do some calisthenics. Hang and stretch twice daily. **Force** your body to become strong! The body was made to work. If it hurts, take some SOC™. If your are weak, be patient and you will become strong.
12. Eat a healthy dinner and enjoy your family/friends.
13. Retire the same time each evening. Sleep outside if possible or in a well ventilated cold room. Pray. Give thanks for being alive. Look forward to better tomorrows.

Microbiology Of Drinking Water

The principal bacterial agents shown to be involved in intestinal dis-eases associated with drinking water are:

Salmonella typhi: typhoid fever
Salmonella paratyphi-Aparathyphoid fever
Salmonella species: enteric fever, salmonellosis
Shigella bacteria: bacillary dysentery
Amebas: Amebic dysentery
Vibrio cholerae: cholera
Leptospira species: leptospirosis
Yersinia enterocolitica: gastroenteritis
Francisella tularensis: tulararemia
Escherichia coli (E. coli): gastroenteritis
Pseudomonas aeruginosa: various infections
Cryptosporidium: cryptosporidiosis

Enteric (pertaining to the small intestine/gut) bacteria like E. coli, Salmonella, and Shigella are classified as *facultatively anaerobic,* that is, they can function and live with or without oxygen. They ferment sugars and produce organic acids (acetic, formic, lactic, etc.) and gases (mixed-acid fermentation).

Unlike bacteria, viruses are **intra**cellular parasites and cannot replicate outside the host's cells. Hepatitis-A (infectious hepatitis) is the product of a notable water born virus. So is poliomyelitis (polio).

Viruses and bacteria are prevalent in raw untreated water. Therefore, conventional treatment of public water supplies involves steps like coagulation, sedimentation, filtration, and disinfection (chlorine, **chloramines,** mercuric acid, etc.) to produce *potable* water. These steps reduce organism count. However, during the warm season, the organisms can multiply in the lines with disastrous results.

Parasites, pathogenic bacteria, and viruses are removed from drinking water by the BEV™ process. In addition, they are **flushed** from the BEV™ system so as not to develop a breeding ground for the spread of dis-ease. No other water system can provide the purity, protection, and elevated ORP potential of the BEV™ and Medical grade Ionized Water™ processes.

The United States is headed for a cataclysmic crisis in public drinking water. Protect yourself!

30

Cancer & Salt

"Well organized ignorance, unfortunately, often passes for wisdom."
anon.

Salt (sodium chloride) is a paradox. It is part of life, yet it is involved in death. A little salt will hurt you a little bit. More than a little will *eventually* kill you.

History can be written according to salt. In ancient China, two big tablespoons of salt was a socially acceptable mode of suicide. Salt has served as money, an item of barter, and a cathartic (laxative). For over 100 years, medicine's focus has centered on salt's relationship to *high blood pressure*. We will instead focus on salt's systemic EFFECTS on the "terrain."

Mankind has chosen to upset Nature's balance. We use salt to *hype* our food and in so doing we hasten old age. Nutritious food does NOT need salt because it has plenty of mineral ions in it to give it flavor. Marginal food requires salt to create the *mirage* of taste—and to keep it from **spoiling**. Look at any can or package of processed food and you will find that it is loaded with salt.

Canned foods came about in 1859 when the H. J. Heinz company produced the first of its Heinz 57 varieties. Salt was used to create a brine environment that was hostile to Clostridium botulinum. Clostridium is a *facultative* anaerobe. It can survive with or without oxygen. Its wastes are the most toxic systemic poisons known. We call the condition produced by these toxins *botulism!*

Sailors of old suffered miserably from *salt*-preserved beef and pork. So did civilian populations. When meat is preserved with salt, it loses its energy force and nutritive qualities. Sodium chloride (table salt) is a preservative that upsets the potassium:sodium balance in the body. Salt puts money in the mortician's pocket.

Organic foods are naturally high in potassium and low in sodium, while bio-junk and processed foods are exactly the opposite. Sodium upsets the ion balance in the body and destroys energy balance in the soil. Salt fertilizers create conditions of EXCESS in the soil, as does table salt in the body. Salt is a concentrated, left-spin energy field that does not belong in the body.

NOTE: A little flour, salt, and water mixed together makes a wonderful play dough for children. However, when it dries, it turns as hard as concrete!

Natural Preservatives

Dr. Carey Reams taught that quality produce will dehydrate before it will rot. He proved his point by entering a watermelon he had grown in the local county fair for three years in a row! Quality, fresh food is high in natural sugars and earth minerals. Quality produce has a right-spin energy signature.

Acres USA once carried a story about a salesman who carted around three cabbages in his car for nine months without spoilage. On the weekends, he would roll them under a shade tree until Monday morning when he would peel away a leaf and hit the road again. When the salesman was challenged, the nine month old cabbages were cut and eaten raw. The point here is that high mineral and sugar content is central to high quality fruits and vegetables.

Homemade ice cream containing too much sugar will NOT set up regardless of the amount of salt applied to the ice to lower the freezing point. Oranges that are high in natural sugars will wither and shrink, but they will NOT rot. Home grown lettuce and greens can be kept in the refrigerator for over a month and will still be crisp and tasty with no spoilage! High sugar levels in the juices of food crops indicates a high mineral content, excellent flavor, and good keeping qualities.

Trace minerals and humic acids applied to plant foliage as a foliar spray raise the sugar/mineral levels in the juices of plants and protect them from frost damage. High sugar levels in a crop is an excellent marker of nutritious food. Proper glucose (sugar) levels in the blood and glycogen levels in the muscles are closely related to peak health. Dis-ease cannot survive in a high energy, right-spin environment where mineral ion levels and sugars are balanced and excesses do not exist.

In the old days, a bushel of fresh green beans weighed 32 lbs. Today, a bushel of beans weighs only 24 lbs. The difference is the lack of earth minerals AND lower concentration of sugar energy. The more concentrated the positive energy fields, the heavier the crop vs. crops raised with salt fertilizers and poisons that produce sick, weak populations of human beings.

SALT: Paul Bragg vs. The Athletes

Here is a true story about how salt affects health and vitality. In the early 1960's, Dr. Paul C. Bragg, a famous health crusader and one of my mentors, challenged a group of college athletes to a 30 mile hike across Death Valley. The temperature in August was 130° Fahrenheit.

The *experts* advised the athletes to take "salt tablets!" The athletes were given all the "cold" water and food they wanted. Bragg drank *only* warm distilled water (in those days BEV water was not available), took NO salt, and fasted—taking no food. Bragg was the only one to finish the hike. The athletes—every last one of them—were carried off for medical care. They suffered from heat exhaustion and heat stroke. Bragg finished the hike in 10 1/2 hours, camped overnight, and repeated the return hike the following day. He was in his mid *sixties!* He was YOUNG and active. **He avoided all salt!**

Rommel's German-Afrikan Corps used no salt in their diets, yet they fought tremendous desert battles. When they were finally captured, they were in peak condition and unaffected by the intense desert heat. The Americans used salt tablets, they salted their food and the heat got to them.

Native peoples consume little salt. When *civilized* man comes along and introduces salt into their diet, their health deteriorates. Salt isn't the only issue in dis-ease, but it is **always** a player in the development of subclinical illness that eventually gives way to SIGNS and the diagnosis of dis-ease.

Cells • Sodium • Mitochondria

When sodium levels are high, the body is in a negative energy condition. A high sodium diet upsets the body's sodium:potassium ratio and speeds the LOSS of potassium from the cells. Potassium is the predominant ion *inside* cell membranes, while sodium is the predominant ion *outside* of cell membranes in the **extra**cellular fluid.

When sodium levels are high, the body steals potassium from the cells and replaces it with sodium. Both ions have a positive (+) charge and both are electrolytes. However, sodium spins left while potassium spins right. **Edema (fluid retention in the tissues) is a SIGN of excess sodium and excess plasma protein wastes in the intercellular spaces.**

Once inside the cell, sodium short-circuits cellular machinery, sedates the mitochondria, and eventually kills the cell. Dead cells create acids that must be removed. Marginal cells that are between life and death produce little ATP and become a drag on the system. The presence of dead and sick tissue needlessly *consumes* vital ENERGY. ATP energy that could be used for growth and repair is squandered in the presence of sodium-imposed stress.

The mitochondria **cannot** function in a high sodium environment. They **cannot** replicate (reproduce) when sodium has invaded their territory.

Energy • Free Radicals

We have spent a lot of time discussing and describing energy using terms like left-spin, right-spin, negative, positive, aerobic, and anaerobic in an effort to help the reader understand the nature of energy and its relationship to aging.

The term "free" radical' is a term that comes to mind in regard to energy and cancer. A free radical is a molecule that contains an *odd* number of electrons. This makes it highly reactive and EXTREMELY unstable.

Free radicals are very much a part of **every** person's life. Poor choices of lifestyle, diet, and water are greatly compounded by environmental poisons that bombard the bioelectric body from every direction.

In a healthy body, free radical reactions take place continuously and look like this: $O^2 + O^2 + H^2 \leftrightarrow H_2 O_2 = + O_2$ (the double arrow means that the reaction can **reverse**). In a stressed body, **reverse** chain reactions cause electron theft to go out of control. The end result is accelerated aging.

Free radical production tremendously influences aging and the formation of cancer in the body. For our discussion here, I want the reader to understand that these *wild* reactions drive the production of **non differentiated** tissue (cancer tissue) and systemic EXCESSES.

Nondifferentiated tissue is the tissue from which we evolve PRIOR to hormonal influences that cause the formation of skin instead of muscle, bones instead of brains, etc. We are talking about OUTLAW tissue with no identity. Tissue *insurrection* best describes the process. Uncontrolled oxidation of the tissues builds EXCESS toxic waste in the system, drives hormone disturbances, and toxic waste overload that eventually manifest as *so called* deficiency conditions occur.

Free radical reactions within the cancerous body are do to loss of control over the "terrain." Cancer absorbs and uses cellular ATP to proliferate. In compliance with the second law of thermodynamics, energy is NEVER lost, it merely changes form. Once excess toxic energy **EXCEEDS** the body's ability to cope, the formation of a tumor or a mass will begin. We will discuss their individual characteristics shortly.

Uncontrolled free radical oxidation can be prevented through detoxification and the use of various racemized™ products and programs outlined thus far. Consumption of Medical Grade Ionized Water™ is perhaps the ultimate tool for terrain control. Do understand this: health is a "cumulative" state of being as is dis-ease. **Health and dis-ease are also a reflection of the choices we make.**

Energy • Cancer

Cancer is a manifestation of a negative energy condition. Cancer **tumors** surround themselves in a zone of SODIUM. They **concentrate** energy by acting as *anaerobic* black holes, siphoning away and isolating the host's life force.

The tumor is NOT the "enemy." Rather, it is a statement by the body that all is not well. Moreover, a tumor is a self-defensive measure taken by the body to preserve itself through the **condensation** of deadly toxic energy. We are talking about toxic energy that the body is unable to neutralize or dispose of through normal exit portals like the lungs, kidneys, bowel, and skin. Tumors—even benign tumors—are a warning SIGN.

In the early stages, a cancer tumor goes unnoticed. As it concentrates more energy, it becomes more "dense." It can now be seen by X-ray, CAT scan, and MRI. It can even be *felt* with the fingers if it is not too deep in the body.

Cancer tumors are NOT the same as cancer masses. Tumors are energy-**importing** clusters of tissue that the body forms to ISOLATE toxic energy fields and get them OUT of circulation.

Tumors are *nationalistic*. They stay within their own territory and import their energy needs. They do NOT spread as commonly believed. When *antagonized by surgical intervention*, the body is weakened sufficiently to precipitate the formation of new tumors rather than son and daughter tumors. Generaly, cancerous tumors should NOT be removed.

Sometimes the body chooses to **dissolve** a tumor. In most cases, however, it chooses to **calcify** (deposit minerals; petrify) the tumor and tie up the toxic energy on a permanent basis. The tumor is an effort by the body to preserve itself rather than the enemy. The enemy is usually the person who inhabits the body. Healing requires focused effort and reprogramming of the way people think. Even if the face of doing everything right, negative thinking will get you because "negative" is what you **believe!. The mind is 90% of the battle.**

Conversely, the positive thinking, happy, loving person can outlast the worst of cancers. However, correct mental choices need to be duplicated on the physical level if success is expected. God performs miracles for people who make correct "choices!" GET IT?

When a **malignant** tumor (or mass) is discovered, immediate action is needed. Radiation and chemotherapy are NEVER wise choices. Torture and financial strain make little sense. Alternative treatment is safer and more humane if the patient has discipline and is willing to face down death.

Alternative therapy requires that a person have a laid-back, happy, 100% happy go lucky attitude and outlook. There is absolutely NO room for doubt, fear, worry, hate, blame, or anger—only love! **The desire to live must be intense and beyond the fear of death.** I highly recommend the book, *Your Body Believes Every Word You Say* and *Holographic Universe* (see Source Page).

The ONLY things cancer tumors and masses have in common is that both are *virus* havens and both like left-spin, anaerobic, high sodium environments.

Cancer Masses

A mass is not a tumor and the terms should NOT be used interchangeably. A mass is not dense like a tumor. It cannot be felt because it has no definitive boundaries. A mass is soft, spongy, porous, and difficult to feel—never hard.

A mass takes form, grows and establishes outposts quietly. Masses exist in the twilight zone *between* life and death. They rarely appear on X-rays, CAT scans, or MRI's and it is almost impossible to differentiate where a mass ends and healthy soft tissue begins with these tools. Masses are *invisible* because they have low density and hide behind other tissues.

Masses are *offensive* in nature. Think of them in terms of outposts for colonial expansionism in a third world country (your body). Masses colonize during a 7 year period, referred to in medical circles as the "occult" period (*occult* means hidden). Long before a cancer *mass* announces itself to the host, it is there, growing and spreading. Masses follow the lymphatic highway and sabotage the host's lymphatic and immune systems, while the host notices nothing and even feels good! By the time a mass announces itself, the host is in **deep** trouble.

Cloaking Period & Sodium

During the occult period, a cancer mass is concealed, invisible and non-detectable by the host and conventional testing. In other words, a mass employs a cloaking technique so as to go undetected. The years preceding the end of the occult period are often some of the very best years in terms of OUTWARD appearance of good health. On the inside however, confirmation of the person's lifestyle, thought patterns, and choices have come home to roost and aging is in full swing.

Masses cause the body to gain weight with little or no increase in body measurements because water is heavier than fat on a volume basis. Therefore, weight gain without inches is reason to question what is occurring in your terrain.

A person who is sodium-toxic always suffers from edema (water logging of the tissues), partly from the sodium and partly from the accumulation of plasma proteins in the **extra**cellular spaces between the cells.

Edema is a SIGN. Edema is abnormal. *Chronic* edema is the equivalent to a quiet proclamation of WAR and must not be ignored. Edema signals the *invasion* of sodium at the cellular level and GROSS accumulation of plasma proteins in the interstitial spaces between the cells. Look for puffy, water filled skin that "dents" easily when pressed and does not spring back quickly. Be alert to swelling in the legs, ankles, feet, and hands. This SIGN also goes with congestive heart failure and is **very** hormone related.

People in the *early stages* of a cancer "mass" formation, often experience substantial weight gain for no particular reason—usually WITHOUT any noticeable change in dietary habits. Near the end of the occult period, they get the *"I just don't feel up to par!"* syndrome. Finally, out of the blue, the person becomes skin and bones. **Their body seems to evaporate!** When this occurs, the *mass* type cancer has removed its cloak, the occult period is over, and the final struggle begins.

Edema is cancer's cloaking device. **People do NOT recognize edema for what it is! They don't understand. They think everything is okay—*"Just a little old age!"*** During the cloaking period, the cancerous body is **cannibalizing** itself. It is experiencing severe free radical oxidation and is digesting its own tissues—a process called **auto digestion.** The body is living on *stored* energy. The body is now in a catabolic state. Once the body has used up its energy reserves—BANG!— the game is over. Because of the *invisible* nature of cancer masses, exploratory surgery is pushed onto the unsuspecting patient by *blind men and women in white robes*. Exploratory invasive surgery sabotages whatever energy reserves remain and weakens the person beyond hope.

A positive confirmation of **CANCER** is seldom a blessing because it does a number on the sick person. By this time, their weight has plunged downward and their energy is nil. The victim becomes skin and bones overnight. Terror sets it.

When sodium levels in the cells and the plasma proteins in the tissues reach the critical point, cancer *turns off* its cloaking device and announces itself.

It's Your Life

There are no tests to determine sodium toxicity at the cellular level, but there are SIGNS. There are no tests for plasma protein toxicity at the **extra**cellular level either, but there are SIGNS. Learn to pay attention to them.

Pay attention when you see people (and children) gaining weight. Be alert to gyrating blood sugar levels that manifest as mood swings/depression. PMS and menstrual problems are serious business. Acne, boils, balding, ongoing "subclinical" illness low energy all tell a story. Bladder infections, prostate problems, bowel conditions, and graying hair have long-term consequences.

If you are in trouble, seek help. But be forewarned that you will be bullied into conventional therapy. People feel **"releived"** when the enemy has been identified i.e., cancer. They want to **"believe"** their physician. Neither count. Identifying the enemy means you are focusing on what you **don't** want. Medical fairy tales are a fraud, and fraud always results in fraudulent decisions. Instead, locate someone who is not held hostage by the AMA (American Medical Association), the pharmaceutical houses, or the FDA. **If you can't find such a person, then strike out on your own.**

Remember, the **body** does the healing. As the steward of that body, it is YOUR job to provide the environment where healing can take place. Control the "terrain!"

Colon therapy is crucial. Limited food intake is wise. Home grown foods are unbeatable. Liver detoxification is mandatory. Hormone issues MUST be addressed. Medical Grade Ionized Water™ is better than any medical clinic in the world—and you can make it right in your own home.

Walking is beneficial. Positive thinking and visualization are crucial. Detoxification is mandatory. Rebounding and lymph rolling should be part of your routine. Laughter and fun are basic prerequisites. Worry and fear are **not** allowed. GUARD your thoughts or you will become a self-fulfilling prophesy. Remember the power of prayer, both for yourself and others. Meditation and deep breathing are powerful tools. Time spent in a garden (bare foot), growing food, and enjoying Nature is as close to heaven as you can get. Take time to focus on and help others. The more you give, the more you receive. Get plenty of rest. Sleep on a Biogenic™ Medical Grade Mattress Pad and turn your rest periods into "healing" periods.

Self Diagnosis & Treatment

The simplest tools for diagnosis are a pendulum and vibration chain. Used properly, they are fantastic devices. Use them to establish the depth of your aura today, so you will have a reference for the future. Combined with your "bio-electric age," you now have TWO reference points. *Tune-in* to your gut instincts.

It is NOT easy to drive sodium from the body—especially a body diagnosed with cancer. Copious amounts of organic potassium are needed, but be careful not to over juice. Eat whole fresh foods like carrots, cabbage, onion, lemon ,and beet. *sip* and *chew* your juices. Do NOT gorge yourself. Remember, it takes 5-10 minutes to properly eat an apple, but only 2 seconds to drink the juice. Juices slam the system, opinions to the contrary notwithstanding. Use moderation and be certain to add a little Yucca Herbal Blend™, DiSorb Aid™, and racemized™ hydrogen chloride for full benefit and as a buffer.

Fresh juices are VERY powerful detoxifiers and can flood the body with wastes to the point that the liver and adrenals become *exhausted* and the kidneys *overloaded*. It's better to go slow. A far superior approach to juices is to have the sick or dying person go off almost all normal food and consume **nothing but the SUPER foods I have mentioned.** The results are incredible! Best of all, you can stay home and heal.

Liver is a wonderful food—if you can stand it! I use **predigested,** organic beef liver tablets. It's a **superb** food. Cancer therapy should **always** include liver. Domestic liver products are contaminated. Avoid them. Do not use *dessicated* liver! It is a high stress food.

Deep "coffee" colonics are therapeutic. Kombucha tea is wonderful. Gentle *rebounding* (mini-trampoline) moves body fluids. Lymphatic rolling is MOST effecive. RHYTHM and regular hours allow you to heal. PACˢ and Aspar-Max™ help.

Detoxification of plasma protein wastes does NOT happen by itself. YOU must assist YOUR body. Once released into circulation, they MUST be gotten rid of fast! Colon therapy, PACˢ, and Yucca Herbal Blend™ make it happen. Avoid tap water. Don't drink distilled water. It is loaded with plasticizers and is biologically "dead" water. Those who advocate it have their feet in cement. Far SUPERIOR choices are available.

Expect To Feel Crummy

EXPECT to feel crummy as you detoxify! You are paying for your sins. Do NOT forget the power of prayer and positive thinking. Try to find strength within YOURSELF. Its nice to have a "strong" person to help you through the transition back to the world of the healthy, but they are few.

Once the potassium begins exchanging places with the sodium inside the cells, the mitochondria will come alive and replicate themselves. The more of them that come alive and multiply—the more *ENERGY* there will be available for your body to rebuild itself. At first, you will feel worse. In time, you will feel better. **It's two steps forward, one step backwards.**

Detoxification can be tough on people. It's a kind of **mind game.** The body shouts, *"I feel crummy!"* but you must ignore and reassure the body that all is **under control.** Talk out loud and tell your body *what you expect* and *what you desire.* Never go hyper at the first sign of a metabolic rebound—guard your energy at all costs! Good days are followed by bad days. In time, you will enjoy more good and fewer bad days. If you panic or cut and run, you will NEVER be healed!

Chemotherapy

Chemotherapy is defined as the prevention or treatment of infectious disease by *chemicals* which act to prevent "antisepsis" in the body while avoiding serious side effects in the patient. If we dissect the word *antisepsis,* we get *anti-*against; *sepsis-*a general fever producing condition, caused by bacteria or their toxic by-products. In light of this dictionary definition, do you think that *chemotherapy* as used on cancer patients meets this description? Did you know that you must sign a form *before* you get your *magic bullet* cancer therapy?

NOT Approved

Drugs used in cancer chemotherapy are *magic bullets.* They are NOT APPROVED as safe for the treatment of cancer. They are administered to unsuspecting people. Medicine and the pharmaceutical companies side step the "liability" problem by having people sign away their rights *beforehand,* so they cannot bring suit for the horrible side effects that follow.

When people sign the *"standard"* form, they are giving the legal AND medical systems *jurisdiction* over them. The name of the game in our legal system is *jurisdiction!* Either medicine and the courts have jurisdiction over a person's body or the person does, but NOT both at the same time.

"Standard" forms are no different than entering a court-room where the judge has committed constructive treason by placing the yellow fringe on a Title 4, U.S.C. 1 flag of "peace" of the united (note small "u") States of America or displaying it inferior to a ball, eagle or spear on the pole, or placing it on the right as you face the flag, or placing it inferior to any other flag. The judges do this to "create" a foreign "state" in order to deny citizens their constitutional rights. JURISDICTION is everything!

When the medical system has jurisdiction, the person does not. When a person grants jurisdiction over their body, medical "science" is free to maneuver with impunity.

For the cancer patient, the options "within" the medical system are nil. Sign the form or be refused treatment because jurisdiction was not granted—a limited liability contract where both sides share the benefits and the patient assumes ALL the risk! The medical system needs *jurisdiction* because they are using EXPERIMENTAL drugs in the treatment of cancer and the destruction of YOUR body—with the blessings of watch-dog agencies, of course.

Everyone MUST come to understand something known in legal AND medical circles as the "Rule of Probable Cause." It states: *"...experimental drugs may be used IF the side effect of the drug is NO worse than the end effect of the untreated disease."*

"For Experimental Use Only"

Regardless of the specie of cancer drug, it will be stamped with the tell-tale sign of a **"magic bullet"** medicine—"For Experimental Use Only."

How do you like that? How does it make you feel to know that the MAXIMUM risk to the poor patient is no worse than if treatment were not rendered at all. What an alternative—sign on the dotted line and let us milk you of your life and savings or go home and die!

"For Experimental Use Only" is a fact that should be sufficient SHOCK therapy to motivate every thinking person to immediately begin the aging reversal process. No matter how you figure it, you are on your own. So go home and live! "Magic bullets" don't work! Self treatment is less risky and the odds of recovery far greater—at a fraction of the cost.

Believe me when I tell you that your health and life are worth more than all the money you can throw at the medical system in the futile effort to buy back your health. **Good health**

isn't for sale! Instead, it requires commitment, discipline, responsibility, and choice. AVOID the horror of cancer and degenerative dis-eases by implementing what you have learned throughout this book.

Cancer & Root Canals

According to Dr. Issels, a German doctor, only 20% of the population has root canals, yet, 90% of cancer victims have root canals in their mouth!

Cancer and root canals in the teeth are related. The implications are scary, but options like dentures, bridges, implants also have severe shortcomings.

I have a problem with root canals if the body's **TERRAIN** is weak. For some people, "dead" teeth in the mouth produce an auto immune response that compromises good health. But if you are in PEAK health or are willing to get yourself in PEAK health, root canals need not become a health issue. Its the "terrain" that dictates whether you can enjoy good health and a long life with root canals in your mouth. From fillings to root canals, ALL dental procedures are less than desirable, so take care of your teeth. Got it?

If you have an **infected** root canaled tooth, get it **OUT** of your mouth. And if you are facing serious dental work, PLEASE call and learn how to prepare your body for amalgam removal to avoid *dental shock* associated with a sick **"terrain."** What you do BEFORE major dental work usually dictates the outcome. Control the TERRAIN and you will become *Young Again!*

PREVIEW: *Our next chapter deals with the world of Time and Space and its relationship to the Fourth Dimension, ageless living, and the vast UNKNOWN!*

Our Stolen Future discusses the "hormone" issue.

It's Your Life!
Some things are worse than death. Becoming a victim of *conventional* cancer treatment is one of them. Never rejoice because insurance is paying the bills. Do be concerned about what "they" are doing to you. Do be independent. Do keep your dignity. Do maintain control of your life. Do stay away from doctors. Do these things and you will leave your loved ones with more than the ugly memory of the **"torture"** that preceded your death!
CHOOSE to live and die on your own terms!

31

Time & Space

*"Time and Space are the shadows by
which man defines his existence."*
Sepio

Time is duration—Space is extension. We do not think
of Time and Space as entities, but we do consider the bodies
and events that occupy them as entities. If we acknowledge the
existence of material bodies because they occupy space, then
what is an event? An event is a group of circumstances that
occupy Time. Therefore, material objects are also events and
both are entities.

Mankind attempts to define those intangibles we call
Time and Space using words and concepts. We have no
physical sense organs for Time and Space. We anticipate them
through our "intuition." Intuition, then, must be a sixth
sense—a projection of the physical body—something we invoke
to comprehend Time and Space.

Philosophy tells us that Time and Space consist of
relations between entities—that there is co-existence and
succession of entities or events. Metaphysics (*meta*: beyond)
tells us that Time and Space are indistinguishable as long as
neither is excluded. Yet, we are aware of the *passage* of Time.

Plato stated, "Time and space is the "substance" which
contains the identity and the diversity in one." If we think of
Space as something that is created, then something must

create it. What? *Metaphysics* answers, *Time.* Okay. If there is creation, then motion must also exist. If there is motion, then there must be a mover or source of motion. Metaphysics tells us that Time is the source of motion, and if this is so, then Time is *ENERGY.*

Is Time *energy* or is energy created in the passing of time? If energy is created, the results are perpetual motion which is not a straight line, but a curved line that returns to itself—like a circle. Therefore, Space becomes Time's trail. But a trail does not move, so Space cannot move either, since it was Time that generated ENERGY in its expansion—creating Space. Time and Space can also be demonstrated to be static, indistinguishable or non-existent. Let us illustrate.

Suppose we are in an airplane that is traveling at the same speed as the Earth's rotation or approximately 1080 miles per hour and we are heading West following the sun at its own speed. We begin our three hour trip in New York City at exactly twelve o'clock noon and when we arrive at Los Angeles it is still exactly twelve o'clock noon.

What has taken place here? Time became a motion of Space and Space the relaxation of Time. We moved from one point to another point on the surface of the earth, but Time did not change. We are in a quandary—caught between Time and Space—a kind of cosmic culdesac. The mathematician working on our dilemma would have difficulty making his calculations respond to our problem—so he would give the *unknown* condition a name: "fourth variable," and reestablish his equilibrium by imposing the ingredient Time so his calculations could continue as if Time were a fixed point.

When we ponder the situation, we must conclude that Time is NOT a fixed point to which we can anchor our lives, but a mirage on a phantom's shroud. Once we admit that Time is not a fixed point, we lose our center and our reference point—yet, our *intuition* tells us there should be such a center.

To compensate, man divides Time into three parts: *present, past,* and *future.* However, this does not solve the problem because the Present is but the transition from Past into Future—a transition that lacks both dimensionality and duration. The Present is the Future before we think of it, and the moment we think of it, it is the Past. Under these circumstances, self examination of our thought processes and sensory experiences becomes impossible. Is Present but the "living fringe" of our memory tinted by expectation? And if it is, what of our dilemma between the poles of eternity—Past and Future?

These extremes—past and future—have delivered us into the *enigma* we call the Fourth Dimension—the "unknowable." Because man *seems* capable of comprehending only three dimensions related to his physical world—that of length, width, and height—the idea of the existence of another dimension that is totally invisible only compounds his dilemma. **Yet, the existence of the Fourth Dimension cannot be denied. Intuition is real. It is more than an intangible tool by which we interpret Time and Space. It is an extension of our mind.**

Perhaps the Fourth Dimension is not unknowable at all, but simply misunderstood? And so, then there is no reason for man to have to die and emerge from his terrestrial envelope before he can come to *know* this *Unknowable* dimension.

Knowledge of the existence of this *other* dimension is quite different than understanding it. Consider Jesus, who passed through the wall in the Temple. He was a Third Dimensional being with a physical body, yet He passed through that wall! Since both He and the wall were solid matter, shall we chalk up this event to Deity? Did He violate some Natural Law? Or did He invoke knowledge of the Fourth Dimension?

When we enter the arena of the Fourth Dimension, necessity demands that we visualize a *hyper-space* that is measured with *meta*geometry (*meta*-beyond). Our three dimensional world of length, width, and height becomes but a section of *hyper-Space*. Let us examine this in more detail.

The *length* of a procession of events is not contained in three dimensional space. Extension in Time is a projection into unknown space—or the Fourth Dimension. Because Space and Time are interchangeable at specific points, Time becomes a dimension of Space. That is, Time is Space in motion becoming the Future or the Past. Therefore, Space is time projected—horizontal Time—Time that persists, Time that moves. And since Space can only be measured by Time, and Time is defined by the speed of light, we must conclude that there is no difference between Space and Time **EXCEPT that our consciousness is defined in Time.**

We are, therefore, *forced* to acknowledge that the Present is eternal—that Time per se does not exist, but is relative to the person with the *notion* of time. **Events do not ebb and flow. It is we who pass them by!** The more we wrestle and try to understand, the deeper we get into the vast unknown.

The creature we call man exists in two worlds: the visible and the invisible. The invisible world is the realm of negative and positive "energy" forces that ultimately determine our perception of reality in the visible world in which we find our existence. The visible world and the physical body, in turn, act as our compass and bridge into the sphere of the unknown — where the *electric* body exists and functions.

People who have become *OLD* tell us, "time seems to *fly*, and the older you get, the *faster* it flies!" Their day disappears before it has begun. Is this a figment of their imagination or is it reality? And if it is reality, by what measure do we scale this phenomenon?

We cannot measure Time phenomenon in Third Dimension terms, for neither Time nor Space exist here, leaving us, once again, wrestling in the shadows of the *unknown*—a Fourth Dimension world where we are totally dependent on our intuition—our sixth sense.

We must invoke our *intuition* to measure the passing of Time because it passes at the **subatomic** level of our existence—the level of the invisible "electric" body. Therefore, it stands to reason that Time DOES pass more quickly for the person who is catabolic, who has passed their anabolic peak, and whose cells are aging at an *accelerated* rate.

Time passes slowly when we are YOUNG—when we are climbing up the anabolic side of the pyramid. When we are young, we experience *slow* Time. After we reach our anabolic peak, we experience *fast* Time as we *slide* down the catabolic side of the pyramid.

We have arrived at the answer we have been seeking. It is the *thesis* of this book, summarized as follows: **Slowing the aging process slows the passing of Time and transcends the physical and material world. And though the physical body is confined in Time and Space, the *electric* body is FREE. It is an extension of the *self* and a fixture of the unknown Fourth Dimension where our mind and emotions are but windows to our soul. The electric body is our spirit and our soul.**

Buying Time! By stopping our bio-electric clock, we buy Time. Time provides us the opportunity to exchange an old body for a young one and is the equivalent of *recycling* the sand in an hour glass. This recycling process does NOT mean that we relive our earlier experiences. Rather, it means that we reexperience Time itself. This is what is meant when we talk about becoming *YOUNG AGAIN!*

PREVIEW: *Our next chapter deals with rejuvenation of the bio-electric body through rest, fasting, and avoidance of self-imposed physiologic stress.*

Bran Muffin Recipe: 1/4 C honey; 1/3 C blackstrap molasses; 1 tbsp. non aluminum baking powder; 1 egg; 2 C unbleached white flour; 1/2—1 C water; 1 C bran; 2 tbsp. olive oil; 1 tbsp. of flax seed; 1/4 C sesame seed; 1 C raisins; 1/4 C wheat germ, 1/2 C chopped walnuts; perhaps a little pumpkin pie spice. Makes six muffins. Bake @ 400° until medium brown. Do not knead.

Taoism & Taoist Super Food

Ancient Chinese Taoists (pronounced *Dowists*) viewed man as a small reflection of the universe. They perceived that **cyclic** change governs all living things. They laid down principles and correlations that described the effect of Nature on man and the response of man to Nature. They described these principles in terms of **Yin** and **Yang**.

Taoist Masters believed that Five Elements describe the natural cycle of life and that man follows Nature's *cyclical* patterns through the "universe within."

Herbals were formulated to help man adapt to nature. Taoist Masters strove for *total* balance and harmony, promoted *self-cultivation*, thought enhancement, *shen* clearing, and *jing* building through manipulation of the Five Elements. Their discoveries are now confirmed by modern advanced physics.

The **Wood** Element represents the liver and gall-bladder which control emotional harmony and the smooth flow of Chi (energy) necessary for a strong nervous system and the clearing of toxins from the body. The **Fire** Element is represented by the heart and small intestine and addresses the blood, lymph, and cerebral systems, plus physical and mental health and growth. The **Earth** Element represents the stomach and spleen and *extracts* and *separates* pure from the turbid within the body. The **Metal** Element represents the lung and colon and is said to dominate respiration and maintain defensive Chi (the immune system). The **Water** Element represents the kidney and bladder systems. Taoists believed that *Jing* (the very *essence* of life) is within body water and is expressed as hormonal and reproductive systems responsible for maintaining youthfulness and glandular function.

Taoist philosophy teaches that the body has the power to **regenerate** itself when stress (physical or mental) occurs. Taoists believe that the body is designed to run on whole food. They teach that *accountability* underwrites superior health and is reflected by the "universe within."

Taoism teaches that people achieve **enlightenment** through balance, awareness, and expression of the *person* within. Enlightenment and of truth bring *understanding*, and Taoist SUPER foods and practices bring health and rejuvenation (see Source Page).

Taoist™ SUPER FOODS are 3500 year old racemized™ formulations.

Especially For You!

This book was written to help people understand the forces in their lives that **CHEAT** them of health and happiness—forces that **CONTROL** them and **LURE** them to an early grave.

The author has endeavored to use examples that are meaningful. Every effort has been made to help the reader develop a practical foundation in the *recognized* sciences and in the *para*sciences.

The reader is reminded that knowledge must be **applied** and that the return of health and rejuvenation requires much **time, focus, and patience.**

Sometimes rejuvenation isn't fun. But if you are willing to devote your energies to this worthy goal, you will be rewarded beyond your greatest expectations.

Each day brings new opportunities to make "healthy" choices. Each step in the right direction brings improved health and slows physical degeneration. Each day is the first day of the rest of **your** life.

Young Again! is a statement, an offer, and a model all in one. It is the product of the author's personal life experiences, observations, philosophy, and lifestyle. It was NOT written to satisfy pretentious *experts.*

The author is not an "expert." *Experts* claim to have answers, but they can't demonstrate proof in their own lives. They suffer from dis-ease despite their knowledge. Their *magic bullets* do not save them. They talk the talk, but they don't know how to walk the walk.

Medical science will not be fond of this book. They will quote chapter and verse in *defense* of themselves. They may scorn and belittle—even accuse the author of oversimplification. They will demand "scientific proof" amd their demands will be *ignored.*

This book was written for those who seek results rather than *endless* debate. It's contents can benefit anyone who is seeking TRUTH.

NEVER forget. Old age is not fun. It is not a joyous process. People age through ignorance. Ignorance is a poor excuse. We can and must do better for ourselves.

Health is a matter of personal choice.

**A person changed against their will
is of the same opinion still!**

32

Rest & Fasting

"Dine with little, sup with less; do better still: sleep supperless."
Benjamin Franklin

We dig our grave with our teeth! Powerful words—and true! Is the problem what we eat? Do we eat too much? Do we eat too often?...or all of the above?

The deleterious effects derived from eating the wrong things have already been discussed. Now let us look at the *degenerative* problems that spring from *other* dietary habits—habits that can accelerate the aging process.

Food a'Plenty

Americans live in a country where food is plentiful and inexpensive. We have become accustomed to treating our dietary habits with total indifference. As children, we are encouraged to eat as much as we want; to gorge ourselves where less would do; to snack between meals and particularly at bed time. We are taught that food is food. We believe that hunger is a signal that it's time to eat. We think a full belly is better than a lean one. We carry our beliefs and habits into adulthood—and eventually to the grave.

It is unfortunate that bio-junk food has become the dietary norm. But it is our failure to develop *dietary discipline* regarding *what, when,* and *how much* to eat that clouds the issue and **compounds** the problem.

Food-Induced Stress

When we are physically tired, mentally fatigued, or spiritually depressed, we think nothing of getting additional sleep. After all, sleep is considered *normal* and everyone accepts this at face value.

Yet, few people realize that the vital organs also need rest. When we eat too much, the organs are *forced* to process that extra food. Overeating stresses the glands. Digestion is NOT a voluntary activity. We eat, the vital organs react. If we eat too much or too often, they become *hyper* stimulated, leading to exhaustion, overload, and crisis.

The digestive tables shown earlier indicate that the body requires a certain amount of time to digest food, called digestion reaction time (DRT). DRT is influenced by stress, physical activity, quantity of food eaten, time of day, how often food is eaten and by the rhythm of our habits.

Vigorous exercise should be avoided for one hour after eating a meal. The body needs time to begin digestion before it must transfer the blood *away from* the abdominal area. This explains the energy drain experienced after a meal. The heavier the meal, the more we experience a drain on energy. If the meal is loaded with toxic substances like food additives, soy or canola, salt and processed sugars, energy drain and free radical formation can be substantial. Snacking creates the same effect as overeating and denies the vital organs rest.

Pot Belly

A distended stomach is seen when the gut hangs over a man's belt line or fills a woman's lower half. People refer to abdominal excess as "fat," but distension (stretching) of the connective tissues that anchor the visceral organs AND a congested, constipated colon are the real problems. In the case of older people, spinal compression and forward extension of the visceral organs [those organs of the abdominal (visceral) cavity which include the liver, intestines, spleen, pancreas, female organs, prostate and bladder] occurs due to settling of the spinal column (see the skeletal depiction of the dowager's hump on page 100).

The gut (small intestine) and colon (large intestine) are held in place by connective tissue called the mesentery (apron). Over time, due to the accumulation of mucoid matter and gravity, the bowel becomes heavy, overly bulky, and *stretches* the mesentery beyond normal—producing the pot belly effect.

Colon therapy combined with lymph rolling restores tone to the viscera and connective tissues. A lymph roler is very simple to use and VERY effective (see Source Page).

If you are older and if you are SHORTER than you once were, hanging and stretching are **mandatory** procedures. I recommend hanging from a bar, rafter, beam, or tree branch several times a day. Start slowly if you are older. Hang for five seconds, then ten and so on until you can hang for several minutes.

The idea of hanging is to s-t-r-e-t-c-h the joints, the connective tissues (ligaments, tendons, muscles), and open the spinal column to blood and lymph flow so it can be rebuilt. In other words, get oxygen and nutrients in, fluids and waste out. Use SOC™ capsules to rid your joints of pain, restore limberness to your joints, and dissolve scar tissue, and use racemized™ hormone precursors to encourage new tissue growth.

Rebound and lymph roll massage every day. Do stretching exercises. Lift weights. Get into colon therapy. Drink BEV™ or Mikrowater™. Eat fresh raw vegetables. Plant a garden. **Train your mind.** Detox, detox, detox! If you will do these things, you will get your life back and get to live it over again in THIS lifetime. I plan to make it to 250 years and will revise it upward accordingly.

Think of the good things people could accomplish with hindsight! Think of all the exciting things the future holds! Life should be a celebration! **Life will be easier the second time around.**

Gluttony

Gluttony is an old word. As a child, I was taught that gluttony was a sin against the sixth commandment. Whether gluttony is a sin is not the issue here. What is a concern is the *premature* old age and death that result from gluttony. When we eat beyond *minimum* satiety (please review chapter nine), we overload the system with waste, free radicals, and more. Proper chewing eases food-induced stress and the tendency towards obesity. Racemized™ products like DiSororb Aid™, R/HCI, and Yucca Blend™ complete the job.

Gluttony is the act; obesity is the effect. Gluttony is one of the primary reasons industrial man is dying of degenerative dis-ease. Gluttony may be driven by genuine hunger, but it's usually the product of "real" dietary starvation. The quickest way to rid yourself of the need to eat is sith SUPER foods like algae, Harmonic™ pollen, biogenic™ liver tablets, Taoist Rice Polish™, Harmonic™ Synergy, and fresh vegetables and fruits.

Space Your Meals

The body was not meant to be under constant dietary load twenty-four hours a day. The organs require rest and an occasional day off and rejuvenation. The glands **must** be allowed to rest between meals. Late night meals and snacking deprive the body of the vital energy it needs for detoxification, tissue repair and growth—all of which occur primarily during the sleep cycle.

Plants have a cycle too. They manufacture food during the day, but they grow and repair their tissues at night. Visit your garden early some morning and "hear" the corn growing. It crackles and pops.

During the day the Earth exhales. At night it inhales. The dew point has special meaning. When the dew forms on the ground, plant and microbial activity are at their PEAK!

Rhythm is vitally important to health and vitality. Structure your life so it adheres to Nature's rhythms.

Sleep • Oxygen • Detoxification • Glycolysis

The body feels refreshed after a "good" sleep because it has processed acid wastes and neutralized abnormal energy fields. Sleep should be a time of energy transformation.

Neutralization of lact**ate** occurs during the sleep cycle. Anyone who has experienced muscle soreness and fatigue from over exertion has experienced the effects of lactate formation in the muscles. *(SOC™ capsules can be taken before or after hard physical work to avoid/ease muscle soreness. SOC™ also speeds healing and reduces scar tissue formation when used prior to any type of surgery.)*

Lactate formation occurs in the early stages of the sugar burning process we call glycolysis. Lactate formation is the result of **insufficient** oxygen in the cells and **incomplete** burning of the sugars. Lactate is a transitional waste product. Rest and sleep provide the vital energy needed to *recycle* lactate. In other words, lactate formation is the product of a system that has gone *anaerobic* at the cellular level.

The *ate* in lactate tells us that lact**ate** is the salt of lactic acid. Salts are *bound* energy. To prevent lactate formation and fatigue, drink plenty of BEV™ or Mikrowater every 30 minutes during work or exercise along with some SOC™. Lactate is a byproduct of *fermentation* process—like alcohol production.

Alcohol is made by "anaerobic" fermentation. Kombucha uses "aerobic" fermentation to produce high amounts of glucoronic acid for healing sick bodies.

Oxygen deficiency in the cells stops the conversion of

glucose into the energy molecule ATP by the mitochondria. An oxygen deficiency sabotages energy production in the *Krebs and Citric acid cycles and in the Electron Transport Systems* (where the mitochondria produce ATP). Aerobic exercise, BEV™ and Medical Grade Water™, rebounding, and lymph rolling heal sick bodies through waste movement and increase tissue levels of oxygen.

Sleep • Digestion • Metabolic Hype

During the sleep cycle, the body uses large amounts of VITAL energy to heal and grow. Sleeping on a full stomach sabotages the detoxification process and blocks healing. *Normal* digestion slows or comes to a halt. We wake up with that *full* feeling—sluggish, not well rested!

Even good food can create a toxic condition if taken before retiring. Sleeping on a full stomach brings on *anaerobic* fermentation and foul gas. **An**aerobic conditions produce **putrefaction** of undigested food in the intestines and releases toxic waste molecules. Avoid late night meals and bedtime snacks if you can. But if you can't, you had best use some DiSorb Aid™, Yucca blend™, and R/HCl with your snack.

Poor digestion and absorption produces excesses and acid wastes. Illness and dis-ease result.

Adequate sleep and dietary rest are important ingredients for good health. Failing to get enough rest is no different than using a battery powered golf cart during the day and forgetting to recharge it at night, with one notable difference. **We are not golf carts!** Without adequate rest and detoxification, the body is forced to draw upon its energy reserves. This kind of lifestyle produces stress and metabolic **"hype."**

Just because we have the ability to hype our body is not justification for doing so. The ability to psyche the body with the power of the brain (Fourth Dimension energy over Third Dimension reality) is a "dangerous" *skill* that comes with a very high price tag.

Discipline • Spacing Of Meals • Snacking

Learning not to overeat requires *discipline.* Learning to space our meals requires *discipline.* Putting *rhythm* in our lives requires even more discipline. Dietary discipline DEMANDS that we NOURISH our bodies!

Allow four hours between meals—including snacks. Snacks are *mini* meals. They interrupt the body's rest break. When we snack, we become a *slave labor boss,* and we force the glands to overwork and become exhausted. How would you like it if every time you tried to get some needed sleep, some inconsiderate person woke you up? So it is with frequent eating. The smart solution to *snacking* is to incorporate the SUPER foods into your diet. In their presence, hunger vanishes. I can attest to this fact. I went from 3-4 meals a day to someone who now eats only once a day. I'm simply NOT hungry, yet I look and feel better than I ever have in my 53 years.

Children are *growing* and *repairing* tissue so they eat more, but children today are malnourished because the food is so poor. Children MUST have nutritious food, good water, and racemic sea minerals. Well nourished children don't snack incessantly. All soft drinks MUST be stopped. Their long term effects are WORSE than alcohol, but in a different way.

Do NOT encourage children to develop habits that will *lure* them to an early grave. Bad habits become an unhealthy lifestyle. Be a good example.

Spacing of meals provides *rhythm* and *control* of dietary habits. Nourishment *tempers* hunger. Home-grown food and the alternative SUPER foods mentioned are examples of foods that build strong bodies and minds.

Nourishment and detoxification strengthens will power. Will power is the product of healthy body and mind. A sick body has little will power. Smoking, drinking, gambling, drugs, gluttony, obesity, etc., have their roots in malnourishment and acidification of the tissues.

The nutritionally deficient person constantly cries for *nourishment.* They snack and eat their way into old age and hasten their appointed destiny with the grave—*decades* ahead of schedule. They are *early birds* in the truest sense.

Rhythmicity

One of the secrets of health and longevity is the establishment of regularity in our lives. Rhythm is so terribly important that reversing the aging process will *stall out* if we ignore this simple secret.

Rhythmicity is rhythm in the sense of the ebb and flow of energy in our daily life. Up each morning at the same time, meals taken within 1/2 hour of the appointed times, plenty of water, exercise, going to bed at the same time, sleeping for 7-8 hours—EVEN if you can operate on less. Practice rhythmicity, and the balance of the lessons in this book will become patterned habit and easy to maintain. **Health and vitality flow on the wires of rhythmicity. The lifestyle of Dr. Paul Bragg and his daughter, Patricia speak's for itself!**

The Miracle of Fasting

This is a true story, told exactly as it happened. I hope you will enjoy it.

It was May 1, 1993, Santa Barbara, California. I was attending a dinner party following a publishing seminar when a cute lady approached me and said, "Did you get one of my apple cider books?"

I answered in the negative, and as she proceeded to hand a book to me, I got a square look at her face and said, "Who are you?"

"I'm Patricia Bragg!" she answered.

At that moment, I knew that the path upon which Bob McLeod—who you met in chapter one—had set me adrift twenty-two years before had reached its destination. I was standing before the daughter of the Great Wizard, Paul Bragg!

"Please come sit down," I said. "We must talk!"

I began, "Your father saved my life. I cannot tell how thrilled I am to meet you! You look exactly like your picture in your father's book on fasting."

So we talked and laughed. The following day I was able to sneak away long enough to visit the Bragg Worldwide Headquarters in Santa Barbara, where I stood in awe of a twenty foot high painting of the wonderful Wizard, Paul Bragg.

"How did you father die?" I asked. "I have heard several rumors and I am anxious to know the truth."

"He died in a surfboard accident in Hawaii. He drowned. They could not revive him!"

"Please tell me, what was his age?"

"My father was 97 years *YOUNG!*—and if he had not died when he did, I have no doubt he would have lived to be 125 years young!" she snapped.

"What is your age, Patricia?" I asked with a lump in my throat.

"I am like my father. I AM AGELESS!"

And so she was. Sweet! Cute! A senior citizen by the calendar, but you would never, ever guess! Patricia appeared to be in her late forties or early fifties.

Paul and Patricia are PROOF positive that each of us can experience agelessness. I am forever thankful for getting to meet this wonderful human being—the daughter of the Great Wizard himself. Like her father, she has helped millions of people. I am proud to be able to continue in their footsteps.

Patricia's father, Paul Bragg, was a Wizard of a man. A recent U.S. Surgeon General (the "highest" *official* medical doctor in the USA, politically speaking) made the comment, "Paul Bragg did as much to help the health and vitality of

American's as any medical doctor." Considering the source, that is one very big compliment.

Many readers will be too young to remember Paul Bragg. When you read his wonderful book, *The Miracle of Fasting*, be sure you are *wide awake!* Bragg speaks simple TRUTHS and in simple terms. He was a "low tech" Wizard, but a Wizard just the same.

God Bless Dr. Paul C. Bragg N.D., PhD. and Patricia Bragg N.D. to whom I dedicated this book. They have helped millions of people find peak health and become *Young Again!*

PREVIEW: *Our next chapter deals with the world's MOST toxic element and it's in YOUR body and drinking water. You will learn what you can do about it.*

Meat Eating vs. Vegetarianism

Please turn to page 367 for a common sense discussion of a volatile health issue. As for your author, *"I've been there! I've done both!"*

Acres USA

This monthly publication has had **profound** influence on my life. If I could only receive one publication, this is the one. Order a trial subscription and see what I mean. Call (800) 355-5313. I accept your thanks in advance.

Ear Candling!

From ancient times to the present, people have had trouble with their ears. Ear wax, infections, water in the ear, pain, poor hearing, ringing, and so on. Candling is used to remove excess wax and restoring healing. It is sometimes referred to as coning or wicking.

As the candle burns, it creates a gentle suction and draws air down the outside of the candle and warms air up the inside. As this occurs, water is drawn out of the inner ear along with wax, bacterial, yeast, and viral infested materials from the outer ear. There is NO pain. The procedure is safer and friendlier than using an ear syringe.

Over 600,000 adenoidectomies and tonsilectomies (ear/tonsil surgeries) are performed each year as a result of ear infections. 50% of all children's surgeries and 25% of hospital admissions are due to ear related complications.

Ear candling is safe and inexpensive home remedy technique. If "ringing" is involved, Yucca™, Aspar-Max™ SOC™ and racemized™ hormone precursors are used.

33

The Camel Or The Palm Tree?

"Truth will come to light; murder cannot be hid."
Shakespeare

"Kibyo" is Japanese for *strange disease*. Kibyo described the series of strange conditions that appeared during the 1950's in the small fishing village of Minamata on the southwest coast of Kyushu, Japan.

The conditions came to be known as "Minamata Disease." In 1957 mercury was discovered to be the toxic agent behind the strange symptomatic conditions and SIGNS.

Cats went crazy. Crows fell from the sky. People experienced dizziness and tunnel vision, their nervous systems failed, numbness was experienced in their extremities, and their legs burned. ALL life forms in the area suffered from the high mercury levels in the air, water, and soil. The mercury came from an industrial plant up the coast from Minamata.

Mercury & Aging

Mercury is the **MOST** toxic substance known to man! It is the only elemental metal that occurs naturally in the "liquid" state. Sometimes it is referred to as *quicksilver* due to its elusive nature. A broken thermometer allows mercury to splatter and run. It **evaporates** like water!

Mercury is of importance to the "aging" story because of its toxic nature and ubiquitous (everywhere) presence in the environment. It has been used in industry for several hundred years. The fur industry used mercury to process animal furs as far back as the time of the Industrial Revolution. Mercury poisoning was diagnosed as long ago as 1865, but it continued to be used by the fur industry into the 1950's!

The expression "mad as a hatter" refers to the tremors and insanity that hat and garment workers suffered. Industrialists did NOT care what happened to the common people. If a doctor dared to create a fuss, he quickly found himself without a license to practice medicine. In those days, a hat worker's widow was given a "gold watch" and a wreath on the casket. Today, we get neither. Mercury has become the equivalent of industrial bio-junk food. Medicine goes about assigning new names to mysterious dis-ease conditions—usually with the word "syndrome" attached. The Japanese equivalent of syndrome is "kibyo!"

About Mercury

Mercury has the ability to cross the placental barrier and deform the unborn fetus. It lodges in our vital organs and short circuits their activity. Mercury poisoning leads to disintegration of the nervous system and damage to the kidney's nephrons (blood filters). **Mercury poisoning usually occurs slowly over many years. It is involved in thousands of diseases plaguing millions of people.**

Acute mercury poisoning leads to vomiting, bloody diarrhea, nervous tremors in the extremities, eyelids and tongue. People with moderate poisoning seldom are aware of what ails them. Fatigue, insomnia, headaches, nervous anxiety, and loss of appetite are common side effects. Erythism (redness as in blushing of the face) is a characteristic symptom of mercury poisoning. So is night time leg pain in older people.

Sources of mercury poisoning include tuna fish, shell fish, water based house paint, insecticides, fungicides (bathroom fungus cleaners), wall sizing, and tens of thousands of products that people come into contact with everyday.

Mercury is so *ubiquitous* that it is in ALL commercially produced food. The only way around it is to grow your own food. The microbes in a healthy soil *denature* mercury, lead, and toxic organic metals and chemicals. The use of Bio-Grow soil rejuvenator (a biodynamic right-spin soil catalyst) is the fastest way to develop a healthy right-spin soil environment.

The GREATEST source of mercury in the United States comes from tap water. Mercury—in the form of mercuric acid salt—is widely used to treat public water supplies. Recent events bear out the severity of the problems we face. For instance, during the fall of 1993, hundreds of innocent people became sick and some DIED from drinking tap water that was contaminated with pathogenic (dis-ease related) bacteria.

The cities were Milwaukee, Washington, D.C., and Chicago. We do not know if more cities were involved because these things are hushed up quickly to prevent panic. In Milwaukee people died! The authorities blamed the bacteria, but the problem was related to mercury.

Here is the problem. Cities throughout the country are treating water with chloramines AND with **mercuric acid** to kill the bacteria. This is done "without" public knowledge and is vehemently denied by authorities. Mercuric acid is used during the "warm months" when demand outruns water processing capability. Population growth creates additional pressure. Cities do NOT have time to treat the water before pumping it into the distribution lines, so they use **mercuric acid** and the latest version of a chlorinated compound called chlor**amine.**

Cities use the same dirty sand filters over and over. They seldom change them! Instead, they use mercuric acid to kill the bacteria and viruses that breed in them, and send the water to the gullible public to drink! Municipal water filters deserve more attention than a cat litter box—which we change regularly. We know better, and so do our water officials.

In the Fall when the hot season is over, cities stop using mercuric acid. If they miscalculate, the results are sick and dead people from an explosion of pathogenic bacteria in the filters and lines—like what happened in Milwaukee, Washington, D. C., and Chicago.

Without mercury, public water supplies are a potential source of an epidemic of pathogenic dis-ease. With mercury, the people are drinking their way to dis-ease, old age, and an ugly death. Mercury creates lots of sick people to fill the hospital stalls—all of them demanding a *magic bullet!* Sick people are good business.

The best solution to the water dilemma is to equip your home or apartment with either BEV™ water or Medical Grade Ionized Water™ which will allow you to "unplug" from the medical system.

SOC™ has a VERY strong affinity for heavy metals and can be used by anyone to rid the tissues of mercury— even if amalgam fillings are still present.

Water pollution in public water supplies is a "time bomb" waiting to explode into dis-ease in the bodies of people who are ignorant enough to drink it. STOP DRINKING WATER FROM PUBLIC WATER SUPPLIES!

Deregulated Death • Bombs & Munitions

The U.S. Department of Agriculture has established a "**zero**" tolerance for mercury. I repeat, a ZERO tolerance! At the same time, the FDA has established a "safe" level for mercury. Safe levels imply safety and a watch dog function. People feel protected. Nothing could be further from the truth.

Federal and state regulatory agencies are *supposed to* enforce food and water purity laws. Powerful interests see to it that mercury's use in industry goes unrestricted. **Mercury is a $6,000,000,000 (billion) dollar industry!** "Corporate" yellow fringe flag government refuses to regulate it. They allow industry to regulate itself.

Mercury is divided into three classes. Elemental vapor (mercury evaporates like water); mercurous/mercuric salt solutions like mercurochrome (for minor cuts; now outlawed)! and mercuric acid; and **a third form that is found bonded to food "proteins."** Every reaction in the body requires **protein** enzymes to occur. Mercury shuts them down and blocks vital biochemical reactions.

"Corporate" U.S. Government, via the Atomic Energy Commission (AEC), is the biggest supplier of mercury to industry. After WWll, they held huge stockpiles of mercury. Government policy shifts allowed this "silver death" element into the market. They know about mercury toxicity, but they dumped it on the market anyway.

The bombing of the Oklahoma City Federal building in April of 1995 may have involved the use of large amounts of mercury to accelerate the explosion. Pictures of the bombed building show that the explosion GAINED velocity as the force went up the face of the building—instead of dissipating as in non-mercury related explosions.

Agriculture uses massive amounts of mercury in the production of FOOD! In 1914, chemists discovered that mercury was an effective fungicide. Over six million pounds of mercury have been used in FOOD production in the past forty years, and over two-hundred million pounds since 1900.

Mercury is used to treat seeds. It is used in the paper industry as a slimicide. **AEROBIC** bacteria convert industrial mercury into highly toxic forms like *methyl* **mercury.** Under normal body protocol, methyl mercury is very difficult to remove from tissues. With SOC™, Yucca Blend™, PAC^s, and Klammath™ algae it is relatively easy to drive from the system. Homeovitic remedies aerobic used to "erase" the vibratory memory of mercury from the tissues. SOC™ is racemized™ carbon and sulfur that have a high affinity for heavy metals.

Mercury Fillings In Teeth

Dentistry has been promoting the use of mercury amalgam (so called "silver" fillings) for over one hundred years. In the mouth, bacteria convert elemental mercury into *methyl* mercury which "bleeds" into the tissues and goes about its dirty work quietly, producing ever new health *syndromes.*

Amalgam fillings are BIG business! Dentists are taught in dental school that amalgam fillings are non-toxic. **Dentistry likes mercury amalgams because they are a quick "drill and putty" operation.** The *ignorant* patient is told the only difference between gold and amalgam is the cost and appearance. Dentistry avoids using the word **mercury** and instead calls these mixed metal fillings *amalgams* or "silver." It is a sin to fill innocent people's teeth with the most toxic element on Earth. Its use renders *predictable* results—just as in the hat industry. Mercury amalgam fillings bring on S-L-O-W death. Professionals who install them claim ignorance and lack of "scientific proof," while their patients lose their health and lives.

Gold also creates problems, but of a different sort. Gold fillings and crowns are composites of dozens of different metals. Elemental metals are toxic to the body. These "anti-life" energy fields are measured in milli-volts (thousandths of a volt). They interfere with body metabolism.

If you have mercury in your mouth, do NOT remove them until your have prepared your system as outlined throughout this book. Removal is FAR more dangerous than placement due to a weaker immune system and an older patient. **I have seen many people sicken and suffer from mercury removal because they did NOT prepare. Allow 6 months minimum!**

NEVER, EVER go to a regular dentist for amalgam removal. They are antagonistic to the idea. They will try to convince you that you have been hoodwinked. They will use the old, professional glass hand approach. AVOID THEM!

Call the phone numbers listed at the end of this chapter to locate a dentist who subscribes to the **protocols** *of holistic dentistry. Be very careful to avoid johnny-come-lately dentists* who are NOT certified holistic, biological dentists! If the dentist even offers amalgam fillings you have the wrong dentist!

Klamath™ algae has the ability to bond to and remove heavy metals—like mercury—from the tissues. So do fresh organic greens. PAC's BUFFER the system and greatly accelerate the process.

The Camel Or The Palm Tree?

Today, more than ever, people are faced with the

dilemma of choosing between conventional medicine and holistic therapies. Making the right choice is easy. Let me emphasize "false" alternatives with a childhood story.

When we were children, one of our favorite jokes involved finding an empty Camel cigarette package and showing it to whomever we could get to listen.

"Assume you are in this picture and it is raining cats and dogs and you must run for cover. Would you get under the palm trees, or would you get under the camel?" (On the face of the package is pictured a camel, some palm trees, and several pyramids.)

Some people answered they would take cover under the palm trees, while others said they would take their chances under the camel.

Regardless of the answer, the person was wrong. You see, we did what conventional medicine does to *desperate* people. We only offered two alternatives, and **BOTH of them were bad choices!** The smart answer was to go around the corner of the package and take lodging in the hotel!

In the world of conventional medicine and expert opinions, you are constantly faced with "camel or palm tree" decisions. Do not allow yourself to fall for false alternatives in matters of health or you will grow old and suffer miserably along the way. Heavy metal poisoning—be it from tap water, food, colloidal minerals, or dental fillings—is a serious problem.

Would you rather drink water that is contaminated with pathogenic microbes, mercury, sodium, chloramines, fluoride or water that is "safe" according to industry standards?"

The answer to this camel or palm tree question is, **None of the above!** Do whatever you need to do to protect yourself from heavy metal poisoning and you will become *Young Again!*

News: The world's second biggest manufacturer of mercury amalgam has agreed to post ALL dental offices in California with signs WARNING patients about the carcinogenic, mutagenic, and teratogenic effects of mercury—especially in children and unborn fetuses.

Scandinavian countries—along with Germany and other European countries—have BANNED mercury amalgam fillings. The American Dental Association and its lackeys are too damned proud and greedy to admit their mistakes!

Dental Alternatives

Mercury removal requires that special protocols be followed for your safety. Composite plastic is the replacement material of choice. They require more skill and time than drill and putty mercury fillings. If they are done correctly, they can last many years. Do not accept porcelain fillings. A dentist that tells you that composites don't hold up probably isn't doing them correctly. Don't be afraid to shop around. Price is not the issue here, but YOUR health is! Call these phone numbers to locate *quality* dental care. American Academy of Biological Dentistry at (408) 659-5385, Huggins Diagnostic Center at 1-800-331-2303, or Clifford Consulting and Research (719) 550-0008. Be prepared to travel. Holistic biological dentists are hard to find, but worth their price.

PREVIEW: *In our next chapter, you will learn about tobacco and how it relates to health and vitality. The American Indians knew the answer!*

Red Flags

Show me a lady with thyroid problems, excess fat, thinning/graying hair, yeast/bladder infections, PMS, fibroid tumors, aching joints, receding gums, or low energy **and I'll show you someone whose ovaries are in trouble and a body whose terrain is our of control. Show me a man who** has grown fat, lost his sex drive, has prostate troubles, low energy and gray or missing hair **and I'll show you a man who is NOT in control of his body terrain.**

Take Time For 12 Things

Take time to **Work.** It is the price of success.
Take time to **Think.** It is the source of power.
Take time to **Play.** It is the secret of youth.
Take time to **Read.** It is the foundation of knowledge.
Take time to **Worship.** It is the highway of reverence and washes the dust of earth from our eyes.
Take time to **Help and Enjoy Friends.** It is the source of happiness.
Take time to **Love.** It is the one sacrament of life.
Take time to **Dream.** It hitches the soul to the stars.
Take time to **laugh.** It is laughing that lightens life's loads.
Take time for **Beauty.** It is everywhere in nature.
Take time for **Health.** It is the true wealth and treasure of life.
Take time to **Plan.** It is the secret of being able to have time to take time for the first eleven things.

Homeovitic Medicine Works!

Homeovitic medicine works at the **subtle energy** level of our existence by manipulating the body's energy fields with substances called *remedies*.
Homeovitic remedies restore the body's vibratory frequency. They are NOT drugs. Some remedies are very specific, others are very general. Some treat substance problems, while others treat emotional problems. Homeovitic remedies are NOT available in health stores and they are SUPERIOR to homeopathic remedies.

Homeovitic remedies have an energy *footprint* that is the same or similar as the offending substance. If the body is sick, *systemic* frequency must be reestablished. Homeovitic remedies provide complementary *biogenic* and *nutritional* support and are *vitalized* to 9x, 20x, 30x, 100x, and 200x fmixed requencies to correct for transitional energy shifts as healing progresses.

Potentiation energizes a substance and makes it more powerful than it originally was. **Succussion** (pounding of a substance so it will vibrate at a specific frequency) and **dilution** (watering down of the remedy) are employed to bring about *resonance* and *transference*—processes that involve the manipulation of Hertz rate, making homeovitics SUPERIOR to common remedies.

Hertz (Hz) rate and frequency are related. When you hear the word Hertz, think "beat." The wavy horizontal line on an oscilloscope represents *beats*. Electricity in the USA is 60 cycles or beats per second. Thus, sixty seconds to a minute, sixty minutes to an hour, etc.

Earth has a wobble in her axis—like a wheel out of balance—heavy on one side. The wobble creates a beat, a thump, a vibration as it spins. The wobble is Earth's Hertz rate or frequency. Until recently, Earth's Hertz rate was 7.8. Today it is about 8.1. By year 2012, Earth changes are expected to bring about a Hertz rate of 13.

Improve your "frequency" is by using homeovitic remedies plus SOC™ capsules to remove mercury residues and memory from body tissues. Homeovitic remedies BLOCK viruses, bacteria, and serum proteins found in vaccines, and protect against nerve and brain damage, hearing loss, and other secondary health crises that proceed from the use of vaccinations and drugs. **Good health is a reflection of vibrational harmony. Use homeovitics to "balance" your system.**

34

The "Sacred" Three Sisters

"First, the Creator gave us tobacco."
Kanonsionni-Kayeneren-Kowa
The Iroquiois

If you control the dietary health of a nation, you control the people. If, in addition, you control the creation of that nation's money supply, you have the perfect monopoly.

When the white man came to the Americas, he discovered that the main staples of the Indian diet were corn, beans, and squash. The Indians called these foods the "sacred three sisters."

The Indians understood the importance of these foods in their diet. They also understood the importance of another FOOD—a food which they held in the *utmost* esteem. That food was TOBACCO!

The Indians told the white man, *"The Creator gave us the sacred three sisters. But before the Creator gave us corn, beans and squash, He gave us TOBACCO!"*

The Indians considered tobacco *sacred*. It was considered sacred because the Indians had discovered tobacco's NUTRITIONAL characteristics. Their discovery was incorporated into their religious beliefs.

The status of tobacco in the Indian psyche was based on DIETARY need, but it was respected on a religious level. Smoking was the extension of the dietary status tobacco held in Indian culture.

When native peoples elevate certain foods and events to religious status, there is a reason. Unfortunately for millions of people, the white man failed to take his cues from Indian dietary habits and religious beliefs. The white man did NOT make the connection between diet and health until four-hundred and ninety-eight years later (1990). The connection was made by a lone individual named Tom Mahoney

Tobacco

Despite its negative image, tobacco has significance to the aging process AND to general health and vitality. Tobacco is **terribly** misunderstood by the American public. They know NOTHING of it's therapeutic or dietary value because their eyes can't see through the smoke, not to mention the TRUTH that they have been denied. They have ONLY heard of the negative aspects of tobacco. They have been told nothing of the real tobacco story. **Their ignorance is NOT an accident!**

Prior to the discovery of America, Europeans did NOT grow or eat corn, beans, or squash. These important foods were absent from European diets. Dietary imbalances created the EXCESSES that plagued the white man and his "civilization."

The *Three Sisters* were taken back to Europe and for a while people's nutritional status improved. Corn was easy to grow and became the "dominant" food staple of the poor. By the seventeen hundreds, corn's dietary dominance manifested as excesses and dis-ease throughout Europe, and particularly in the Mediterranean countries of Italy, Spain, Greece, and Portugal. The condition of *excess* had no name—yet!

Casal's Necklace

In 1735 the Spanish physician Casal described a disease condition by one of its key SIGNS. He called it *mal de la rosa.* This means "red sickness." People on farms who ate a lot of corn suffered the most. They typically had a red ring around their neck which came to be called *"Casal's necklace."* In the American South, corn's dominance among farmers and the poor, caused the phrase "red neck" to come into usage.

In 1771 an Italian doctor described the SIGNS of an unknown dietary EXCESS condition when he wrote of "rough, painful skin." *Pellagra* is the English corruption of Italian and summed up the condition nicely. Until the 1900's, however, no connection was made between corn intake and the condition of EXCESS that had come to be called *pellagra.*

Like most conditions, pellagra operates behind a cloak in the early stages. It includes loss of energy, weight loss, and poor

appetite. The four 'D's' dizziness, depression, dementia and delusion best describe pellagra's SIGNS. There are tens of thousands of people suffering from these SIGNS today.

In the United States, similar dis-ease conditions occurred beginning in the 1850's. After 1859 when H. J. Heinz produced the first "canned" food, the problem grew worse. Canned food contains salt to keep down botulism. In addition, heat processing destroys and denatures food enzymes. This was the beginning of bio-junk food.

The Civil War wrought massive upheaval in people's dietary habits—especially farm people in the South. Excesses became very prevalent. Economic conditions were blamed, but *pellagra* had its roots in the shift from a *balanced* agricultural society to an unbalanced *industrial* one. The poor did not eat a balanced diet. They ate too much corn and not enough greens and proteins. An unbalanced diet produces EXCESSES in people, plants, and animals—no matter what the food. *Excess* corn creates an acid pH condition with many side effects.

By the turn of the century, the dis-eases of pellagra and beriberi became widespread. Poor people were eating too much corn—hominy, corn meal, grits, and corn meal mush—especially in the South. (The South continues this practice to this day.) Worse, the corn being consumed was "bolted." Bolted corn has had the germ removed. The germ is what causes a seed to sprout and grow. It is the seed's LIFE force!

The food processing companies discovered that bolted, *de-vitalized* corn meal keeps better. It was one of the first "natural" bio-junk foods. Bolted corn meal is like white bread. Both were and are perceived by an ignorant public as *status* foods. Processed food became "value added" food and commanded higher prices and higher profits. People didn't realize they had been taken. They are **STILL** being taken.

Pellagra became *endemic* (related to certain geographic areas and diets). Tens of thousands of people suffered from *pellagra* and *beriberi.* In dogs, pellagra is called black tongue. These dis-eases could have easily been prevented IF the white man had payed attention to the Indian diet—which included tobacco. Tobacco contains the "entire" vitamin B-12 complex. Tobacco is very valuable FOOD!

Non-hybrid, non-bolted corn is good food. Too much corn, like anything, brings on excesses and acid driven dis-ease conditions in the body. Excesses are easily offset with a diet that includes fresh green leafy vegetables (alkaloids), high quality proteins, and VARIETY. Digestive short falls and hormonal imbalances all affect how the body responds to even the best of food—which brings us back to the "terrain."

The Mexican custom of soaking corn in lime water offsets corn's acidity and prevents the incidence of pellagra in Mexican populations. The custom was adopted from the Indians, along with the combining of corn and beans for dietary balance.

The B-vitamin Story

The B-vitamins (B's) offset dietary excesses and do away with pellagra and beriberi by rebalancing the system. Specifically, "niacin" has been credited as the active pellagra cureative agent. **(This is NOT true, but for the time being, let us *assume* it is true.)**

Niacin is referred to as vitamin B-3. Niacin is involved in ALL of the body's metabolic pathways. These pathways are a very complex series of reactions that keep us alive, healthy, and happy. The healthy *bio-electric* body is a reflection of strong activity in the reactions of these critical pathways.

Niacin contains two molecules, NAD (*nicotine* dinucleotide) and NADP (*nicotine* adenine dinucleotide phosphate). These substances are used in the Krebs and Citric Acid Cycles and the Electron Transport System where the energy molecule ATP is created, burned and converted into cellular lightning!

All of the B's, including niacin, are involved in the FUSION reactions of the gut and liver. The mitochondria need B's to produce energy to fuel the body, build, and repair the tissues and to keep our immune system strong.

B Vitamins • pH • Soft Drinks

The Indians knew about tobacco's life giving properties. Tobacco is the richest natural source of the B's in the world—nothing compares to it—**nothing!** Concentrations of the B vitamins run as high as 30%! When **"small"** amounts of green or dried tobacco are put into stews, beans, and salads, we get the B's. Care must be taken in the choice of variety. Most importantly, fresh lemon juice or apple cider vinegar MUST be used to bring green tobacco within digestion range.

The pH of edible tobacco is Ph 10-11. Lemon juice and vinegar have a pH of 2. Stomach acid (HCL) is between pH -1 and +1. For each # up or down the scale (pH 7 is neutral, above is alkaline, below is acid), pH changes by 10 times. So, a pH of 10 is 1,000 times more alkaline than pH 7.

The side effects of soft drinks **loaded** with phosphoric acid is incomprehensible and goes beyond just pH. When ingested, the body is **forced** to draw on bone calcium to "buffer" the acid introduced into the blood stream which skews the calcium:phosphorous ratio and *grossly* alters body physiology. When the side effects of *aspartame* sweetener (think red, white and blue swirl) are added, it's a wonder we don't just die!

Synthetic vs. Natural B's

Real B vitamins are potent right-spin substances, even in small amounts. ALL commercial B-vitamins—unless derived from a natural FOOD source—are "synthetic" and left-spin, and require high doses to *mimic* the real thing.

REGARDLESS of claims on the label promoting "natural," unless B vitamins are food derived, they are **synthetic.** Synthetic niacin, B's, vitamins A, D, and E, are not the same as naturally occurring vitamins. The body is UNABLE to build healthy tissue with synthetic vitamins. When the body's supply of natural B's diminish, energy fusion reactions slow, and pernicious anemia (chronic shortage of oxygen carrying red blood cells) announces itself—and if ignored, will eventually bring down the immune system.

When we are sick, white blood cell count should go UP. If this fails to occur in response to a threatening condition, health are lost dis-ease manifests. Without sufficient B's, the body CANNOT defend itself. Other excellent sources of "real" B vitamins is racemized™ Biogenic™ liver tablets, Klammath™ algae, Harmonic™ pollen, Harmonic™ Synergy, Taoist Rice Polish™, fresh green leafy vegetables and organic RED meat (if available).

Green tobacco is loaded with B's. Dried tobacco is even more concentrated. Green tobacco juice contains nicotine as an alkaloid. Dried tobacco contains nicotinic acid. Nicotinic acid, niacin, and nicotinamide are the acid forms of nicotine.

Niacin is promoted as the 'heart' vitamin, which is true IF it is from a natural food source. Natural niacin improves blood circulation and has anti-agglutination (anti-clumping) qualities. The *experts* tell us the FLUSH that accompanies niacin ingestion is due to its vitamin activity, but, this is NOT true. The *flush* effect is a mild "shock" type allergic reaction to *synthetic* niacin molecules and binders. Food sources are the only safe sources of B-vitamins.

Fresh organic greens are one of the best sources of the B's. Meat has limited amounts of the amino acid trytophan which the liver converts to niacin (60 mg of trytophan=1 mg niacin). It is most suspicious that government authorities (FDA) outlawed this amino acid. Personally, I prefer to get my amino acids from WHOLE super foods like Biogenic liver tablets and Klammath™ algae.

Food alkaloids can be **poisonous** if you overdo. Alkaloids are nitrogen-containing compounds with "marker" physiologic properties. In other words, alkaloids make things happen in the body! Alkaloids are alkaline on the pH scale. Other alkaloid foods that we commonly eat are SPINACH and SWISS

CHARD which explains why many people have difficulty digesting them. These nutritious vegetables must be eaten or prepared with lemon or vinegar to be of benefit to the body. Other well known plant derived alkaloid drugs are digitalis (foxglove), belladonna (nightshade), lobelia, and marijuana. There are many kinds of Indian tobacco (Rustica, Lobelia, Aztec, etc.), but they are NOT for consumption. Do not confuse garden and commercial tobacco varieties with edible tobacco. (For seed, see the Source Page).

The Niacin Story

Nicotine was named for Jean Nicot—the French ambassador to Portugal who sent tobacco seeds to Paris in 1550. By 1571, crude nicotine had been isolated. In 1828, purified nicotine was isolated. In 1867, *nicotine* was demonstrated to cure black tongue and pellagra, but it was ignored.

Natural nicotine is a FOOD nutrient source of the B's. Nicotine is EXTREMELY poisonous if **purified** or **synthesized**. When eaten in leaf form and in small amounts, it is not a problem. The Indians used it judiciously.

Nicotine from dried tobacco is not as toxic as we have been led to believe. If it were, people who smoke and chew would react and die on the spot. I would remind the reader that the mucous membranes of the respiratory tract are the avenue of choice where fast absorption is desired. Cigarettes are BAD news because of what is in them —and I am not talking bout "tobacco!." Cigars do not share the dangers of cigarettes—and you can tell the difference by the smell.

History Of Vitamin P-P

From the turn of the century, nicotinic acid was known by the disguise name—"P-P factor," short for **P**ellagra **P**reventive. (This name was used until the generation then alive had died. Later, in the 1930's when the word "vitamin" was coined, P-P factor became known as "vitamin P-P.")

In 1899, Dr. Joseph Goldberger of the United States Public Health Service, launched a study into the effects of P-P factor and its relationship to pellagra. He dragged his feet for 16 years before he penned his study regarding the relationship between P-P factor and pellagra—something that had been known since 1867! This was NO accident. There was a reason for the delay.

In the meantime, pharmaceutical and oil industry interests went to work developing "synthetic" P-P factor. They did NOT want people to know they could treat pellagra, beriberi—and the spin-off dis-ease conditions that resulted from them—by **"growing"** their own cure in the form of tobacco. They did NOT want people to make the association between P-P factor, nicotine, and tobacco.

Pharmaceutical interests figured out a way to manufacture SYNTHETIC "P-P" cheaply and easily using pyridine carbon rings from inexpensive charcoal and petroleum. Synthetic P-P factor is not the same. Real vitamin P-P spins right and supports good health. The other spins left.

The pharmaceutical companies could NOT 'patent' tobacco, but they could patent "synthesized" molecules. This is exactly what they did to women with their damnable hormone analogs contained in estrogen supplements and birth control pills.

Keep The People Confused!

Niacin is a *bogus* term. It is a coined name—like canola! It was invented by the medical establishment and pharmaceutical interests in the 1950's. It was coined to hide the fact that "nicotinic acid" (the acid form of nicotine in dried tobacco) is the *active* ingredient that balances the **excesses** that bring on pellagra and beriberi.

Certain "corporate" interests wanted control over America's health. There was a massive effort to VILIFY tobacco. That effort continues to this very moment.

To create confusion and cover their tracks, the *experts* divided the B-12 vitamin complex into separate vitamin *factors*, called B-1 through B-12. They even went so far as to give vitamin B-12 a special name—"intrinsic factor." You will find this term in all medical and nutrition texts. **Intrinsic factor MUST be present in gastric juices for proper digestion.**

Intrinsic factor is critical to FUSION reactions in man's gut and liver. Fusion reactions provide us with vitality and energy and are part of biological *alchemy*. This is "cold fusion." Without intrinsic factor, pernicious anemia rears its head and the immune system takes a nose dive.

Intrinsic factor is also known as **cobalt blue** or cobalt 60. Look on a vitamin bottle and you will find that vitamin B-12 is called "cyanocobalamin." Dissected, the word looks like this: *cyan*-blue; *cobal*-short for cobalt; *mine*-short for *amine*.

Cobalt & Health

Cobalt 60 is a *naturally occurring radioactive substance* that must be present in order for life to exist. It is a crucial element in the fusion reactions in the bio-electric body of man and animal. It is involved in the production of the massive amounts of energy needed to keep us alive. Tobacco is loaded with cobalt blue. It is full of the B-vitamin complex. When we eat whole natural foods like fresh green leafy vegetables and tobacco—we provide the body with natural NAD and NADP, cobalt 60, and all of the B-vitamins it needs to assist the mitochondria in the production of ATP.

Everyone should grow tobacco. It is legal to grow so far. It can be eaten fresh or steamed and can be frozen or dried. The tobacco cultivar of which I am speaking is a beautiful plant. It stands 6-10 feet tall and 3 feet wide. The bugs will not eat tobacco. It is simply too potent.

The Dilemma

On one hand, the public is told that tobacco and nicotine are bad for them. On the other hand, they are told that niacin and the B's are good for them. We are NOT being told the whole truth!

A long-term campaign began early in this century to get people to stop using tobacco in all forms. Today the effort is **massive!** The public is being DRIVEN into a frenzy over the smoking and chewing of tobacco. Every dis-ease condition from lung problems to cancer is being blamed on tobacco. **Tobacco is a scapegoat, and the experts are LIARS!**

The TRUTH of the matter is that less expensive, cheaper, substances—synthetic substances—have been *substituted* in many tobacco products. People have been smoking and chewing TOXIC substitutes instead of the real thing! If you want to smoke, get a good cigar and go outside.

Lies & More Lies

Personally, I do NOT like smoking or chewing. However, the issue here is not personal preference, but the fact that we have been lied to about something that can powerfully boost our immune system at a time when our food supply is deteriorating at a fantastic rate!

At the same time that tobacco is being vilified, the U S Government is "the" biggest grower of **hybridized** tobacco in the world! The implications are scary, but tobacco isn't the issue. What is the issue is the parallel "corporate" government called the "U"nited States Government, which is NOT the same as the "u"nited States Government. The former operates under the yellow fringe flag—a war flag; the latter under the Title 4 USC, Section 1 American Flag of Peace.

One reason tobacco is being socially vilified is to cover

the deleterious side effects of billions of tons of toxic waste chemicals being burned in waste incinerators across the USA. Tobacco is the perfect cover. The pharmaceutical companies and "corporate" big government are the problem, not tobacco. People MUST wake up and realize that their health can be improved by growing and eating tobacco in SMALL amounts.

The more something is believed to be true, and the greater the number of people who believe it to be so, the greater are the odds that it is NOT true!

Old time farmers from Tennessee and thereabouts knew that if you wanted to have the finest horses in the world, you had to feed them TOBACCO! It seems to me that people count as much as horses. You can also use tobacco in **small** quantities in stews, salads. Freeze it green or dry it for later use during the year.

Tobacco was the American Indian's gift to the white man. We accepted the Sacred Three Sisters, BUT we ignored the greatest gift of all. Home grown tobacco strengthens the immune system, improves mitochondrial oxidation (energy production), and boosts metabolic reactions in the liver.

Pellagra's disappearance in 1935 had nothing to do with "enrichment" of the food supply with *synthetic* vitamins. Pellagra ceased to be a problem when **dietary variety** and **quality proteins** found their way onto people's dinner plates.

Today people are suffering with *subclinical* pellagra, living *marginal* lives, and suffering from dietary excesses. When health breaks down, medical science says *"Syndrome."* The Japanese would say *"Kibyo."* I call it *"Old age!"*

PREVIEW: *Our closing chapter is only one page. Its title comes from a poem by the same name. Please read it and think about its meaning.*

If you can't see it, and your don't understand it, then it must be from the devil!

The Appendix

The appendix extends downward from the cecum, which is the most toxic spot in the body (see drawing page 46). It was put there to siphon away "excess" toxic energies from the cecum area of the colon. The appendix is surrounded by clusters of lymph nodes called Peyer's patch. The cecum is the end of the small intestine ends and the beginning of the large intestine. It's where parasites hang out. It is 6 feet up from the anus and the end of the road during colon therapy.

Making It Happen In Your Life!

Good health is a one step at a time process in reverse. Here are some basic steps to health and vitality.

1. Drink only biologically-friendly water.
2. Begin a *serious* detoxification program.
3. Eat fresh, raw, home grown food if possible.
4. Avoid extremes. Seek balance in ALL areas of your life.
5. Get into therapeutic fasting.
6. Use only <u>food</u>-based racemized™ supplements.
7. Level your hormones and open your receptor sites.
8. Avoid all bio-junk food.
9. Get plenty of aerobic exercise.
10. Use racemized™ hormone precursors EVERYDAY!
11. Stay away from doctors.
12. Get control of your mind.
13. Laugh! Love! Help others!
14. Don't buy into hate, anger, greed, envy, blame, etc.
15. Avoid medications, recreational drugs, alcohol.
16. Follow to your instincts.
17. Visualize the body and life you desire.
18. Refuse to think anything negative.
19. *Erase* vaccine energy fields from your body.
20. Remove mercury and heavy metals from your tissues.
21. Develop a healthy, regular prayer life.
22. Use a rebounder to move lymphatic fluids.
23. Do lymphatic role downs morning and evening.
24. Use ETVC™ for energy; leveling blood sugars; burn fat.
25. Live today. Forget yesterday. Leave tomorrow alone.
26. Drink Kombucha tea to grow hair or restore color.
27. Do load-bearing work everyday.
28. Simplify your life in every way possible.
29. Remove those mercury dental fillings from your mouth.
30. Use racemized™ sea minerals in your water.
31. Grow a garden! Grow a garden! Grow a garden!
32. Learn to use a pendulum and vibration chain.
33. Use Taoist SUPER foods for superb health.
34. Eat only organic foods.
35. Don't consume soy or canola oils or soy products.
36. Give thanks each day to be alive.
37. Be patient with yourself. Give your body a chance.
38. Experience the *miracle* of rejuvenation.
39. Live life 90% correct and don't worry about the 10%.
40. Do whatever it takes to enjoy a healthy life.

The Young Agian! philosophy and use of racemized™ products allows for HEAVY overlap during transitional changes in the terrain.

35

Unforgiven

"Most wonderful; with its own hands it ties
And gags itself-gives itself death and war
For pence doled out by kings from its own store.
Its own are all things between earth and heaven;
But this it knows not; and if one arise
To tell this truth, it kills him unforgiven."

Tomasso Campanella, The People

Reversing the aging process is a one step at a time
process that occurs one day at a time—in reverse.

Ask yourself these questions. *"Am I willing to take*
responsibility for my future and create the miracle of agelessness
in my life? Am I willing to do whatever it takes to keep my youth
or gain back the years I have lost? Am I willing to act in my own
best interest today? Right now?

Everything in life comes at a price. Pain! Suffering!
Money! I hope you will join me and pick up your yoke no matter
how difficult it may be. Never scream *"Uncle!"* Health and
vitality belongs to he or she who is willing to pay the price.

May you become *Young Again!*

Sincerely,

John Thomas

Hormones & Detoxification

What's can I do to speed the aging reversal process?" is the question I'm asked most.

I respond, *"Start with your liver. Clean it up! Get rid of the liver and gall bladder stones are blocking the flow of bile wastes from exiting your body!"*

It stands to reason that the body can't return to a more youthful condition when **excess** wastes have accumulated in all of the soft tissues of the body!

All necessary information and supplies needed to complete a series of liver and tissue purges come as a package. The process takes 8 weeks to complete. During this period, your lead a normal life in every respect.

The only time special provision is made is the night of the purge and the following day. Most people do their purges on a Friday or Saturday night so they can rest up the following day. It takes three weeks to prepare the body for the first of six purges, thereafter, they are performed each week. There is nothing dangerous or difficult about the purge process. Think of the process as being akin to breaking out of jail—in this case, your own jail!

Of Equal Importance

Balancing of the body's hormonal system and "deblocking" of the body's hormonal receptor sites is of **equal** importance to liver and tissue purging.

It is ideal to begin the 90 day hormone program at the **same time** as the liver and tissue purge program.

Think of it this way. Purging of the waste lightens the body's load, while the racemized™ hormone precursors act to "polish" the neuro and hormonal receptor sites so the body can once again take charge of itself.

Liver/tissue purging gets you out of jail, while the hormone program "flips" the breaker switches on your electrical panel and allows the current to flow—literally!

Products are available to open and turn on women's AND men's hormonal systems. The program improves nerve function, reduces joint pain, clears the mind of that "foggy" feeling, normalizes menstrual problems, improves energy, reduces body fat, rids you of that "cold" feeling, improves sex drive, grows hair, stops yeast and blader infections, normalizes prostate problems, and rids the body of fibroid tumors in the breasts and uterus.

Far Infrared Sauna Now Available!

The Earth is bombarded with energy rays that belong to the FIR band of the light spectrum. Humans can't see FIR energy, but it's there nevertheless. Soldiers use special equipment and FIR light to see at night. The Japanese have DISCOVERED how to use FIR energy to promote **health** and **longevity.**

FIR *energy* is **right-spin** energy and is, therefore, both safe and good for the body. The most practicable FIR technology available is the **Far Infrared Sauna** that uses as little as 15¢ a day by converting normal electricity into healthful FIR energy.

FIR Saunas have captured my attention because they fit into most any home or apartment. FIR saunas produce and direct FIR energy that heals the body without the need for water, or heat, or lights.

FIR heat is sometimes referred to as "soft heat." One thing for sure, FIR heat dissolves and rids the skin and sub cutaneous tissues of acid wastes. Translated, that means an end to acne, aching joints, winter time blues, old age complaints, and body odor.

Acid wastes produce inflammation, swelling and pain if allowed to build up in the tissues. **Excess** waste brings on degenerative dis-eases like cancer, arthritis, and diabetes, just to name a few. Older people move more freely and their temperament "sweetens" when they incorporate the use a FIR sauna into their daily lives.

FIR energy also **stimulates** basal metabolic rate. People with degenerative disorders like fibromyalgia, systemic lupis and hypertension find relief with the therapeutic effects of FIR energy. Heart and stroke patients can safely enjoy a Far Infrared sauna, too!

FIR saunas are well engineered, modular in design, easy to set up and move around, carry a 5 year warranty, and have a beautiful cedar interior and furniture grade beautiful pine exterior. FIR saunas come fully equipped with stereo speakers, phone jack, and reading lamps.

Use a FIR sauna to "unplug" from the medical system.

One of the best and safest hair and body soaps I know of is Dr. Bronner's. It's available at most health stores. Avoid peppermint if you have a perm in your hair.

**Biogenic™ Lymph Roller
A Powerful Health Building Tool!**

**Rebounder or Mini Trampoline
Available from many department stores.**

**The Aurameter is a very useful measuring
device. Highly Recommended!**

The Way It Is!

Meat Eaters vs. Vegetarians

"The savvy person is neither a heavy meat eater nor radical vegetarian. Balance is the key!"

Deep within the heart of the health movement is the **dogma** that vegetarians are smarter and healthier than meat eaters because they don't eat meat. In fact, any vegetarian worth his lettuce knows that when sick, aging meat eaters go "vegetarian" their health improves and they soon look and feel better.

The question is "why" do heavy meat eaters enjoy improved health when they include fresh vegetables in their diet? Because heavy meat eaters need **"balance"** and fresh, live food provides balance.

Having been on **both** sides of the fence, first a heavy meat eater and then a radical vegetarian, I returned to my senses many years later, mellower and smarter. Here is what I learned first hand.

1. All foods impose stress on the body.
2. How we digest food dictates the results.
3. Dietary balance is the key.

It is our ability or inability to fully process "food" that dictates long term health and longevity—NOT whether we are meat eaters or *vegetarians*. **In fact, the less we eat, the longer we will live.** Therefore, see that you eat fresh, live "low stress" vegetables, reduce both meat and *total* food intake, and use racemized™ organic, predigested liver tablets for optimum health.

Racemized™ liver is a ZERO stress food because it is **predigested.** It is my **"meat"** of choice. I take 2 tablets 2x daily with racemized™ hydrogen chloride and DiSororb Aid™ to insure rapid assimilation.

Vegetarians **enjoy** better health and maintain their appearance longer than people who eat too much meat. However, vegetarians DO experience secondary health problems due to lack of *variety* and the **inability** to PROCESS proteins (same problem for meat eaters) cauing both to experience connective tissue problems. The "vegan" suffers far worse and ages much faster!

Here are a few other tips. Red meat is better for you than chicken. Fish is in between. Butter is good for you. Margarine is bad news. Soy and canola are deadly.

"Eat your vaccine, dear!"

Did you know that government, the medical establishment, the pharmaceutical companies, and the multinational food giants have hatched a devilish plan that will have disastrous effects on the health of people worldwide and especially in the USA?

The scheme involves using genetically altered fruits and vegetables to transport the likes of hepatitis B, polio, measles, mumps, tetanus, swine flue, and rubella into YOUR body via the food you eat.

Gene splicing of the food supply will produce millions of sick people. It will render "forced" immunization moot while it keeps the hospital rooms full.

If you want to live a healthy, happy life, you MUST plant a garden, grow some fresh food in containers on your patio, share a community plot, or hire someone to grow "safe" vaccine and chemical-free food for you.

Home grown food—even in small quantities—produces astounding effects on health. The best way to get into gardening is to start today! Normally it takes many years to build up your soil and neutralize the negative energy fields in the soil. Now, with the use of a product called Bio-Grow™, it is possible to convert dirt into live soil in less than 30 days. Bio-Grow™ creates a positive energy soil environment where microbes and plants prosper. This is a Fourth Dimension ENERGY product that duplicates the effects of Biodynamics, but with a lot less work. Biodynamics l, ll are available if you want to understand this agricultural energy phenomenon (see Source Page).

Hyper Active, Attention Deficit Children

One thing these children have in common is that their neuro receptor sites are "locked up." Worse, their hormonal receptor sites are not able to read and regulate their systems and learning is VERY difficult. Read this book carefully , you'll know how to solve this learning dilemma.

End Your Cravings!

If you "crave" food, cigarettes, alcohol or drugs, "purge" your liver, eat SUPER foods and use racemized™ hormone precursors and your cravings will simply...........go away.

Anal itching often accompanies detoxification.

Glossary

AIDS-Acquired Immune Deficiency Syndrome.
ATP-energy carrying and storage molecule of body; product of mitochondrial oxidation of blood sugars (glycolysis).
Acetylcholine-a nerve impulse transmission chemical.
Acetylcholinease-an enzyme that splits acetylcholine.
Acid-any substance that liberates hydrogen ions; ion donor.
Acid stomach-common term for upset stomach; cause is an really alkaline stomach; poor digestion; lack of HCL.
Acupuncture-alternative modality; manipulates energy fields in bio-electric body with pins or their electrical equivalent.
Adenovirus-a virus associated with upper respiratory infections, associated with AIDS/HIV.
Adhesion-water's tenedency to coat the surface of things.
Adrenals-a pair of ductless glands; located on top of each kidney.
Aerobes-bacteria that require an oxygen rich environment.
Aerobic-with air.
Aerobic exercise-exercise that produces a high oxygen state.
Aging process-begins at anabolic peak and ends with death; cumulative
Agglutination-clumping of the red blood corpuscles; see soy.
Albumin-a blood protein; abnormally found in the urine.
Alcohol-end product of fermentation; anaerobic process
Algae-lowest of plants; some edible (klamath, spirulina, chlorella)
Alkaline-above pH 7.0.
Alkaloid-alkaline plant juices; physiologically active.
Allopathic medicine-conventional cut, burn, and drug medicine.
Alum-double sulfate of aluminum; toxic; food additive; pickles.
Aluminum-a metal that releases toxic ions into food and water.
Alzheimer's -atrophy of brain; produces dementia, violence, anger in elderly.
Amalgam-mixture of toxic metals used to fill the teeth; up to 60% mercury; erroneously referred to as "silver" fillings.
Amenorrhea-absence or suppression of menstruation.
American Dental Association-"official" dentistry.
Amyloid-a complex protein substance without structure.
Anabolic, anabolism-build up of tissues; repair of tissues.
Anabolic Peak-high point of anabolism; end or youth, beginning of old age.
Anaerobes-bacteria that can live in the absence of oxygen.
Anaerobic-without air; oxygen deficient.
Analog-a synthetic molecule; "—R" group moved; a patented drug.
Andropause-male version of menopause in women.
Angina pectoris-chest pain due to lack of oxygen in muscles.
Anemia-low number of circulating red blood corpuscles.
Anions-the smallest form of energy released during a reaction.
Antibiotic-anti: against; bio: life; ic: pertaining to; drug.
Arthritis-deterioration/inflammation of the connective tissues and joints.
Arteriosclerosis-hardening of arteries; see atherosclerosis
Antenna-device that receives a radio (energy) signal.
Antibody-product of a previous infection; immunity related.
Aspartate-salt form of aspartic acid; aspartame (Nutrisweet™); toxic.
Atherosclerosis-plaque formation/deterioration of arteries.
ATP-adenosine triphosphate; the energy carrying molecule of the body.
Atrophy-deterioration and death of body tissue/gland/organ.
Avogadro's #-number of atoms in 12 grams of carbon-12.
Aura-the electric body; invisible body; see Fourth Dimension.
Bacteria-microorganisms; microbe.
Bactericidal-a non-selective killer of bacteria, antiseptic.
Balding-loss of hair; related to O_2 deficiency and toxicity.
Basal metabolism-minimum resting energy expenditure.
Basement membrane(s)-primary support/connective tissues.
B-12: vitamin #12 of vitamin B complex; related to cyanocobalamin; called intrinsic factor; contains cobalt blue.

BAT-brown adipose tissue; not related to WAT (see).
Bent molecule-the water molecule. Also known as a polar molecule.
BEV-biologically friendly, conception point drinking water.
Bile-liver and body waste product; fat emulsifier; digestive enzymes.
Biogenic-stimulation of body to produce new, healthy tissue and heal self.
Bio-dynamic-term describing energy friendly agriculture.
Bio-electric age-true age based on health of the vital organs.
Bio-electric body-the physical and energy body's combined.
Bio-junk food-adulterated food; toxic; negative spin effect.
Biological alchemy-transformation of the elements in liver, gut via bacteria; fusion reactions.
Biological Theory of Ionization-life is the product of the energy released by the breaking of ionic bonds that hold minerals together.
Bio-magnetics-the use of therapeutic magnets in healing.
Bio-magnetic Irrigator-dental hygiene device; prevents/dissolves/removes plaque from the teeth; manipulates hydrogen ions and the water molecule; plaque (-) minus charge; treated water (+); joining of these is called oxidation.
Bladder-the urine storage organ in animals.
Blood-one of two key body fluids; lymph is the other.
Body odor (BO)-odoriferous product of microbial oxidizing of skin waste.
Bonds-the energy link within molecules.
Bone spur-abnormal mineral deposit in/on joints and bones.
Bowel-the colon or large intestine.
B-vitamins-the B-12 complex; B-1 through B-12; see intrinsic factor.
Brix-a unit of measure of the sugars in plant juices.
Brown fat-see BAT.
Calcify, calcification-soft tissue invasion by mineral salts (calcium).
Calcium-mineral element; a metal; elemental; anion.
Calculus-dental plaque; tartar.
Cancer-systemic deterioration/collapse of immune system.
Canola oil-same as rape oil; toxic; mustard family; see soy oil.
Capillaries-smallest blood vessels; can be venous or arterial.
Carbohydrate-sugars, starches, dextrins, and cellulose; contains carbon, oxygen, and hydrogen; classes of nutrient; other classes are protein/fats.
Carbon-essential element to all living things; atomic element #12.
Carbon cycle-the path of carbon from atmosphere through bacteria, soil, plant, animal, ocean, and back to the atmosphere; requirement for life/creation of positive energy food.
Carbon dioxide- atmospheric gas; animal waste gas, CO_2.
Carcinogenic-poisonous.
Cardiovascular disease-dis-eases of the circulatory system.
Carpal Tunnel Syndrome-occlusion/deterioration of nerve & nerve paths in bones of wrist; loss of motion and/or function.
Carrion-spoiled animal flesh.
Casts-albumin/amyloid, proteins, salts; wastes deposits of the kidney's tubules; indicates deterioration of nephrons.
Catalyst-a substance that causes a chemical reaction that would not occur without its presence; used over and over.
Cataract-the clouding of the lens of the eye or its capsule.
Cation-smallest form of (-) energy released during a reaction.
Catabolic, catabolism-break-down or self-digestion of body's tissues; failure/inability to rebuild or repair tissues; old age; opposite of anabolism.
Cavities-rotting away of the teeth; decay.
Cecum-junction of small/large intestine; gut/colon (bowel).
Cellulose-a carbohydrate; fiber.
Chemotherapy-treatment of dis-ease w/negative energy drugs.
Chloroform-toxic substance; source: chlorinated water/drugs.
Chlorine-a halogen; a gas; "a wildcat," used to treat water.
Chloride-a salt form of chlorine (sodium/pot./alum chloride).
Chi Gong-Chinese modality; transference of energy via the hands.
Chiropractic-modality for correction of alignment of spine.
Chiropractic (Network)-advanced holistic form of chiropractic
Chloramine-highly toxic form of chlorine; absorbed while bathing; avoid.
Chlorinated water-water treated with some form of chlorine.
Cholesterol-a body fat; an alcohol; part of bile; a phospholipid.

Cilia-hair like projections in small intestine/respiratory tract.
Cirrhosis-hardening of glandular tissues; inflammation of.
Clinical Disease-a diagnosed medical condition with measurable signs.
Cloak(ed)-under cover; hidden; can't be detected; subclinical; occult stage.
Cobalt blue-natural radioactive isotope; related to anemia/ vitamin B-complex/B-12/intrinsic factor; fusion reactions.
Co-enzyme-necessary for the function of an enzyme.
Cohesion-water's tendency to stick together; hydrogen bond.
Colloid-substance that stays in suspension; mineral colloids not as effective in nourishing body as minerals in racemic ionic form.
Colon-large intestine; bowel.
Colonic irrigation-washing of colon; forced acceleration of body wastes/bile.
Collagen-connective tissue; 30% of body protein.
Comfrey-garden plant grown for spinach like leaves; heals ulcers.
Coral Calcium-biogenic coral; used for rejuvenation.
Crypts of Lieberkuhn-where food nutrients are absorbed in the gut (small intestine) ; located between intestinal villi.
Crystal-a salt; combination of halogen and a metal ions.
Currency, electrical-energy money; mineral ions.
Cyanide-contained in rape (canola) oil; toxic.
Cyanocobalamin-cobalt blue; synthetic B-12/intrinsic factor.
Cytoplasm-fluid inside the cell.
DNA-genetic code of living things; deoxyribonucleic acid.
Defecate-a bowel movement.
Degenerative dis-ease-systemic oxidation and acidification of the tissues.
Denature-alteration in form, function and/or shape of food enzymes/proteins.
Holistic dentistry-biologically friendly dentistry.
De-energize-neutralization/synchronization; loss of effect.
Deodorant-a chemical used to mask BO; most are toxic.
Dermis-the true skin; beneath the epidermis (outer skin).
Detoxify-removal of waste from the body.
Devitalized food-loss of vitality; neutralization of energy.
Diabetes-malfunction/dis-ease of vital organs; insulin related; blood sugar too high; obesity related; old age sign.
Digestion-breakdown/conversion of nutrients into energy.
Dilution-homeopathic remedies.
Dirt-unproductive, dead, synchronized soil.
Dis-ease-the opposite of health; a left-spin condition.
Diuretic-drug that sheds the body's extracellular fluids.
Dogma-established authoritative opinion.
Dowager's hump-hunchback condition due to loss of bone mass and connective tissue; degenerative; hunchback.
Dowsing-technique for measuring nature of energy and direction of spin.
Drugs-chemical substances that cause a physiologic effect.
Ductless glands-glands that do not excrete into a lumen or duct.
Dynamic Reflex Analysis-kinesthetics.
ETVC™-racemic food that builds muscle, burns fat, boosts energy, levels sugars.
E. coli-un/friendly bacteria of the gut.
Eczema-acute/chronic inflammation of the cutaneous layers of the skin (dermis); dermatitis; toxicity related.
Edema-excess tissue fluids; plasma protein/lymph toxicity; potassium loss;
Enema-a swallow, partial cleansing of the lower colon.
Electrolytes-mineral ions capable of electrical conductivity; nerve fiber transmission; nerve pathway related.
Electron flow-movement of electrons along metal wires.
Endocrine system-the body's hormonal system for transmission of energy and messages via the blood/glands.
Energy-electrical phenomenon.
Energy field-a field of electrical influence; signature may be left/right spin.
Energy imbalance-bio-electric stress; dis-ease.
Energy manipulation-alteration of signature and frequency of an energy field.
Energy meridian-an energy highway or path.
Energy (scrambled)-effect of radiation/irradiation/food additives/halogens on food energy molecules and/or enzymes.

Enzymes-biological catalysts; all body functions require them.
Estrogen-a group of female horones (estrone, estradiol, estratriol, etc.)
Exit portal-waste removal avenue(s) in bio-electric body.
Exocrine glands-glands that secrete hormones/enzymes into lumens or hollow organs like the stomach or gut.
Extracellular fluid-fluid between (outside) cells; interstitial.
Fabale-a family of plants; parent family of the soy bean.
Facultative anaerobes-bacteria that can function with or without the presence of oxygen.
Fats-food category that may be healthful/bad; excess adipose body tissue.
Far Infrared-healing part of the light spectrum; therapeutic.
Fever (febrile)-elevated body temperature due to infection/toxins.
Fission-splitting of atoms/molecules; catabolic; nuclear.
Fluorine-a halogen gas; toxic; a wildcat.
Fluoride-the form of fluorine gas combined with metal ions to form a salt..
Fluorosis-fluoride toxicity.
Food-nutrient energy; energy footprint may be lert/right.
Footprint-descriptive term indicating spin direction, intensity and depth.
Fourth Dimension-an invisible/intangible energy dimension.
Functional cells-healthy tissue cells; parenchyma cells; vitality producing.
Fusion-anabolic transmutation/formation of molecules.
Gallbladder-holding sack for liver's bile; dumps into gut.
Gallstones-deposits of precipitates from bile.
Gas-free moving matter; non-solid; invisible energy; w/o form.
Gastric-related to stomach.
Genetically engineered-manipulated life forms; synthetic.
Germ Theory of Disease-allopathic medical theory; disease diagnosis.
GI tract-gastrointestinal tract.
Glaucoma-a group of eye dis-eases involving atrophy of retina.
Glucose-blood sugar; in storage form called glycogen; energy fuel for body.
Glycerol-glycerin with alcohol(s) attached; present in fats.
Glycine-a nonessential amino acid; sweet; glycine max.
Glycolic acid-a natural substance used to peel skin; rid face of wrinkles.
Glycosides-inhibit muscle enzymes; soy/canola contain them.
Glycolysis-splitting & oxidation of glucose; Krebs cycle; formation of ATP.
Glands-body organs with special functions and tissues.
Goiter-swollen thyroid gland; stressed ovaries, pancreas, liver and adrenals.
Gout-uric acid toxicity in blood and joints; degenerative.
Gua Sha-acupuncture without needles; lymphatic manipulation.
Greens-collards, broccoli leaves, spinach, cabbage, chard, etc.; good food.
Gut-small intestine (includes duodenum, jejunum, ileum.
HCL-hydrochloric acid; stomach acid; breaks down proteins.
Halogen-an extremely unstable, acid gas; a wildcat; toxic.
Harmonic-a healthy frequency; causes body to resonate health/vitality.
Heart attack-insufficient oxygen available to heart muscle.
Herbicides-man made organic poisons.
Hemorrhoids-swollen, congested, displaced veins in the anus.
Hepatitis-inflammation of the liver (hepatocytes).
Hepatocytes-the functional cells of the liver.
Herpes-group of viral conditions; sex/non sex types.
High blood pressure-hypertension; abnormal; sign of systemic problems.
HIV-Human immunodeficiency virus; the precursor virus to AIDS.
Hologram-a multidimensional energy message.
Homeopathic medicine-the medicine of similars; remedies.
Homeovitic-qualities of homeopathy plus energy and nutritional support.
Hormone-chemical messenger; powerful energy field; product of vital glands.
Howdy Doody Lines-Facial lines that indicate stress in vital organs/colon.
Hyaline-albuminoid tissue substance that reflects amyloid degeneration.
Hyalinization-infusion of hyaline into cells or tissue.
Hybrid food-food produced from genetically weak seed.
Hydration-the water level in the tissues of the body.
Hydrochloric acid-see HCL.
Hydrogen-an element; high energy; bonds easily; bioactive; acidic.
Hydrogen peroxide-H_2O_2; therapeutic; antiseptic; oxidizer; ages tissues.
Hype-unrealistic thinking; mind over matter; biojunk food induced stress.

Hyperspace-Fourth Dimension energy space.
Hypertrophy-increased/abnormal change in organ function.
Hypoglycemia-low blood sugar.
Hypotrophy-decline; abnormal change in organ function.
Hypovolemia-low blood fluid volume (also lymph).
Ileum-end of small intestine; joins colon at cecum.
Ileocecal valve-gatekeeper between small intestine and cecum (lg. intestine)
Immune system-our bio-electric defense system.
Immunization-bogus introduction of foreign microbial protiens into body.
Impotence-inability of male to get an erection; female clitoris non responsive.
In-camera-consideration of all body systems as a whole; not isolated.
Inflammation-redness; swelling; edema.
Indols-toxic whole molecules produced/absorbed in the gut.
Insulin-A blood protein; controls glucose flow into the cells.
Integument-the skin (subcutaneous, dermis, epidermis).
Internal environment-status of the cells/fluids/tissues.
Intercellular substance-mix of materials between the cells.
Interstitial fluid-fluid between the cells; extracellular fluid.
Intestine-small intestine (gut) and large intestines (colon).
Intima-innermost layer of the artery blood vessel wall.
Intoxication-alcohol saturation of tissues beyond liver's to breakdown and the kidneys to excrete; or, toxic acidic waste condition of the tissues.
Intracellular fluid-fluid inside the cells.
Intrinsic factor-needed for digestion; vitamin B-12/tobacco related.
Intuition-instinct; extension of the min beyond 3rd dimension.
Invisible-not seen; the electric body; Fourth Dimension.
Iodine-an element; needed for health; related to thyroid goiter.
Ion-an atom that has gained or lost an electron.
Ionic bond-bond between two mineral ions.
Ionic minerals-minerals that have gained/lost electrons.
Ionization-exchange of energy and electrons; anions/cations.
Irradiation-destruction/scrambling of food molecules/tissues.
Iridology-reading/interpretation of health via iris of eye.
Ischemia-reduced oxygen supply to heart muscle.
Isotope-an atom with same number of protons, but different number of neutrons; a different molecular form of the same element.
Jaundice-toxic liver effect; bilirubin; yellowing of eye sclera.
Juice capsules/tablets-concentrated right-spin dried plant juices.
Kombucha tea-dynamic home preparaton used for rejuvenation.
Kidney-primary excretory organ of the body; exit portal.
Kidney stones-mineral/fat/waste precipitates in the kidneys.
Kinesiology-study of body movement.
Kinesthetics-muscle sense tests; identify toxic food/drugs.
Lactate-the salt form of lactic acid.
Lactic acid-product of anaerobic fermentation; incomplete oxidation of glucose; acid waste; produces muscle soreness; liver recycles and oxidizes.
Laying on of hands-healing through energy transfer; similar to chi gong.
Lecithin-emulsifier and component of oils/fats/bile; soy derived.
Left-spin-negative energy; catabolic; anti life;
Lemon juice-powerful de-toxifier(if fresh); acidic.
Lice-creatures that live on filth and negative energy.
Life expectancy-length of time we can expect to live.
Lightning, cellular-energy produced by the mitochondria.
Limb regeneration-regrowth of bone, nerve and tissues.
Liver-primary chemical/fusion/detox organ of the body.
Liver breath-bad breath resulting from stress liver; onions.
Liver stones-natural waste product of body; slows bile flow; accelerate aging.
Load-bearing work-work involving movement and weight.
Localized condition-a condition that is not systemic.
Lungs-organs of external breathing.
Lye soap-saponification of fats/oils with lye (sodium hydroxide).
Lymph-fluids in lymph vessels; a body fluid.
Lymphocyte-immune system cell; B-cell; part of lymph. systen
Lymphotrophic-change in lymph fluid; T-cell.
Lyse-to split, cleave or break apart.

Macrophage-non circulating immune system 'attack' cell; defensive.
Magic bullets-medical science hype; false hope; drugs.
Magnetic line devices-protection from electrical fields.
Magnetism-the effect of a magnetic field.
Magneto hydro dynamics-dental plaque removal therapy.
Malathion-a toxic man-made organic poison.
Malnutrition-insufficient right-spin food energy.
Manganese- trace mineral; builds serum iron via bioalchemy.
Mastication, masticate-chewing of food.
Matter-condensed energy.
Matriarchal society-blood line follows the woman.
Matrix-collagen framework for deposition of bone minerals.
Meat-dead animal tissue; may be right/left spin energy.
Menopause-negative shift in hormonal flow; the "climactic."
Menstruation-end of normal, monthly, hormonal, female cycle.
Mental age-how old a person thinks.
Mercury-extremely toxic element; quicksilver; evaporates.
Mercuric acid-extremely toxic heavy metal agent for treatment of water during warm months; an acid form of elemental mercury.
Metabolic process-metabolism.
Metabolism-a change in energy via biotransformation; energy transmutation.
Metabolite-waste products of metabolism.
Metaphysics-beyond normal physics of length, width, height.
Microbes-microscopic life forms; bacteria.
Mikrowater-ionized water that is highly reduced or oxidized; acid or alkaline.
Microwave oven-a negative energy cooking device.
Medical Grade Ionized Water™-reduced/oxidized water with very high ORP pH in both acid and alkaline forms; a therapeutic water; made from BEV™ water plus mix of racemized™ liquid minerals; NEVER make from "tap" water; used in Japan to heal people with diabetes, cancer, arthritis and cardiovascular disease; acid form capable of destroying virus, bacteria, fungi and yeast; water BEYOND conception point.
Mitochondria-bacteria that produce the ATP energy molecule.
Modality-a form of therapy.
Molds-lowest life forms.
Molecular bond-bond between molecules.
Mononucleosis-inflamed lymph nodes/liver; severe immune system stress.
Monosodium glutamate (MSG)-a salt of sodium and glutamine.
Morbid-dis-ease related; death related.
Multiple sclerosis-inflammation of the central nervous system; deterioration of the myelin sheaths of the nerves.
Muscle tone-resistance of muscles to elongation or stretch.
Mustard gas-chemical agent of war; made from rape oil.
Myocardial infarction-see heart attack.
Myelin-protective nerve fiber sheath; destruction pH related.
Myelinoma-deterioration of the nerve sheaths.
Myxedema-low thyroid function/metabolic rate; thyroid atrophy; low BMR.
Naturopathic-alternative therapeutic modality; similars.
Necrotic flesh-dead, non-gangrenous tissue; not same as carrion.
Negative energy-left-spin energy; catabolic.
Negative inhibition-feedback system to control metabolism.
Nephron-kidney blood filter; critical to detoxification.
Nerve gas-toxic agent of war; blocks enzyme function.
Neurolema-the outer sheath of nerve fibers (includes the Schwann cells).
Neuropathy-syndrome of nerve fiber (myelin) deterioration; pH related.
Neutralize-denature; detoxify; energy shift; synchronize.
Niacin/niacinamide-names for bogus vitamin B-3; synthetic.
Nicotine-if natural, a good source of complete B-vitamins.
Nicotinic acid-acid form of nicotine; natural source: dry tobacco.
Nitrogen-essential element; contained in proteinous foods.
Nodes-part of lymphatic system; also known as nodules.
Nonfunctional cells-cell that do not grant permission to life.
Nonshivering thermogenesis-heat produced w/o shivering.
Nourishment-positive food energy that fuels anabolism.
Obesity-slowdown in metabolic & vital organ function.

Old age-dis-ease; loss of vitality; acidification/breakdown of conective tissues
Open pollinated seeds-seeds that produce true to type; non hybrid.
Opportunistic-condition where microbes proliferate; low tissue vitality.
Organic-a misnomer; a molecule containing carbon; healthy food.
Organic poisons-poisons built on a carbon skeleton.
ORP-Oxidation/reduction potential; measure of life force (electrons) in Medical Grade Ionized Water™; symbol (+) means water is in oxidized state and missing electrons; and exact opposite (-) for reduced water; high pH plus high ORP is rejuvenating to body; electrons fuel mitochondrial production of ATP;
Osteoporosis-loss of bone mass; acidification of tissues and fluids; aging.
Ovaries-glands that produce female reproductive cells (egg).
Oxidation-glycolysis; conversion of glucose (sugars) molecule to ATP; chemistry term indicating loss of electrons indicated by symbol (+); describes energy state of Mikrowater™ (oxidized); destructive to tissues; produces free radicals.
Oxygen-gas; atomic element; oxidizer; aerobic; anabolism.
Ozone-O_3; therapeutic; bactericidal to pathogenic organisms.
PAC*-racemic formulation of powerful antioxidants and phytochemicals.
P-P Factor-pellagra preventive agent; part of the B-complex; known as B-3, niacin; most commercial sources are synthetic.
Palliation-relief of signs/symptoms without cure of cause.
Pallor-poor color; abnormal color.
Pancreas-vital digestive organ; both duct and ductless; stress linked to liver.
Paradigm-a new model along side an older model.
Paralysis-loss of muscle function; degenerative.
Parasympathetic nervous system-involuntary system; we have no control.
Parathyroid-four tiny glands next to thyroid; (ductless).
Parenchyma cells-functional cells of a gland or organ.
Pathogenic-pertaining to dis-ease; dis-ease causing; stress terrain.
Patriarchal society-blood line follows the male.
Peer review-undressing in public; submission to convention; following the protocols of "legitimate" medical science; control of independent thought.
Pellagra-dis-ease related to unbalanced dietary intake; B-vitamin related.
Pendulum-an antenna; a tuning device; a transmitter; a tool.
Peristalsis-intestinal wave-like motions that move food/waste.
Pesticide-organic poison; man-made; attached to carbon atom.
pH scale-normally from 1-14; 7 is neutral; ea. # increases 10x.
Phagocyte-a cell that eats the body's invading enemies/antigens.
Phenols-toxic whole molecules produced/absorbed in the gut.
PHG-phytohemaglutinin; a vegetable protein glue; soy beans.
Phytates-substance that interferes with digestion; heaviest in soy.
Phytohemaglutinin-see PHG.
Plants-nature's antennas; mediate cosmic energy; build soil; food energy.
Pituitary-important ductless gland; linked to all other glands.
Plicae circularis-undulating folds in the walls of the gut.
Plaque-toxic waste deposits in the artery walls; on teeth produce decay.
Plasma Protein-see lymph.
Poison-carcinogenic; deadly; produces negative effects.
Polar molecule-the water molecule; a bent molecule.
Poly/pleomorphic-microbial ability to change "specie" to suit body "terrain."
Polluted-toxic; loaded with poisonous waste; tap water.
Positive energy-right-spin; anabolic.
Positive thinking-mind over matter; helpful if real; no hype.
Post mortem-after death; examination after death.
Potassium-atomic element; (+) charge; sodium's twin; alkaline.
Precipitate-formation of a solid & settling out of solution.
Precursor-a substance that precedes another; beta carotene/vitamin A.
Proof-something medical science demands, but can't deliver.
Prostate-male ejaculatory organ; surrounds urinary tube.
Portal-an exit point or avenue or system for waste disposal from body
Protein-one of three food forms; see fat, carbohydrates.
Proanthocyanidins (PAC)-plant derived antioxidant/free radical scavengers.
Puberty-onset of secondary sex charistics (breasts/body hair).
Pulmonary system-blood movement from heart to lungs and return.
Pulse rate-beats per minute of heart muscle.
Pure water-H_2O only minus all comtaminants; toxic memory erase.

Purine-a nitrogenous protein waste from the digestion of animal tissue, or self digestion of body tissue; catabolic; adenine, guanine; nucleic acid end product.
Pyridine ring-a synthetic organic molecule used to make artificial B-vitamins; left-spin; will not support life; toxic to body.
R-group-a chemical group that gives an organic molecule its characteristic(s).
RNA-Ribonucleic acid; nucleic acid; genetic template material.
Racemize™-process that increases spin rate and energy field to boost biological availability and usefulness to body by a factor of 10x.
Radiation-energy radiating from a source (nuclear/solar); left/right spin)
Radionics-broadcasting of energy frequencies in agriculture.
Radiomimetic-ability of a substance alter body frequency to left/toxic state.
Rape oil-canola oil; toxic; not a food; radiomimetic.
Rebounder-a mini trampoline used to circulate lymphatic fluid.
Reduced-opposite of oxidized, oxidation. A high energy state.
Refractometer-device for determining dissolved mineral levels in the juices of plants using glucose levels as standard.
Rejuvenate-to rebuild; start anew; anabolism; opposite of aging.
Remedies-home/vitic/opathic substances that neutralize negative energy.
Replication-multiplication; reproduction.
Repolarization-stimulation of cellular matrix and organelles (mitochondria) to normalize cellular function and increase production of ATP.
Resiliency-return to previous condition; bounce back.
Respiration, external-O_2/CO_2 exchange in the lungs.
Respiration, internal-O_2/CO_2 exchange in the cells.
Reticular-fine network of tissues that form the glands/organs.
Retrovirus-a virus capable of using a reverse enzyme to access the host; HIV virus is said to be a retrovirus.
Right-spin energy-anabolic; positive; aerobic.
Rouleau effect-toxins in blood that produce clumping of blood corpuscles.
Root canal-removal of tooth's nerve; retention of dead tooth; toxic.
Rotenone-a toxic poison from the soy bean.
Roten-Japanese for derris: plant family to which soy belongs.
Rhythm-scheduled; systematic; regular; habit.
Rhymicity-routine; systematic; regular lifestyle and habits.
Saliva-secretion of the salivary glands; digestive juice; pH sensitive/indicative.
Salt-combination of halogen and metal ions.
Satiety-fullness beyond desire; nutritionally full.
Saponification-soap making; the hydrolysis or splitting of fat by an alkali; hydrolysis of an ester; (*sapo*-soap;*facere*-to make).
Scar tissue-a negative energy memory field; dysfunction in the skin's parenchymal cells during repair due to low energy state; acidification of tissues.
Scientific Method-medical sciences official system of information gathering.
Schwann cells-nerve synapse cells; polish receptors for peak signal function.
Sea water-naturally balanced mineral ion water; right-spin.
Sedentary lifestyle-lack of exercise and load bearing work.
Senility-loss of mental faculties.
Shallow breathing-insufficient exchange of lung gases.
Signature, energy-4th Dimension energy profile; combination of spin and intensity; specific to all substances and organisms.
Signs-measurable dis-ease conditions; will support diagnosis.
Silica-important element; body transmutes to calcium.
Similar(s)-homeopathic principle; cancellation of one energy field by another.
Single factor analysis-a form of scientific myopia; "head in the sand."
Sixth sense-intuition; Fourth Dimension; extension of mind.
Skatols-toxic whole molecules produced/absorbed via the gut.
Skin-our outer tube; halographic; an organ; exit portal.**Sleep**-detoxification period, rejuvenatiion of tissues; ATP production..
Smoking-oxidation of dried tobacco via flame.
Sodium-an element; a metal; alkaline; always involved in cancer.
Soft drink-acid forming; accelerates aging; toxic; heavy metals; avoid.
Soil-biologically alive dirt.
Solar energy-anionic energy; right spin; anabolic; life giving.
Solvent-a substance that dissolves solids creating a solution; alcohol dissolves fats (non polar); water dissolves polar substances (all other).
Soy bean-toxic plant of Derris family.

Soy bean oil-degenerative left spinning energy field; toxic.
Space-extension of the mind; related to Time.
Sperm-male reproductive cells.
Spin-direction of energy flow of a substance or thought.
Spinach-an alkaloid; Goosefoot family; eat with vinegar/lemon.
Spirulina-a complete algae protein; good nutrient energy.
Sprouts-sprouted seeds eaten as food.
Spurs-mineral/body waste deposits in joints/on bones.
Standard-a defined reference point; a known yardstick.
Stannous-a tin containing compound.
Stannous fluoride-a toxic fluoride/tin containing compound.
Static-standing still; not changing; no motion; synchronized.
Stomach-food receptacle; digestive organ.
Stress-bad energy; negative effect on body, mind and spirit.
Stroma cells-nonfunctional structional cells of the glands.
Sub-atomic-below atom level; fusion; transmutation; alchemy.
Sub-clinical-not diagnosable; symptoms only, prior to signs.
Sub-cutaneous-below the dermis or dermal layer of skin; shallow fascia; deep fascia; connective tissues composed of skin, muscle, ligaments, and tendons.
Sugar-glucose or other energy molecule; may be right/left-spin; glycolysis.
Sun-source of anionic energy; life giver; causes Earth to spin.
Supplement-vitamin, mineral, misc. factors added to diet.
Sweat-a waste product; extracellular fluid; heat regulator.
Swiss chard-an alkaloid; a Goosefoot; eat with vinegar/lemon.
Symbiotic-one life form helps the other; buddy system.
Sympathetic nervous system-under our conscious control.
Symptoms-subclinical; undiagnosable; early stages of dis-ease; Fourth Dimensional; bio-electric; energy related.
Synapse-juncture points along nerve fiber where signal is transfered.
Synchronization-temporary neutralization of energy (electron) transference.
Synergy-the coming together of two or more energy forces.
Systemic-affecting the entire body; fever for example.
Synthesis-energy forces coming together to form a new substance.
Synthetic-artifically prepared; man-made analogous molecule.
T-cells-defense cells of the immune/lymphatic systems.
Tartar-calculus; dental plaque.
Terrain-the TOTAL energy state of the bio-electric body.
Testes, testicles-glands that produce male reproductive cells, (sperm).
Therapeutic-having healing qualities; promotes health.
Therapeutic touch-healing through energy transfer; chi gong.
Thermogenic hyperphagia-production of heat & the eating of body WAT (fat) through oxidation by mitochondrial brown fat.
Thixotrophic-substance that when disturbed turns to liquid state, and then reverts to a gel state when left undisturbed; silicone (breast implants).
Thymus-gland of the immune system and lymphatic systems; above heart.
Thyroid-Major gland of body; affected by ovaries and liver stress.
Time-extension of mind; related to Space; Fourth Dimension.
Time & aging-passing of Time defines speed of aging.
Time made visible-signs of aging in the mirror.
Tin-stannous; see fluoride; toothpaste.
Tissue-cells of the body; grouped by type, function, and organ.
Tobacco-richest source of natural, complete B-vitamin complex in the world; up to 30%; alkaloid when green; acid when dry; a good food; must be food grade tobacco; must be eaten with lemon or vinegar.
Tone-resistance of muscles to elongation or stretch; that state in which body functions/parts are healthy and normal; retention of muscular shape, strength.
Toxic-poisonous; acidification; causes tissues to age.
Toxins-poisonous; negative energy fields; acidic;
Trace minerals-minerals needed in minute amounts; electrolytes.
Transmutation-conversion of one mineral or energy field into another in the gut/solar plexus, or liver of animals, or in soil by bacteria.
Trophy-change related to nutritional deficiencies or excesses.
TRUTH-something that can be ignored, but not denied; something that is.
Tumors-abnormal energy importing energy fields in the body; cancer/benign.
TVP-textured vegetable protein; avoid; usually soy derived.

Unopposed estrogen dominance-female condition where progesterone is lacking or receptor sites are "blocked" by hormone analogs.
Uric acid-a waste product of nitrogen tissue breakdown.
Urine-waste product of the body; useful therapeutic if drank fresh AM daily.
Vaccines-live or attenuated microbes in animal protein serum; toxic.
Vascularization-blood vessel invasion into tissue or bone.
Vibrational medicine-manipulation of energy for healing.
Villi-finger-like projections of the gut wall.
Vinegar-acidic; if naturally produced, good for body; aerobic product.
Virus-a non-life form; parasitic; steals converts body's energy; proliferate when the terrain is supportive; opportunistic.
Visible-tangible; length, width, and height; Third Dimension.
Vital organs-ductless glands: ovaries/testes, pancreas, thymus, thyroid, pituitary, parathyroid.
Vital force-the effect generated by the vital organs on body, mind, spirit.
Vitamins-co-factors; important to health and vitality; use only food derived.
Waste-acid byproducts of metabolism.
Water-h_2o; food; energy source; primary substance in body; polar solvent; most important substance to enter the body; use BEV™ or Mikrowater™.
Water molecule-H_2O if "pure"; otherwise contains toxic waste and mineral passengers, impure water is partially synchronized water, polluted water; one oxygen and two hydrogens.
Water substitutes-soft drinks, beer, milk, etc.; not acceptable substitutes for water; BEV is world standard.
Weeds-negative energy antenna; detoxify the air/soil; natures garbage crew.
White blood cells-part of the immune defense system.
Wildcats-name give to the halogens (fluorine, chlorine).
Wrinkles-confirmation of the passing of Time; aging of the vital organs; toxicity in the dermal/subcutaneous skin; acidification of the surface fascia.

IMPORTANT EXERCISES FOR KEEPING THE EXTERNAL AND THE INTERNAL MUSCLES OF THE ABDOMEN - FIRM AND HEALTHY.

Index

Healthy Baby Formula

3 1/2 C. BEV™ or Medical Grade Ionized Water™, 2 ea. Biogenic™ liver & Klammath™ algae tabs, 1 Disorb Aid™, 1 tbsp. coconut oil, 1 tsp. each TRP™, cod liver oil, & "blackstrap" molasses, 2 ea Taoist 5 Elements™/High Performance™; add contents of 1 SOC™ cap. Crush/soak/liquify; refrigerate; makes 32 oz. (thin with water; perforate nipple as needed).

Popcorn • Oil • Salt • Brewers Yeast

Popcorn is a good food—as long as it isn't cooked in soy or canola oil and covered with salt. And for a real treat, sprinkle brewers yeast on your 'buttered' popcorn. It adds zest, and you won't need any salt. You'll love it!

Are You Feeling Overwhelmed?

Making the transition from the "normal" good old American diet to a healthy one can be challenging.

New ways to healthfully prepare food and new types of strange foods is challenging for conventional cooks. The person eating "strange" new foods often doesn't appreciate tampering. Go slow. *Invest in a good vegetarian* cook book like *Foods That Heal* or a healthy "meat" cook book like *Nourishing Traditions* (see Source Page). Visit a health food store or food co-op and buy a supply of basic food staples. Mix them among your regular food dishes on the dinner table. Home made bread is a good dietary addition. AVOID soy products, canola oil, and tofu. Avoid ALL prepared foods. They are a guaranteed ticket to the grave. Convert your family one step at a time!

"Nothing transforms a person as much as changing from a negative to a positive attitude." Paul C. Bragg

"If we eat wrongly, no doctor can cure us. If we eat rightly, no doctor is needed." Victor Rocine